INTRODUCTION TO PHYSIOLOGICAL PSYCHOLOGY

INFORMATION PROCESSING IN THE NERVOUS SYSTEM

INTRODUCTION TO PHYSIOLOGICAL PSYCHOLOGY

INFORMATION PROCESSING IN THE NERVOUS SYSTEM

JACKSON BEATTY

University of California, Los Angeles

BROOKS/COLE PUBLISHING COMPANY
MONTEREY, CALIFORNIA

A Division of Wadsworth Publishing Company, Inc.

For my family,
Jackson, Marian, and Scott Beatty

ISBN: 0-8185-0123-5
L. C. Catalog Card No.: 74-17631
Printed in the United States of America

10 9 8 7 6 5 4 3 2

Production Editor: *Lyle York*
Interior Design: *Linda Marcetti*
Cover Design: *John Edeen*
Illustrations: *John Foster*
Typesetting: *Holmes Composition Service, San Jose, California*
Printing & Binding: *Kingsport Press, Kingsport, Tennessee*

Preface

This book is written in the belief that the excitement of current research in physiological psychology should be communicated to the student in an introductory text. *Introduction to Physiological Psychology: Information Processing in the Nervous System* is organized around major problem areas and current research questions in psychology. As the title suggests, special importance is placed on the information-processing properties of the nervous system in order to provide a unified framework for the understanding of topics such as perception, attention, sleep and wakefulness, motivation, and language. Current neuroanatomical, neurochemical, and neurophysiological data are presented. The book reflects my belief that a good introductory text should be interesting to those students not previously acquainted with the field of study, should address the major problem areas of the discipline, should provide a coherent conceptual framework for understanding these problems, and should be factually current and accurate.

This book evolved slowly during several years of teaching physiological psychology at the University of California, Los Angeles. I am, therefore, pleased to acknowledge my debt to those hundreds of students who were responsible in part for the selection of material, who gave me awareness of the ease or difficulty of learning particular segments of this body of knowledge, and who, with their questions, led me to a treatment of general principles of nervous function and behavior whenever possible. This book is a product of that course and of my students.

I am also indebted to my colleagues at the University of California, Los Angeles, and elsewhere, who critically reviewed the various chapters during writing and revision of the manuscript: David D. Avery of Colorado State University, Charles M. Butter of the University of Michigan, Harry J. Carlisle of the University of California, Santa Barbara, Ray A. Chism of Bakersfield College, Walter Dowling of UCLA, Franklin Krasne of UCLA, Eric H. Lenneberg of Cornell University, Donald B. Lindsley of UCLA, Donald Novin of UCLA, Kelyn Roberts of UCLA, and William R. Uttal of the University of Michigan. I also thank Edward Walker of the University of Michigan who, as consulting editor for Brooks/Cole, critically read and commented on the manuscript at several stages in its development. I owe special thanks to Nancy V. Peter, with whom I have spent long hours of reading and editing as the manuscript developed. Her good taste is reflected in this final version.

I also thank David Finch for his collaboration in preparing the glossary, and Arana Greenberg and Rhoda Freeman, whose efforts in the production of the manuscript greatly eased my task.

Jackson Beatty

Contents

Chapter 4   Information Processing in Audition and Somatosensation   78

Chapter 5   Information Processing in Vision   120

Chapter 6   Motor Systems and the Control of Movement   146

Chapter 7   Sleep and Wakefulness   169

Chapter 8   **Attention**   **188**

Chapter 9   **The Timing of Behavior**   **209**

Chapter 10   **Language**   **230**

Chapter 1

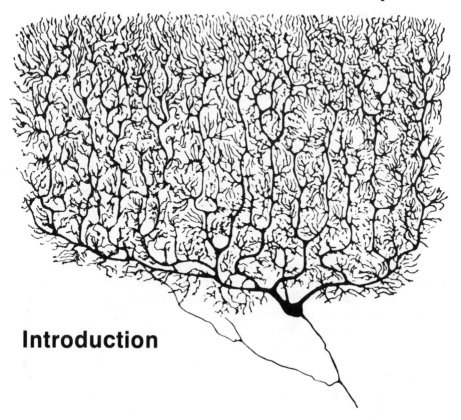

Introduction

If I begin chopping the foot of a tree, its branches are unmoved by my act, and its leaves murmur as peacefully as ever in the wind. If, on the contrary, I do violence to the foot of a fellow-man, the rest of his body instantly responds to the aggression by movements of alarm or defense. The reason of this difference is that the man has a nervous system whilst the tree has none; and the function of the nervous system is to bring each part into harmonious cooperation with every other [James, 1890, p. 12].

With these words, William James, the great American psychologist and brother of Henry James, the novelist, began the chapter in his classic text of 1890, in which he examined the functions of the brain. James' text was neither a medical work nor a physiological treatise. Instead, his *Principles of Psychology* was devoted to behavior and the mental life. Why, then, should he discuss brain physiology? James phrases his argument in this way:

If the nervous communication be cut off between the brain and other parts (of the body), the experiences of those other parts are nonexistent for the mind. The eye is blind, the ear deaf, the hand insensible and motionless. And conversely, if the brain be injured, consciousness is abolished or altered, even although every other organ in the body be ready to play its normal part. A blow on the head, a sudden subtraction of blood, the pressure of an apoplectic hemorrhage, may have the first effect; whilst a very few ounces of alcohol or grains of opium or hashish, or a whiff of chloroform or nitrous oxide gas, are sure to have the second. The delirium of fever, the altered self of insanity, are all due to foreign matters circulating through the brain, or to pathological changes in that organ's substance. The fact that the brain is the one immediate bodily condition of the mental operations is indeed so universally admitted nowadays, that I need spend no more time in illustrating it, but will simply postulate it and pass on. The whole remainder of the book will be more or less of a proof that the postulate was correct [p. 4].

James' faith in his postulate was well founded. The study of correspondence between the brain activity and behavior has indeed been fruitful. The spinal reflexes that modulate motor behavior, the sensory structures that process incoming information, the chemical changes that occur in learning, the brain structures that underlie motivated behavior, the cortical mechanisms necessary for language, and even the basic neuronal nature of brain tissue are among the discoveries that have followed the acceptance of the postulate of a mechanistic brain, which controls bodily functions and behavior. This book, like James', is evidence of the utility of the mechanistic concept.

The Brain as a Machine

Psychology shares with other sciences the hope and aim of providing a mechanistic understanding for natural phenomena. The phenomena of concern here are behavioral in nature, and to understand in this context means to provide a complete demonstration of the mechanical processes necessary to account for a phenomenon. Only rarely has this ambitious goal even been approximated. We must temporarily be contented with less satisfactory explanations. We cannot yet disassemble the machinery of behavior and expect it to function again upon reassembly. Thus, our understanding of biology is less complete than our understanding of man-made artifacts. In the latter realm, we can indeed demonstrate some level of understanding a system's function by assembling that system from raw materials.

Although we do not have the capacity to create a functioning human brain, we may indeed demonstrate that we know something about it if we can establish plausible functions for that brain and verify our hypotheses by appropriate measurements. Without constructing a detailed wiring diagram of the nervous system, we may construct functional diagrams that indicate the roles played by aggregate sections of neuronal tissue. I emphasize function because it is the function, or performance, of brain tissue that is of primary interest to psychology. The ultimate output of the nervous system is behavior.

The comparison of biological problems and engineering problems is not specious, for biological science and engineering are not as separate as is often supposed. The British zoologist J. Z. Young has pointed out that engineers are often given the task of creating machines to perform selected functions of living organisms. For example, simple machines assist man in mechanical chores. Thus, a functional parallel exists between man and certain of the machines he creates. It is not surprising that the language and techniques of the engineer are often assimilated by the biologist to understand the biological function that the man-made machine models. When the laws of mechanics are applied to the movements of muscle tissue and bone, an orderly and powerful conceptual system is formed for understanding a limited set of functions in living tissue.

Similar dependencies exist between engineering technologies and the neurosciences. Various mechanical devices have been constructed to perform information, or control, functions, and in these respects such machines are similar to biological control systems. Most notable today is the computer technology, but in earlier times more primitive models were used. Pavlov, for example, modeled his conceptual physiology of conditioned reflexes on a railroad switchyard.

Thus, a pattern often appears. Advanced physical sciences develop a set of concepts that are appropriate to a range of physical phenomena. Engineering technologists then may use some of this knowledge to model biological functions in the form of useful machines. The biologist may adopt the physical concepts directly or in the adapted form of the technological model. This usage assumes that an analogy, or similarity, exists between the biological and artificial systems that share common functions. If the analogy is useful, then the language and methods of the engineer are adopted by the biologist and used in preference to other modes of description. Conversely, engineers may use biological models to suggest methods for construction of the analogous artificial device. Neurophysiological concepts of sensory-system function, for example, have been employed in the design of computer-based, pattern-recognizing machines. The possibilities for fruitful interchange are increased when strong functional analogies between man and machine exist.

As with any analogy, the identity between man-made informational systems and the brain must not be pushed past its point of utility. As Arbib has noted, to say that "my love is like a red, red rose" does not mean that she would appreciate being soaked with cold water at regular intervals. But, where an analogy is applicable, its use may be beneficial.

A Preview

In the pages that follow, I have tried not to lose sight of psychology in the study of physiology. I have sought to pose meaningful psychological problems and to use neuroanatomical, neurochemical, and neurophysiological information in discerning possible solutions. As James wrote, "Our first conclusion is that a certain amount of brain-physiology must be presupposed or included in Psychology" (1890, p. 5). But the psychology must never be lost. This text begins with an examination of neuroanatomy and neurophysiology—the part that must be presupposed—and examines the properties of nervous tissue that enable the brain to process information. In addition, Chapter 2 develops some conceptions of the organization of the nervous system.

Chapters 3, 4, and 5 are concerned with the sensory systems. Much is known about the function of sensory systems; these systems provide excellent examples of the ways in which neuronal mechanisms filter and transform information to solve the important problems of perception. Such systems do not operate in isolation from the rest of the brain; perception must be considered an integrated process of the nervous system.

Chapter 6 investigates the output mechanisms of the nervous system, the muscle tissue, and the neuronal systems that control the muscle tissue. Here the idea of feedback control is discussed. The integration of muscle with other bodily tissue and the varying patterns of muscular innervation permit the diversity of action that characterizes man.

The states of consciousness, especially sleep and wakefulness, are the subjects of Chapter 7. Here we see that the pattern of organization within the brain is altered as the transitions between states are made.

Chapter 8 examines the problem of attention, both in selecting stimuli to which the organism will attend and in setting the momentary level of activation. Discussed here are those brain mechanisms that mobilize all major bodily organ systems as internal or environmental events dictate.

Chapter 9 approaches the joint problems of the ordering and the timing of behavior. Time is a crucial dimension of behavior, and temporally sensitive mechanisms are distributed throughout the nervous system. Single cells may serve as clocks in some organisms and are capable of triggering behavior cycles independently of any environmental stimulation.

The neuropsychological basis of language is examined in Chapter 10, where the brain properties that underlie the capacity for speech and symbolic thought, as well as the possibility that man is not the only primate capable of language use, are discussed.

Chapter 11 attempts to bring some physiological evidence to aid in understanding the problems of motivation and the emotions. Explored here are brain systems that mediate pleasure and pain and that seem to underlie emotional expression. This chapter also stresses the importance of both cognitive and bodily events that determine the form of emotion.

Chapter 12 examines the critical capacity of the nervous system for change. Through learning, organisms are able to modify their behavior on the basis of their own past experience, enhancing the adaptive capability of individual members of each species. Some current concepts of this ubiquitous process are discussed in an attempt to understand the mechanisms by which the nervous system can alter its own organization through experience.

The result of this endeavor is the concept of man as an organism, linked in evolution with other animals and endowed with a nervous system capable of complex processes and profound adaptability. Such a view of man provides a biological perspective within which problems of human existence may be considered.

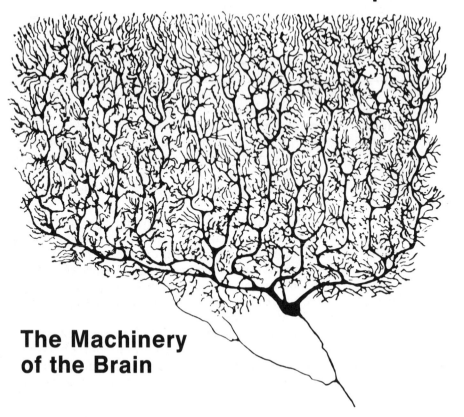

Chapter 2

The Machinery
of the Brain

It is the nervous system that controls and coordinates behavior, allowing the organism to respond adaptively in a complex environment. How does the nervous system perform these functions? A variety of explanations have been offered. For example, in the seventeenth century René Descartes reasoned that the responsible substance appeared to be "spirits" that flowed through the "tubes and spaces" of the brain. Descartes saw as crucial to this process the centrally located pineal gland, which acts as a valve, deflecting "spirits" from both halves of the body to motor centers, where action is initiated. Figure 2.1 shows Descartes' conception of this process.

Concepts of the nervous system have changed in the intervening 300 years. The fluids and ventricles of the brain are important but not in the control of behavior. However, the mechanistic concept relating brain and behavior that Descartes championed is still the keystone of the neurosciences. To understand the control of behavior, the structure and the function of the brain must be understood as well. For that

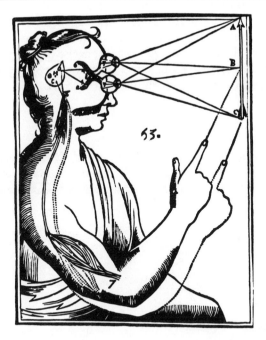

Figure 2.1. *An early view of the brain.* René Descartes ascribed the control of behavior to the mechanistic flow of "spirits," which enter through the eyes and proceed through the optic nerve to the pineal gland where they are reflected to the pores of motor nerves, giving rise to movement. Although the concept of spirit has not proved fruitful for the neurosciences, the mechanistic concepts that Descartes championed form the foundation of modern biological thought. (From Magoun, H. W., *The Waking Brain*, 1963, p. 8. Courtesy of Charles C Thomas, Publisher, Springfield, Illinois.)

reason, the study of physiological psychology begins with the non-behavioral concepts of neurophysiology (the study of neuronal functioning) and neuroanatomy (the study of the structure of the nervous system).

Modern neurophysiology has focused not on the fluid-filled ventricles of the brain but on its cellular matter instead. The brain and nervous system are composed of two types of cells, the neurons and the glia. Glial cells outnumber neurons in the brain by a factor of ten to one, but most glia are much smaller than neurons. Therefore, by weight, the brain has equal amounts of glial and neural tissue. Although some theorists have proposed that glial cells share in the information-processing functions of the brain, their only firmly established role is that of supportive elements for the neuronal cells. Glia are probably responsible for carrying oxygen and nutrients from the blood to the neurons and for transporting waste products back in the opposite direction. Some glial cells appear to perform special insulating functions by wrapping themselves about the axons of neurons (see Figure 2.10). Still others remove dead or damaged cells from the brain. But the role of the brain in guiding behavior seems to depend upon the activity of the other major constituent of brain tissue, the neurons.

The Neuron

Neurons are cells that are especially adapted to perform information-processing functions. Figure 2.2 illustrates many of the structural features of a typical neuron. Three major regions are of

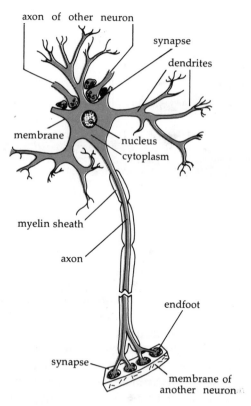

Figure 2.2. *The idealized neuron as commonly conceived.* The major structural elements of the soma, dendrites, and axon are shown. Notice also the synaptic input from other neurons. An idealized neuron is not an actual neuron, but the structural elements shown here are present in most neurons of the nervous system.

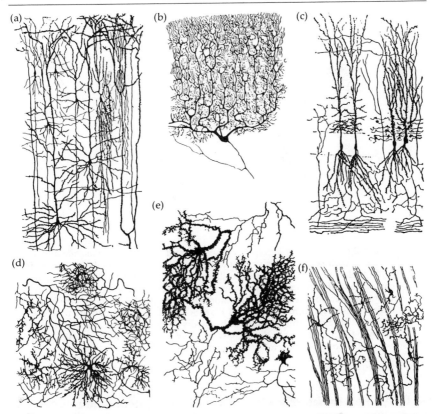

Figure 2.3. *Structural variations in neurons.* A sampling of neurons, drawn from various areas of the brain, exhibits great diversity of form. (From Ramon y Cajal, S. 1955, as reprinted in Purpura, D. Comparative physiology of dendrites. In G. Quarton, T. Melnechuk, & F. Schmitt (Eds.), *The Neurosciences: A Study Program*, 1967, p. 373. Used by permission of The Rockefeller University Press.)

importance. First is the cell body, or soma, which contains the nucleus of the cell. Second are the dendrites, which are fibers or processes that extend from the cell body. While often relatively short, the dendrites may be extremely complex (see, for example, Figures 2.3 and 2.4). Dendrites function to collect information from other neurons and transmit that information in an integrated form to the soma of the neuron. The complex dendritic trees—a term suggested by the branch-like structure of many dendrites—probably determine the form that information processing will take in the dendrites of these neurons. Thus, dendritic structure may be related to cellular function. The third major region of the neuron is the axon, usually a single process and often rather long. The axon functions to transmit information from the

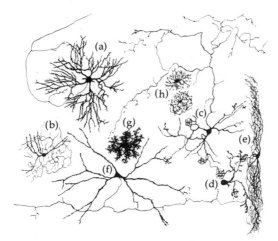

Figure 2.4. *A series of different cell types drawn from a single thalamic nucleus in the cat.* Each cell displays structural characteristics appropriate to its function: (a) a thalamocortical projection cell, (b)–(e) local circuit cells, each showing somewhat different structural properties, making connections entirely within the ventrobasalar nucleus, (f) an integrator cell with a double axon, (g)–(h) glial cells of the thalamus. (From Scheibel, M. E., & Scheibel, A. B. Elementary processes in selected thalamic and cortical subsystems—the structural substrates. In F. Schmitt (Ed.), *The Neurosciences: Second Study Program,* 1970, p. 445. Used by permission of The Rockefeller University Press.)

cell body to other neurons within the nervous system or to muscle and glandular tissues. The axon hillock is the region of the neuron connecting the axon and the soma.

Neurons communicate through synapses, which are specialized structures for information transmission. Each synapse has three important regions: the presynaptic membrane, the synaptic cleft, and the postsynaptic membrane. The presynaptic membrane is always the membrane of an endfoot, a tiny bulblike swelling at the end of the axon. (An axon may divide into many small branches, each with its own endfoot, as the axon is about to contact other cells.) The postsynaptic membrane may be the surface of a cell body, a dendrite, or even another endfoot, although most synapses are probably of the axodendritic form (a connection between a presynaptic axon and a postsynaptic dendrite). Separating the pre- and postsynaptic membranes is the synaptic cleft, a small space filled with extracellular fluid. The synapse is a polarized structure; information passes only from the presynaptic to the postsynaptic neuron. No communication in the reverse direction appears possible.

The Neuronal Membrane

An understanding of psychological information-processing functions depends upon knowledge of the representation of information within the nervous system. It appears that information is coded as a series of electrochemical events within the brain. These electrochemical events are themselves reflections of complex changes occurring within the neuronal membrane, the thin barrier separating the intracellular fluid of the neuron from the extracellular fluid that surrounds the cell. Membrane events thus form the basis for information processing in the nervous system.

The membrane itself is very thin, only about 50 to 75 angstroms wide (an angstrom is one ten-thousandth of a micron or one ten-millionth of a millimeter). This tiny barrier separates two fluids that are chemically quite different (see Figure 2.5). The intracellular fluid contains much more potassium (K^+) than does the extracellular fluid; whereas the extracellular fluid has greater concentrations of both sodium (Na^+) and chloride (Cl^-). These ions are electrically charged particles that combine with molecules of water. In this form, the ions are said to be hydrated. Under proper conditions, the movement of such particles can produce electrical forces.

If the membrane were totally impermeable to these three and all other ions, no ions could ever cross the membrane, and the two fluids would be totally isolated and without effect on each other. If, at the other extreme, the membrane were completely permeable, sodium, potassium, and chloride would cross the membrane freely, and soon no electrical or concentration differences would exist between the intracellular and extracellular fluids. In fact, the membrane is only slightly permeable to any of the three ions, and even that permeability is differential. The membrane is more permeable to potassium than to sodium by a factor of about 100 to 1.

If the membrane were permeable only to potassium, what would be the result? Think of the membrane as a solid structure with pores through which hydrated potassium ions can just pass. Hydrated sodium is larger than hydrated potassium and therefore cannot pass through these pores. But potassium ions would be relatively free to move in both directions, into and out of the cell body. Since ions in solution are constantly moving about, there is some probability that a potassium ion will strike a pore and pass through it. Because there are far more potassium ions on the inside than on the outside, it is much more likely that an inside potassium ion will enter a pore and pass through it. Ions diffuse from a region of higher concentration to a

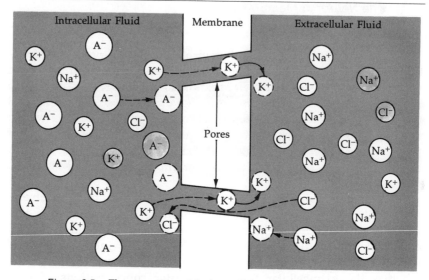

Figure 2.5. *The composition of the intracellular and extracellular fluids, separated by a semipermeable membrane.* In the resting state, only hydrated potassium and chloride can pass freely through the membrane. Both ions have the same effect, driving the membrane potential to a compromise voltage of about −70 millivolts, the inside being negative with respect to the outside. The development of the resting potential is discussed in the text using the K^+ ion, although other ions are also present. Cl^-, for example, functions in the reciprocal manner to K^+. Since the Cl^- ion is a negatively charged particle and, unlike K^+, is concentrated outside the cellular membrane, the movement of either ion species along its own concentration gradient across the membrane produces inside negativity. Large anions (A^-), which cannot pass through the membrane, are nonetheless attracted to the positive ions in the extracellular fluid, resulting in a clustering of anions along the inside membrane.

region of lower concentration. For example, if a speck of ink is dropped into a glass of water, the dye molecules diffuse (from a region of high concentration to regions of lower concentration) until the water is of uniform color (no concentration differences exist). In the case of the neural membrane, it makes sense to think of concentration forces tending to push potassium ions out of the cell into the extracellular fluid, a region of low potassium concentration.

But little potassium will actually pass into the extracellular fluid when the membrane is permeable only to potassium. Other forces act to stop the outward movement. Potassium is an ion and therefore electrically charged. The movement of even a single ion across the membrane creates an electrical force. When an intracellular potassium ion moves across the membrane, the cell loses a positive charge and the extracellular fluid gains a positive charge. Therefore, the inside of the cell becomes negative with respect to the outside. How can the situation be rectified? A potassium ion could move back into the cell, but that is not very likely. There are some potassium ions in the extracellular fluid, but they are relatively rare; so the odds are against the movement of an extracellular potassium ion across the membrane. Could another kind of positive ion move in to replace the potassium ion that left the cell? This time the answer is definitely no, since this membrane by definition is impermeable to all other ion species. Extracellular sodium, for instance, cannot move in to replace the lost potassium. An electrical charge results when a membrane is permeable to only one ion species and the concentration of that ion is not uniform across the membrane. It is the movement of an ion along its concentration gradient (from greater to lesser concentration), across a membrane permeable only to that ion, that generates electrical force in living cells. This force is the membrane potential since it is the membrane that is primarily responsible for its generation.

Since opposite electrical charges attract each other and the membrane is very thin, ions tend to be trapped on either side of the membrane. A positive potassium ion having left the cell through a pore is attracted to available negative ions still inside the cell. Since the cell wall blocks the positive ion's return, the charged particles on both sides cling to the membrane. Charges separated by the membrane congregate along it, giving rise to what is known as a capacitive charge. The electrical forces generated by the movement of ions across the membrane remain at the membrane that gave rise to those forces.

Just as opposite electrical charges attract each other, similar charges repel each other. Positive ions are driven from a positive electrical field. With this in mind, it is easy to see why potassium does not keep flowing out of the cell until internal and external concentrations of the ion are equal. With the movement of each additional potassium ion outward, the strength of the positive electrical field outside the cell increases. Eventually it will reach a point at which the electrical forces exactly equal the force of concentration. From that moment until conditions change, potassium will be in electrochemical equilibrium. No more potassium will move in than moves out. If the outward flow were to slow, the membrane potential would drop, encouraging more outward movement. If outward movement were to increase, the membrane potential would correspondingly increase, forcing more potassium back into the cell. But, at the equilibrium potential, concentration and electrical forces exactly balance to produce no net movement. Thus, it should be clear that, if a membrane is permeable only to one species of ion, the membrane potential is determined by the concentration difference across the membrane. Very small concentration differences are counteracted by very small electrical fields. Very large differences in concentration, which make unidirectional movement of the ion across the membrane very likely, require relatively large electrical forces to limit the ionic flow.

The membrane of actual neurons at rest fits reasonably well with this model. The neuronal membrane is much more permeable to potassium than to sodium. Therefore, the resting membrane potential depends primarily upon the concentration differences for potassium. Ions that cannot cross the membrane, or that can cross only in very small amounts, contribute nothing or little to the actual membrane potential. The resting potential is a compromise among the equilibrium potentials of all ions involved, but the compromise is made in accordance with the relative permeability of the membrane to the various ions it separates. Ions that cross the membrane most freely contribute most to the membrane potential.

In the mammalian nervous system, membrane permeability and the concentration differences of several ions combine to produce a resting potential of about −70 millivolts (mV), the inside being negative with respect to the outside. For the sake of understanding, it is useful to think of this resting membrane as primarily a potassium membrane, a membrane permeable only to potassium; although this is a severe oversimplification.

The ability of neurons to communicate with each other over long distances rests on the ability of the axonal membrane to change its state when appropriately stimulated. Under certain conditions, a patch of axonal membrane may suddenly transform itself from a potassium-permeable to a sodium-permeable structure—a change that would produce a shift in the membrane potential toward the equilibrium potential of sodium.

Sodium, like potassium, is a positive ion, but, unlike potassium, it is concentrated outside the cell. If the membrane passed only sodium, positive sodium charges would be likely to move from the extracellular fluid, where they are most dense, to the intracellular fluid, where they are scarce. The inside of a cell with a sodium membrane would then be positive. With the concentration differences in sodium that exist in the mammalian nervous system, a purely sodium membrane, which passed no other ions, would maintain an equilibrium potential of about +60 mV (the inside being positive with respect to the outside).

If the membrane were suddenly to change from a potassium to a sodium membrane, the membrane potential would shift from the potassium equilibrium (−90 mV) to the sodium equilibrium (+60 mV). At first, sodium ions would be driven into the cell both by the sodium concentration gradient and by electrical forces. Remember that the inside is still negative and that sodium is a positive ion. The electrical attraction diminishes as more and more sodium ions enter the cell, replacing the potassium ions that had gone out before and making the inside less and less negative. Soon the deficit of positive ions in the intracellular fluid is more than made up, and the inside of the cell becomes positive. This process continues until the sodium equilibrium is reached.

The Nerve Impulse

Changes in membrane permeability actually occur in neurons, giving rise to an electrochemical event of crucial importance to neuronal functioning—the nerve impulse. If a cell is electrically stimulated near its axon in such a way as to depolarize the membrane (making the resting potassium membrane less negative), a brief and stereotyped sequence of events takes place in the membrane. For a very short period of time, on the order of 1 millisecond (msec), the membrane becomes more permeable to sodium. The molecular basis of this change within the membrane is unknown, but some mechanism within the membrane itself is responsible for the sudden switch from potassium permeability to increased sodium permeability. The result of this process is the expected change from the resting membrane potential of −70 mV to a sodium-dominant membrane potential of +30 mV. Immediately thereafter the membrane transforms itself again into a primarily potassium-permeable structure, and the membrane potential again becomes negative. These electrical changes are shown in Figure 2.6, which illustrates the action potential—the electrical representation of the nerve impulse.

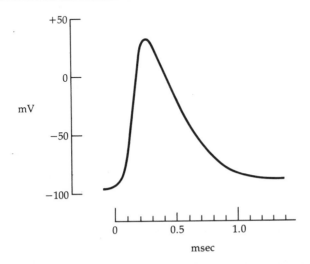

Figure 2.6. *The action potential, or spike.* The graph shows the action potential in detail. The duration of the primary electrical event is less than 1 msec.

How does depolarization produce a shift in membrane permeabilities? Whatever the responsible molecular mechanism might be, it involves the circular process of positive feedback. Sodium permeability depends heavily upon membrane depolarization. When a membrane becomes depolarized, either as a consequence of electrical stimulation or in the normal functioning of the neuron, sodium is able to pass through the membrane more freely. Since sodium is a positively charged ion, its entry further depolarizes the membrane. In response to the increased depolarization, the membrane increases its permeability to sodium and thus permits the entry of additional sodium ions at an ever increasing rate. This feedback process is called the Hodgkin cycle after its discoverer and is illustrated in Figure 2.7.

The Hodgkin cycle appears to be self-limiting. The increase in sodium permeability lasts only for about 1 msec, even when the cell is artificially maintained in a depolarized state. Inactivation of the heightened permeability to sodium appears to be an intrinsic and fundamental property of the membrane itself. Also, the return to a potassium equilibrium potential is facilitated by a temporary increase in the membrane's normal permeability to potassium. By opening the membrane still more to potassium, the recovery from the sodium equilibrium potential is hastened. Figure 2.8 depicts these processes.

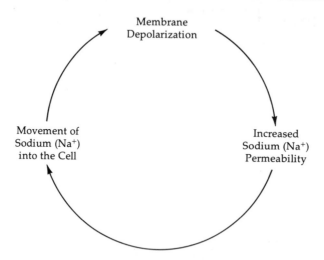

Figure 2.7.   *The Hodgkin cycle—a positive feedback loop that characterizes excitable membranes.* Depolarization of the membrane increases the membrane's permeability to sodium, which, under normal conditions, results in the increased influx of sodium, further depolarizing the membrane.

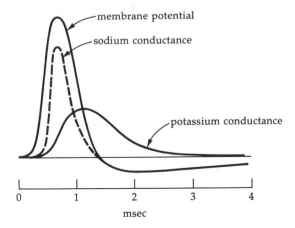

membrane potential

sodium conductance

potassium conductance

0   1   2   3   4

msec

Figure 2.8. *The membrane events underlying the action potential.* Sodium conductance increases dramatically as the action potential begins, but the sodium channels are quickly inactivated. An increased potassium conductance, which begins at the peak of the spike, aids in the recovery of the resting potential.

Weak depolarizing stimuli are not sufficient to trigger the Hodgkin cycle. The Hodgkin cycle and the action potential that it produces require depolarization of the membrane at or beyond the threshold, usually several mV above the resting potential. If depolarization does not reach threshold, no action potential is produced. When depolarization exceeds threshold and the membrane is at rest, an action potential always occurs. Depolarization triggers the action potential, or spike, but does not determine its form. Once triggered, the Hodgkin cycle proceeds independently of the stimulus. The size of the spike, its shape, and its duration are fixed for a given neuron. The action potential, generated by energy within the axon, does not depend upon the energy of the stimulus once the threshold has been reached. Stronger stimuli do not produce larger spikes. For this reason, the spike is an "all or nothing" response. The analogy is often drawn between the generation of a spike in a neuron and the firing of a bullet from a rifle, since the speed of the bullet does not depend upon the force with which the trigger is pulled. Once triggered, the device responds in its own fixed manner.

Although the switch to the sodium membrane occurs very quickly, the recovery from this altered state takes somewhat more time. Because of the nature of the membrane properties, a second action potential cannot be triggered while the first is still taking place. During this time period, the absolute refractory period, the neuron is completely impervious to further stimulation. In the mammalian nervous system, the absolute refractory period is about 0.5 to 1 msec in duration. Immediately thereafter, during the relative refractory period, the cell continues to restore potassium equilibrium. During this relative refractory period, which typically continues for up to 100 msec, the threshold of the cell is raised.

The effect of the relative refractory period is to preserve information about the strength of the depolarizing stimulus. Stronger, long-lasting stimuli are able to trigger the action potential for a second time at an early point in the relative refractory period, as the threshold level slowly drifts back to normal. The result is that strong stimuli can fire a cell at a faster rate than can weaker stimuli. This relation between stimulus strength and rate of spike production is an important principle in understanding the processing of sensory information within the nervous system.

Propagation of the Nerve Impulse

The nerve impulse normally originates in the axon hillock of the neuron as the result of excitatory (depolarizing) synaptic activity in the dendrites. Nerve impulses do not arise in the dendrites or soma since the membrane in these regions of the neuron presumably is not excitable; that is, it does not respond to increasing depolarization with increases in sodium permeability. Therefore, the axon hillock, which, like the axon itself, is excitable, becomes the usual site of nerve-impulse generation.

The function of the nerve impulse is to transmit information in a reliable manner from the soma to the endfeet of the axon. Information is transmitted as the nerve impulse is propagated down the length of the axon. Propagation occurs in the following manner. With the initiation of the nerve impulse at the axon hillock, the membrane at the site of the nerve impulse becomes inside positive and current flows into the cell at this point. At the same time, current flows out of the cell at points surrounding the active site, with the density of current flow decreasing with increasing distance from the active site. Current flowing out of the cell acts to depolarize the membrane through which it flows. Thus, the existence of a nerve impulse at the axon hillock depolarizes the surrounding membrane and, by this process, triggers the generation of a nerve impulse in the immediately adjacent portion of the axon. Thus, the nerve impulse is propagated in the axon, passing as a smooth wavefront from the axon hillock, where it originates, to the endfeet of the axon, where it terminates. The nerve impulse does not travel back into the soma because the membrane of the soma is not excitable. The nerve impulse does not travel from the endfoot to the soma because, under normal conditions, there is no mechanism in the endfeet capable of depolarizing the axon and generating the nerve impulse. Thus, under normal conditions, the flow of information in the axon proceeds in an orderly fashion from soma to endfeet as a propagated nerve impulse.

The nerve impulse travels at a fixed rate of propagation in the particular neuron, which is determined by factors such as the diameter of the axon. The amplitude of the nerve impulse is similarly dependent upon properties of the axon, particularly the concentration difference of Na^+ across the membrane. Thus, the propagated nerve impulse is a relatively robust biological signal, continuously regenerated as it passes down the membrane of the axon and capable of faithfully representing information over great distances.

If a nerve impulse is initiated in an axon not by the activation of excitatory synaptic events but by the artificial application of electric current, the neuron responds in much the same way. Stimulation of the axon hillock generates a nerve impulse that is propagated down the length of the axon. If the stimulating probe is applied not to the axon hillock but to some portion of the axon itself, a nerve impulse is also generated (see Figure 2.9). However, this nerve impulse is propagated in two directions, with one wave of depolarization traveling toward the soma and another toward the endfeet. This splitting occurs because the axon itself is not a directionally polarized structure. The normal soma-to-endfeet information flow is strictly a function of the fact that excitatory events occur in the axon hillock and not in the endfeet. But even under normal conditions a spike may be present in the axon as it is being propagated from the axon hillock to the endfeet. Why does this nerve impulse not divide and return to the soma as is the case when the axon is artificially stimulated? The nerve impulse does not divide under these conditions since to do so would require that the impulse be propagated in a region of the axon through which it had just passed. This is impossible since, having just generated a nerve impulse, the region immediately behind the advancing wavefront is in its absolute refractory period. Thus, even though current flows in both directions in the axon from the site of the nerve impulse, the depolarizing effects of this current can trigger a nerve impulse only in the region of the axon that the impulse is invading and not in the refractory portion of the axon through which it has just passed.

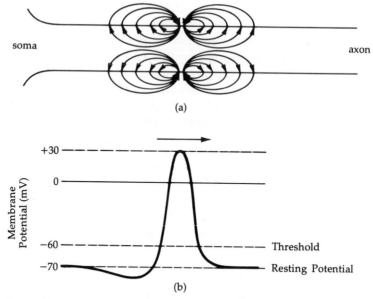

(a)

(b)

Figure 2.9. *An action potential being propagated along an axon.* (a) The action potential begins with an inrush of sodium and concludes with the outward movement of potassium as the spike moves down the membrane. The arrows indicate the pattern of the flow of current (movement of positive ions) depolarizing the membrane both preceding and following the site of the action potential. The current flow depolarizes the membrane but triggers a spike only in front of the advancing wave, since the tissue behind it is in the absolute refractory state. (b) The graph shows the membrane potential of the same axon. The peak of the spike corresponds to the point of maximum ion movement in (a). The single arrow indicates the direction of spike propagation along the axon.

Saltatory Conduction

The speed with which an axon can propagate a nerve impulse is largely a function of the distance from the active site that a significant depolarizing current may travel. Arrangements that facilitate the flow of current through the axon act to increase the rate of spike propagation, since the electrotonic flow of current is quite rapid compared with the slower membrane events necessary to regenerate the nerve impulse. Thus, larger axons have higher propagation rates since their increased internal volume facilitates the flow of current down the axon.

Another method for extending the range of current flow in vertebrate axons is the insulation of the axon with myelin sheaths (see Figure 2.10). These sheaths are about 2 mm in length and are composed of the tightly wrapped membrane of a specialized glial cell. Each

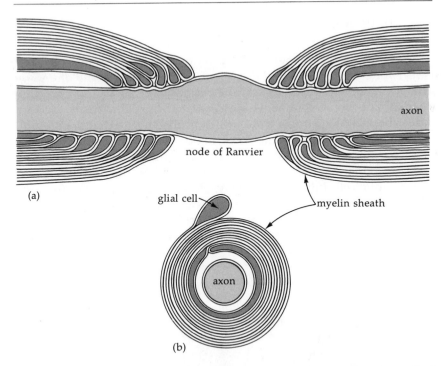

Figure 2.10. *The myelin sheath and a node of Ranvier.* In (a), a longitudinal section of a myelinated axon is shown. The break in the myelin sheath is a node of Ranvier. At this point, the membrane is in contact with both the intracellular and the extracellular fluids. Only at these nodes on a myelinated axon can an action potential be produced. Drawing (b) shows the myelin sheath in cross section, revealing its many layers, and the glial cell from which it originates.

segment is separated from the next by a small space, the node of Ranvier. It is only at these nodes that the membrane of the axon may make contact with the extracellular fluid. Between nodes, the thick coating of myelin separates the intracellular fluid and the axon membrane from the extracellular fluid. This has the effect of decreasing dramatically the density of ions normally capacitively bound to the membrane and thereby increasing the distance of effective current flow in the axon. In the myelinated axon, therefore, the nerve impulse may be generated only at the nodes of Ranvier and thus seems to jump from node to node, a form of propagation termed saltatory conduction (from the Latin "saltare," to jump). Myelination of axons was a crucial development in vertebrate evolution, since it permitted high-speed, long-distance communication without requiring significant increases in axon width. This in turn allowed for the evolution of large, quickly responding, complicated organisms such as man.

Synaptic Structure and Synaptic Transmission

A synapse is the point of connection between two neurons. The presynaptic component is the endfoot of one neuron, and the post-synaptic component is a dendrite, a cell body, or an axon of the other neuron. The two components are separated by the synaptic cleft—a space about 200 angstroms wide, which is filled with extracellular fluid. Although the endfoot and the postsynaptic membrane come very close to each other, they do not touch. Through the synaptic structures, a spike arriving on the presynaptic axon affects the activity of the postsynaptic cell. Information always flows in one direction, from the endfoot across the cleft; there is no known mechanism by which the postsynaptic membrane can affect the activity of the endfoot. Figures 2.11, 2.12, and 2.13 show this synaptic structure in detail. As with other

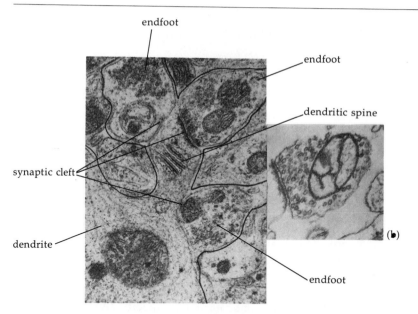

Figure 2.11. *Some endfeet synapsing on a dendrite and a dendritic spine.* In (a), three endfeet are shown; the upper two synapse on a dendritic spine, a small protuberance from the main dendrite. The third endfoot synapses on the dendrite itself. Notice that all three synapses possess a synaptic cleft, separating the endfoot from the dendrite. Concentrations of vesicles at the presynaptic membranes may also be seen. In (b), a single synapse is shown. (From Whittaker, V. P. The investigation of synaptic function by means of subcellular fractionation techniques. In F. O. Schmitt (Ed.), *The Neurosciences: Second Study Program.* New York: Rockefeller, 1970. Reprinted by permission.)

cellular structures, there is much variability in the form of synaptic connection. For example, synapses may be classified by the portion of the postsynaptic neuron contacted by the endfoot. Axodendritic synapses, terminating on a postsynaptic dendrite, are believed to be excitatory in function. Conversely, axosomatic synapses, which include a portion of the soma as the postsynaptic element, are thought to be inhibitory. The third form of synapse involves endfeet as both the pre- and postsynaptic elements. Such connections may be either inhibitory or excitatory, but the firmest evidence to date confirms only one type of interaction in which the activation of the presynaptic endfoot lessens the effectiveness of the postsynaptic endfoot in effecting the release of neurotransmitters at the synapse between the second endfoot and a third cell. This rather complex form of interaction is termed presynaptic inhibition; presynaptic refers to the connection between the second and third cell. Presynaptic excitation may also occur.

How does a nerve impulse, arriving at an endfoot, change the electrical activity of the postsynaptic neuron? Since the synaptic cleft is filled with extracellular fluid, current could simply flow through the space to the postsynaptic membrane. Such an explanation is, however, unlikely for several reasons. First, although the nerve impulse is always uniform, the postsynaptic changes can result in either an increase or a decrease in membrane polarization. An explanation based on the simple flow of current could not explain such events. Second, there is no electrical activity at the postsynaptic membrane when the spike is at its height in the endfoot. Electrical transmission across the membrane would be nearly instantaneous. In fact, however, there is a delay of 0.3 to 0.5 msec before any potential change occurs at the postsynaptic membrane. A more valid explanation is that the transmission of information across the membrane is chemical, not electrical. Different chemicals could produce different effects on the postsynaptic membrane. Electrical changes should not appear postsynaptically until after a transmitter substance is released from the endfoot and diffuses across the synaptic cleft. The time estimated for the diffusion of a substance across 200 angstroms of extracellular fluid is about 0.3 msec. Thus, the nature of communication between neurons in the mammalian brain appears to be primarily chemical.

The structure of the endfoot also suggests a chemical, rather than electrical, phenomenon. Figure 2.13 is a photograph of one endfoot, the synaptic cleft, and the postsynaptic membrane. Notice the collections of small spherical objects within the endfoot. These synaptic vesicles are thought to be tiny packets, each containing a small amount of chemical transmitter. When a spike reaches the endfoot, unknown changes take place within the membrane to cause a release of the neurotransmitter from the vesicles into the synaptic cleft. Chemicals that could perform

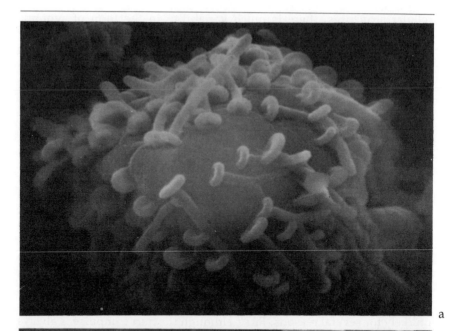

a

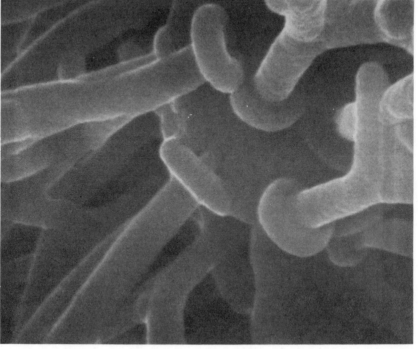

b

transmitter functions are indeed found in isolated synaptic structures. Studies of electrical activity in the neuromuscular junction, a synaptic-like structure joining motor neuron with muscle fiber, also indicate that the packets contain transmitters. Through careful recording, tiny electrical events that are always exactly the same size and that occur at random intervals have been detected on the postsynaptic membrane. These miniature endplate potentials, as they are called, are probably the result of the random release of individual packets, each containing the same amount of transmitter substance. Sometimes, observations are made of postsynaptic changes that are exactly two or exactly three times larger than the usual miniature endplate potential, suggesting that two or three packets have been released simultaneously.

In the peripheral nervous system, it has been possible to identify with some certainty the neurochemicals that function as synaptic transmitters. Acetylcholine (ACh) performs this function at the neuromuscular junction, at all synapses of the parasympathetic branch of the autonomic nervous system, and at the preganglionic synapses (between spinal neurons and ganglia cells) of the sympathetic nervous system. The postganglionic neurons of the sympathetic nervous system employ another neurochemical, norepinephrine (also known as nor-adrenaline). The positive identification of neurotransmitter agents within the central nervous system, however, has been far more difficult.

A number of conditions must be met to assert with certainty that a particular agent functions as a transmitter for a specified class of synapses. First, it is necessary to demonstrate that the endfeet of the presynaptic neurons actually contain the transmitter substance and that activation of the presynaptic neuron causes release of that substance. Moreover, another chemical agent that functions to break down or deactivate the transmitter agent must be present within the synaptic system. Such enzymes are necessary to reverse the effects of the neurotransmitter on the postsynaptic membrane and to maintain the stability of the synaptic system. Further, the postsynaptic membrane must respond to the supposed transmitter agent when experimentally

Figure 2.12. *Photomicrographs of synapses in Aplysia, the California sea hare.* The scanning electron microscope provides a great depth of field, allowing a more three-dimensional view of the subject. Here, a large number of endfeet are shown synapsing on a single neuron at low (a) and high (b) magnification. (From Lewis, E. R., Everhart, T. E., & Zeevi, Y. Y. Studying neural organization in Aplysia with the scanning electron microscope. *Science,* 1969, **165,** 1142. Copyright 1969 by the American Association for the Advancement of Science. Reprinted by permission.)

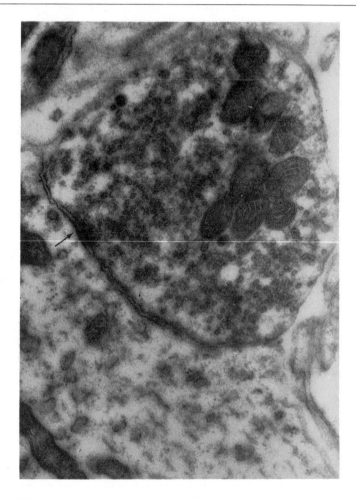

Figure 2.13. *An electron micrograph of a single endfoot.* Individual spherical vesicles can be easily distinguished. The arrow points to the synaptic cleft. (From Palay, S. L. The morphology of synapses in the central nervous system. *Experimental Cell Research*, 1958, Suppl. 5, 280. © 1958 by Academic Press, Inc. Used by permission.)

applied to the synaptic structure. This demonstrates that the neuro-chemical is sufficient to produce postsynaptic activation. Finally, pharmacological agents that interfere with the function of the transmitter agent must also interfere with the normal functioning of the synapse. These criteria are quite stringent. Nonetheless, it has been possible to meet all these requirements in the identification of the peripheral transmitters, acetylcholine and norepinephrine. No single chemical compound has been identified with any certainty as a CNS transmitter agent. Acetylcholine is often suggested as an excitatory transmitter within the CNS, whereas various investigators have proposed gamma-aminobutyric acid (GABA), norepinephrine, dopamine, and 5-hydroxytryptamine (5-HT) as inhibitory agents. The difficulty in the identification of central neurotransmitters is primarily a function of the complexity of central nervous system tissue.

Excitatory Postsynaptic Potentials

Within the central nervous system, the effects of transmitter release may be either excitatory or inhibitory, depending upon the chemical contained in the vesicles of the endfoot and the reactivity of the postsynaptic membrane. Different neurotransmitters are released by different neurons, but each neuron appears to use only one neurotransmitter at all of its endfeet. If the effect of transmitter release is to depolarize the postsynaptic membrane, the synapse is considered to be excitatory, since its action tends to induce spiking in the postsynaptic neuron. The immediate depolarizing response of the postsynaptic membrane to the release of an excitatory transmitter substance is termed an excitatory postsynaptic potential (EPSP).

An EPSP is a longer lasting event than the presynaptic spike that triggers it. Unlike the action potential, the EPSPs vary in size. Depending upon certain conditions in the endfoot, different numbers of packets may be released on different occasions, leading to greater or lesser changes in the postsynaptic membrane. The EPSP is thus a graded potential.

Excitatory transmitters appear to depolarize the membrane by interfering with its normal selective permeability. Since the selective permeability of the membrane produces the membrane potential in the first place, opening the membrane to many kinds of ions allows normally excluded ions, such as extracellular sodium, to rush into the cell, making it less negative. Unlike the membrane in the nerve impulse, however, the opened membrane will not permit the buildup of a sodium equilibrium potential, since positive potassium ions can flow outward with equal ease. The voltage across a nonselectively permeable membrane will be zero if given sufficient time for the necessary movement of ions.

The membrane does not, however, completely depolarize when an excitatory transmitter is released. Within the membrane are complex chemical systems designed to deactivate the transmitter substance and return the membrane to its normal condition. The process of deactivation is responsible for the termination of the EPSP.

Inhibitory Postsynaptic Potentials

Other synapses, containing different chemical transmitters, act to hyperpolarize, or increase the negativity of, the postsynaptic membrane and drive it away from the threshold level necessary to produce a spike. Since these synapses tend to prevent neural firing, their hyperpolarizing responses are called inhibitory postsynaptic potentials (IPSPs). IPSPs tend to drive the postsynaptic membrane toward −75 mV. The inhibitory neurotransmitter liberated in the synapse increases the permeability of the postsynaptic membrane for both potassium and chloride. A compromise between the equilibrium potentials of these two ions would be about −75 mV under normal concentrations in the intracellular and extracellular fluids. Inhibitory transmitters, like excitatory agents, are deactivated within the postsynaptic membrane.

Spatial and Temporal Summation

Action potentials are triggered when the axon hillock reaches the spike threshold. Neurons normally have only one axon but make many synapses with input fibers. The effects of all synapses must interact to determine whether a spike will be produced.

The capacity of a neuron to integrate information is apparent when the structure of a complex neuron is examined. Figure 2.14 shows the many synapses of a single neuron. Clearly, no single synapse can dominate the activity of the others, although synapses nearer the axon are relatively more important in the initiation of spike activity, since these synapses exert a greater electrotonic effect on the axon's excitable membrane. EPSPs and IPSPs from each of the synapses summate, triggering an action potential if the resulting depolarization reaches threshold in the axon hillock. This process of combined influence from many different areas of the membrane is called spatial summation.

If a number of spikes arrive at one synapse in a short period of time, each release of transmitter will summate with prior and subsequent releases, resulting in a larger EPSP if the synapse is excitatory or a larger IPSP if the synapse is inhibitory. This is temporal summation, or the integration of activity in time.

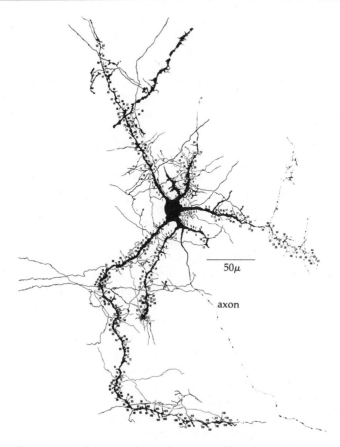

50μ

axon

Figure 2.14. *Synapses of a single neuron.*   Neurons act to integrate information from a large number of inputs. Here, many synapses (each indicated by a number) act on the dendrites of a single neuron. (From Calvin, M. Chemical evolution of life and sensibility. In G. Quarton, T. Melnechuk, & F. Schmitt (Eds.), *The Neurosciences: A Study Program,* 1967, p. 796. Used by permission of The Rockefeller University Press.)

The Organization of Nervous Tissue

The ability of the nervous system to control behavior depends not only upon the information-processing properties of individual neurons but also upon the ways in which single cells are combined to form functional units. The patterns of connections among cells and the organization of neurons into larger anatomical structures are critically important to the understanding of neuropsychology. A conceptual map of the nervous system is necessary before the control of any specific function can be examined.

Figures 2.15 through 2.23 depict the brain and nervous system from several vantage points. What organizational patterns do these drawings reveal? Several major concepts have influenced neuroanatomical thinking in the last century. None is completely adequate by itself, but together these concepts give a reasonably accurate idea of the complexity of brain structure.

Magoun, in reviewing the historical development of neuroanatomical concepts, has distinguished three major models that have contributed to neuroanatomical theory. The first of these is an evolutionary model, developed in the nineteenth century and based on the ideas introduced by Lyell and Darwin. It considers the complex mammalian nervous system as a series of levels, each controlling approximately similar functions at different degrees of complexity. The primitive nervous system is a relatively simple structure, sensitive to some environmental changes and capable of triggering a limited set of behavioral responses to those changes. In the process of evolution, organisms acquire the ability to detect increasingly subtle events in the world about them and to respond in more complicated and adaptive ways. Each such major evolutionary step results in the elaboration of a higher neuronal level that dominates those below it. From this viewpoint, the nervous system of man is comprised of a number of levels, the most primitive being the spinal cord and some brainstem structures, the highest being the great cerebral cortex. The regulation of basic internal functions such as breathing, digestion, and similar processes is controlled in the brainstem. The sensory and motor areas of the cortex, which developed later, serve the higher functions of adaptation, including the establishment of conditioned reflexes and learned, complex behaviors in general. Finally, in man, the development of the enlarged association areas of the cortex, which are neither clearly sensory nor clearly motor, permits language and sophisticated symbolic processes. The evolutionary model stresses the increased encephalization, or growth of the cerebral hemispheres, as one ascends the phylogenetic tree.

A second model stresses the pattern of growth in an individual animal as representing a fundamental principle of organization within the brain. This embryological concept emphasizes lateral differentiation in the nervous system. Viewed horizontally instead of vertically, the central core of the brain appears to be general in function and undifferentiated in structure. As one moves sideways, increasingly specialized patterns of neural organization appear. Central structures tend to be nonspecific, whereas lateral areas are highly specific. The lateral structures are added to the primitive neural tube as the nervous system of the embryo matures.

The third major stream of neuroanatomical thought centers on a technological model. Modern control theory concerns itself with the flow of information in man-made as well as biological systems. Anatomists influenced by this approach search for fiber pathways that can serve to control functions. Fundamental to this thinking is the concept of feedback. Adaptively controlled processes must have information about their own output, or behavior, in order to control their performance in the future. Informational pathways in a feedback-controlled system therefore tend to form loops, relaying information between various levels within the system. Viewed from this perspective, the brain is formed of many pathways linking different structures throughout the nervous system to produce finely regulated, adaptive behavior.

Directions in the Brain

In discussing the nervous system and its function, it is often necessary to describe the location of one area in relation to another. A special vocabulary is used to refer to directions. For example, dorsal refers to the back of the four-legged animal and ventral to the front or belly side, divided along the horizontal plane. Along the nose-to-tail axis, the head is anterior, or rostral, and the tail is posterior, or caudal. Medial refers to the center of the organism, or its brain, and lateral refers to structures located to either side of the midline. Ipsilateral refers to two points on the same side of the body, and contralateral refers to points on opposite sides.

These directions become somewhat distorted in man, the biped. In standing, the horizontal plane has been rotated. But, because the vertebrate brain retains its same orientation within the skull, the same terms can be applied to the same regions of the brain in all vertebrates. (See Figure 2.15.) Thus, ventral refers to the base of both the standing human and the quadruped brain. If one imagines man walking on both his legs and his arms with head pointing forward, these differences disappear.

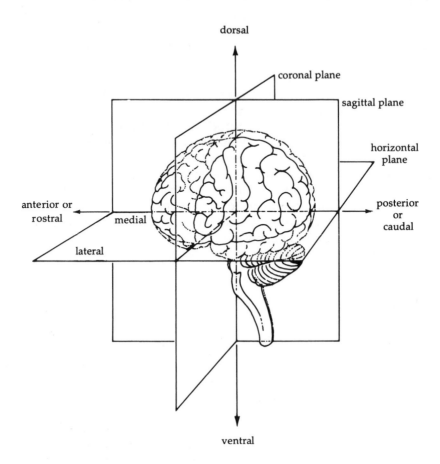

Figure 2.15. *Anatomical terms that refer to position, direction, and location within the central nervous system.*

The Development of the Nervous System

The structural plan of the nervous system emerges very early in embryological development. Since, in the very first stages of growth, extensive differentiation has not yet taken place within the brain, only the great functional divisions are present. Development provides an excellent opportunity to observe first the fundamental divisions of neuronal tissue and later the emergence of successively smaller units of organization.

The brain and the spinal cord, which together form the central nervous system (CNS), develop from a single tube of neural tissue. The nerves that connect the CNS to the sense organs and effector systems of the body grow from two separate streaks of primitive tissue. During development, these streaks become the peripheral nervous system, entering the spinal cord through the dorsal and ventral roots to make their connections with the CNS (see Figure 2.21).

Figure 2.16 illustrates three early stages of CNS growth. The upper, closed end of the tube, which will later become the brain, grows more quickly than the lower end, which will form the spinal cord. Three major swellings soon develop in this primordial brain. These enlargements correspond to what will later become three primary sectors of brain tissue—the forebrain, the midbrain, and the hindbrain. Other divisions of brain tissue follow: the forebrain is separated into the

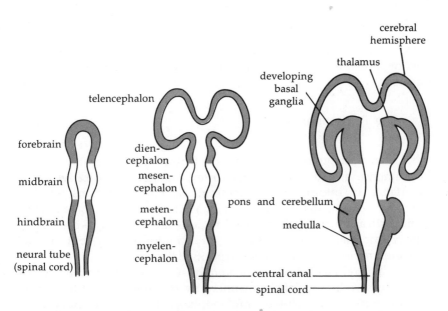

Figure 2.16. *The pattern of growth and differentiation within the neural tube.* Initially, only three brain sections can be reliably distinguished. Later, the five major levels of the brain are discernible. (From Gardner, E. *Fundamentals of Neurology, Fifth Edition*, 1968. Used by permission of W. B. Saunders Company.)

telencephalon and the diencephalon, and the hindbrain is separated into the metencephalon and the myelencephalon. In this more detailed terminology, the midbrain is called the mesencephalon. Below all these cephalic structures is the spinal cord.

Within each of these brain regions, substructures form and further subdivide as growth continues. All identifiable brain structures are present in man at birth, but the process of development is not finished. Single cells within the areas of the central nervous system continue to grow, increasing the complexity of their dendritic structures and elaborating their connections with other neurons. Figure 2.17 shows such a pattern of growth of cortical cells in the human infant, continuing through the first two years of life.

Major Structures of the Human Nervous System

The adult human brain is considerably more complex in structure than the embryonic brain. Within each of the great divisions of CNS tissue, specialized tissues have developed. A listing of these tissues does not explain brain function but does provide a conceptual map of the brain that emphasizes the spatial relations among brain areas. Such a conceptual map is necessary for understanding the functional relationship between brain activity and the behavior of the organism.

The Telencephalon

The most prominent anatomical feature of the human brain is the immense size of the cerebral cortex. Its size is indicative of its importance in information processing; the cortex contains three of every four neurons in the human brain. Yet much remains to be learned about cortical function. Specialized regions are devoted to processing sensory information and to the control of motor activity, but most of the cortex remains functionally unspecified.

The cerebral cortex is a bilaterally symmetrical structure, separated into a right and left hemisphere by the longitudinal fissure. In man, the cortex is convoluted, or folded, in a pattern of gyri (ridges) and sulci (valleys). The pattern of convolution greatly increases the surface area of the cortex, which is composed of gray matter, the cell bodies, and dendritic processes of cortical neurons. Beneath this gray layer is the white matter of the cortex, the shiny myelinated fibers that connect the gray matter of the cortex to other cortical and subcortical areas.

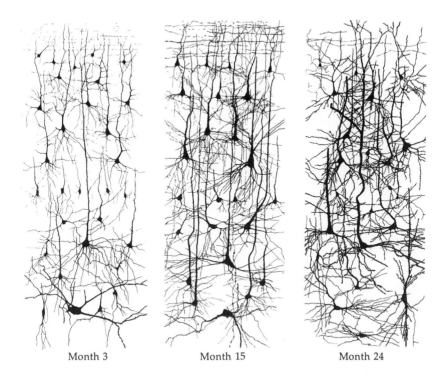

Month 3   Month 15   Month 24

Figure 2.17. *Cerebral cell development.* The process of cerebral development does not stop at birth. Shown above are sections of the human cortex at the third, fifteenth, and twenty-fourth months of life. Whereas the number of cells appears constant, there is a dramatic elaboration in the dendritic structures. Many more processes are apparent in the twenty-fourth month, and the opportunity for communication between individual cells is very much increased. (From Conel, J. L. *Postnatal Development of the Human Cerebral Cortex,* Vols. I-VI, Harvard University Press, 1939–1963; used in Altman, J., Postnatal growth and differentiation of the mammalian brain with implications for a morphological theory of memory. In G. Quarton, T. Melnechuk, & F. Schmitt (Eds.), *The Neurosciences: A Study Program,* 1967, p. 731. Used by permission of The Rockefeller University Press.)

Each cerebral hemisphere is divided into four principal lobes or regions. Figure 2.18 shows these divisions, several of which are defined by the major sulci of the brain. The central sulcus separates the frontal lobe from the parietal lobe. The lateral sulcus divides temporal lobe from frontal and parietal lobes. The occipital lobe, lacking a major sulcus for its demarcation, constitutes the most posterior section of the cerebral cortex.

These anatomical divisions are of some functional importance. The occipital lobe of the cortex is especially important in visual

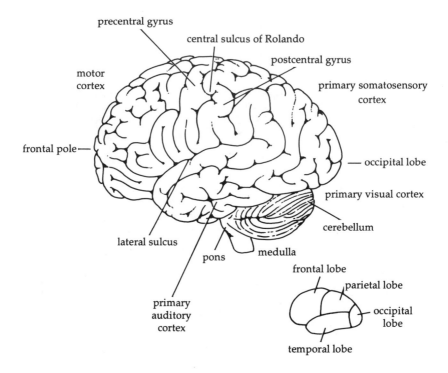

Figure 2.18. *Lateral view of the brain.* (Modified from Noback, C. R., and Demarest, R. J. *The Nervous System: Introduction and Review.* Copyright © 1972 by McGraw-Hill, Inc. Used by permission of McGraw-Hill Book Company.)

information processing. It contains the primary visual cortex (the area of cortex that directly receives visual information from thalamic visual relay nuclei—the lateral geniculate nuclei). Secondary visual areas that receive input from the primary visual cortex are also located nearby in the occipital lobe. The temporal lobe contains the primary auditory cortex and secondary auditory areas. In addition, temporal lobe structures of the left hemisphere appear to be especially important in language processing.

The central sulcus that divides the frontal and parietal cortex separates gyri in which bodily functions are represented. The precentral gyrus of the frontal cortex is the primary motor cortex in man and is concerned with control of muscular activity at the cortical level. The postcentral gyrus of the parietal cortex serves in a complementary manner as the primary somatosensory area of the cortex, receiving sensory input from various bodily structures in an orderly manner.

Aside from these sensory and motor functions, relatively little is known about the precise functional significance of the remaining cortical tissue. These areas have been labeled association cortex, since it is easy to assume that they might contain interneurons linking sensory and motor events; but such weak theory has proved less than useful. The localization of function within the cortex is a topic to which we shall often return in later chapters.

Two other neocortical structures deserve mention: the corpus callosum and the anterior commissure are fiber bridges linking the left and right hemispheres. The corpus callosum is by far the larger of the two and provides a communications link between the two cortices from the frontal to the occipital pole. The anterior commissure links more limited portions of the frontal lobes.

Some neuroanatomists distinguish a fifth region of the cortex, which they term the limbic (meaning "border" or "rim") lobe. The limbic lobe lies deeply buried beneath the neocortex and forms a ring of evolutionarily old cortex surrounding the brainstem. Two of the most prominant cortical structures in the limbic ring are the hippocampus and the septum. Limbic system activity has been implicated in a variety of functions, from the expression of emotion to the formation of memory.

The basal ganglia (ganglia is really a misnomer; nuclei would be a more proper term) are also telencephalic structures located at the junction between the telencephalon and the diencephalon. Globus pallidus, putamen, and the caudate nucleus are the three nuclei regularly considered to form the basal ganglia, but the amygdala is sometimes included as well. Together, the putamen and caudate nucleus form the striatum. With the exception of the amygdala, basal ganglia function is primarily concerned with the control of motor activity. The amygdala has been implicated in limbic lobe functions, including the control of aggression.

The Diencephalon

Two major groups of nuclei—the thalamus and the hypothalamus—form the diencephalon. The thalamic nuclei (see Figure 2.19) may be divided into three groups, based on their patterns of connection: sensory relay, association, and intrinsic thalamic nuclei. The sensory relay nuclei receive input from lower stations of the specific sensory systems and project (send axons) to the primary sensory areas of the cortex. The lateral geniculate nucleus receives input from the retina and projects to primary visual cortex. Similarly, the medial geniculate nucleus functions as the thalamic relay nucleus for audition.

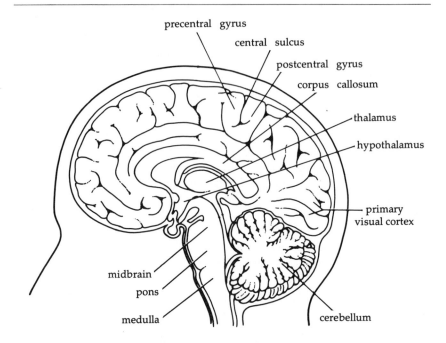

precentral gyrus

central sulcus

postcentral gyrus

corpus callosum

thalamus

hypothalamus

primary
visual cortex

midbrain

pons

medulla

cerebellum

Figure 2.19. *Median sagittal section of the brain.* (Modified from Noback, C. R., and Demarest, R. J. *The Nervous System: Introduction and Review.* Copyright © 1972 by McGraw-Hill, Inc. Used by permission of McGraw-Hill Book Company.)

Somatosensory information is relayed to the somatosensory cortex through the ventrobasal nuclear complex.

The association nuclei also project to the cortex but, unlike the sensory relay nuclei, do not receive input from the special senses. Instead, the thalamic association nuclei are anatomically related to the cortical association areas. Thus, the term "association" should not be taken too literally. It may be wise to conceive of both types of nuclei as important components of an integrated but as yet relatively unspecified system of thalamocortical connection.

The intrinsic nuclei of the thalamus do not project to the neocortex but instead make connections with other thalamic nuclei, limbic lobe structures, and the reticular formation of the brainstem. The intrinsic nuclei are also called midline nuclei on the basis of their medial location.

The hypothalamus is formed by a cluster of small nuclei at the base of the thalamus near the junction of the diencephalon and midbrain. These nuclei separately and in combination regulate food

and water intake, sexual function, endocrine activity, emotional behavior, and other related bodily processes. Hypothalamic nuclei make
numerous connections with other brain structures, especially the various nuclei of the limbic system. The pituitary gland is also directly
controlled by hypothalamic nuclei. For the psychologist, the
hypothalamus is particularly important in understanding processes of
motivation and emotion.

The Midbrain

Compared with the telencephalon and diencephalon, the midbrain (mesencephalon) is a relatively undifferentiated structure. It is
tubelike in form and, in this way, resembles the hindbrain and spinal
cord below it. (Figure 2.20 shows the midbrain in cross section.) In
the center is the cerebral aqueduct, containing cerebrospinal fluid,
which is similar to the central canal of the spinal cord below. The
aqueduct is surrounded by the central gray matter—a dense collection
of cell bodies and cellular processes. Other prominent midbrain structures include the cerebral peduncles, which connect the forebrain with
the hindbrain and spinal cord, and the superior colliculi, which arise
from the superior dorsal surface of the midbrain tube and serve
visual-information-processing functions (particularly localization of
visual information). Immediately below the superior colliculi lie the
inferior colliculi, which are involved with processing auditory signals.
Through the dorsal core of the midbrain runs the tegmentum, which

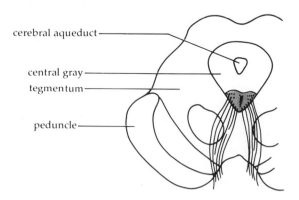

Figure 2.20. *A cross section of the human mesencephalon.* (From Ranson, S. W., &
Clark, S. L. *The Anatomy of the Nervous System, Tenth Edition,* 1959. Used by
permission of W. B. Saunders Company.)

contains the midbrain portion of the reticular formation. The reticular formation, which extends through the hindbrain, is a complex and interconnected structure of tiny fiber tracts and small nuclei. The reticular formation was originally conceived to be undifferentiated in its structure, but some anatomical regularity has been discovered in recent years. The reticular formation of the brain stem has been the focus of intense research interest since the late 1940s, when the alerting effects of reticular-formation stimulation were first noted. The reticular formation appears to function as an activating system for the organism and has been implicated in studies of sensory integration, attention, learning, and memory.

The Metencephalon

The metencephalon is composed of two great structures, the pons and the cerebellum. The pons is the tubular extension of the brainstem. As in the midbrain, the reticular formation extends through the tegmental region. Reticular tissue in the metencephalon joins the raphe nuclei at the midline. The raphe nuclei appear to be involved in the regulation of sleep states. Other distinguishable nuclei are found in the metencephalic tegmentum, including the cochlear nuclei, which receive input from the auditory nerve, and the superior olivary nuclei and the trapezoid bodies, both of which also function in processing auditory information. Other nuclei in the metencephalon make connection with various cranial nerves as the nerves enter the central nervous system.

Ventral to the tegmentum of the pons are a series of fiber pathways linking higher brain areas with lower structures. At the caudal portion of the pons, these fiber tracts begin to form the pyramids of the medulla below. Transverse fibers in this region cross the midline, forming a large bundle of fibers that connects pontine nuclei with contralateral cerebellar cortex.

The cerebellum is a convoluted bilateral structure of primitive cortex that lies behind the brainstem at the level of the pons. Between the two cerebellar cortices is a central cerebellar structure, the vermis. The cerebellar complex, a phylogenetically old structure, receives input from all sense systems and many brain areas. Cerebellar damage is usually accompanied by disorders of movement and coordination, suggesting that the normal function of the cerebellum is concerned with the modulation and control of motor activity. The massive amount of information available to the cerebellar cortex and the wide variety of structures to which it sends output suggest that the cerebellum may have other functions as well.

The Myelencephalon

This lower portion of the hindbrain forms the medulla, which links the upper brainstem with the spinal cord. The internal structure of the medulla changes considerably from the caudal to the rostral border. The pattern of spinal fiber tracts changes in numerous decussations, or crossings of the midline, throughout the medulla. The complex systems of fiber paths and small nuclei that mark the reticular formation elsewhere in the brainstem are also present in the medulla. At the caudal boundary of the medulla, the reticular formation makes contact with the spinal cord.

Various larger nuclei also appear in the myelencephalon. These include relay nuclei for several cranial nerves, somatosensory nuclei such as the gracile and cuneate nuclei, and the superior and accessory olivary nuclei, which form part of the complex brainstem auditory system.

The Spinal Cord

The spinal cord, which together with the brain forms the central nervous system, begins below the skull at the vertebral column, in which it is encased. The spinal cord is bilaterally symmetrical and segmentally organized. Between each pair of vertebrae, sensory nerves enter the cord through the dorsal roots and motor nerves leave through the ventral roots. Figure 2.21 presents a representative cross section of the spinal cord, although substantial differences in the form of rostral and caudal segments do exist. The dorsal and ventral roots of peripheral nerve fibers are evident, as are numerous sensory and motor tracts. The sensory tracts are found primarily in the dorsal portion of the cord. The cuneate and the gracile tracts carry somatosensory information to the brain where they synapse on their respective sensory nuclei in the medulla. In the lateral portion of the cord are the lateral spinothalamic tract and the spinocerebellar tracts. The anterior spinothalamic tracts are seen in the ventral border of the cord.

The efferent fiber tracts, which terminate on motor neurons in the spinal cord, may be divided into two broad classes—pyramidal and extrapyramidal motor tracts. The pyramidal tracts originate in the cortex and descend through the brainstem to form the pyramids of the medulla. There, pyramidal fibers cross the midline as they enter the spinal cord to form the lateral and ventral corticospinal tracts. This system is prominent in the human brain. The remainder of motor tracts in the spinal cord are classified as extrapyramidal and originate in subcortical areas of the brain.

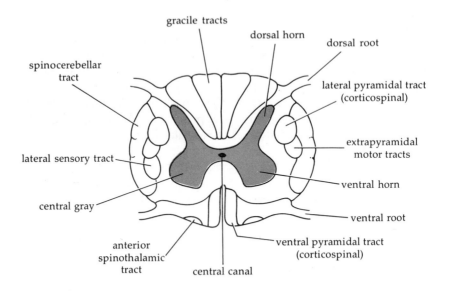

Figure 2.21. *The spinal cord.* Motor tracts are shown on the right, and sensory tracts are shown on the left. (From Milner, P. M. *Physiological Psychology.* © 1970 by Holt, Rinehart and Winston, Inc. Redrawn with permission of Holt, Rinehart and Winston, Inc.)

In the center of the spinal cord is the central canal, which is surrounded by gray matter—a dense neuropile of small cell bodies and dendrites. This central gray matter forms an H-shaped structure with horns of gray matter protruding in the lighter tissue toward both the dorsal and ventral roots. Thus, the spinal cord is a structure that receives sensory information, issues motor commands, makes connections of both afferent (sensory) and efferent (motor) fibers with higher centers of the brain, and, in the dense neuropile of the central gray, integrates and processes information in a variety of ways. The question of sensorimotor integration within the spinal cord appears in the study of spinal reflexes (see Chapter 6).

The Peripheral Nervous System

The peripheral nervous system includes all neuronal tissue except the brain and spinal cord. The peripheral nervous system, developing from separate embryological streaks of tissue, invades the central nervous system, linking cord and brain with other bodily tissues. The spinal nerves enter the spinal column in the 31 pairs of dorsal and ventral roots. These nerves (a nerve is a collection of axons that is large enough to be seen by the naked eye) are mixed until they near the spinal cord, where they separate into afferent and efferent nerves to form, respectively, the dorsal and ventral roots. Cell bodies of the efferent fibers are contained within the gray matter of the ventral horn, whereas the soma of sensory neurons are located in the dorsal root itself, outside the spinal column. These cell bodies form the dorsal root ganglia, which appear as a slight bulge in the dorsal root.

In addition to the 31 sets of spinal nerves, 12 cranial nerves are also part of the peripheral nervous system. These nerves originate at various levels of the brain stem and selectively innervate various structures of the head and viscera (internal organs). Table 2.1 lists the 12 cranial nerves and their functions. It should be noted that the optic nerve is not really a part of the peripheral nervous system at all. Rather, the tissues of the retina and the optic nerve originate from CNS tissue in the development of the embryo.

Table 2.1. *Cranial nerves and functions.*

Name	*Functions (Major)*
1. Olfactory nerve	Smell
2. Optic nerve	Vision
3. Oculomotor nerve	Movements of eyes; pupillary constriction and accommodation
4. Trochlear nerve	Movements of eyes
5. Trigeminal nerve	Muscles of mastication and eardrum tension; general sensations from anterior half of head including face, nose, mouth, and meninges
6. Abducens nerve	Movements of eyes
7. Facial nerve	Muscles of facial expression and tension on ear bones; lacrimation and salivation; taste; visceral; sensory
8. Vestibulocochlear nerve	Hearing and equilibrium reception
9. Glossopharyngeal nerve	Swallowing movements; salivation; taste; visceral sensory
10. Vagus nerve and cranial root of 11	Swallowing movements and laryngeal control; parasympathetics to thoracic and abdominal viscera; taste; visceral sensory
11. Spinal accessory nerve (spinal root)	Movements of shoulder and head
12. Hypoglossal nerve	Movements of tongue

Modified from Noback, C. R., and Demarest, R. J. *The Nervous System: Introduction and Review.* Copyright © 1972 by McGraw-Hill, Inc. Used by permission of McGraw-Hill Book Company.

The cranial nerves, unlike the spinal nerves, do not divide into afferent and efferent branches as they enter the central nervous system. Instead, they remain mixed, the ratio of afferent to efferent fibers varying widely among the cranial nerves.

The Autonomic Nervous System

The autonomic nerve fibers constitute a special portion of the peripheral nervous system, innervating the visceral organs and glands. Within the central nervous system, the limbic system and the hypothalamic nuclei are involved in the regulation of autonomic activity.

The autonomic nervous system may be anatomically and functionally divided into two branches—the sympathetic and parasympathetic. These branches appear to be reciprocally related so that increased sympathetic activity is accompanied by decreased parasympathetic activation. The sympathetic branch functions in part to prepare the organism for action, whereas the parasympathetic branch is associated with nonstressful vegetative functions, such as digestion and sleep.

Within the peripheral nervous system, the two branches of the autonomic nervous system maintain differing patterns of organization (see Figure 2.22). Sympathetic efferents leave the spinal column through the ventral root, as do motor neurons of the somatic nervous system. However, sympathetic efferents synapse immediately in the sympathetic ganglia, which are adjacent to the spinal column. Fibers originating in these ganglia (collections of cell bodies in the peripheral nervous system) then exit through the spinal nerves and proceed to the target organs that they innervate. Visceral afferent fibers enter the spinal nerves and pass through the sympathetic ganglia without synapsing as they proceed to the dorsal root ganglia and enter the spinal cord, where they synapse in or near the dorsal horn. Efferent sympathetic fibers originate only in the thoracic and lumbar segments of the spinal cord in the upper and lower back.

The parasympathetic branch of the autonomic nervous system originates in the sacral (tail) segments of the spinal cord and the cranial nerves. The ganglia for the parasympathetic branch are located not near the spinal column but near the target organs that they innervate. Thus, a parasympathetic efferent leaves the cord through the ventral root and proceeds directly to the visceral structure, where it makes contact with a short-axoned ganglionic fiber. This parasympathetic ganglionic fiber innervates the target organ. Figure 2.23 illustrates both branches of the peripheral autonomic nervous system and the internal organs with which they connect.

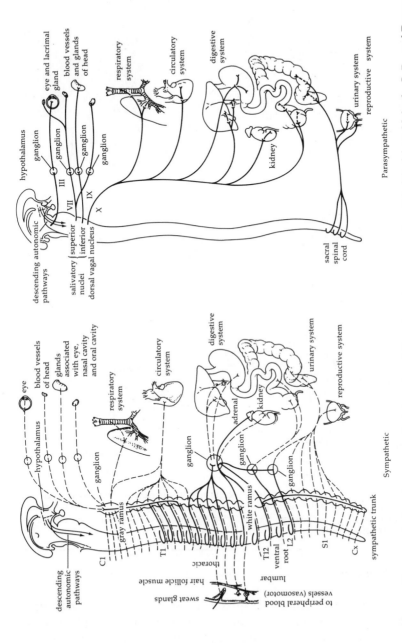

Figure 2.22. *The sympathetic and parasympathetic branches of the autonomic nervous system.* (Modified from Noback, C. R., and Demarest, R. J. *The Nervous System: Introduction and Review.* Copyright © 1972 by McGraw-Hill, Inc. Used by permission of McGraw-Hill Book Company.)

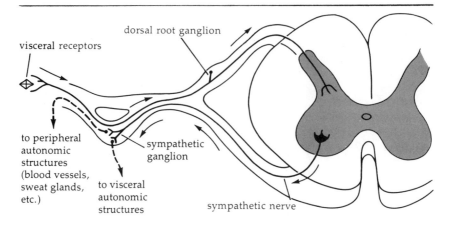

dorsal root ganglion

visceral receptors

to peripheral
autonomic
structures
(blood vessels,
sweat glands,
etc.)

sympathetic
ganglion

to visceral
autonomic
structures

sympathetic nerve

SYMPATHETIC PORTION OF AUTONOMIC SYSTEM

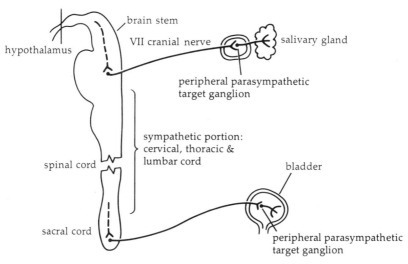

brain stem

hypothalamus

VII cranial nerve

salivary gland

peripheral parasympathetic
target ganglion

sympathetic portion:
cervical, thoracic &
lumbar cord

spinal cord

bladder

sacral cord

peripheral parasympathetic
target ganglion

PARASYMPATHETIC PORTION OF AUTONOMIC SYSTEM

Figure 2.23. *Patterns of innervation in the sympathetic and parasympathetic branches of the autonomic nervous system.* (From Thompson, R. F. *Foundations of Physiological Psychology.* © 1967 by Richard F. Thompson. Redrawn with permission of Harper & Row, Publishers, Inc.)

Summary

The understanding of the control of behavior depends upon knowledge of the structure and function of the nervous system. Thus, neuroanatomical and neurophysiological information is important to the behaviorist.

Two broad classes of cells, the neurons and the glia, compose the brain and the nervous system. Glia act to support the neurons; they provide nutrition, dispose of waste products, and generally provide the glue (glia in Latin) that holds the nervous system together. Neurons perform the information-processing functions of the brain. The neuron consists of a membrane, separating the intracellular and extracellular fluids, and various internal structures. The principal portions of the neuron are the cell body and its processes, the axon and the dendrites. Swellings at the tips of the axon are the endfeet, which synapse on other cells.

An understanding of the nature of the neuronal membrane and the fluids it separates is crucial to the understanding of the electrical activity in the neuron. Potassium is highly concentrated within the neuron, whereas sodium and chloride are more densely concentrated in the extracellular fluid. It is helpful to conceive of the membrane of the resting neuron as being permeable only to potassium. Therefore, only potassium can pass through the membrane along its concentration gradient into the extracellular fluid. Since potassium is positively charged, the inside becomes more negative and the outside more positive as the outward flow of ions continues. This movement generates electrical forces that counteract the further efflux of potassium. When the electrical forces are sufficient to block any further net flow of the ions, potassium is said to be in equilibrium.

If the membrane were permeable only to sodium, sodium would flow into the cell, along its concentration gradient, until the sodium equilibrium potential of +60 millivolts (mV) is reached. In producing an action potential, or spike, the neuronal membrane switches from a primarily potassium permeability to a sodium-dominant permeability. This permeability change results in a shift in the membrane potential from its normal resting state (−70 mV) to a positive +30 mV. Because of unknown processes within the membrane itself, this change is transient, and the neuron quickly returns to its resting state.

Excitable membranes, capable of producing an action potential, show a positive feedback pattern characterized by the Hodgkin cycle. Since the amplitude and duration of an action potential depend only upon the intrinsic properties of the membrane and its surrounding fluids, all spikes within a single section of axon are identical.

The action potential is triggered when the membrane reaches a critical state of depolarization, which may be produced by excitatory input, by intrinsic properties of the membrane, or by the occurrence of an action potential in nearby tissue. In an axon, the generation of a spike stimulates the production of another spike in immediately adjacent tissue. If, however, the axon is myelinated, the spikes are produced at the nodes of Ranvier. In either way, an action potential of the axon is propagated, permitting communication between the soma and the endfeet of the neuron.

Endfeet contact other cells at a synapse by releasing a chemical transmitter into the synaptic cleft. If such a neurotransmitter enters the postsynaptic membrane and induces depolarization, the synapse is excitatory. Hyperpolarization results from inhibitory synapses. Postsynaptic events summate both in time and in space to determine the activity of the postsynaptic cell.

Neurons and glia are organized to form the great structural elements of the nervous system. The organization of this tissue has been characterized by several models. The evolutionary model emphasizes vertical organization, with higher levels being added later in evolution. The embryological model stresses the increasing lateral differentiation and specialization that develop in the maturing embryo. The technological model emphasizes the patterns of connection between different structures within the nervous system as pathways for feedback and the flow of control information. Each of these models contributes to the understanding of neuroanatomical organization.

As the embryo develops, anatomical divisions are quickly apparent. The central nervous system (CNS) and the peripheral nervous system grow from separate tissues in the developing organism. The neural tube, which forms the CNS, begins its vertical differentiation by rapid growth in the anterior areas. The forebrain, midbrain, and hindbrain are easily distinguished. Later these three divisions become five: the telencephalon, diencephalon, mesencephalon, metencephalon, and myelencephalon. Within each of these five areas, increasingly fine substructures appear.

The peripheral nervous system, developing separately, includes the spinal nerves, which enter the spinal column to make contact with the CNS, and the cranial nerves, which enter the CNS at higher levels. The portion of the peripheral nervous system that innervates the viscera constitutes the autonomic nervous system, which is divided into sympathetic and parasympathetic segments. The former is classically associated with arousal of the body to action, and the latter is related to vegetative functions such as digestion and sleep.

The central and peripheral nervous systems together constitute an information network responsible for the coordination of behavior in complex organisms, including man.

Chapter 3

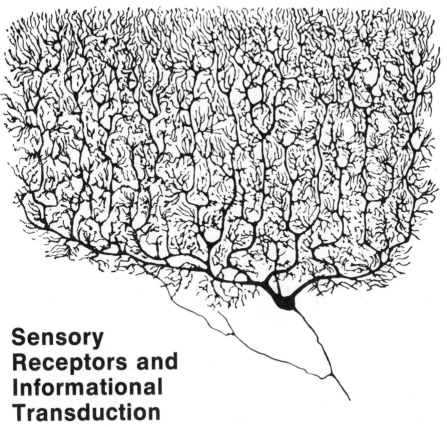

Sensory
Receptors and
Informational
Transduction

How does the eye respond to light, the ear to sound, the skin to pressure? These are specific questions about specific sensory systems. We can also inquire about the general nature of sensory systems, since at least some common principles of organization and function govern the different modalities of sensation. The emerging general theory is filled with exceptions, differential particulars, and many limitations, but the conceptual similarities among the various senses—both in structure and in function—make the general questions worth asking. Thus, the strategy I have taken here is to consider the different senses as examples of biological information-processing systems. Each sensory system, because it is designed to handle particular kinds of information, is unique. However, because the sensory systems use similar arrangements to process information, they are general. This interplay between general functions and specific features makes the study of sensory processes exciting.

Two broad questions must be considered. The first question, which is treated in this chapter, concerns the nature of receptor function and the ways in which environmental information is coded into a form that the nervous system can use. The second question concerns the way in which the nervous system recodes these signals to extract meaningful information about the world. This latter question is the subject of the following two chapters.

Some General Principles of Receptor Function

Receptor cells are the first neurons in any sensory system, at the interface between the organism and its environment. The rods and cones of the eye are receptors, as are the nerve endings in the skin and the hair cells in the ear. All receptor cells share certain features. Receptors transfer information from one form of physical energy to another. Although the nature of the input signal varies among the senses, the output of all receptors is a bioelectric change that can affect the behavior of the neurons to which the receptors are connected. Receptors have traditionally been called transducers; however, this term should be modified to emphasize the informational nature of their function. Transducers transfer power from one energy system to another. But it is not the transfer of power that is crucial to understanding the action of a receptor. All the power in the output of a receptor, the bioelectric response, is supplied from biological sources of energy. The input, the sensory signal, serves a control function by triggering a response in the receptor. It is the information about the stimulus that is transmitted; information, not energy, is the commodity with which the nervous system deals. Receptors must be thought of as informational transducers, or recoding devices, translating information about the energy impinging on them into a neuronal representation.

Encoding Quality

Psychologists have classically drawn a distinction between the quantity and the quality of sensory stimuli. The quantity of a stimulus is a function of its intensity. Quality is a function of the kind of energy that excites the receptor. Heat and light are, to the physiological psychologist, energies of different quality. How is quality information encoded? A receptor transmits to the nervous system its degree of excitation at each point in time. Therefore, information about the quality of the stimulus can be extracted by the nervous system only if it has knowledge of the properties of the individual receptors from which it receives that information.

Because they respond to many kinds, or qualities, of signals within a broad range of energies, individual receptors are said to be broadly tuned. For example, a sense receptor near the surface of the skin might respond to gentle pressure as well as to heat. However, this receptor does not respond with equal efficiency to all stimuli. Sometimes differences in sensitivity are extreme; the eye does not respond to sound, nor the ear to light, for example. But subtle differences in quality are also important. Differential sensitivity to the quality of energy forms the basis of quality encoding in receptors. For example, a sensory receptor that responds to a wide variety of stimuli could be very sensitive to small temperature changes but could require fairly substantial levels of mechanical stimulation to entice it to respond. Such a cell would be well suited to provide thermal information. By comparing its output to that of other nearby cells with different patterns of response sensitivity, higher neuronal centers would be able to distinguish warmth from pressure. The quality of stimulus energy to which a particular receptor is most sensitive is its adequate stimulus (which really means "most adequate stimulus").

The problems that broadly tuned receptors pose for the nervous system should not be underestimated. The difficulties become quite real when qualitative judgments are made within a sense modality. For example, information about color must be extracted from the differential responsiveness of three classes of cones to light of different wavelengths. These cones are very broadly tuned receptors, and yet very fine judgments can be made about color. Similar problems arise in encoding pitch in the ear and localizing skin pressures in the body senses. To obtain fine sensitivity of behavior from broadly responsive receptors takes a clever neuronal arrangement that is able to decode the confounded information produced by those receptors.

What is the basis for this differential sensitivity? The nature of the receptor itself may determine much of its selectivity. Rods and cones in the eye, for example, contain a complex biological arrangement, making them exquisitely sensitive to light energy. No other mammalian receptor could begin to equal their responsiveness to visual stimuli. In other sensory systems, however, the adequate stimulus is only partially determined by the receptor. Selectivity is also determined by the accessory structure or the nonneural tissue in which the receptor is embedded. For example, the frequency-selective receptors in the auditory system depend upon nonneural tissue for their selectivity. Neuronally, these cells are alike. The selectivity depends not upon their nature but upon their location in the cochlea of the ear, since the initial frequency analysis is performed mechanically by the basilar membrane.

Similarly, in the skin, sensory receptors optimally recode very different kinds of information. This differential sensitivity depends primarily upon the location of receptors in the body. The mechanical setting of a receptor can thus be crucially important in determining the quality of information it will transmit.

Charles Sherrington, a pioneering neurophysiologist who, early in this century, outlined the nature of the spinal reflexes, put forth an idea about the role played by the differential sensitivity of receptors in the body: receptors lower the threshold of excitability of reflexive behavior to the adequate stimulus and raise it for other stimuli. Here, adequate stimulus really means "adequate to elicit a reflexive response." Such a view is terribly limited when one considers the whole animal, not just his spinal cord. But it wisely emphasizes the relation of sense receptors to the behavior of the animal, which is easy to overlook. Sherrington's view also implies that the nervous system is innately wired to respond to certain kinds of stimuli but not to others. We do not perceive everything; we perceive only certain classes of events.

Encoding Quantity

The quantity of a stimulus is a function of its intensity. Most receptors encode quantity in a similar and straightforward way. In general, the stronger the stimulus, the more the receptor will respond. However, there are important exceptions to this rule. First, receptor cells, like man-made sensors, have limits to their sensitivity. The lower limit is commonly called the threshold. Stimuli that are weaker than the threshold value have no effect on output of the receptor. As more is learned about sensory systems, difficulties arise with the threshold concept. For example, the sensitivity of some receptors approaches the theoretical limit for any mechanical device. Rods in the eye seem capable of responding to a single quantum of light. The ear is nearly sensitive enough to detect the random movement of atoms, or thermal noise. Signals weaker than these are not signals at all, in the conventional sense, but rather expressions of the underlying randomness of the universe. The notion of a threshold makes little sense here.

There are, however, receptors that give no apparent response to weak, but physically measurable, signals. Does the idea of a threshold, a lower boundary to sensitivity, apply in this case? The answer is yes, in the sense that the cell gives little useful information about signals below some minimal strength. Since different receptors show very different lower boundaries, the threshold provides a convenient method of categorizing receptors. But the answer is also no, in the stricter sense that threshold is a firm boundary. The response of the receptor does not disappear at threshold but instead becomes more difficult to detect. Responses to subthreshold stimuli are small enough to be lost in noise—that is, in the spontaneous activity of the cell that is not related to incoming stimulation.

To measure threshold, one needs a rule to determine whether a response has occurred. For example, a response could be defined as an increase in the cell's firing rate of at least five spikes per second. Stimuli failing to meet this criterion would be considered subthreshold. However, if a different rule were chosen, the estimate of the cell's threshold would also change. Both the experimenter and the organism must use decision rules to determine whether a stimulus is present. If the rule is very strict (ten spikes per second, for example), weak stimuli are often not detected. If it is very lenient (for example, one spike per second), weak stimuli are detected more frequently. However, the use of a lenient decision rule increases the chance of deciding that a stimulus is present when in fact the cell is merely showing an excess of spontaneous activity. Therefore, the lowest possible value in the decision rule is not always the best. Sensitivity must be balanced against the need for accurate detection in the decision process. This is especially true for the organism, which must base a course of action on this information.

Some receptor cells show an approximate lower boundary of sensitivity, or a threshold. Some cells also show an upper boundary of their ability to code intensity information. Some signals are too strong to produce an informative response in those receptors that have an upper boundary. Between the lower and upper boundaries is the effective intensity range of the receptor. Figure 3.1 shows this range for a hypothetical cell. Within this range, the receptor gives larger responses to stronger stimuli and smaller responses to weaker stimuli. Thus, the response is monotonic with the stimulus intensity. If the receptor produces the same response to all stimuli above its upper boundary, the cell shows saturation. Nonmonotonic relationships between stimulus intensity and response magnitude have also been reported. For example, the receptor response might actually decrease with further increases above the receptor's upper boundary. Nonetheless, the pattern shown in Figure 3.1 is quite typical. Information from cells with different effective ranges may be combined to provide the organism with information about stimuli over a wide dynamic range.

Within the effective dynamic range, most receptors do not relate input to output by a linear rule. Instead, they show a compression function—a stimulus-response function that compresses a large range of stimulus intensity onto the restricted range of neuronal response. If the rule were linear, then a constant change in stimulus strength would produce a constant change in receptor response, no matter what the initial level of the stimulus. The function in Figure 3.1 relating stimulus

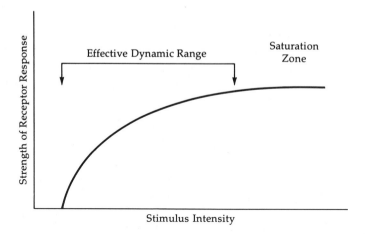

Figure 3.1. *Response of a receptor to stimuli of increasing intensity.* Many receptors show both upper and lower boundaries to their capacity to signal intensity information. The lower boundary is often termed threshold. Between the threshold and the upper boundary lies the effective dynamic range of the cell. Within this range most receptors display compression functions, producing a smaller response to a fixed increment of stimulus intensity at higher absolute levels of intensity. Even this monotonic relation breaks down in the region of saturation, in which the cell may no longer signal intensity information in a meaningful way.

to response would be a straight line throughout the effective range of the cell. It is not. Instead, it is a curve that shows smaller response changes at higher stimulus levels. Therefore, the receptor is able to signal very small changes in intensity when the level of stimulation is low. At high levels, the receptor is much less sensitive to small changes and requires larger stimulus changes to produce a similar change in its response. The compression function greatly increases the range of intensity to which the receptor is able to respond with the same relative sensitivity.

Relative sensitivity implies a constant fixed-increment of response to a fixed-percentage increase in the strength of the input throughout the effective range. There is currently some debate as to whether this relation is best characterized by a logarithmic function or a power function with an exponent of less than one. Both functions, however, take the form of a compression function for normal sorts of stimuli. Intensity compression functions are well suited for many important environmental stimuli. In vision, for example, the light reflected by objects varies dramatically with the level of illumination, but the percentage of the energy that an object reflects is fixed. Therefore, two objects of somewhat differing reflectivity are equally distinguishable over a wide range of illumination.

The response of a receptor to a stimulus may depend in part on previous stimulation of that receptor. Many receptors maintain their initial response for a continuing stimulus. Other receptors, by adapting, may reduce the size of their response. Figure 3.2 illustrates some typical responses to a prolonged stimulus. Receptor A, which adapts completely, shows only an initial, or phasic, response; that is, it re-

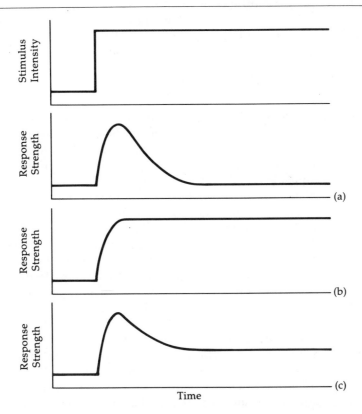

Figure 3.2. *Patterns of temporal adaptation by receptors to stepwise increases in stimulus strength.* Receptor (A) shows complete adaptation with only a phasic response at the onset of the stimulus. Receptor (B) shows no adaptation whatsoever; therefore, its response mirrors exactly the distribution of stimulus energy in time. Receptor (C), like most cells in the nervous system, responds more vigorously to a changing stimulus than to a fixed stimulus, but its temporal adaptation is not complete. Between the extremes of complete adaptation and no adaptation, many unique patterns of temporal responsivity may be formed. This diversity of response contributes to the processing of temporal information in sensory systems.

sponds only during change. Receptor B shows no adaption; its initial response does not diminish over time. Receptor C gives both a phasic and a sustained, or tonic, response. The tonic level of response is lower than the initial, or phasic, level and depends solely upon the intensity of the stimulus. The size of the phasic response, however, depends upon both the absolute intensity of the signal and the amount of time taken to reach that intensity. Thus, the phasic component takes into account the rate of change. By knowing the adaptation rates of its various receptors, the nervous system is able to extract information concerning the presence or absence of stimulus change as well as the intensity of the stimulus. Stimulus intensity and its changes through time are encoded in the size of the receptor potential.

Receptor, Generator, and Spike Potentials

Receptor cells produce receptor potentials, which are strikingly similar in all sensory systems. Like the postsynaptic potentials of neurons, receptor potentials are graded. They vary continuously with the strength of the stimulus. Further, they are local electrical events; they are not propagated, and they are strongest at the point within the receptor at which they are initiated. The receptor potential grows exponentially weaker as the distance from its source is increased. Receptor potentials differ from spike potentials, then, in two ways: they are graded and local, whereas spikes are uniform and propagated.

To communicate sensory information to the central nervous system, receptor potentials must be recoded into spike patterns in the axons of afferent sensory neurons. Figure 3.3 illustrates the recoding process for sensory subsystems in which the receptor is separate from the sensory neuron. Here, environmental energy, as modified by the accessory structures, triggers a receptor potential within the receptor itself. Through synaptic interactions, the receptor potential induces a similar graded potential in the sensory neuron. Because the graded dendritic potential in the sensory neuron can lead to the generation of an action potential, the graded response of the sensory neuron has been termed the generator potential. In this respect the generator potential resembles the excitatory postsynaptic potentials seen elsewhere in the nervous system.

Because not all sensory systems possess distinguishable receptors and afferent neurons, difficulties in terminology arise. For example, the receptor in the Pacinian corpuscle system is simply the distal portion of the membrane of the sensory afferent. Slow potentials generated at the receptor surface lead directly to spike production by electrotonic flow to the axon. Thus, all graded potentials in the sensory

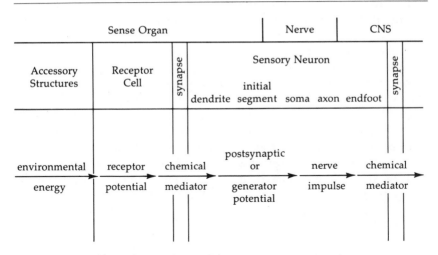

Sense Organ			Nerve	CNS

Accessory Structures	Receptor Cell	synapse	Sensory Neuron initial dendrite segment soma axon endfoot	synapse

| environmental

energy | receptor

potential | chemical

mediator | postsynaptic
or
generator
potential | nerve

impulse | chemical

mediator |

Figure 3.3. *An outline of the general structure of information processing in accessory structures, receptors, and sensory afferent neurons.* The receptor potential is depicted separately from the generator potential. In some systems, these two potentials are identical, and there is no synapse between receptor cell and sensory afferent. Instead, the receptor potential triggers spikes directly in the axon of the receptor cell. (Adapted from Davis, H. Some principles of sensory receptor action. *Physiological Reviews*, 1961, **41,** 404. Used by permission.)

afferent may be said to be generator potentials. But they are also electrical events produced in response to environmental stimulation, which argues for their inclusion as receptor potentials. This difficulty is more one of phrasing than of substance, however. While most authorities regard the slow potential of the Pacinian corpuscle as a generator potential, others prefer to consider it as a receptor potential.

In the relationship between receptor and spike potentials, in the response to stimuli of varying intensities, in the broad coding of sensory quality, and in the capacity of informational transduction, most bodily receptors share common governing principles. Important differences exist among different receptors, however, in both structure and function, across and within the various sensory systems. We now turn our attention to these differences.

Information Transduction in Hearing

Purely mechanical systems—nonneural systems—play crucially important roles in sorting and analyzing biological information. Nowhere is the importance of the nonneural systems more obvious than in hearing, because the preneuronal structures of the ear perform the initial frequency analysis on which all further frequency processing is based.

Waves of compression in the air are generated whenever a sound is made. Therefore, the first task of the ear is to effectively harness these waves and transmit them to the auditory receptor cells in the inner ear. The external ear funnels the vibrations onto the tympanic membrane, a drum-like structure separating the outer ear and the middle ear. (See Figure 3.4.) From the tympanic membrane, vibration passes through three bones called the ossicles, which consist of the malleus, the incus, and the stapes, to the oval window of the cochlea, or inner ear. The ossicles increase the effectiveness of conduction by mechanically matching the air-driven vibrations with the characteristics of the fluid-filled inner ear. Their action is less efficient if the middle-ear muscles are contracted. In this way, the nervous system can use a

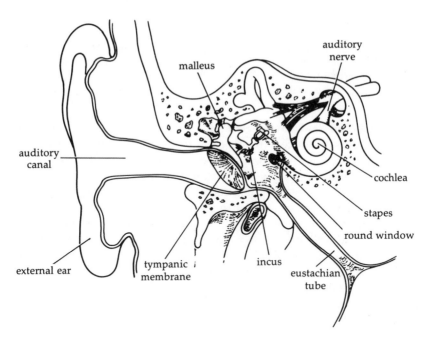

Figure 3.4. *The inner, middle, and outer ear.*   The outer ear and the auditory canal function to guide air-driven vibrations into the middle ear, where a series of three bones—the malleus, incus, and stapes—efficiently transfer this energy to the fluid-filled inner ear. The inner-ear structure forms a coil. Sound energy enters the inner ear and causes deflections of the basilar membrane, on which the receptors for audition are located.

nonneuronal mechanism to reduce the effects of a loud signal. Such adjustments in response to intense stimuli occur reflexively.

Information processing begins in the inner ear. The outer ear and the middle ear make connections and adjust pressures. The inner ear performs the frequency analysis that is the basis for the perception of pitch. Sound energy may be characterized by frequency and intensity, which, in perception, roughly correspond to pitch and loudness. As in most sensory systems, the intensity of the stimulus is signaled by the size of the receptor potential. The cochlea, an accessory structure for audition, performs frequency analysis mechanically. The cochlea is a spiraled canal with several compartments. Figure 3.5 illustrates a cross section of the cochlea. Sound energy, translated into mechanical vibration at the oval window, generates a traveling wave that moves down the cochlea's fluid-filled canals. Figure 3.6 indicates the effect of a traveling wave.

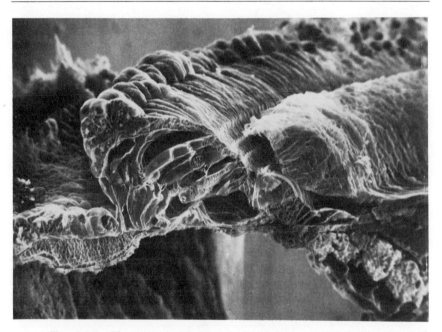

Figure 3.5.   *The structure of the inner ear revealed in a scanning electron micrograph of the organ of Corti.*   Notice the thinness of the basilar membrane upon which the organ rests, the hair cells that appear to be the receptors for audition located within the organ, and the tectorial membrane that overlies the hair cells. (From Bredberg, G., Lindeman, H. H., Ades, H. W., West, R., & Engstrom, H. Scanning electron microscopy of the organ of corti. *Science,* 1970, **170,** 861–866. Copyright 1970 by the American Association for the Advancement of Science. Used by permission.)

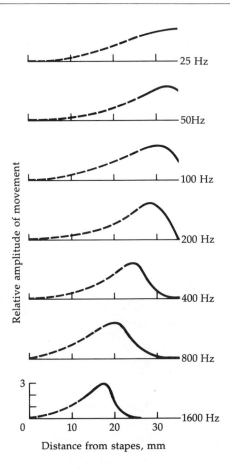

Figure 3.6. *Basilar membrane displacement to pure tone stimulation*. Different frequencies of vibration yield different patterns of cochlear movement. Low-pitched tones tend to produce vibration of the entire basilar membrane, whereas high-pitched tones are limited in their effect to the region near the stapes. The graphs show the amount of displacement by a vibratory stimulus of varying frequency at different points along the basilar membrane. (From von Békésy, G. Effects on fluid movement of destroying the apical portion of the cochlea. In E. G. Wever (Ed.), *Experiments in Hearing*, McGraw-Hill, 1968. Used by permission.)

The basilar membrane of the cochlea, which introduces frequency selectivity into hearing, is the only membrane that offers mechanical resistance to the traveling wave. The degree of resistance varies according to the membrane structure in different parts of the cochlea. At the base of the cochlea, the basilar membrane is quite firm and narrow. Further from the base, it becomes looser and wider. A firm membrane transmits high-frequency vibrations in a manner similar to that of a rubber band, which resonates at higher and higher pitches the more tightly it is stretched. Although the basilar membrane probably does not resonate, it rapidly loses its ability to transmit high-pitched sounds as it becomes flaccid.

Movement of the stapes displaces the basilar membrane and sets up a traveling wave that reaches maximum displacement further down the membrane. At this point, excitation of the receptor cells is also maximal. The point of maximum displacement shifts down the membrane, away from the oval window, as the pitch of the stimulus tone is lowered. Figure 3.6 shows the displacement for sounds of different frequency. Notice that, as the frequency is lowered, the region of significant movement of the membrane becomes wider. For very low-pitched tones, the entire cochlea is involved, and the resulting frequency analysis cannot be highly selective. The responses of the cochlea to discriminatively different tones of neighboring pitches are quite similar. Therefore, as a receptor organ, the cochlea is broadly tuned; but its responses to tones of different frequencies are sufficiently different to allow the nervous system to extract detailed information about the pitch of sounds.

The receptor mechanism necessary to relay information of cochlear motion to the auditory neurons is provided by the organ of Corti, which rests on the basilar membrane. The organ of Corti is a remarkably sensitive device. It can respond to a movement of the tympanic membrane that measures one tenth the diameter of a hydrogen atom. Were the ear any more sensitive, we would hear, when all else is quiet, a constant buzz—the sound of atoms randomly moving through the universe.

As in other sensory systems, the details of receptor action in the ear are not completely understood. It is known that the hair cells of the organ of Corti play a crucial role in sensory transduction. When sound energy moves the basilar membrane, the cilia atop the hair cells are pressed against the tectorial membrane, which lies over them. The movement distorts the cilia, and the particular geometry of the angles at which tectorial membrane, hair cell, and basilar membrane meet magnifies the distortion.

The movement of the hair cells does not provide the energy used to produce the electrical response of the ear. Here, as is generally true in sensory systems, stimulus energy serves to trigger or control the release of biologically generated energies. In the organ of Corti, membrane potentials provide this energy. The hair cells maintain a membrane potential that is inside negative. However, the endolymph of the cochlear duct, into which the cilia project, is positively charged (+80 mV). Therefore, the difference in potential between cochlear duct and hair cell can be as high as 180 mV—a very powerful source of energy for a living system. Movement of the basilar membrane alters this standing voltage, producing a fluctuation voltage, the cochlear microphonic, which is an exact electrical replica of the vibrations present in the membrane. If one records the cochlear microphonic of a cat and plays the resulting signal through a high-fidelity amplifier, the listener will hear the sounds present at the cat's ear. If the cat is listening to music, the reproduced sound will be an almost perfect reproduction of the same music.

The cochlear microphonic appears to be produced by the action of the basilar and tectorial membranes on the outer hair cells that results in the mechanical distortion of the hair cells. The reduction in the amplitude of the cochlear microphonic as hair cells are destroyed by intense auditory stimulation indicates that the cochlear microphonic arises specifically from hair-cell activity. A nearly linear relationship exists between the number of remaining hair cells and the strength of the cochlear microphonic. Such evidence linking the cochlear microphonic with hair-cell activity strongly suggests that the cochlear microphonic may represent the summation of the actual receptor potentials.

Hair cells appear to make contact with the auditory nerve fibers by more or less conventional synapses. Auditory neurons that enter the cochlea and proceed toward the organ of Corti lose their myelin sheaths as they penetrate the basilar membrane. Following routes of varying complexities, these afferent fibers finally synapse on the inner and outer hair-cell bodies. The presence of small vesicles and mitochondria in hair cells near these fibers is indicative of synaptic connections.

The arrangement of hair cells, membranes, and nerve fibers shown in Figure 3.7 continues down the length of the cochlea. The place theory of pitch perception states that sounds of varying pitches produce different patterns of spike activity in the nerve fibers innervating the array of hair cells. Different neurons respond maximally to different frequencies of sound; quality is encoded by the place of maximal response.

Thus the outer, middle, and inner ear function as an integrated system for encoding acoustic signals into a representation that is interpretable at higher levels of the nervous system. The mechanical properties of these structures are exceptionally important both for maintaining high sensitivity to low intensity acoustic signals and for the initiation of the frequency analysis.

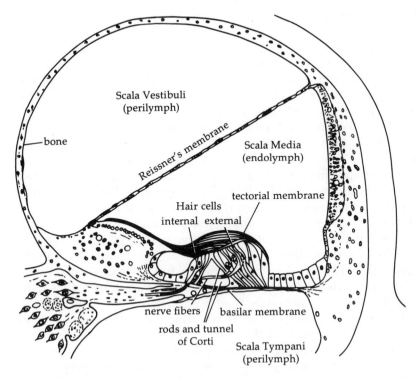

Scala Vestibuli (perilymph)

bone

Reissner's membrane

Scala Media (endolymph)

tectorial membrane

Hair cells
internal external

nerve fibers basilar membrane

rods and tunnel of Corti

Scala Tympani (perilymph)

Figure 3.7. *A detailed cross section of the cochlear duct.* Notice especially the relation of the basilar membrane, the tectorial membrane, and the hair cells that lie between them. Movement of the basilar membrane alters this relationship, producing distortion of the hair cells. (From Davis, H., Benson, R. W., Covell, W. P., Fernandez, C., Goldstein, R., Katsuki, Y., Legouix, J. -P., McAuliffe, D. R., & Tasaki, I. Acoustic trauma in the guinea pig. *Journal of the Acoustic Society of America,* 1953, **25**, 1182. Used by permission.)

Information Transduction in Touch and Pressure

The critical question of quality encoding has also been a focus of concern in the study of bodily sensation. Because many different kinds of receptors found in the skin vary in shape and size, it was once universally believed that dissimilar receptors performed different functions. Four principal anatomical types of sensory receptors in the skin were held to be of major functional importance: Krause endbulbs for cold, Ruffini corpuscles for warmth, and Pacinian and Meissner's corpuscles for touch. In addition, the free nerve endings in the skin were believed to carry information about pain. Much of this categorization, which rested on weak evidence, has been challenged recently. While acknowledging that some of the endings, such as the Pacinian corpuscles, serve a useful purpose, Weddell and his colleagues argued that the correlation between structure and function in other cells is often illusory. There are anatomically many different sorts of endings, and to believe that there are only four is, in the first place, falsely simplifying the anatomy. Further, and much more to the heart of the matter, most endings might be of no functional importance; it has not been possible to correlate the quality of sensation arising from a particular tiny spot of skin and the appearance of the receptor that lies nearby. Many complex endings may be no more than benign little growths. Perhaps the most telling evidence comes from the investigation of the cornea of the eye. Stimulation of the cornea can produce sensations of touch, heat, cold, and pain; yet the cornea contains only free nerve endings—receptors without any encapsulation at all. Here, at least, one anatomically defined receptor can mediate many kinds of functionally defined sensations. It follows that the nervous system must extract information about the quality of somatic sensation from the patterns in the firing of many broadly tuned somatosensory receptors. This view of quality encoding is in general agreement with the analysis of the other sensory systems.

Most somatosensory receptors respond to mechanical deformation; sometimes, the accessory structure surrounding the receptor may be of functional importance. One such case is the Pacinian corpuscle (shown in Figure 3.8), which is found, among other places, in the mesentary of the abdomen of the cat. Like other somatosensory receptors, the Pacinian corpuscle is very small, only a little over 1 mm in length. The corpuscle is very sensitive to tiny mechanical displacements, responding to movements as small as 2/10,000 mm; but it adapts very quickly to prolonged pressure. The Pacinian corpuscle generates a receptor potential and spikes in its axon only when a stimulus is first applied and when a stimulus is removed. Thus, it signals changes in pressure, but it does not signal the continued presence of pressure. The very rapid adaptation of the Pacinian corpuscle is produced by the accessory structure, the corpuscle itself, and not by the neuronal receptor that lies inside the corpuscle. With its many fluid-filled compartments, the corpuscle acts as a shock absorber for the neuron. When pressure is applied, the corpuscle and the receptor are distorted, but the fluid-filled compartments quickly adjust themselves to accommodate the pressure so that the inner compartments return to their original shape. The compensatory movements of fluid release the receptor from displacement and terminate its response. When the stimulus is re-

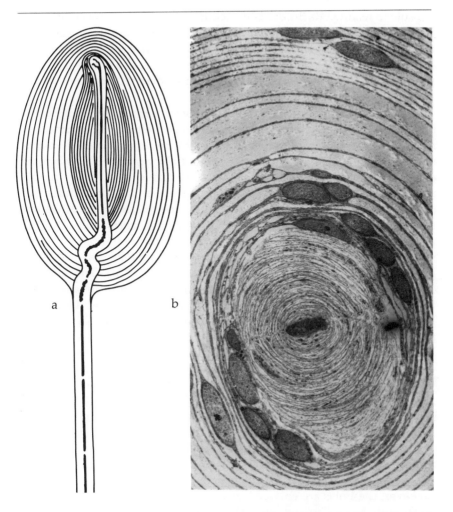

Figure 3.8. *Pacinian corpuscle.* Because of the insulating function of the fluid-filled compartments of the corpuscle, mechanical pressure on this receptor yields only phasic responses. External displacement is quickly compensated by movements of the fluid, which release the receptor from mechanical distortion. Removal of the stimulus induces phasic activity in this receptor as the fluid flows into its normal arrangement. (a) Schematic drawing illustrating the laminar structure of the corpuscle. (b) An electron micrograph of an actual corpuscle. (a. From Quilliam, T. A., & Sato, M. The distribution of myelin on nerve fibers from Pacinian corpuscles. *Journal of Physiology,* 1955, **129,** 173. Reprinted by permission. b. From E. R. Lewis, unpublished photomicrograph, used by permission.)

moved, the accessory structure itself stimulates the receptor to respond (the off-response). The receptor is distorted by the movements of the capsule to readjust its fluids. The Pacinian corpuscle is a case in which a nonneural accessory structure modifies the actual stimulus presented to the receptor. By extracting information about changing pressures and discarding information about the absolute pressure to which it is subjected, the corpuscle filters the information that will be sent to the central nervous system.

The process of transduction in the somatosensory mechanoreceptors is still incompletely understood. Nonetheless, all methods of research suggest a common mechanism by which mechanical displacement is translated into membrane-potential changes. The electrical events in mechanoreceptors appear to be ionic in nature. In this respect, a mechanoreceptor functions in a manner similar to that of an excitatory central synapse. In the synapse, the release of an excitatory transmitter causes a breakdown in the selective permeability of the postsynaptic membrane to the small ions. Neuronal membranes in their resting state are relatively impermeable to sodium (Na^+) but relatively permeable to both potassium (K^+) and chloride (Cl^-). The unequal concentrations of these ions across the membrane create a voltage that is inside negative. At rest, the membrane's charge is relatively close to the K^+ and Cl^- equilibrium potentials but quite far from the Na^+ equilibrium voltage, which is inside positive. If the membrane's selective permeability is destroyed temporarily, Na^+ flows into the cell and depolarizes the membrane. If nonselective permeability is maintained long enough, the membrane potential reaches a new equilibrium of zero.

In a synapse, an excitatory transmitter opens up the postsynaptic membrane to let ions pass freely. In a mechanoreceptor, displacement of the membrane performs the same function. It has been proposed that the membrane has holes that are normally not large enough to permit the passage of hydrated Na^+. When the membrane is stretched, however, the holes are enlarged, permitting all ions, including Na^+, to cross with ease. The size of the depolarization varies with both the amount of stretching and the area of the membrane that is deformed. The receptor potential is graded and is localized at the point of displacement, triggering spikes in the cell's axon in the conventional way; the electrotonic spread of current into the axon region depolarizes that excitable membrane.

Receptors signal different qualities of information for various reasons. Undoubtedly, some highly specialized cells exist in the somatosensory system, but most somatosensory receptors differ from each other primarily in sensitivity, or threshold, and in the way in which they are fitted into the tissue of the body. Accessory structure, in the broad sense of the mechanical arrangements around a receptor, is an exceptionally important informational filter for the body senses.

Information Transduction in Vision

The visual system is probably the most intricate of all sensory systems, either natural or man-made. From patterns of reflected light energy, it creates three-dimensional maps of an environment too distant to touch. It defines objects not only by their brightness and darkness but also by the wavelength of light that they reflect. The maps contain brightness, contour, and color information. Moreover, the visual maps, or perceptions, are integrated with other information about position of the body, head, and eyes. Visual perception is a model of the environment, not simply a representation of the pattern of light on the eye. Tilt your head and the map does not change. As you read this page, your eyes dart back and forth, but the perception stays still. Hold the page a full arm's length away. The size of the page does not change, but its image on the retina changes radically.

Much of visual perception is a function of exceptionally complex brain control systems. To believe that we "see" with our eyes and a little bit of visual cortex is utter nonsense. Building a stable map of the visual world depends upon many brain processes. However, because vision begins in the retina and because what the retina encodes is determined in part by the mechanical structures of the eye (the accessory structure for vision), it is worthwhile to consider the mechanical structure of the eye before examining the properties of the visual receptors themselves.

The structure of the human eye is shown in Figure 3.9. The human eye has the form of a round camera; light enters through the pupil and is imaged by the lens onto the retina. A pattern of light and dark is focused on the rods and cones, the visual receptors of the eye. Without the lens, no focus is achieved and the illumination of the retina is relatively uniform; the result is blindness, as there is no patterned information available for the visual system to process.

By controlling the musculature of the eye, the brain can select portions of the environment that it wishes to monitor. For example, the ciliary muscle controls the shape of the lens. Increasing ciliary tension thickens the lens, bringing closer objects into focus. This process is accommodation. You can easily see the effects of accommodation by focusing on a very close object—2 or 3 inches from the eye—and observing the change in the clarity of objects in the background.

The central nervous system also controls the extraocular muscles that determine the position of the eyes. Some movements of these muscles are automatic, such as convergence movements that turn the eyes toward each other. When looking at a distant object, the eyes are parallel, and corresponding points on the two retinas receive virtually the same image. But when the gaze is shifted to a nearby object, the two

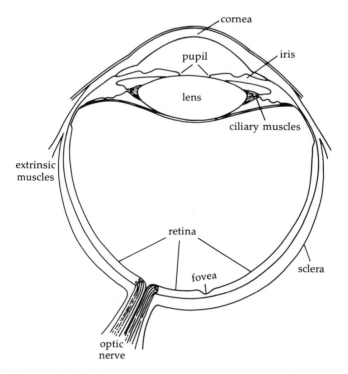

Figure 3.9.   *The mechanical structure of the eye.*

eyes point slightly toward each other if the same correspondence between the two retinas is to be maintained. Convergence and accommodation processes are both involved when the gaze is shifted from near objects to far objects or vice versa.

Three patterns of eye movement, in addition to the convergence processes, are typical. First, the extraocular musculature is in a continual state of limited oscillation, producing small amplitude tremors. The exact function of these oscillations is unknown, if any, in fact, exists. They may simply be the result of the structure of the neuronal control mechanisms within the brain that are responsible for regulating eye position and producing the other types of eye movements. The second common pattern is slow drift. Eye position is rarely fixed but instead wanders slowly from a point of fixation. These deviations are in contrast to a third type of movement, the large, rapid saccades. Saccadic eye movements are powerful ballistic movements that redirect the gaze from one portion of the environment to another. If eye movement is eliminated, visual perception quickly stops. The visual system responds to change; eye movements are one way of providing such change. Saccades reposition the retinal image on new groups of receptors. Without these movements we would be functionally blind.

The presence of eye movement and the production of a stable perception present some important problems for information processing. Moreover, to localize an object, the brain needs information about the position of the object's image on the retina and the position of the eyes in relation to the head. There appear to be two visual systems—one concerned with recognizing objects and the other with localizing them. The latter system, located in the brainstem, is intimately connected with the control of the extraocular muscles.

Within the eye, a neuronal tissue, the retina, contains the receptors for vision. Figure 3.10 shows the retina in cross-section. Although it seems unlikely, the receptors are not on the surface of the retina

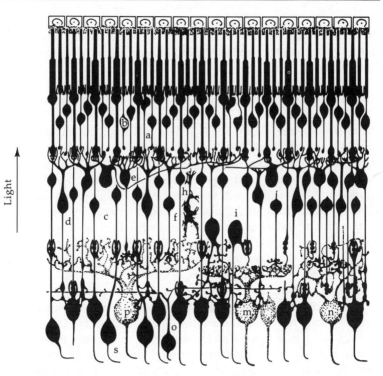

Figure 3.10. *A detailed but highly idealized drawing of neuronal retinal tissue.* Notice that light enters the retina through nonreceptive neuronal tissue—the ganglion cells and their axons, the amacrine cells, the bipolar cells, and the horizontal cells—and passes through these layers before it reaches the receptors—the rods and the cones. Cells are designated as follows: rods (a), cones (b), horizontal cells (c), bipolar cells (d, e, f, h), amacrine cells (i, l), and ganglion cells (m, n, o, p, s). (From Polyak, S. *The Retina.* © 1941 University of Chicago Press. Used by permission.)

facing the lens; instead, they are buried at the bottom of the retina. Light must pass through all other retinal tissues before striking the receptors. Apparently this design is of little practical consequence, although it could hardly be expected to improve visual acuity.

The fovea, or most central portion of the retina, appears as a slight depression of the retina in Figure 3.9. The mass of neural and vascular tissue that overlays much of the retina is shunted aside in the fovea, presumably to improve the optical resolution in this small patch of tissue. Not surprisingly, the fovea is involved in high-acuity visual-information processing.

Although fundamentally similar, rods and cones, the receptors of the visual system, differ in general shape (rods are longer and thinner than cones) and in the photochemicals they contain. The fovea is comprised entirely of cones. A great many optic nerve fibers innervate the fovea, which accomplishes detailed, high-acuity color vision. Rods, which as a system are more sensitive than cones, predominate outside the fovea. Because many rods connect with only a few optic nerve fibers, vision is more sensitive, but less accurate, in the periphery than in the fovea.

Rods and cones function in much the same way, despite their structural differences. Figure 3.11, which shows one vertebrate rod, illustrates its complexly layered outer segment, which has been estimated to contain about 1,900 separate discs. The discs of the outer segment appear to be destroyed through use; they disappear from the tip of the photoreceptor but are replaced at its base at an average rate of 30 discs each day. Each disc in the rod contains the photochemical rhodopsin. It is in these discs that the crucial step in visual transduction, the absorption of a quantum of light energy by a single molecule of rhodopsin, takes place. The rigid structure of the outer segment appears to play some role in the generation of bioelectric receptor potentials, since the electrical response of the receptor is dependent upon the integrity of the disc structure.

The photochemical rhodopsin is composed of 11-*cis* retinene (a bent form of the retinene molecule) bound with a large opsin molecule. Retinene can only bind with the opsin in the 11-*cis* form. When a photon of light is absorbed by the intact rhodopsin molecule, the retinene is likely to change into its more stable, straightened form, all-*trans* retinene. All-*trans* retinene cannot bind with the opsin, so the molecule is split. The breaking of rhodopsin into retinene and opsin is apparently the basic act of visual transduction in the rods.

Although the splitting of the rhodopsin molecule begins the process of visual-information transduction in the rods of the vertebrate eye, the physical events that link this action with the production of a receptor potential remain unknown. The process is apparently complex,

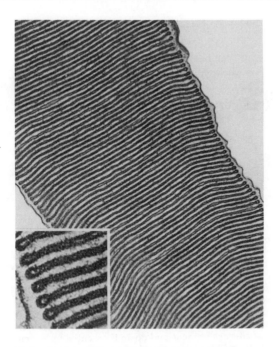

Figure 3.11. *A single rod in cross section.*   Notice the precisely layered structure of the section of the rod containing rhodopsin, which is shown at two levels of magnification. (From Hogan, M., Alvarado, J. A., & Weddell, J. E. *Histology of the Human Eye,* 1971, pp. 425, 428. Used by permission of W. B. Saunders Company.)

but nonionic electrical events that could be of some significance have been discovered. An early receptor potential (ERP) can be recorded from the intact rod in response to a bright flash of light. The ERP's amplitude, which depends upon the availability of rhodopsin in the cell, grows smaller when the supply of available rhodopsin has been reduced by prebleaching the eye with intense light. The amplitude of the ERP varies also with the wavelength of the stimulus energy in a manner exactly paralleling the spectral absorption characteristics of rhodopsin. That the ERP is photochemical and not ionic is indicated by the fact that it may be obtained from the frozen retina. The structure of the outer segment of the rod also is an important determinant of ERP activity, since ERPs cannot be recorded from rhodopsin in solution.

The most important question, however, remains unanswered. Does the early receptor potential, despite its name, actually function as a receptor potential in the visual system? Some suspect that the ERP may be an electrical phenomenon with little biological consequence.

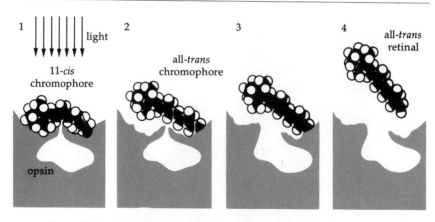

Figure 3.12. *Photochemical basis of vision.* Photochemicals in both the rods and the cones are composed of opsin and retinene in its bent, or 11-*cis*, form. The 11-*cis* form is not stable. When excited by a photon of light, the retinene molecule is momentarily free to rotate on its axis. The probability is high that, when the state of excitation passes, the retinene portion of the photochemical molecule will return not to its 11-*cis* form but to its more stable all-*trans*, or straightened, form. In the all-*trans* form, retinene can no longer bind with opsin, and the photochemical molecule is necessarily decomposed. Little else is known about this molecular process except that the splitting of a photochemical molecule into separate molecules of all-*trans* retinene and opsin is essential for visual-information transduction. (Used by permission from Hubbard, R., & Kropf, A. Molecular isomers in vision. *Scientific American,* 1967, **216**, 76. Copyright © 1967 by Scientific American, Inc. All rights reserved.)

The relation between the ERP and the receptor potential of the rod remains to be elucidated.

In the vertebrate eye, the receptor potential, measured intracellularly in the soma of the photoreceptor, is a hyperpolarizing response. Unlike the ERP, the receptor potential is indeed ionically mediated. Changes in membrane permeability selectively alter the flow of the small hydrated ions across the membrane of the soma. However, the connections between these ionic events and the processes that occur in the layered outer segment of the photoreceptor remain obscure.

The nature of the receptor response also is puzzling. In invertebrates, the response of rods to light stimulation is depolarization. This fits very well with the idea that depolarization triggers spikes that carry information to higher centers. In vertebrates, however, the response of the receptor is hyperpolarization, which does not usually precede impulse generation. There have been several suggestions to resolve the quandary. One is that the visual system is inhibited by light, but this idea will not get us very far; little evidence for massive inhibition exists in the outer retinal layers. Another possibility is that hyperpolarization

Figure 3.13. *Rods in the bullfrog retina.* The scanning electron microscope shows the orderly structure of the rods in the eye of the bullfrog. (From E. R. Lewis, unpublished photomicrograph, used by permission.)

at the receptor poses no special problem. In the vertebrate eye, receptors are several cells removed from the spike-generating process. Whereas depolarization is necessary to trigger spikes in the peripheral retinal layers, either sort of polarizing change may convey information by electrotonic conduction.

Cones differ from rods not only in their structure but also in the photochemicals they contain. There appear to be three classes of cones, each characterized by a unique photochemical. The chromophore in all these molecules is retinene, in the 11-*cis* form, but the opsins differ slightly. The variety of opsins gives each class of visual receptor a distinguishing spectral-absorption characteristic. Each class of cones differs from the others in the wavelength of light that is absorbed most efficiently. (Figure 3.14 illustrates the spectral absorption characteristics of a number of cones.) Therefore, each of the three classes of cones responds most vigorously to a different wavelength.

In a survey of single cones in the vertebrate eye, Tomita and his colleagues noted three different responses to light stimuli of varying

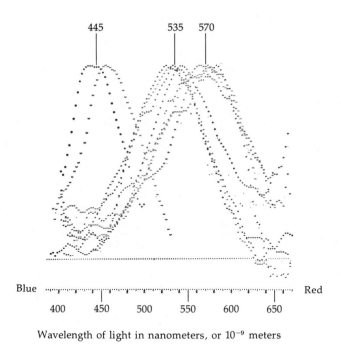

Wavelength of light in nanometers, or 10^{-9} meters

Figure 3.14. *The absorption spectra of ten separate cones from the primate visual system.* Notice that these ten cones cluster into three groups of slightly different spectral sensitivities, giving rise to the terms blue, green, and red cones. Color-detection mechanisms within the retina operate on these differences in spectral absorption. (From Marks, W. B., et al. Visual pigments of single primate cones. *Science,* 1964, **143,** 1181–1183. Copyright 1964 by the American Association for the Advancement of Science. Used by permission.)

wavelength. One peaked at 462 millimicrons, another at 529, and the third at 611. For convenience, color names (blue, green, and red) are often used to denote these three classes of cones; although it is improper to speak of color-sensitive cones, since "color" is a psychological, not a physical or physiological, term. Therefore, "red cone," for example, must always be interpreted to mean "a cone that responds maximally to stimulus energy of a wavelength that a human observer would call red." It would be more proper to speak simply of short-, medium-, and long-wave-cone systems, but such terms are somewhat unwieldy. Therefore, color words are handy to distinguish the classes of cones if it is understood that color is not a property of any retinal system.

The discovery of three spectrally distinguishable cone systems in the fovea of the vertebrate eye lends confirmation to Thomas Young's original postulate (1802) that three types of photoreceptors are necessary to mediate color vision. Although this trichromatic structure may not persist beyond the level of the retina (see the discussion of the opponent color systems in Chapter 5), the differential spectral sensitivities of these three classes of cones do indeed form the basis for color vision. Without this diversity of receptor characteristics, wavelength and intensity information would be inextricably confounded within the human visual system.

Summary

Although many differences exist among the receptors of the various sensory systems, common principles appear to govern their functions. The differences stem from the unique problems that each sensory system must solve, whereas the similarities result from the evolution of common modes of resolving problems of information transduction and processing in the context of the mammalian nervous system.

Receptors recode information present in environmental stimuli into bioelectric events, which are the language of the nervous system. Stimuli serve control functions in these highly specialized cells.

Most receptors respond to stimuli of different qualities and, for this reason, are said to be broadly tuned. The type of stimulus by which a receptor is most efficiently stimulated is the adequate stimulus for that cell. Differential sensitivity results from both the intrinsic properties of the receptor and the accessory structure in which the receptor is located. Place theories of quality encoding assert that knowledge of the receptor's tuning properties is necessary for proper decoding of stimulus quality within the nervous system.

The quantity of stimulation refers to the intensity of the stimulus. Within the effective range, most receptors respond to increasing stimulus intensity with a monotonically increasing response. Whereas certain receptors possess near-maximal sensitivity, others are characterized by an effective lower boundary to their responsiveness, or a threshold. The definition of a threshold depends in part upon the decision rule adopted to determine the presence of response. Cells also show an upper boundary to their dynamic range, above which saturation occurs. Within the effective stimulus range, most receptors display a compression function that relates input to output in a nonlinear but monotonic fashion; some receptors, however, exhibit nonmonotonic response functions.

Receptor potentials, unlike action potentials, are graded and nonpropagated. In these respects they resemble postsynaptic events. In some receptors the receptor potential acts as a generator potential, directly triggering the production of spikes in the axon of the cell. Other receptors are closely coupled to afferent neurons, so that the receptor potential induces a generator potential in a dendrite of the afferent neuron, which in turn generates spiking.

Accessory structure is of major importance in hearing. The outer and middle ear funnel vibrations from the air into the inner ear with proper impedance matching. The middle ear muscles provide a mechanical method for attenuating these vibratory signals.

The cochlea and its basilar membrane act as a frequency analyzer. Sounds of differing frequency maximally displace different portions of the basilar membrane. The receptors in the auditory system are the hair cells, which project their cilia against the tectorial membrane. Movements of the basilar membrane distort the cilia, giving rise to bioelectrical potentials in a manner as yet unknown. A large standing voltage (180 mV) between the cochlear duct and the interior of the hair cell appears to be gated in some fashion, giving rise to the cochlear microphonic, which may represent a summation of the actual receptor potentials. Since frequency differentiation by the basilar membrane is crude, the hair cells respond as broadly tuned receptors. The hair cells appear to be innervated by fibers of the auditory nerve through synaptic-like structures.

Mechanoreceptors of the somatosensory system generate bioelectric forces by modulation of the flow of ions. Distortion of these pressure-sensitive structures appears to render the membrane permeable to all small ions, including extracellular sodium. Therefore, pressure results in the depolarization of the membrane of the mechanoreceptor.

Although great anatomical diversity exists among the receptors of the somatosensory system, many of these anatomical structures may be without functional significance. A variety of sensations can be appreciated from appropriate stimulation of the cornea of the eye, which contains only free nerve endings. Moreover, little correspondence exists between the sensitivities of small spots of skin and the somatosensory receptors located beneath the spots. However, some anatomical structures within this system are functionally important. For example, the layered, fluid-filled structure of the Pacinian corpuscle is responsible for the rapid habituation of this receptor to prolonged stimulation.

The eye acts as a camera, imaging the visual world upon the retina of the eye. Neuronal control mechanisms regulate the position of the eye and the convergence and accommodation processes to select the range of objects in the environment that receive visual processing. In addition to these motor acts, the eyes show three patterns of movements: tremor, slow drift, and saccades. At least some of these movements are necessary to assure continuity of visual perception.

Rods, located in the periphery of the eye, and cones, in the fovea, are the receptors of the mammalian visual system. Rods and cones contain photochemicals essential for visual-information transduction. When a photon of light strikes such a molecule in the receptor, it is split into two parts—retinene and an opsin. The process of transduction in the photoreceptors is complex and only poorly understood. Nonionic photoelectric events, such as the early receptor potential (ERP), may be recorded, but the relation of this activity to the production of the functional receptor potential remains obscure. The receptor potential measured at the somatic membrane appears to be ionically mediated.

In the three classes of cones, the combination of retinene with different opsins results in slightly different spectral-absorption characteristics. This forms the basis for color vision in mammals.

Sensory receptors provide the only mechanisms by which the nervous system may obtain information about the environment. Some receptors are highly specialized, but most are characterized by broad responsivity to stimuli. The result is the ambiguous encoding of information that must be resolved by more central neuronal mechanisms.

Chapter 4

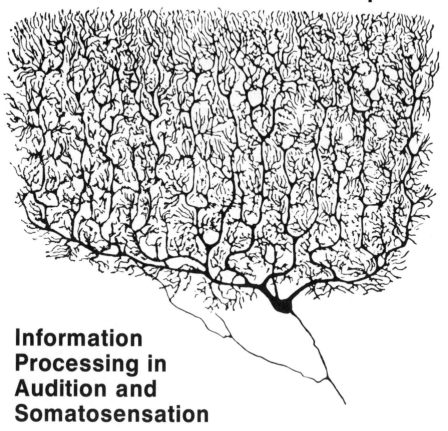

Information Processing in Audition and Somatosensation

Just as general principles appear to govern the process of information transduction in the receptors of the various sensory systems, similar patterns of organization may be found in the structure and function of the nervous tissue that processes sensory information at successively higher centers of the brain. In this chapter, we shall first attempt to identify some of the general principles of information processing that are common to all of the major sensory systems. Then we shall examine the ways in which these principles are realized in specific sensory systems, each with its own unique set of restrictions and requirements. The higher-order processes of the auditory and somatosensory systems are treated in this chapter; information processing in the visual system is explored in the following chapter.

Law of Specific Energies and Place Theories

If one's ears were connected to the optic nerve and one's eyes to the auditory nerve, what would happen? Could one hear a sunset or see a song? Or would one simply be deaf and blind? Unfortunately, the latter is probably the most likely outcome of such an experiment; the senses would not work. But the questions posed by this unlikely situation are sensible and have received some serious attention. How much does the nervous system need to know about the receptors to which it is connected? Apparently such knowledge is extremely important; the nervous system, for all its senses, depends upon exact knowledge of the nature and location of receptors in gathering information about the environment.

One of the first clear presentations of the idea that the perception of quality depends upon the excitation of different types of neurons was proposed by Johannes Muller. Muller believed that the brain structures responsible for the various sensations were qualitatively different— that is, each structure had its own nerve energy. In detail, he was wrong: the form of energy in the brain is the same for all senses. His law of specific nerve energies, however, does contain an important general truth that underlies what is known as the place theory of the representation of sensory quality: that the quality of sensation often depends upon which neurons are excited and not upon the quality of the stimulus energy. Although a receptor can be excited by stimuli other than its adequate stimulus, the response of the receptor is the same to all stimuli. Thus, for example, hearing sounds depends on the excitation of auditory system structures, not on the kind of stimulus that is employed. Electrical stimulation of auditory structures produces auditory sensations, not visual percepts.

Processing Information

That the sensory pathways of the brain form an information-processing system is a fundamental concept for understanding brain function in perception, but one only recently established. For example, it was once held that the optic nerve and radiations (the fibers which connect the eye to the cortex) simply relayed the pattern of light on the retina onto the cortex. Aside from solving no important questions, since the relay concept simply raises the problems of perception to a higher and more mysterious level, this early formulation is empirically wrong. As sensory information is transmitted from receptor to the cortex, signals are rearranged to emphasize different aspects of the total information. Features are extracted from patterns of stimulation. Sensory information-processing systems are intelligent systems, and some major problems of perception are solved before information ever reaches the brain.

The various sense systems face similar problems in processing their receptors' signals. One common problem stems from broad tuning of sensory receptors. Broadly tuned receptors show relatively small differences in response to stimuli that are perceptually easily distinguishable. In audition, for example, the peripheral frequency analysis performed by the cochlea is crude; the cochlear responses to two tones of similar pitch—that ultimately are easily distinguished by the listener—may differ very little. Neuronal systems are needed to sharpen the selective response of the sensory transducers to account for the selective behavior of the whole organism. If stimulus frequency is encoded by the rate of firing in specific neurons, the broad response of the cochlea and auditory nerve must be transformed at some point within the nervous system to a more finely tuned response, which lets the point of maximum displacement, and hence the frequency or pitch of the tone, be known more exactly.

Other sense systems share the problem of resolving information for broadly tuned receptors. For example, our visual world is so sharp and clear that it seems natural to think of our eyes as very fine optical systems. Nothing could be further from the truth. Normally, there are significant impurities floating in the vitreous humor of the eye that could only cloud the visual image. Moreover, the visual receptors themselves are buried at the very back of the retina. Therefore, no matter how perfectly it is formed by the lens, the visual image will be blurred by the blood vessels and nervous tissues through which it must pass. A stimulus that we see as a fine line is received at the receptors as a broad band of light or dark. The nervous machinery must reconstruct the line from the response of many receptors. Figure 4.1 shows the effects of retinal blur. Neuronal circuits sharpen the image.

A simple demonstration confirms the presence of sharpening mechanisms in the bodily senses as well. Light finger pressure upon the body surface is easily localized. As pressure is increased, ever larger areas of the surface are deformed, yet sensation remains limited to the point of maximum pressure. The perception of only the pressure maxima in a wider area of deformation is an instance of sharpening.

In processing information, the nervous system often retains information about the point of maximum or minimum stimulation—that is, about points of greatest change in the pattern of stimulation—at the expense of information about the absolute levels of stimulation. This is

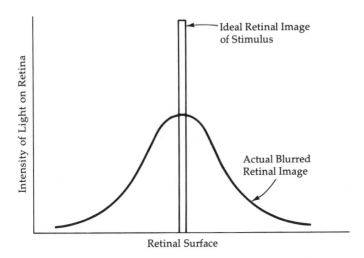

Figure 4.1. *Retinal blur.* The optical properties of the eye are less than perfect. Here, the distribution of light on the retina, produced by a fine bright line about the width of a single receptor, is shown. Various degrading influences spread this narrow band of light into the actual distribution of illumination. Neuronal image processing is required to minimize this effect of blur.

an issue to which we will often return. The nervous system extracts some features of the stimulus—such as point of maximum pressure—and discards other kinds of information—such as the total area affected. Stimulus change, either in space or in time, is usually emphasized, whereas information about absolute strengths is often discarded. Sometimes different features are extracted by separate parts of the same sensing system, each acting upon the same information at the same time. This is parallel processing.

Concepts of parallel processing and multiple feature extraction in sensory systems are meaningful only when the process of feature extraction itself is well understood. Therefore we shall first examine the neural mechanisms by which the ubiquitous sharpening process is accomplished.

Lateral Inhibition

The nervous system sharpens the representation of the stimulus through neuronal arrangements in which the neurons involved act upon each other. Figure 4.2 shows the intensity of the stimulus falling on each of a series of receptors. Parallel receptors of this sort, which can

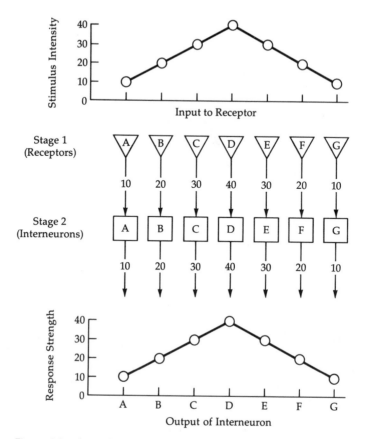

Figure 4.2. *A set of receptors with independent neuronal connections.*

be found in virtually any sense system, are similar in function and arranged in a logical order as indicated in Figure 4.2. If there are no connections among units, the response of these cells will mirror the distribution of stimulus strengths, and no sharpening will occur. (In fact, if the receptors show typical compression functions, the curve of responses will actually be flatter, not sharper.)

Figure 4.3 shows one mechanism by which the information coming from the various receptors may interact. Each receptor excites not only a single second stage (stage-2) cell, but also inhibitory interneurons, which act to turn off the adjacent stage-2 cells. Together these cells form a neuronal network with lateral inhibition. Each cell inhibits the influence of its neighbor at the next stage in the chain. The effect of such a network is to increasingly emphasize points of stimulus change

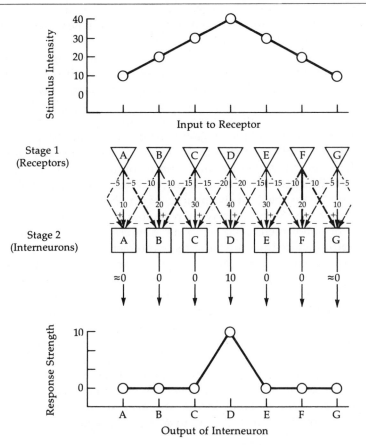

Figure 4.3. *A set of receptors with lateral inhibitory connections.* Lateral inhibitory interactions often act to sharpen sensory information. The connections from receptors A, B, and C, to stage-2 cell B are darkened to illustrate the convergence of information. The connections from receptor F to stage-2 cells E, F, and G are darkened to emphasize the divergence of sensory information.

at successive stages. The distribution of activity will become sharper and sharper.

A numerical example helps to clarify the argument. Suppose that the inhibitor cells are half as effective at turning off a neighboring cell as the direct excitatory connections are at turning it on. (This choice of values makes for a dramatic example, but the logic is the same for many arbitrarily chosen constants.) Figure 4.2 illustrates what happens without inhibition. Figure 4.3 shows lateral inhibitory sharpening. Consider neuron B in stage 2. As in Figure 4.2., where no inhibitory connections exist, this neuron receives an excitatory input of 20. But, as it also receives inhibitory inputs of −5 from A and −15 from C, the result is 0, or no activity. The same holds true of C, where positive input of 30 is counterbalanced by negative inputs of −10 and −20. For this network, any point along a linearly increasing, decreasing, or stationary function will be represented by a stage-2 cell that gives no response. Cell D, however, is not on a constant function but instead is at a peak. It receives an excitatory input of +40, but, because its inhibitory inputs are only −15 and −15, its response will be not 0 but 10. The representation of the stimulus by the stage-2 neurons has been sharpened.

Lateral inhibitory systems function in approximately this manner. However, they may be much more complicated. First, cells may have inhibition/excitation ratios that yield less striking sharpening. In such cases, many levels of sharpening might be used to produce successive refinements. Second, arrays of receptors are often two-dimensional instead of one-dimensional, as in the numerical example. Third, cells may produce more intricate patterns of interaction by affecting not only their most immediate neighbors but also many other cells in the same general region, resulting in a more complex representation of their function. Finally, inhibitory connections not only go forward from one stage to the next but may also feed back on the stage-1 neurons themselves, in which case they are said to be recurrent. All these factors contribute to the complexity of actual lateral inhibitory systems. Nonetheless, the basic concept is straightforward. By inhibiting neighboring units, the maximally excited cell stands out in sharp contrast to the surrounding cells. Conversely, the most weakly stimulated cell may be made notable by its absence, since in minima in the stimulus distribution it will result in an enhancment of inhibitory input to the corresponding cell.

Some perceptual effects of lateral inhibition can be seen in Figure 4.4. Dark gray patches appear at the intersections of the white stripes. The intersections appear to be darker than the remainder of the stripes since these areas are inhibited from four sides instead of just two.

Convergence and Divergence

At each successive stage of a lateral inhibitory network, a larger number of receptors influences the activity of each neuron. In the example shown in Figure 4.3, the stage-1 neurons receive input from a single receptor. At stage 2, each neuron receives input indirectly from three receptors. Although some connections are excitatory and others are inhibitory, a change in the activity of any of the three receptors will produce an alteration in the stage-2 cell into which they feed. The three receptors, A, B, and C, together map the receptive field for the stage-2

Figure 4.4.   The effects of lateral inhibitory mechanisms in vision can be seen at the intersections of the white lines by focusing on the dot.

cell B. A receptive field is a list or a map of the receptors that influence the cell under study.

The receptive field is not always uniform. In the numerical example above, the receptive field has an excitatory center—receptor B—and an inhibitory surround—receptors A and C. Theoretically, the receptive field can be determined for any cell that is responsive to sensory stimuli. The receptive field of a cell, no matter where the cell is located, is always a collection of receptors. In vertebrates, however, the receptors are not named and numbered as they are in the example. Therefore, the receptive field is usually defined as a map. For example, the receptive field for a somatosensory cell located in the cerebral cortex might be the receptors in a large area of the right forearm, and, as was the case in the numerical example, the receptive field might be divided into excitatory and inhibitory regions. Since many receptors ultimately send signals to this one cell, complex receptive fields show the convergence of information. Convergence simply means that information from many sources is channeled to one analyzer.

In Figure 4.3, the receptive field of stage-2 cell B is outlined to demonstrate convergence. The opposite relation, divergence, is shown for receptor F. Divergence of information occurs when a receptor sends signals to many higher sensory neurons—here, the stage-2 cells. Even in the highly simplified system illustrated here, both convergence and divergence may be demonstrated.

Through the systematic use of convergent and divergent patterns of connection, the nervous system processes incoming patterns of stimuli to extract various stimulus features. Sharpening is often employed in an array of similar receptors, but other procedures of sorting signals are possible. Information is transformed by using precisely determined connections among receptors and by employing excitation and inhibition to sort out relevant features.

Temporal Adaptation

Like lateral inhibitory processes that are spatial, temporal inhibitory processes also serve to filter and select information. Temporal inhibitory processes are observed in neuronal networks in which inhibition is not determined by the spatial pattern of the stimulus but rather by its time pattern, or history. Usually the response to a stimulus becomes smaller the longer the stimulus is present. The effects of such networks are similar to the temporal adaptation effects of some receptors, but these central networks operate on different sets of stimulus information. Just as lateral inhibitory mechanisms emphasize spatial changes in the stimulus pattern, temporal inhibitory systems selectively transmit information concerning temporal change by responding only to an alteration of the stimulus. If the stimulus does not change, temporal adaptation suppresses further input to more central sensory areas.

Most sensory cells show some temporal adaptation. Many cells respond only when a stimulus appears or disappears, and some respond to both stimulus onset and offset. Still others, and these are certainly a minority, are free of the effects of temporal adaption and respond continuously for the duration of the stimulus. However, substantial numbers of sensory cells strike a compromise between these extremes. Most show a heightened response to change and a steady, but smaller, response to a maintained stimulus. The response to change is the phasic response; the response to a continuing stimulus is the tonic response.

Spontaneous Activity

Sensory messages are always processed in the brain against a background of other activity, since the brain is a complex organ with multiple functions. What might be startling, however, is that the sensory systems themselves are always active, even in the absence of stimulation. For example, most optic nerve fibers show a considerable amount of activity when the organism is in the dark. In fact, optic nerve activity actually decreases when the eye is diffusely illuminated, since inhibitory mechanisms then are brought into play.

Spontaneous activity is present even in the first-order neurons of sensory systems. The source of these impulses is not definitely known, but chance discharge of the receptor seems a likely explanation. Such discharges may result from thermal or other probabilistic variations. Detailed analysis of the temporal pattern of spontaneous activity in many cells shows a Poisson form, a statistical distribution that characterizes many kinds of random processes. Other cells show different temporal patterns of spontaneous activity, however, so that one explanation cannot hold for all cases.

Central sensory neurons also display substantial levels of spontaneous activity. These discharges may be attributed to several sources. First, the excitatory influence of more peripheral neurons that are spontaneously active is important. Second, there is nonspecific input to the sensory systems from reticular formation neurons, which may control the overall level of sensory activity from moment to moment. Third, at each level, many connections are made with neurons originating at higher stations in the same sense system. Cortical modulation of subcortical processes, for example, is not uncommon. All these sources of input may contribute to the spontaneous activity of central neurons.

Spontaneous activity provides a background against which the activity of inhibitory processes takes place. Information is conveyed in the brain not only by excitation but also by inhibitory mechanisms, which require ongoing signals that may be modulated. Spontaneous activity may fulfill other roles as well. For example, in some man-made communication systems nonsense information is used when there are no real messages to be sent, to make sure that the system remains in working order.

Central Processes in Hearing

Successful analysis of a biological system depends upon finding the proper units for analysis. By this token, the study of the auditory system has been partially successful. Frequency analysis—classifying sounds by the amount of energy present at each frequency at each point in time—has provided a key to understanding the lower levels of the auditory system, where cells appear to act mainly as frequency analyzers, encoding in their discharge rate the intensity of the auditory signal in a particular frequency range. Other codes, however, also are present in the brainstem auditory systems, which emphasize different informational aspects of the stimulus such as the location of the sound source in the acoustic environment. A major shift in coding parameters appears to occur in the cortex. The frequency-analyzer concept, which is so helpful in understanding quality encoding in the brainstem, is markedly less useful in the cortex, where neurons, while utilizing frequency information, appear to be responding to another code. The auditory cortex appears to sort auditory information differently than do the subcortical structures. Thus, because the scientific problem is conceptual rather than technical, the understanding of the cortical processing of auditory signals is quite incomplete.

Anatomy of the Auditory System

The auditory nerve enters the brainstem in the medulla, where it synapses upon cells in the cochlear nuclei on either side of the midline. The pathways from cochlear nucleus to cortex are multiple and overlapping, as may be seen in Figure 4.5. The anatomical complexity of the auditory system may have evolved for several reasons. First, the fiber systems that bypass and cross each other might provide delay lines that route the signal into the same nucleus at different times to facilitate analyses of the acoustic patterns. Second, the auditory system has primitive evolutionary roots, and its complexity may result from the building of higher upon lower structures. Third, the auditory system is intimately related anatomically to the vestibular system, which controls balance. The long evolutionary history and extensive comingling with another sense system probably account for much of the anatomical distribution of auditory system nuclei.

Figure 4.5 shows the gross anatomy of the principal nuclei of the auditory system. The auditory nerve enters the brainstem at the medulla, where it splits into three parts that terminate in the dorsal and the two ventral—one anterior and one posterior—cochlear nuclei. Each of the cochlear nuclei receives fibers from the entire cochlea. Moreover, each is arranged in an orderly tonotopic fashion by the frequency of the adequate stimulus. Thus, connections are distributed within each nucleus by the location on the cochlea from which the auditory nerve fibers originated.

Fibers originating in the cochlear nuclei pass directly to the superior olive (which physically resembles an olive) to the ascending auditory nucleus of lateral lemniscus or to the inferior colliculus of the midbrain. Fibers originating in the superior olive and in the lateral lemniscus proceed to the inferior colliculus. The inferior colliculus in turn projects to the medial geniculate nuclei of the thalamus. Medial

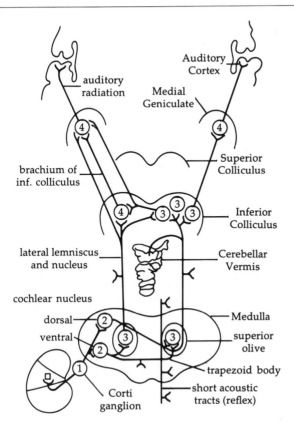

Figure 4.5. *The principal nuclei of the auditory system.* The numbers indicate the order of the cell—that is, the number of steps it is removed from the auditory periphery. (From Davis, H. Psychophysiology of hearing and deafness. In S. S. Stevens (Ed.), *Handbook of Experimental Psychology,* © 1951 by John Wiley & Sons, Inc. Used by permission.)

geniculate nuclei send their axons, which together form the auditory radiations, to the primary auditory cortex of the temporal lobe. Our diagram stops there. It is possible to trace the projections from the primary auditory cortex to other cortical areas, but exact definition is very difficult past this point. Certainly there is auditory information in widespread areas of the cortex, but, for these areas, the term sensory would be a misnomer, as this distinction is probably not meaningful at high levels. The concept of a sensory system as a strictly sensory structure is very hard to maintain, even at much lower levels. For example, Harrison and Irving suggest, on quantitative anatomical evidence, that the medial superior olivary nucleus, which has long been thought to play a role exclusively in sound localization, is found only in animals with well-developed visual systems. They argue that this nucleus may be responsible for moving the eyes and head in the direction of a sound. What kind of structure is this? Sensory? Motor? Sensorimotor? Such categories seem to be too restrictive.

Signal Processing in the Auditory Nerve

In the auditory nerve, single cells are responsive to pure tones, presented either alone or in combination. If a cell responds to pure tones, its tuning curve can be computed (see Figure 4.6).

A tuning curve plots the amount of stimulus energy needed at various frequencies to produce a fixed change in the rate of firing of the cell. The tuning curve is an equal-response curve; each point indicates a particular combination of frequency and intensity that produces the same response from the cell as does any other combination on that curve. Therefore, it is also a curve of ambiguity; given only the response of the cell, there is no way to decide which combination of frequency and intensity is actually present when the neuron is responding. The nervous system must simultaneously utilize information from other similar sensory cells, with slightly different tuning curves, to actually solve the problem.

One further note: A minimal excitatory shift from the spontaneous firing rate is often used to define a tuning curve. But inhibitory tuning curves also have been computed by using a decrease from spontaneous level as the measured change. Taken together, the excitatory and inhibitory tuning curves provide a more complete description of the behavior of the neuron.

Figure 4.6 shows tuning curves for a number of cells in the auditory nerve. Notice that each curve forms a "V" at its bottom. Each cell has a well-defined frequency for which it is most sensitive. Tones at frequencies either higher or lower than this best frequency must be considerably more intense to produce a response from the cell. Notice that the curve is steeper above the best frequency than below it. Auditory nerve cells have a sharp high-frequency cutoff, which is a direct consequence of the distribution of energy in the traveling wave in the cochlea. Low-frequency tones displace the whole basilar membrane, whereas higher frequency sounds affect the basilar membrane only in its first turns. The asymmetries in cochlear displacement shown in Figure 3.6 are reflected in the tuning curves in the auditory nerve.

The tuning curves are a way of diagramming the receptive field of auditory neurons. Since it is impossible to actually list the receptors involved in this complex mammalian sense system and impractical to

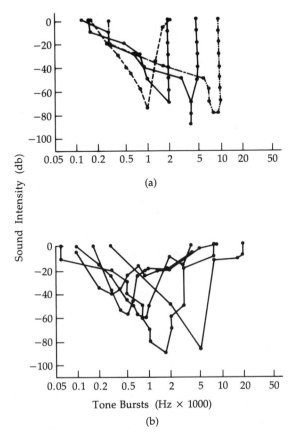

Figure 4.6. *Tuning curves of afferent fibers in the auditory nerve.* (a) Normal asymmetric pattern of response, extending from the adequate stimulus into lower-frequency ranges. (b) Other units in the auditory nerve in which the high-frequency cutoff is not so sharp. (Used by permission from Katsuki, Y., Neural mechanism of auditory sensation in cats, *Sensory Communication: Contribution to the Symposium on Principles of Sensory Communication*, W. A. Rosenblith (Ed.), The MIT Press, Cambridge, Massachusetts. © 1961 the MIT Press.)

physically map them, the tuning curve represents a convenient shorthand. The best frequency of the tuning curve corresponds to a point along the basilar membrane where the nerve fiber must make most of its connections. The spread of the curve most likely reflects the coarseness of frequency coding by the cochlea. Each spot is moved substantially by intense vibrations of many frequencies.

Notice, however, that the auditory-system tuning curves are substantially sharper than the cochlear displacement curves shown in

Figure 3.6. The increased selectivity results from lateral inhibitory connections. But inhibition can be observed more directly. When stimulated with a continuous tone at its best frequency, a cell in the auditory nerve maintains a rate of discharge above its spontaneous level. If a second tone burst is then sounded at a slightly different frequency, the response of the cell is substantially reduced or completely suppressed. If the tone burst is of a very different frequency, however, no inhibition occurs. The method of paired stimuli can be used, therefore, to determine exactly the range of inhibitory frequencies surrounding the best frequency of a cell.

Inhibition of higher tones by lower ones is both more common and more powerful than the reverse. The inhibitory region for auditory nerve cells is normally asymmetric. Since frequency is determined by place in the cochlea, the paired stimulus procedures actually map the spatial extent of the inhibitory surround of the receptive field. Receptive fields divided spatially into excitatory and inhibitory areas characterize all major sensory systems at peripheral levels.

Signal Processing in the Brainstem

There are about 30,000 hair cells in the cochlea, about 30,000 fibers in the auditory nerve, and about 90,000 cells in all three of the cochlear nuclei together. Connections are not simply one to one, of course. There is much convergence and divergence in the pattern of connections. The maintenance of a constant number of channels suggests a system that transforms information while discarding little of the available data. Man-made electronic and mathematical systems built in this way often show the property of information conservation, which also seems a reasonable property for the auditory system. The triplication of neuronal connections in the cochlear nucleus begins the pattern of multiple representation of information, which continues into more central auditory areas.

Tuning curves of cochlear nucleus neurons appear to have the same form as those in the auditory nerve. No appreciable broadening or narrowing of these selectivity functions appears at this stage. Because of the tonotopic organization in each of the cochlear nuclei, coupled with the excitatory-center/inhibitory-surround receptive field, simple tonal stimuli result in patches of excitation in each of the three fields. The size of these excited regions increases with the intensity of the stimulus. The response to natural sounds is much more complex.

In terms of frequency characteristics, the other brainstem auditory nuclei process information in much the same manner as does the cochlear nucleus. Figure 4.7 shows typical tuning curves for cochlear

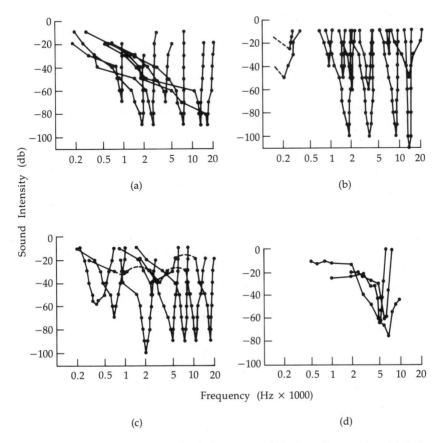

Figure 4.7. *Tuning curves for single neurons within the auditory system.* (a) Cochlear nerve. (b) Inferior colliculus. (c) Trapezoid body. (d) Medial geniculate body. (Used by permission from Katsuki, Y., Neural mechanism of auditory sensation in cats, *Sensory Communication: Contributions to the Symposium on Principles of Sensory Communication*, W. A. Rosenblith (Ed.), The MIT Press, Cambridge, Massachusetts. © 1961 The MIT Press.)

nucleus, inferior colliculus, trapezoid body, and the medial geniculate nucleus of the thalamus. The tuning curves appear narrower in the more central nuclei. Most data indicate that this process of ever-sharper frequency tuning climaxes in the medial geniculate bodies, where some neurons show marked frequency selectivity. The sharpening of frequency response is probably built upon the familiar base of converging excitatory and inhibitory signals.

Some investigators question, on methodological grounds, the data that support the theory of increasing frequency selectivity. They argue that, when relatively intense stimuli are used for testing, little narrowing of the tuning curves is seen in the ascending auditory stations of the brainstem. One exception might involve responses to low-frequency stimuli, where sharpening undoubtedly is present between the auditory nerve and the cochlear nucleus. A revision in the widely held concept of brainstem processing of frequency information would be necessary if it were established that the pattern of frequency-selective tuning curves shown in Figure 4.7 reflects methodological curiosities rather than the functional patterns of the neurons from which the data were obtained.

Single Cell Activity in Auditory Cortex

The primary auditory cortex, which receives fibers directly from the medial geniculate nucleus of the thalamus, is surrounded by the secondary auditory areas of the cortex. The secondary areas do not communicate directly with the medial geniculate to any large degree. Instead, their input comes primarily from collateral, or secondary, projections and from other thalamic nuclei.

Single cells in the primary auditory cortex are more difficult to characterize than are the subcortical auditory units. Many respond to pure tones, and, of these, some fire only at the onset of the tone, showing very rapid and complete adaptation. Others show adaptation but maintain a low level of response as long as the tone is present.

Tuning curves of cells in the primary auditory cortex are diverse. Figure 4.8 shows some typical examples. These curves are broader than those of the medial geniculate. Many are multipeaked, indicating that the cell has several best frequencies.

Pure tones do not seem to be the best type of stimuli for testing neurons in the primary auditory cortex. Animals in nature are faced with problems of pattern perception, and it may be to these problems that auditory cortex makes its unique contribution. Many cortical units that respond to complex natural sounds fail to respond to continuous pure tones, no matter what frequency and intensity are used. Some of these cells, however, discharge in the presence of tones of changing pitch. Some are direction sensitive and fire only when the tone sweeps through its acoustic receptive field in one direction, up or down. Other units are responsive in both directions. Even when moving tones are employed, many cells in the primary auditory cortex remain silent; yet these same cells will fire in the presence of natural sounds. Clearly, these neurons participate in auditory perception. The difficulty in understanding auditory information processing in the cortex is conceptual. Until the proper stimulus dimensions are determined, the neurophysiological problem will remain unsolved.

Frequency information, however, is not discarded into the

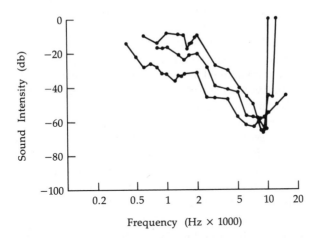

Figure 4.8. *Tuning curves for single units within the primary auditory area of the cortex.* Unlike cells in the higher brainstem nuclei, cortical units show broad patterns of responsivity. (Used by permission from Katsuki, Y., Neural mechanism of auditory sensation in cats, *Sensory Communication: Contributions to the Symposium on Principles of Sensory Communication*, The MIT Press, Cambridge, Massachusetts. © 1961 The MIT Press.)

cortex. The primary auditory cortical area maintains the precise tonotopic organization observed in subcortical auditory nuclei. Tunturi, for example, has mapped the auditory cortex of the dog after first applying strychnine to a small cortical area. (Strychnine in small quantities is a central nervous system excitant, allowing the effects of tiny signals to be detected in the cortex.) Frequency is distributed from the front to the back of the primary auditory cortex in an approximately linear manner. Two millimeters of cortical tissue represents a one-octave shift in the adequate stimulus.

Further, the auditory cortex, like the other sensory cortices, is composed of discrete cortical columns within which individual neurons are likely to display the same best frequency. Thus, frequency information is certainly present in the primary auditory cortex. The ways in which cortical neurons transform their thalamic input, however, remain to be discovered.

Frequency Following in Pitch Perception

All the evidence presented above suggests that the frequency of a sound is encoded by selectively exciting some neurons but not others. Most cells in the brainstem and in the auditory nerve have well-defined tuning curves that show a best frequency; for any intensity of stimulation, the cells respond more vigorously at this frequency than at any other. Frequency seems to be signaled by which cells are firing, and intensity by how much these cells discharge.

Other explanations of pitch perception have been offered, but none seems to fit the data as well as the scheme just outlined. The most time-honored alternative concept is frequency following. In the auditory nerve, cells discharge in phase with low-pitched, strong tones. Cells respond once or twice per cycle up to about 400 cycles per second (Hz). Above this frequency, cells miss some cycles and fire for others, but each time they do fire, they fire at the same phase of the stimulus waveform. Groups of cells can, therefore, follow a signal up to about 5000 Hz, above which frequency following is unlikely. However, the discharge of cells in phase does not necessarily indicate that frequency following encodes pitch for higher nervous centers; more likely, frequency following is simply a consequence of the construction of the receptor and is ignored by central processes.

There are, then, serious difficulties with the frequency-following theory of pitch perception. First, animals seem to need auditory structures as high as the inferior colliculus to make pitch discriminations, yet frequency following is difficult to demonstrate beyond the auditory nerve. Second, the frequency-following theory demands that rate of discharge signal both stimulus frequency and stimulus intensity—a difficult requirement. Third, since the volleys are not maintained at higher auditory stations, there must be, if the theory holds true, some decoding neurons that transform the stimulus-linked volleys into some more durable central code; however, no such neurons have been found. Few neuroscientists currently support a frequency-following theory of pitch perception.

Critical Bands and Auditory Masking

Studies of auditory masking, or the capacity of one sound to interfere with the detection of another sound, provide some purely behavioral evidence concerning the extent of the auditory receptive fields. Most of the recent studies use a pure tone as the test stimulus—the signal that is to be detected—and narrow-band white noise as the masking stimulus. Acoustic white noise is a signal that has the same amount of power at all audible frequencies, sounding something like an electronic hiss. Narrow-band noise is similar to white noise except that its frequency range is restricted by an upper- and lower-boundary frequency; between these two limits, the power of the signal is divided equally among all frequencies. Band-limited noise is a useful masking stimulus, which, by uniformly exciting a given area of the cochlea, facilitates determination of auditory receptive fields. In contrast to a pure 1000 Hz tone, which has all its power at precisely 1000 Hz and is perfectly predictable, a narrow-band noise between 990 and 1010 Hz will contain no frequencies above and below these limits and will be of uniform intensity within them.

If a pure tone (the test stimulus) is presented with a masking wide-band white noise in the same ear, the ability of the mask to prevent detection of the test signal increases almost in direct proportion to the intensity of the mask. But does all the energy in the white-noise mask contribute to this interference? Perhaps only a small part of the signal, which activates the same part of the cochlea as the test signal, is involved. This is the concept of the critical band.

Experiments using various bandwidth masks seem to demonstrate the presence of a critical band surrounding the test tone. Only a small range of frequencies near that of the test stimulus are involved in masking. When the width, or frequency range, of a narrow-band mask is increased (with the power at each frequency held constant), the efficiency of the mask also increases until the limits of the critical band are reached. Further broadening of the masking signal has no effect on detection.

As might be predicted from knowledge of the movement of the cochlear membrane and the tuning curves of auditory nerve fibers, critical bands are asymmetrically distributed about the test frequency, with lower frequencies being the more effective maskers. The width of the critical band, which increases exponentially as a function of test signal frequency, is much broader for high pitches than for low. When this data is measured in terms of the cochlea, however, the critical band appears to be of constant size, about 1 mm wide, regardless of the frequencies used in measurement. This finding reflects the compressions of high frequencies into smaller areas of the cochlear structures. Correspondingly, the width of a receptive field measured in other ways is also about 1 mm, but it is not known to what level in the auditory system this width should be attributed. Further, receptive field width suggests some limits for the interaction of tones; it does not, however, imply that tones must be separated by 1 mm on the cochlea to be detected as different. Much finer frequency resolution is possible because of diverging signals and the overlapping of receptive fields. In addition, the width of a neuron's best frequency is much narrower than the width of its entire receptive field.

Localizing Auditory Signals

Localizing sounds in space depends upon hearing with two ears. Sounds are localized by analyzing differences in intensity, frequency pattern, or arrival time between the right and left ears. Unfamiliar sounds cannot be localized with only one ear.

Figure 4.9 shows a head with several sound sources. If the sound source is directly ahead (A) of the listener, both ears receive exactly the same stimulus. When the sound source is displaced to one or the other side, the two ears receive slightly different messages. Sounds coming from C will reach the right ear slightly before they reach the left ear. This very small difference in arrival time produces a phase difference between the two ears. Each ear receives substantially the same message but at slightly different times; the sound always reaches the closer ear first. Phase differences are especially prominent for low-pitched sounds, in which each cycle repeats itself very slowly. The minimal detectable difference in arrival times is about .03 msec, or 3/100,000 sec, but signals arriving as much as 2 msec apart are still perceived as a single sound.

The near ear receives also a slightly more intense signal than the far ear does because intensity quickly falls off as distance from the sound source increases. This is important if the sound source is both weak and close to the ear, but the distant ear receives a weaker signal also because it is in the acoustic shadow of the head. Shadow effects account for a substantial part of the intensity difference between the ears for lateral sound sources. High-pitched sounds are especially susceptible to acoustic blocking.

The differential susceptibility of high-pitched sounds to acoustic blocking suggests that there may be a way to discriminate between sounds coming from the front and from the rear. If the sound is familiar and possesses high-frequency components, it will appear slightly less brilliant if the source is behind the head because the pinnae, or external ear, casts a shadow for higher frequencies that partially blocks their pathway to the inner ear. A more accurate way of distinguishing front and back, of course, is to turn the head; then the problem of front and back becomes the simpler problem of right and left.

If directional hearing is built on such subtle cues, there must be highly specialized central mechanisms capable of detecting small changes in the phase and intensity of the auditory signal. Investigations of single cells in the brainstem auditory nuclei have revealed such specialized neuronal systems. The superior olivary complex is the lowest auditory center in the brainstem in which information from both ears is available to single cells. It is divided into two parts, a medial and

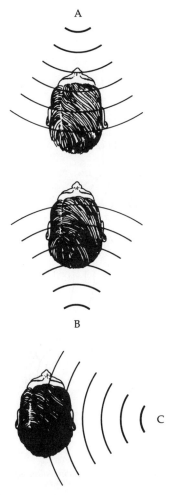

Figure 4.9. *Three sources of auditory signals yield slightly disparate patterns of auditory input, from which localization may be accomplished.* Sounds emanating from source A arrive at the two ears with equal latencies and intensities, as do sounds originating from source B; however, high-frequency information is attenuated from B by shadow of the ear. Source C results in a shorter-latency, higher-intensity signal at the right ear.

a lateral nucleus, both of which have cells that respond differently to a sound when the location of its source is changed.

In the medial olivary nucleus, cells have two large dendrites. One extends medially and receives input from the contralateral ear through the contralateral cochlear nucleus. The other dendrite projects laterally

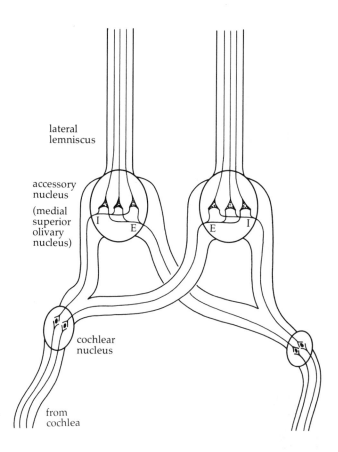

Figure 4.10. *The arrangement of neurons within the medial superior olivary nucleus by which auditory localization can take place. "E" indicates excitatory synapses and "I" inhibitory.* (From Variation on a theme of Bekesy: A model of binaural interaction, by W. A. Van Bergeijk, *Journal of the Acoustic Society of America*, 1962, 34, 1434, with permission of the publisher and Mrs. W. A. Van Bergeijk.)

and makes contact with fibers that originate in the cochlear nucleus on the same side of the brain. (There are two olivary complexes, one on each side of the brain; each is the mirror image of the other.)

Most cells in the medial olivary nucleus increase their rate of firing when either ear is stimulated, but about one in four is excited by stimulation of one ear and inhibited by stimulation of the other. These excitatory-inhibitory (EI) cells are responsive to intensity differences between the two ears.

EI cells in the medial olivary nucleus that respond to low frequencies (have low-pitched tuning curves) are responsive also to phase differences between the ears. Each cell has a best time difference and will respond maximally when the arrival time of signals at the two ears differs by that fixed amount. As the arrival times are made to differ from this value, the size of the response diminishes. If a low-pitched pure tone is used, a shift of 180 degrees (one-half a cycle) abolishes the response of the cell, which then responds less actively than if only one ear were stimulated. Such a neuron is ideally suited for extracting phase information from low-pitched tones. The EI cells localize high-pitched sounds by comparing intensity differences.

Cells in the lateral olivary nucleus show a similar specialization for localization. The lateral olivary nucleus is prominent in echo-locating animals such as bats and dolphins, where cells that are normally very quiet have been reported. These cells have well-defined tuning curves and respond to auditory input from the ipsilateral (same side) ear. The cells are responsive also to input from the contralateral ear. The tuning curves for the two ears are virtually identical for any lateral nucleus cell. Contralateral input, however, is inhibitory. Such cells extract information about intensity differences between the ears and discard information about absolute intensity—exactly the appropriate pattern for a localizing mechanism.

Similar results are seen in cells higher in the brainstem. Localization-relevant information is passed on to more central auditory nuclei, but it is not clear whether these centers add anything to the analysis made in the olivary complex. They probably do reprocess and, in doing so, refine localization information. It is a question for future investigation.

Central Processes in Somatosensation

The neuronal organizations of the auditory, skin, and body senses are quite similar. All involve processing information from many sense receptors distributed over a spatial area. Lateral inhibitory interactions are common. Von Békésy has argued that this neuronal similarity has perceptual counterparts as well. Partially to demonstrate this correspondence, von Békésy constructed an artificial cochlea, large enough to rest one's arm on and driven by vibrations slow enough to be processed by the skin senses. Like the cochlea, its rubber surface conducts a traveling wave that peaks in different places for different frequencies of vibration. The result is a sensation of stimulation at a single spot on the forearm that changes with frequency. Thus a pattern of skin stimulation that is very similar to cochlea excitation results in highly selective localization of the stimulus. In the auditory system, cochlea localization is translated to signal pitch.

Anatomy of the Somatosensory Systems

That the anatomy of the somatosensory systems of the CNS is complicated should not be surprising. Somatosensory information is needed by the most primitive organisms to permit control of their own behavior. In the course of evolution, additional receptors are introduced, and, as alternate mechanisms for processing bodily information develop, a complex, hierarchical neuronal system results.

Much sensory information is processed at the spinal level, where spinal mechanisms act to modulate and organize behaviors initiated by more central processes. In mammals, multiple analysis of somatosensory information is the rule; the output of each receptor reaches many different neuronal analyzers. Multiple analysis reflects the divergent property of sensory neural nets.

The axon from a primary somatosensory receptor enters the spinal cord through the dorsal roots—collections of sensory fibers that enter the spinal cord from the rear between each pair of vertebrae—of the cord (see Figure 2.21). Once inside the spinal columns, the axons branch and synapse upon several of many spinal nuclei. The pattern of connections is very complicated, and many connections are unknown.

Lemniscal Pathways.   One of the best known of the somatosensory subsystems is the lemniscal system, which, at the level of the midbrain, forms the medial lemniscus. This tract synapses in the thalamus in the ventrobasilar complex. The ventrobasilar complex, a thalamic sensory-relay nucleus, projects to the primary somatosensory cortex.

Three major pathways originate in the spinal cord and eventually form the medial lemniscus. (See Figure 4.11.) The first and most prominent of these pathways is the dorsal column, which is divided into the cuneate and gracile tracts. The dorsal column is formed of axons from receptor cell bodies outside the spinal cord that enter at the dorsal roots and band together as they pass through the spinal cord and terminate in the medulla, at the base of the brainstem. There, they synapse in either the gracile nucleus or the cuneate nucleus. The gracile nucleus receives axons that originate in the legs and lower body; the cuneate receives axons that originate in the arms or upper body. These two nuclei, like most brain structures, are bilaterally symmetrical. Fibers from these nuclei cross the midline and form a part of the medial lemniscus.

The spinocervical pathway (named for a synapse made in the cervical or neck portion of the spinal cord) is a second contributor to the medial lemniscus. Axons from receptors that utilize the spinocervical pathway synapse in the dorsal roots as they enter the spinal cord. The axons from these second-order fibers ascend and, in turn, synapse on

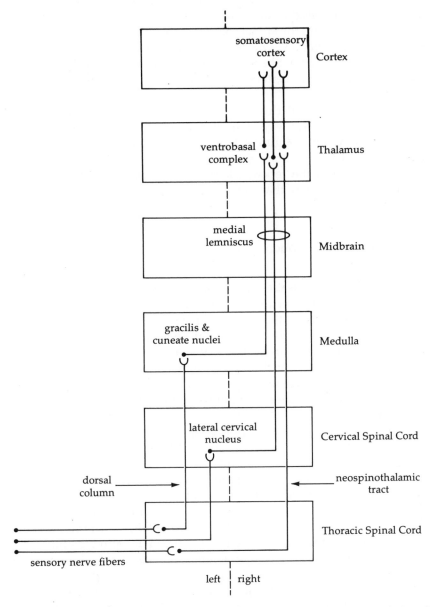

Figure 4.11. *Major portions of the lemniscal system from spinal cord through forebrain.*

the lateral cervical nucleus high in the spinal cord. Axons from the lateral cervical nuclei cross to the other side of the spinal cord and project upward, where they join other fibers of the medial lemniscus.

Finally, fibers of the lateral sensory tracts, which originate in the dorsal horns, are second-order fibers that receive input directly from receptors. They cross the spinal column at the level of entry and proceed directly to the thalamus, where they join the medial lemniscus in the midbrain. These latter fibers form the neospinothalamic system and have been found with certainty only in high primates and man.

Extralemniscal Pathways.   The numerous other somatosensory fibers that make their way to higher areas of the brain form the extralemniscal systems. Figure 4.12 shows some of the more prominent extralemniscal tracts; many others certainly exist. As a result of the intensive study of the reticular formation in the 1950s and 1960s, the extralemniscal systems that involve the reticular formation are among the best known.

The Sense of Touch

Touch is the sensation of pressure produced when the surface of the body makes contact with an object. This definition does not include very intense pressures that may be regarded as pain. Temperature sensitivity must also be distinguished from touch, although the two are not independent. Pressure sensitivity changes with temperature. For example, the sense of touch is most refined when the object is a few degress above normal skin temperature; one is less able to make very fine judgments of pressure or texture when the object is either warmer or colder than that.

The imprecision of the preceding definition of touch points to one of the largest problems in studying the body senses, the determination of the qualities—the psychological dimensions—of the somatosensory perception. Touch, pain, warmth, cold, and kinesthesia (position and movement of the joints and musculature) are generally considered the five important qualities of bodily sensation. At least some of these are not totally separable from others. The interdependence of temperature and pressure has been mentioned, but other ambiguities also exist. The distinction between strong pressure and pain is often difficult to make. Similarly, the separation of pain and the sensation of burning or freezing is not always clear. Moreover, some bodily sensations—itching and ticklishness, for example—do not seem to fit properly within the five-part division of somatosensation. Perhaps it is best to think of touch, pain, warmth, cold, and kinesthesia as the major classes of sensation produced by a partially differentiated, partially unified sensory network.

Two types of fibers, both of which participate in tactile sensation, appear to innervate the hairy skin of the cat. One group, showing

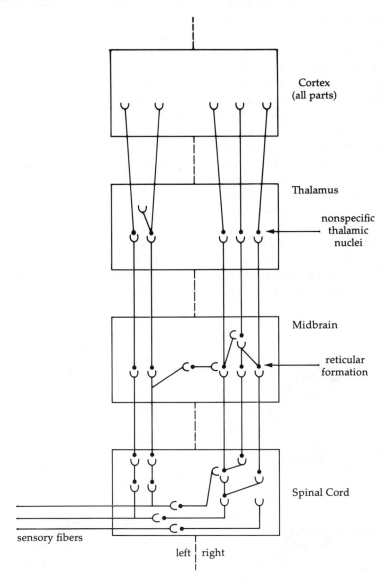

Figure 4.12.   *The extralemniscal sensory pathways of the somatosensory system.*

only phasic on-and-off discharges and, therefore, signaling only movement or stimulus change, adapts quickly to the application of the stimulus. The axons of the neurons of this group are myelinated and range in size from very small to large. Their receptive fields are small and localized. Each fiber innervates many receptors in uniform receptive fields. No center-surround organization can be seen in these first-order afferents. (See Figure 4.13.)

The second group of afferents displays a more complex response, which has both phasic and tonic components. The phasic response is a burst of activity, the intensity of which is a function of the rate of change. The tonic response depends solely upon the intensity of the stimulus. Figure 4.14 illustrates both the phasic and tonic components of one afferent nerve fiber in the monkey. These afferent fibers innervate discrete spots on the skin (see Figure 4.15), and, although each normally innervates only one receptor or spot, sometimes as many as five receptors may be contacted by the branching afferent. In this system, no complex receptive field organization is possible. Such afferent fibers show the compression functions common in sensory systems that carry quantity information.

The relatively well-defined lemniscal systems appear to serve the function of epicritic sensation, which was Head's term for the sensitive, exact sensations of light touch and pressure. (In contrast, the extralem-niscal systems subserve protopathic sensibilities such as diffuse touch, pain, and temperature.) The lemniscal systems, therefore, are necessary

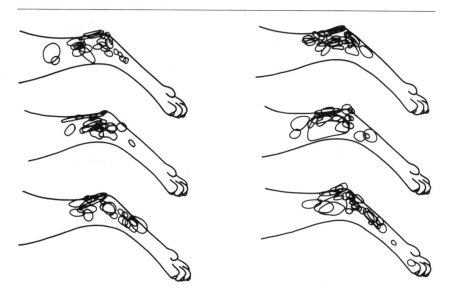

Figure 4.13. *A number of receptive fields for afferents in the somatosensory system of the cat.* (From Hunt, C. C., & McIntyre, A. K. An analysis of fibre diameter and receptor characteristics of myelinated cutaneous afferent fibres in cat. *Journal of Physiology,* 1960, **153**, 103. Used by permission.)

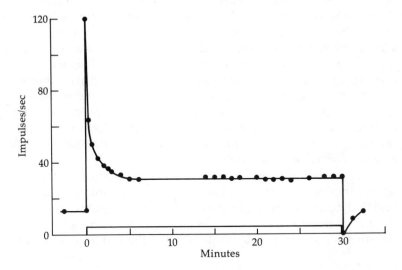

Figure 4.14. *The response of a somatosensory afferent neuron in the monkey, showing both phasic and tonic components.* Notice the stability of the tonic response for stimulus maintained for a period of ½ hour. (From Iggo, A. An electrophysiological analysis of afferent fibres in primate skin. *Acta Neurovegetativa*, 1962, **24,** 229. Used by permission.)

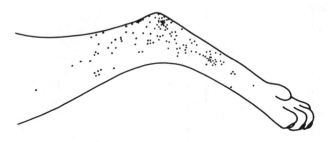

Figure 4.15. *The punctate receptive field of afferent fibers, innervating only single receptors.* (From Hunt, C. C., & McIntyre, A. K. An analysis of fibre diameter and receptor characteristics of myelinated cutaneous afferent fibres in cat. *Journal of Physiology*, 1960, **153,** 106. Used by permission.)

for the precise localization of tactile stimuli and the construction of a tactile map of the immediate environment.

Some indication of the complexity of the lemniscal systems can be gathered from the study of cortical neurons that receive lemniscal input. Receptive fields of neurons within the somatosensory cortex possess larger receptive fields than are seen in the primary afferents. Under anesthesia, most of these neurons display only excitatory innervation, the strength of which varies within the receptive field. Figure 4.16 illustrates the receptive field of one typical neuron within the somatosensory cortex of the anesthetized monkey. The neuron receives converging excitatory information from the wrist, thumb, and forefinger of the contralateral hand. The point of maximal excitatory efficiency usually lies in the central portion of the field, but the pattern of excitation can be eccentric, with the most efficient point lying near the edge of the field. Multipeaked fields, in which several separated maxima are present, also exist.

A smaller fraction (about 1 in every 12) of these cortical units in an anesthetized animal are characterized by an antagonistic receptive field that displays well-defined excitatory and inhibitory regions. In the absence of anesthesia, this percentage may well be very much larger. Anesthesia appears to selectively deprive the somatosensory cortex of

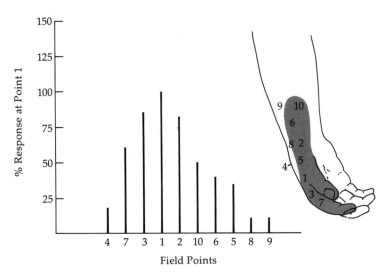

Figure 4.16. *The receptive field of a single somatosensory cortical neuron.* Within that receptive field, the excitatory response to stimulation is not uniform. On the left is graphed the percent of maximal response that occurs when different points within the receptive field are electrically stimulated. The receptive field is defined by the response of the cortical neuron to light tactile stimulation. (From Mountcastle, V. B., & Powell, T. P. S. Neural mechanisms subserving cutaneous sensibility, with special reference to the role of afferent inhibition in sensory perception and discrimination. *Bulletin Johns Hopkins Hospital*, 1959, **105**, 205. © 1959 The Johns Hopkins University Press. Used by permission.)

inhibitory input under most conditions. Consequently, the cortical units described above may possess inhibitory surrounds that were not detected. Figure 4.17 shows one such cell. Stimulation of the central excitatory area alone increases the firing rate of this cortical neuron above the spontaneous level of discharge. Concurrent stimulation of the inhibitory surround not only attenuates the excitatory effect but also suppresses even the spontaneous discharge of the neuron. On release from inhibitory stimulation, the cell shows rebound firing, which in form may approximate the initial, purely excitatory response in both phasic and tonic components. Figure 4.18 illustrates other patterns of receptive field organization, some of which differ from the more common center-surround pattern.

The lemniscal system maintains strict topographic mapping of its projections in both the thalamus and the cortex. Figure 4.19 shows this mapping in the postcentral tactile area of the somatosensory cortex of the monkey. Other somatosensory cortical areas contain similar topographic arrangements. Such representations are a distortion of bodily proportion, but they faithfully mirror the innervation density of peripheral tissue. Highly innervated regions such as the face and the

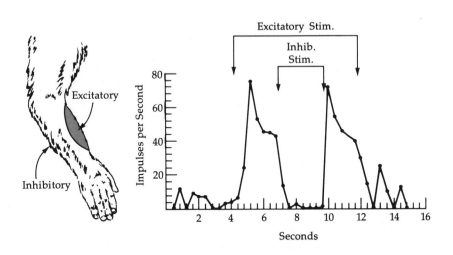

Figure 4.17. *Center-excitatory, surround-inhibitory receptive field of a somatosensory cortical neuron.* Inhibitory stimulation completely suppresses the response to stimulation of the excitatory portion of the receptive field. (From Mountcastle, V. B., & Powell, T. P. S. Neural mechanisms subserving cutaneous sensibility, with special reference to the role of afferent inhibition in sensory perception and discrimination. *Bulletin Johns Hopkins Hospital,* 1959, **105,** 218. © 1959 The Johns Hopkins University Press. Used by permission.)

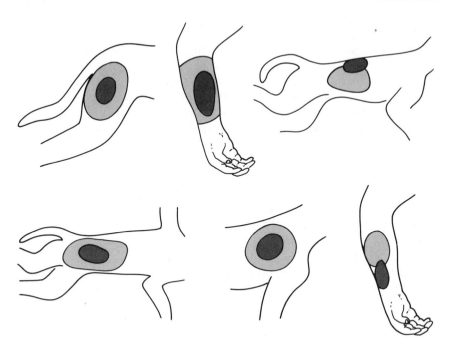

Figure 4.18. *Some typical receptive fields of somatosensory neurons in the monkey.* Notice that asymmetric relationships are sometimes present. (From Mountcastle, V. B., & Powell, T. P. S. Neural mechanisms subserving cutaneous sensibility, with special reference to the role of afferent inhibition in sensory perception and discrimination. *Bulletin Johns Hopkins Hospital,* 1959, **105,** 221. © 1959 The Johns Hopkins University Press. Used by permission.)

hands are heavily represented, both in the thalamus and in the cortex. Receptive fields of neurons that represent these areas tend to be smaller than those of units connected to less sensitive tissue such as the skin of the back.

The somatosensory cortical tissue displays a columnar form of intrinsic organization. Electrode penetrations that are perpendicular to the cortical surface encounter individual units that respond to the same type of stimulus. Moreover, the receptive fields of such cells are quite similar, as are their latencies of response. Transverse penetrations contact a wider variety of cells, which suggests that columns of cells in this area constitute functionally integrated subsystems that can process sensory information with some precision.

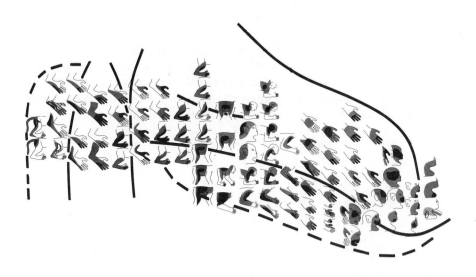

Figure 4.19. *Topographic presentation of somatosensitivity receptive fields within the primary somatosensory area of the monkey.*   The extent of cerebral representation appears to depend upon the degree of innervation of bodily structures and not upon the absolute size of those structures. (From Woolsey, C. N. Organization of somatic sensory and motor areas of the cerebral cortex. In H. F. Harlow & C. N. Woolsey (Eds.), *Biological and Biochemical Bases of Behavior.* © 1958 by The University of Wisconsin Press. Reprinted by permission.)

Kinesthesia

Mountcastle and his colleagues have devoted much of their attention to the problem of kinesthesia, the sense of the position and movement of the limbs. Kinesthesia, like touch, is the product of a finely graded, information-rich system capable of reliably signaling the exact state of position for each of the limbs and any changes in that state. Movements of the major joints of the shoulder and hip as small as 1 degree and as slow as 1 degree per second are detectable. The more distal joints are less sensitive; movement thresholds up to ten times as large as those in the major joints are common in the toes and fingertips. It is tempting to think that less precise information is necessary in the more distal joints to maintain adequate knowledge of body position since the bones that they move are quite short. Larger errors of positioning at the major joints would result in greater absolute errors of limb position.

The tissues surrounding the joints of the limbs contain many receptors, each of which is situated to respond in a characteristic manner to movement of the joint. As in other sensory systems, a variety of patterns of temporal adaptation characterizes these receptors. Some, acting as detectors of movement but providing little additional informa-

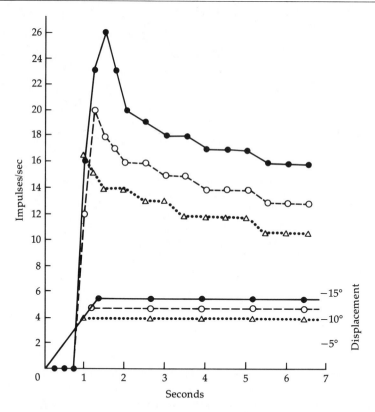

Figure 4.20. *Response on the single kinesthetic afferent from the cat's knee to rotation stimulation at the rate of 10°/sec through three different angles.* Notice that the tonic response depends upon the final placement of the limb. (From Boyd, I. A., & Roberts, T. D. M. Proprioceptive discharges from stretch-receptors in the knee-joint of the cat. *Journal of Physiology,* 1953, **122,** 46. Used by permission.)

tion, display only phasic activity. Receptors that adapt more slowly seem able to provide more detailed information on which kinesthetic sensitivity must depend. The phasic response of these cells is determined by the rate of movement, whereas the tonic level of response depends solely on the position that the limb assumes when the movement is completed. It is useful to think of these cells as describing a particular sector of all possible movements of the limb. The receptor is activated in only a subset of positions, which together constitute the excitatory angle of the cell. Within that region, the tonic level of firing is dependent upon position; it may continue to respond for hours if the position is maintained. Outside the excitatory angle, movement of the limb produces neither phasic nor tonic activity. Figure 4.20 shows the response of one such cell to the movement of the limb to three different resting positions within its excitatory angle. Excitatory angles of receptors range between about 10 and 30 degrees and may be positioned anywhere within the arc of movement of the limb.

Movement receptors are connected to thalamic sensory nuclei by dorsal column fibers of the lemniscal system. Lemniscal fibers synapse upon neurons within the ventrobasal nucleus of the thalamus, which in

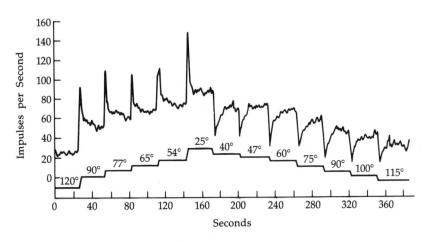

Figure 4.21. *Response of a single thalamic neuron in the ventrobasal nucleus to flexion of the contralateral knee in the unanesthetized monkey.* Both phasic and tonic components are clear. The lower tracing depicts the actual movement of the limb in this experiment. (From Mountcastle, V. B., Poggio, G. F., & Werner, G. The relation of thalamic cell response to peripheral stimuli varied over an intensive continuum. *Journal of Neurophysiology,* 1963, **26,** 812. Used by permission.)

turn projects to the postcentral gyrus of the somatosensory cortex. Convergence is implied by the orderly widening of excitatory angles at higher levels within this system. Figure 4.21 illustrates the response of one thalamic neuron to discrete movements of the knee through its excitatory angle of about 75 degrees. Such a neuron must systematically receive input from a series of receptors, each of which provides information concerning a small portion of the thalamic excitatory angle. This neuron gives its maximum excitatory tonic response when the limb is fully flexed (25 degrees). Thalamic neurons have excitatory angles that exceed one-half of the range of possible movement of the limb. Because they respond maximally when the limb is either fully flexed or fully extended, thalamic neurons are said to be single-ended. Figure 4.22 depicts the excitatory angles of a series of cells within the ventrobasal nucleus of the thalamus in the monkey. Because of the single-ended response pattern with maxima at either extension or flexion, thalamic cells form two populations, responding reciprocally as the limb is moved from full flexion to full extension. These two classes of thalamic neurons together provide sufficient information to determine limb position with reasonable accuracy.

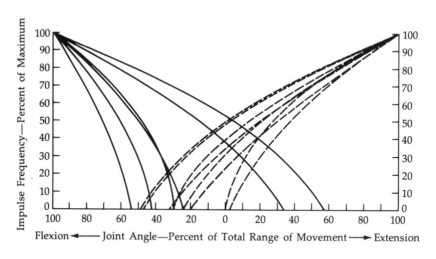

Figure 4.22. *Excitatory angles of 14 kinesthetic neurons in the thalamus of the unanesthetized monkey.* Such excitatory angles are single-ended, as neurons respond maximally at either full flexion or full extension. Movement of the limb throughout its possible range produces a reciprocal pattern of firing in these two groups of thalamic neurons. (From Mountcastle, V. B., Poggio, G. F., & Werner, G. The relation of thalamic cell response to peripheral stimuli varied over an intensive continuum. *Journal of Neurophysiology*, 1963, **26,** 828. Used by permission.)

Pain

The perception of pain and the neurophysiological substrates of pain perception are only poorly understood. The most common model for this system is the specificity theory, which postulates that pain is perceived through the activity of a specific sensory system that is activated only by painful stimuli. This traditional theory maintains that small peripheral fibers with free nerve endings are the receptors for pain. The fibers enter the spinal cord and proceed through the lateral spinothalamic tract, an extralemniscal system, to the thalamus of the brain. Despite its apparent simplicity, the specificity theory of pain perception has been remarkably difficult to defend.

For example, the specificity theory demands the existence of identifiable receptors, yet such receptors are not easily located. In studies of large populations of somatosensory fibers, only a few fibers respond exclusively to very intense stimuli. Even these may not be pain receptors but rather may represent units high on the distribution of threshold intensities; no evidence suggests that stimulation of these units produces only pain. Second, lesions of the lateral spinothalamic tract are not uniformly effective in the termination of peripheral pain. If these pathways were the transmission link in a specific sensory system for the perception of pain, the absence of pain should result from lesion just as blindness results from optic tract damage. Third, under certain clinical conditions, pain in one area of the body may be triggered, often after long delays, by gentle stimulation of another, unrelated area of the body surface. Such facts, and others like them, are difficult to understand if the simple specificity theory is true.

Melzack and Wall have proposed an alternative conception of the physiological mechanisms serving pain perception. In their gate control theory, which is similar to the arguments of Weddell, they propose that pain is not the result of the activation of a limited set of pain receptors but rather a state triggered peripherally by the presence of a unique pattern in the massive flux of somatosensory input. A particularly dense region of the spinal cord, the substantia gelatinosa, may act as a gate to control access of peripheral information to the central activating structures involved in the reaction to a painful stimulus. Activity in the small, slowly adapting fibers of the somatosensory system, which typically are characterized by high thresholds to stimulation, opens the gate. Conversely, large, fast, quickly adapting, low-threshold fibers inhibit the substantia gelatinosa and close the gate. Controlling access to more central pain mechanisms, such a device within the spinal cord would act as a pattern detector by monitoring information concerning the balance of activity within the large- and small-fiber systems. A prolonged intense stimulus, which is perceived as painful, would tend

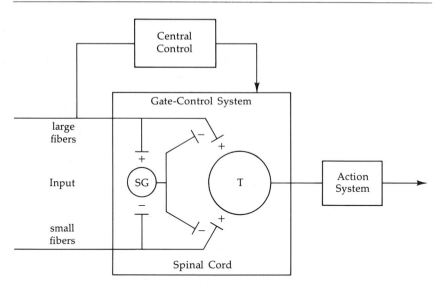

Figure 4.23. *A spinal mechanism proposed by Melzack and Wall in their gate-control theory of pain.* Large-fiber input excites the substantia gelatinosa, which acts to close the gate for both large and small fibers to the T cells. Small-fiber input has the opposite effect. Accessibility of input from either the large or small fibers to the T cells depends upon the balance of activity between these two classes of afferents. For this reason, the postulated gate acts as a spinal pattern detection device for the perception of pain. Central control of this mechanism probably also occurs as indicated above. T cells project to activation and motivational systems within the mammalian brain. (From Melzack, R., & Wall, P. D. Pain mechanisms: A new theory. *Science,* 1965, **150,** 975. Copyright 1965 by the American Association for the Advancement of Science. Used by permission.)

to maintain excitation in the high-threshold, slowly adapting, small fibers long after the activity of the quickly adapting, large fibers had been habituated. Reactivation of the large fibers would restore the balance to a more normal level and thus reduce perceived pain. Perhaps this is why rubbing a wound often makes the pain disappear temporarily.

Although Melzack and Wall's gate control theory is by no means firmly established, it represents an attempt to formulate an alternative concept of a problem for which the traditional concept has been less than productive. The problems of pain perception are not yet solved.

Temperature

Rather little is known of the neural mechanisms that underlie the sense of temperature. Temperature-sensitive receptors have been localized in thermally sensitive organs such as the tongue. These units differ in the temperature to which they maximally respond, giving rise to distinctions between "warm" and "cold" fibers. However, there is little evidence that the distribution of peak sensitivities is not continuous.

Temperature-sensitive fibers apparently transmit information to the ventrobasal complex of the thalamus through the lateral neospinothalamic tract of the spinal cord. The ways in which information from various receptors may be integrated at spinal, thalamic, or cortical levels is not known.

Summary

Sensory processing is necessary within the nervous system to extract those features of stimuli that are biologically relevant to the animal from the mass of ambiguously encoded sense information present at the receptors. Sensory systems are, thus, information-processing systems that maintain and maximize certain classes of information at the expense of other, less important classes.

The nervous system commonly uses lateral inhibitory mechanisms to sharpen spatial informational patterns. In the cochlea of the ear, in the retina of the eye, and on the skin of the body, discrete stimuli affect a large number of receptors as a result of either the broad-tuning characteristics of the receptors or the close mechanical coupling of receptors through accessory tissue. Lateral inhibitory networks emphasize spatial change—minima, maxima, and shifts in the rate of stimulus change—at the expense of information about the absolute intensity of the stimulus or its degree of dispersion.

Implicit in this organization is the convergence and divergence of sensory information. Convergence refers to the availability of information from many receptors at a single, more central detector cell, whereas divergence emphasizes the contributions that a single receptor makes to a number of detectors. Complex patterns of convergence and divergence form the basis of information processing in sensory systems.

Inhibitory processes that operate in time as well as in space give rise to a diversity of temporal adaptation patterns. Phasic responses emphasize stimulus change and, sometimes, the rate of that change. Tonic responses typically depend upon the quantity of the stimulus. Spontaneous activity in sensory systems may operate as a base against which inhibitory phenomena, both spatial and temporal, may be seen. The depression of CNS activity below its spontaneous level may convey as much information as its enhancement does in other circumstances.

The auditory system embodies many of these principles in its function. Auditory information enters the CNS from the cochlea via the auditory nerve. Following a complex set of interactions within the brainstem, auditory signals are relayed to the medial geniculate nucleus of the thalamus and thence to the primary auditory cortex. The tuning curves of auditory neurons within this system suggest increasing frequency selectivity at higher levels of analysis, which culminates in the finely tuned responses of single cells in the thalamus. Apparently, another as yet undefined principle of analysis governs the response of cortical neurons, which display much broader tuning curves, often with multiple peaks of responsivity. Many cortical units fail completely to discharge to any simple tonal stimuli but respond vigorously to natural sounds of various sorts.

Behavioral data in auditory masking experiments suggest that the width of auditory receptive fields is approximately 1 mm of cochlear surface. Not all masking noises are equally effective in interfering with the detection of a pure tone; instead, a critical band exists about the test stimulus within which random excitation interferes with detection. These data correspond to other measures of receptive field size within the auditory system.

Special mechanisms are used to localize auditory signals in space. Cells in the superior olivary complex seem first to perform this function by employing both intensity and phase information in determining localization.

The somatosensory system, like the auditory system, is complexly organized below the level of the thalamus. Many separable pathways exist, some of which reflect the increasing complexity of sensory-motor integration encountered in the evolution of mammals. The lemniscal systems seem to relay precise information of touch and body position, whereas extralemniscal systems may be important for the more diffuse body sensations.

Although some pressure-sensitive afferents adapt with exceptional speed, most afferents within the lemniscal system show both phasic and tonic responses. The phasic response is determined by the rate of pressure change; the tonic response signals absolute pressure.

Under normal conditions, the receptive fields of most central neurons, on which information from these afferents converges, are marked by an excitatory center and an inhibitory surround, although these fields need be neither simple nor symmetric. Stimulation of the inhibitory surround alone may completely antagonize the effects of excitatory stimulation and spontaneous discharge.

Within the lemniscal system, at both the thalamic and cortical levels, strict topographic mapping of the body surface is preserved. The area of the cortex devoted to any particular portion of the body is related to the extent of innervation in that tissue and not to the absolute size of the innervated structure. Within the somatosensory cortex, a columnar structure of organization is maintained. Within a cortical column, single cells display similar properties in their receptive field organization. Columns appear to constitute functionally integrated sensory subsystems.

Like information of touch, kinesthetic information is processed within the lemniscal system. Joint receptor afferents signal limb position and the rate of its change within narrow excitatory angles. In the thalamus, where the excitatory angles of single units are greatly increased, two classes of cells respond maximally at either full flexion or full extension. Tonic activity reliably signals limb positions within the excitatory angle of the cell.

Other body sensations of less precision depend, in part, upon extralemniscal activity. The specificity theory postulates a specific subserving system of pain perception that involves free nerve endings as receptors, small-diameter peripheral fibers as afferents, and the lateral spinothalamic tract as the relay system that terminates in the thalamus. The specificity theory has been remarkably difficult to document. Alternative theories emphasize pattern-detection devices within the spinal cord that extract configurations of discharge within the somatosensory system characteristic of painful stimuli. Neither theory is well established.

The auditory and somatosensory systems constitute complex mechanisms for processing sensory information. Each system seems to operate under similar general principles, but those principles are often uniquely employed to treat the special problems of each sensory modality. Although the precise rules of their operation are not yet known, the more central structures in both systems appear to function to extract increasingly general features of the sensory stimulus.

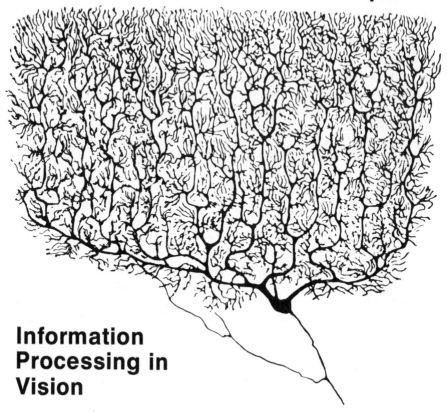

Chapter 5

Information
Processing in
Vision

The neurons of the visual systems of the brain transform, process, and recode information present at the retina to extract the information necessary to create a map of the visual world. That map, usually called a percept, is a more or less stable representation of the environment. The percept is constructed from sensory information, but it is not the product of an exclusively sensory process. When sensory information is not adequate to completely identify the object seen, additional information is supplied from other sources such as memory. Visual percepts usually begin with information available at the retina, which is then sorted, coded, and recoded by the visual system into its ultimate form. Visual information-processing neurons and the rules by which they operate are the subjects of this chapter.

Information Processing in the Retina

The initial major transformations of visual information occur in the retina of the eye, but until recently little was known about these processes. The small size and complicated anatomy of the cells of the retina are major barriers to the discovery of retinal function. Werblin and Dowling, however, side-stepped the problem of retinal neuron size by studying an unusual experimental animal, the mudpuppy. The eye of the mudpuppy is very much like the mammalian eye. In the retinas of both are five layers of neural tissue: receptors, horizontal cells, bipolars, amacrine cells, and retinal ganglion cells, the axons of which leave the eye to form the optic nerve. The receptive fields of the ganglia cells have the same general properties in both mudpuppies and primates. Because each cell in the mudpuppy eye is larger, intracellular recordings can be made directly from each type of retinal cell to determine the conditions under which the cell is active. Such record-

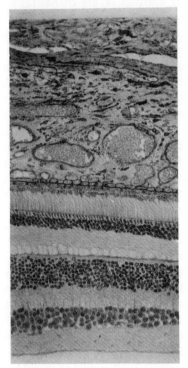

Figure 5.1. *Cross section of the human retina magnified approximately 150 times.* (From Polyak, S. *The Vertebrate Visual System.* © 1957 The University of Chicago Press. Used by permission.)

ings require the use of a pipette microelectrode, a very thin glass tube filled with an electrically conducting salt solution. Its tip is so small that it cannot be seen with a light microscope. Not only does this electrode make possible the measurement of the internal electrical events in retinal cells; it also allows the cells to be marked with a stain when the recording is completed so that later the cell can be identified microscopically. Microelectrode recordings of the mudpuppy eye partially solved the riddle of retinal information processing.

In the course of development, the retina emerges from the same tissues that also form the brain. (See Figure 5.1.) The complex connections that occur in such tissue form the anatomical basis for visual-information processing. Figure 5.3 is a schematic, or conceptual, drawing of the retina that shows five layers of cells. In the flow of information, the first cells to be activated are the receptors, the rods and cones. In these cells, light energy triggers the production of neuroelectric activity.

Beneath the receptors lie four distinct layers of neural tissues. Each layer is characterized by a unique type of cell, some of which carry information across the retina, whereas others transmit information between layers of the retina. Laterally oriented horizontal cells comprise the first layer of neurons beneath the receptors. The anatomy of the horizontal cells seems to be suited to gathering information from a number of individual receptors; their processes transverse the retina and make contact with many receptors. (See Figure 5.3.) Beneath the layer of horizontals are the bipolar cells, which make vertical connections in the retina and contact both the horizontal cells and the receptors. Bipolar cells are well suited to carry information from the receptors and the horizontal cells to the lower levels of the retina. The amacrine cells comprise the third layer. Like the horizontals, the amacrine cells can make lateral connections. The ganglion cells, which appear to receive information from either amacrine or bipolar cells, are the last cells in the retinal system of information processing. Their axons project out of the retina to the lateral geniculate nucleus in the thalamus of the brain. The axons of all the ganglia cells together form the optic tracts, the fiber bundles that connect the eyes to the brain.

In the mudpuppy, the receptive field of the receptor is the receptor itself. The receptor responds only to light falling directly on it, not to light falling on its neighbors. It thus appears that receptors are not interconnected; each receptor functions as a separate, independent photodetector. A rod or a cone responds to the extent to which it is excited, regardless of the activation of other rods or cones.

Activation of a receptor in the mudpuppy eye produces hyperpolarization; that is, the interior of the receptor becomes increasingly negative with respect to the extracellular fluid. When first illuminated,

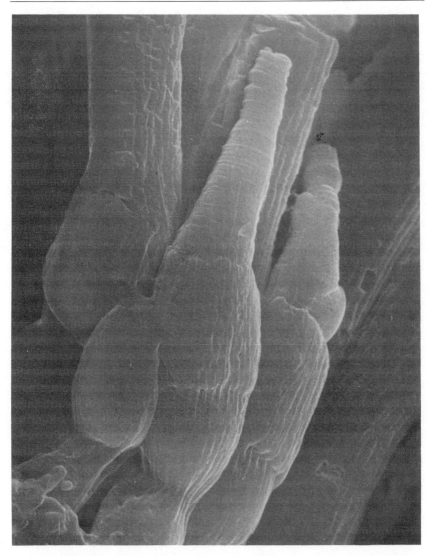

Figure 5.2. *Rods and cones from the mudpuppy retina.* The scanning electron microscope shows the outer structure of the rods and cones, which are distinguishable by their shapes. (From Lewis, E. R., Zeevi, Y. Y., & Werblin, F. S., unpublished photomicrograph, used by permission.)

the receptor hyperpolarizes in proportion to the strength of the illuminating energy. The gradual decay of initial activity to a lower, steady level is also related to stimulus intensity. When the stimulus is terminated, the receptor returns slowly to its dark resting state, but, in

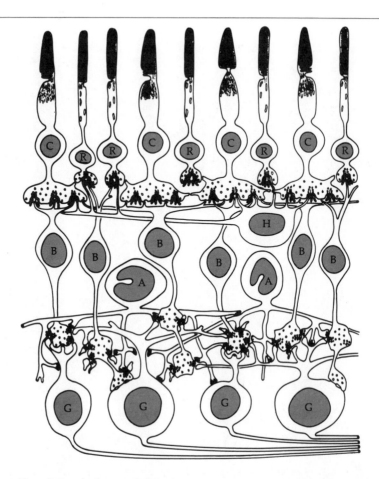

Figure 5.3. *A schematic diagram of the mudpuppy retina showing receptors, the rods (R), cones (C), the bipolar cells (B), horizontal cells (H), amacrine cells (A), and the ganglion cells (G).* (From Dowling, J. E., & Boycott, B. B. Organization of the primate retina: Electron microscopy. *Proceedings of the Royal Society of London: Series B,* 1966, **166,** 104. Used by permission of the Royal Society of London.)

so doing, it slightly overshoots its mark. The result is a slight depolarization, or a small "off" response, opposite in direction to the hyperpolarizing "on" response. The intracellular potential is then somewhat less negative than in the resting state. Thus, the receptor shows three discrete responses to the onset and offset of stimulation: (1) a large initial phasic hyperpolarizing response; (2) a smaller tonic response; and (3) a slight depolarization that occurs when the light is turned off and the cell adjusts itself to the dark resting level. (See Figure 5.4.) In its three responses, a receptor encodes information about both the intensity and the duration of the stimulus.

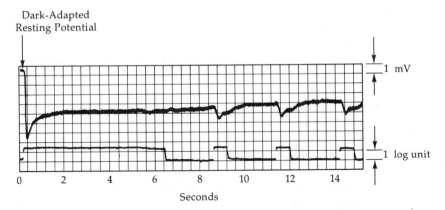

Figure 5.4. *The response of a dark-adapted receptor to stimulation.* Stimulus intensity is indicated in the lower tracing. The response of the receptor to stimulation is graded hyperpolarization. When the stimulus is removed, the response begins to decay to the original resting potential. If additional stimuli are presented before the readjustment process is completed, the cell returns to the hyperpolarized state more quickly than it did originally. (From Werblin, F., & Dowling, J. Organization of the retina of the mudpuppy, *Necturus maculosus.* II. Intracellular recording. *Journal of Neurophysiology,* 1969, **32,** 346. Used by permission.)

The first cells in the visual system to combine information obtained from a number of receptors are the horizontals. The lateral orientation of horizontal cells enables them to receive and integrate information from many receptors. Like the responses of the receptors that excite them, the response of the horizontal cells is hyperpolarization. The exact nature of the contact between receptors and horizontal cells is not known; it might be either electrical or chemical. No more is known of the connections between any of the other neuronal elements within the retina.

As do the receptors, the horizontal cells exhibit increasingly large hyperpolarizing responses to increasing levels of stimulation. Horizontals probably summate the excitatory activity of the receptors that their dendrites contact. The size of the receptive field of the horizontal cell measured optically is about the same as the size of the cell and its dendrites measured microscopically. This correspondence lends support to the belief that the horizontal cell makes connections with many receptors in a single area and responds when any of them are excited. The strength of the horizontal cell's response depends upon both the number of excited receptors and the strength of the excitation. Some important properties of perceptual behavior appear to result from the retinal patterns of connection.

Human observers are poor judges of the absolute intensity of light but are quite good at discerning changes in the relative brightness of objects in the visual field. To understand what absolute or relative intensity means, consider the following example. Words printed on the pages of a book look very much the same when read in a library, at home, or out of doors. Indeed, the relative difference in intensity between the letters and the page is the same in all cases. The absolute intensity of light, however, is many times greater in the library than at home, and even that level of intensity is a poor second to the absolute intensity of outdoor light at noon. Yet the words, relative to the page, look much the same. The neural basis of this phenomenon first appears at the bipolar cells. The visual system discards most information about absolute intensity and preserves information about the differences in intensity between objects in the visual field. Objects are recognized by shape, contour, and color, not by absolute intensity of reflected light. The visual system is primarily a pattern recognizer rather than a brightness detector.

The process of retaining information concerning relative differences illustrates the concept of feature extraction. The visual system does not process all available incoming information. Instead, the complex patterns of stimuli must be reduced to proportions commensurate with the information-processing capacity of the nervous system. Not all information is equally useful; relevant features are extracted at the expense of other information, which is virtually discarded. The information available on the receptor mosaic of the retina is transformed or reorganized. Only certain classes of reorganized information are preserved and passed on to higher levels of the nervous system.

Retinal mechanisms that first perform this feature extraction permit pattern recognition at widely differing levels of light intensity. Bipolar cells, which receive information both from single receptors and from horizontal cells, respond with graded potentials and do not generate neuronal spikes. The bipolar cells combine information in a more complex manner than do the horizontal cells. The receptive field of the bipolar cells is divided into two regions—a small circular central area and a larger concentric surrounding area. The central area corresponds roughly in size with the area of the bipolar's dendritic tree, a set of processes that connect the bipolar and the layer of receptors. The dendrites probably make direct contact with receptors. Light falling on this central area of the receptive field excites the bipolar cell. Excitation takes one of two forms: in some bipolar cells, central stimulation produces hyperpolarization; in others, stimulation of this area produces depolarization. The two response patterns occur equally often.

Stimulation of receptors in the surround antagonizes the response to central stimulation. For example, if a bipolar cell is hyperpolarized when the central portion of the receptive field is stimulated, illuminating the surround reduces this hyperpolarization. Similarly, in the other type of bipolar, illuminating the surround reduces the effectiveness of central stimulation in producing depolarization. In neither case does stimulation of the surround have any effect on the polarization of the cell if the center is not also illuminated. The surround, by antagonizing or eliminating the response of the cell to central stimulation, performs only a veto action. Information from the surround probably arrives at the bipolar cells through the horizontal cells.

The organization of the bipolar's receptive field into a center with an antagonistic surround creates a contrast detector, which is relatively insensitive to the absolute level of light. If the receptive field is evenly illuminated, the cell makes no response in the steady state. The cell will not respond to maintained uniform illumination regardless of the strength of the stimulus. Instead, the bipolar polarizes or depolarizes, as its nature dictates, to differential illumination of the center and the surround. Werblin and Dowling have shown that the bipolar functions as a contrast detector, responding to the ratio of illumination between the center and the surround. Contrast detection is the first step toward pattern recognition in the visual system.

Although a bipolar cell shows no tonic response to uniform illumination, it does show a phasic response to changes in the level of uniform stimulation. Because the transmission of information from the receptors in the surround through the horizontal cells to the bipolar is slower than the transmission of information from the central receptors, which affect the bipolars directly, a phasic response occurs to a uniform change in illumination and is maintained until the horizontal input to the bipolar arrives. Only a change in center illumination relative to the surround, however, can produce a change in the tonic response.

The bipolar cell performs the first contrast detection in the visual system. It compares center with surround and responds only when there is a difference. By the nature of the system, there are two types of bipolar cells. Half respond to central stimulation by polarizing and half by depolarizing. Both types of response are maintained through later stages of processing. The introduction of center-surround antagonism at the bipolar cell is the last change in receptive field organization that occurs in the retina.

The remaining two layers of cells in the retina, the amacrine and ganglion layers, differ from the other layers in that they are capable of generating propagated action potentials. Whereas hyperpolarization is the rule in the receptors, in the horizontals, and in half of the bipolars, the amacrines and the ganglia produce conventional depolarizing responses that lead to spikes. The amacrine cells depolarize and

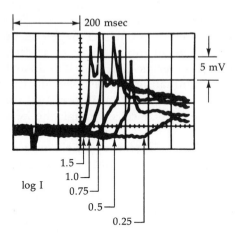

Figure 5.5. *Amacrine cell response.* Amacrines respond to stimulation by the production of one or two spikes. Variations in stimulus intensity produce no change in the number of spikes but rather a shortening of the latency of that response. Here, spike patterns to stimuli of five intensities (log *I* 0.25 to 1.5) are shown. (From Werblin, F., & Dowling, J. Organization of the retina of the mudpuppy, *Necturus maculosus.* II. Intracellular recording. *Journal of Neurophysiology,* 1969, **32,** 349. Used by permission.)

generate one or two spikes with every change in input intensity. Increasing the intensity of stimulation does not increase the number of spikes that an amacrine cell produces but, instead, decreases the delay that precedes their occurrence.

Many amacrine cells have a center-surround organization in their receptive fields like that observed in bipolars. The amacrine cells fire either when the center of their receptive field is illuminated or when the illumination of the surround is reduced. Other amacrine cells have very large uniform receptive fields—that is, have no center-surround organization in their receptive fields—and respond with spiking to the onset or offset of illumination anywhere within this area. Amacrine cells could behave in this way if they made connections with several bipolar cells that have different center-surround organization but that originate in the same general area of the retina.

Amacrines respond during the phasic response of bipolars but not during tonic bipolar activity. Werblin and Dowling suggest that each amacrine cell can inhibit further input from the bipolars as soon as the phasic response is begun. In close proximity to each synapse between bipolar and amacrine, there is a return synapse that carries information in the opposite direction. If this latter connection is inhibitory, the excitatory input from the bipolar can be quickly cancelled, and only sudden large changes in bipolar activity can be transmitted to the amacrines. These neuronal connections facilitate temporal adaptation, which emphasizes stimulus change.

The remaining retinal cell is the ganglion, which, like the amacrine cell, generates spikes. Unlike that of the amacrine, however, the rate of spike production of the ganglion cell depends upon stimulus intensity. The axons of ganglion cells leave the retina and form the optic nerve, which carries visual information to the brain. In the absence of any visual input, ganglion cells still fire, showing spontaneous activity.

Ganglion cells have different types of receptive fields. Some respond only to transient changes in the level of illumination. Of these, some respond to increases and others to decreases in light intensity. Still others—the so-called on-off cells—respond to both. Another class of ganglion cells not only fire when illumination changes but maintain firing as long as illumination is constant. These cells show the same center-surround organization in their receptive fields as do the bipolars. Moreover, their receptive fields are of the same size as the bipolars'.

The receptive field organization in the ganglion cell, together with the cell's anatomy, suggests that ganglia make connections with either amacrine or bipolar cells. The function of ganglion cells seems to be the generation of frequency-coded spike trains that may be transmitted to the CNS. Their receptive fields bear the stamp of the cell with which they connect. At present, no data contradict this interpretation.

Again, it is worth noting that the patterns of receptive field organization in the mudpuppy eye are very similar to those in the optic nerve of higher animals. The retinal mechanisms involved in both cases are probably similar. The receptors function to transduce the information encoded in the distribution of light energy to a form that the subsequent neuronal elements can process. The other neuronal tissue serves to emphasize change. The horizontal and bipolar cells emphasize spatial change—contrast and contours—whereas the amacrines signal the presence of temporal change—movement, or other changes, in time. The ganglia relay these transformations of the retinal image to more central stations in the nervous system.

Other as yet unknown neural mechanisms for information processing may exist in the retina. The data presented above characterize about 80 percent of the retinal neurons studied; further experiments may reveal additional functions in these same cells. However, there is no reason at present to believe that all possible retinal signal-processing mechanisms are known.

Anatomy of the Thalamocortical Visual System

In higher mammals, the pathways leading from the retina to the thalamus and the primary visual cortex are normally designated as the visual system. Other visual systems exist, but far less is known about their structures and functions. These other channels for visual information involve brainstem structures, and one seems to be important in orienting the organism toward visual targets and in coordinating vision with the bodily senses. However, the thalamocortical visual system is crucial for pattern recognition and color detection. Much more is known about this system than the other visual systems; moreover, in terms of its sheer size, it is the dominant visual system.

Figure 5.6 shows the thalamocortical visual system. The axons of the ganglion cells leave the retinas and form the optic nerves, which proceed into the thalamus, where they terminate on the lateral geniculate nucleus. Some fibers in each of the optic nerves cross the midline of the body at the optic chiasma. These same axons comprise the optic tracts as they proceed from the chiasma to the thalamus. Fibers that originate in the nasal hemiretina cross, whereas axons from the lateral hemiretinas do not cross. Therefore, visual information encoded on the left hemiretinas of each eye is passed to the left thalamus and the left cortex, and the converse occurs on the right. An object seen in the left visual field will be imaged by the lens onto the right half of each retina, and the corresponding images from both the right and the left eyes will go to the same half of the brain. Termination in the same half of the brain is necessary for the integration of corresponding binocular information from the two eyes.

The fibers of the optic tract do not terminate randomly in the lateral geniculate nucleus; they are arranged retinotopically—that is, by the location on the retina at which they originate. The spatial arrangement of the retinal receptors is at least partially preserved in the thalamus.

Cell bodies located in the lateral geniculate nucleus send their axons to the primary visual cortex. The axonal fiber tracts of the lateral geniculate cells are the optic radiations, which synapse systematically with cortical cells. Again, retinotopic organization is preserved.

From primary visual cortex, axons transmit signals to the surrounding cortical tissue, the secondary visual areas. The patterns of connection at this point become less clear.

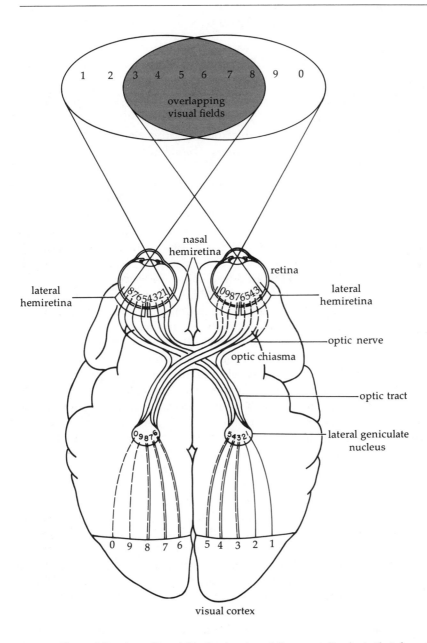

Figure 5.6. *An outline of the visual system of the mammalian brain that shows the correspondence of points in the retina, thalamus, and visual cortex.* Notice that, in the optic chiasma, fibers of the nasal hemiretinas cross and proceed to the contralateral thalamus, whereas fibers of the temporal hemiretinas proceed directly to the ipsilateral thalamus.

Information Processing in the
Thalamocortical Visual System

Spatial Organization of Receptive Fields

The receptive fields of the ganglion cells in cats and in monkeys (including some monkeys whose visual system is behaviorally indistinguishable from man's) resemble the receptive fields of the bipolar and ganglion cells of the mudpuppy. Most ganglion cells in high vertebrates show center-surround organization with circular or near circular form. Some cells, however, show strikingly different patterns; they have very large, uniform receptive fields and show a sustained discharge dependent upon the intensity of stimulation. Such a cell, lacking the inhibitory interactions necessary for contrast detection, could function to provide an indication of the overall intensity of illumination. It could not, however, be very precise, since a neuron has a response range of only a few hundred spikes per second, whereas the levels of light in which the visual system can function vary over a range of a million to one. Moreover, single cells are not usually sensitive to small changes in the rate of firing when response rates become high. For these reasons, it appears that a cell with a uniform receptive field can give only a general indication of the brightness of an object.

Little change in receptive field organization appears to occur in the thalamus. The receptive fields of lateral geniculate cells are much like those of the ganglia. Circular center-surround organization is the rule. If any transformation occurs at this level, it is directed at increasing the antagonism between center and surround. Thus, the thalamic cells will be even less affected by diffuse, unpatterned light than the ganglia cells were. Thalamic cells are more efficient contrast detectors.

Hubel and Wiesel have conducted many of the experiments that led to the descriptions of ganglion and thalamic cell activity presented above. They mapped the receptive fields in cats by moving a small spot of white light across a dark field in front of the anesthetized animal, noting changes in the firing pattern of the cells under study. They have extended this procedure to the study of cortical cells and, in so doing, have generated a conceptually elegant scheme of processing patterned information in these areas.

Cortical cells do not show the small, circular center-surround organization so typical of the cells below them. Instead, the first cortical cells in the primary visual cortex respond to lines. Figure 5.7 depicts various arrangements of receptive field organization that Hubel and Wiesel attribute to simple cortical cells. These cortical cells receive input

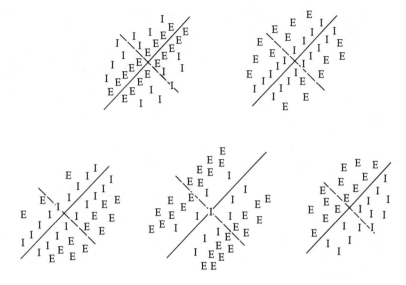

Figure 5.7. *Various receptive-field arrangements in simple cortical neurons.* Excitatory and inhibitory responses are indicated by E and I, respectively. Notice that the preferred stimulus for these cells appears to be linear rather than circular in form. (From Hubel, D., & Wiesel, T. N. Receptive fields, binocular interaction and functional architecture in the cat's visual cortex. *Journal of Physiology*, 1962, **160**, 111. Used by permission.)

from several thalamic cells, the receptive fields of which lie along a line on the retina. If the centers of the receptive fields of the thalamic cells are simultaneously illuminated (assuming for the moment that they are center-excitatory/surround-inhibitory), the simple cortical cell is maximally excited. If the line of light on the retina is rotated, fewer thalamic cells respond and, therefore, the response of the simple cortical cell is also diminished. Whereas thalamic cells respond most effectively to spots, simple cortical cells respond most effectively to lines.

The visual cortex is functionally organized into cortical columns. Cells directly above and below each other communicate freely, whereas cells separated laterally by more than a small distance appear to be virtually independent. A vertical cluster of cells that function as a unit define a cortical column. All the simple cortical cells within a cortical column show the same angle of orientation in their receptive fields. Moreover, their receptive fields lie in reasonably close proximity to each other on the retina. Simple cortical cells send output to another type of cell within the same cortical column, a cell that Hubel and Wiesel have labeled the complex cortical cell. The result is that the complex cortical

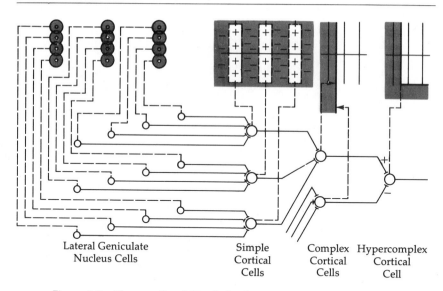

Lateral Geniculate   Simple   Complex Hypercomplex
   Nucleus Cells   Cortical   Cortical   Cortical
                           Cells   Cells   Cell

Figure 5.8. *The receptive fields of visual-system cells with a plausible pattern of interconnection.* Lateral geniculate cells, with circular center-surround receptive field organization, may send their output to the simple cortical cells. Simple cortical cells receive excitatory input from a number of thalamic units, the receptive fields of which form a line. The complex cortical cell receives excitatory input from a number of simple cortical cells, all of which show the same angle of preferred orientation. A hypercomplex cell receives excitatory input from one complex cortical cell and inhibitory input from another. The result is a cell that responds maximally to a line in a particular orientation that is terminated before entering the receptive field of the inhibitorily connected complex cell. (From *Neuropsychology: The Study of Brain and Behavior,* by C. Butter. © 1968 by Wadsworth Publishing Company, Inc. Reprinted by permission of the publisher, Brooks/Cole Publishing Company, Monterey, California.)

cell has a larger receptive field than does a simple cortical cell. The best stimulus for the complex cell is still a line, but the line can occur anywhere in its receptive field, as long as it is in the proper orientation. The complex cell responds equally well to any correctly oriented line within the receptive field. As the line is rotated, however, the cell's response is diminished. The transformations introduced by the cortical cells organize visual information into larger, more general features. In simple cortical cells, specific lines replace spots as the best stimuli; in complex cortical cells, lines of a particular orientation within the receptive field replace fixed-position lines as the requisite for cellular response. Cortical cells seem to function to extract increasingly more general features from the mosaic of light and dark originally present at the receptors of the retina.

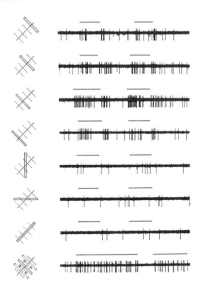

Figure 5.9. *The response of a complex cortical cell to a moving line.* As with simple cortical cells, a line stimulus must maintain the proper angle of orientation if a response is to be produced. Movements of a line perpendicular to that orientation produce no response whatsoever. (From Hubel, D., & Wiesel, T. N. Receptive fields, binocular interaction and functional architecture in the cat's visual cortex. *Journal of Physiology,* 1962, **160,** 116. Used by permission.)

Outside primary visual cortex, the process of combination and recombination of input to extract specific features from the stimulus continues. Hubel and Wiesel, for example, have identified cells they term hypercomplex. Hypercomplex cells function like complex cells except that, in hypercomplex cells, the line must be terminated at one or both edges of the receptive field. Another line, proceeding from the first at a right angle, functions as a termination, so that some have suggested that hypercomplex cells might function as corner detectors.

Although it is inconclusive, some behavioral evidence suggests that these neuronal units, lines and corners, are the elements from which visual percepts are constructed. If a person is shown a figure, using special methods so that the object is always imaged on exactly the same place in the retina, an interesting perceptual phenomenon occurs. The stabilized retinal image at first gives rise to a normal perception; soon, however, parts of the figure disappear. (See Figure 5.11.) As neuronal units become adapted or fatigued, whole lines or corners disappear at once. If units recover, these lines return, while other parts may disappear. The image does not become blurred or fuzzy or become

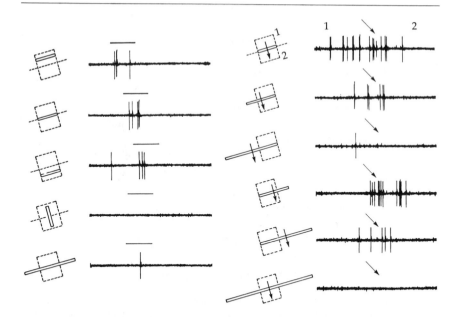

Figure 5.10. *A hypercomplex neuron in the cat.* Notice that this unit not only has a well-defined receptive field with an optimal angle of orientation but, in addition, requires that the linear stimulus be terminated in the receptive field. (From Hubel, D. & Wiesel, T. N. Receptive fields and functional architecture in two nonstriate visual areas (18 and 19) of the cat. *Journal of Neurophysiology*, 1965, **28**, 250. Used by permission.)

dim. The elements of perception are features such as lines that either are or are not detected. That this phenomenon depends upon the existence of single-cell line detectors, however, may be an unprovable assertion.

Single Cells and Color Vision

The spatial organization of receptive fields can be mapped by stimulating the retina with small spots of white light. However, visual systems are sensitive not only to the intensity of light but also to its wavelength. How, then, do single cells process information about color? Using the macaque monkey, whose color vision appears identical to man's, De Valois found that about 80 percent of the lateral geniculate nucleus (LGN) cells, which receive information from the cones of the fovea, are color-sensitive. Their response varies when only the wavelength of the light is changed.

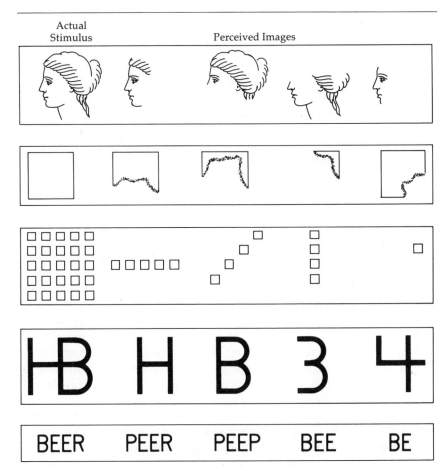

Figure 5.11. *Some images (left) and the ways in which they decompose under stabilized conditions (right).* In all cases, the decomposition seems to maintain the integration of the perceptual stimulus. (Used by permission from Pritchard, R. M. Stabilized images on the retina. *Scientific American,* 1961, **204**(6), 75. Copyright © 1961 by Scientific American, Inc. All rights reserved.)

There are three types of cones in the fovea, all of which have slightly different spectral sensitivities. Spectrally sensitive LGN cells compare one class of cone with another to extract the relative difference between their strengths of response. Only by determining the relative difference, or ratio of excitation, between at least two classes of cones can color information be extracted.

Consider a single cone, the excitation of which suddenly increases. The change of response indicates an alteration in the light falling on it; the light could have become more intense, or its wavelength could have shifted to one that the cone absorbs more readily. Because intensity and wavelength are inextricably confounded in any single cone system, color information cannot be reliably extracted from a single type of photoreceptor. Only by comparing the activity of two or more cones with at least slightly different spectral sensitivities can color information be extracted.

A brief excursion into history is appropriate here. Two major theories have been proposed to explain color vision. Thomas Young (1802) postulated that there are three different classes of photoreceptors for color vision and that each class has a unique set of spectral characteristics. This trichromatic theory appeared necessary to account for the phenomena of color mixture and chromatic adaptation. However, other important perceptual data cannot be understood within the framework of the trichromatic theory. Why should a red circle appear redder against a background of green? Or why, after staring at a blue figure, should one see a yellow after-image? Such facts compelled Ewald Hering (1905) to propose an opponent-process theory of color perception. Although he was wrong in detail (he suggested that a single receptor could act at different times to either signal, red or green), Hering provided an important beginning for the study of neuronal processes in color perception. The cones themselves appear to be organized as Young suggested, but the neurons to which they connect are arranged in a manner more congruent with that proposed by Hering. This is the opponent-process organization of wavelength-sensitive cells of the visual system.

Just as a contrast-detection cell does not alter its tonic output when the intensity of light is changed, a purely wavelength-sensitive cell shows no change unless the wavelength of the light is altered. There are two systems of spectrally opponent cells in the visual system. The larger of the two is the red-green system, where cells receive excitatory input from one class of cone, either the red or the green, and inhibitory input from the other. About half the cells are excited by red cones and the other half by green. As the wavelength of the light changes, the ratio of excitatory to inhibitory input also changes, and the cell alters its rate of firing. But if the intensity of the light is increased or decreased, there is no change in the ratio of inhibition and excitation, and therefore there is little change in the output of the cell. Because spectrally opponent cells extract information about color and discard information about intensity, they too are feature extractors.

A second set of color-sensitive neurons in the brain forms the blue-yellow system. Like the red-green system, it compares classes of cones. The blue cones are opposed to yellow, but there are no yellow cones. Yellow is constructed by combining the output of red and green cones. Summating the activity of red and green cones results in a spectral-sensitivity curve that peaks between red and green at yellow. Combining red and green yields a result very different from that obtained by contrasting them, as in the red-green system. The blue-yellow system, therefore, involves all three classes of cones.

Since the spectrally opponent systems keep color information and discard information concerning intensity, the brain uses another mechanism for preserving intensity at the expense of color. This mechanism is composed of the broad-band brightness detectors, which combine the output of all three cone types. Therefore, in exciting the cell, any perceptible color of light is approximately as effective as any other. Color information is removed by adding the output of the different cones.

If 80 percent of the geniculate cells are color-sensitive and if most geniculate cells act as contrast detectors with a center-surround organization in their receptive fields, many cells must be performing both functions. Wiesel and Hubel have shown that, in fact, the cells do perform both functions. By mapping the receptive fields with small spots of colored light, it is possible to determine both the spectral properties and the spatial characteristics of the geniculate cells. In a cell that shows both types of feature extraction, the neuron apparently makes connection with one class of cones in the center of its receptive field and with another in its surround. (See Figure 5.12.) By comparing the various combinations of center-surround and spectral-opposition cells, the nervous system would obtain the information necessary to decode separately spatial and spectral information.

Natural Stimuli

The experiments that have been discussed so far are analytic in nature. Receptive fields are mapped with spots of light. The supposition is that this method of mapping reveals most of the interesting information about the cell and its function. Other investigators who have proceeded with a different strategy argue that the animal is adapted to fit his environment. Therefore, it might be profitable to test cells with stimuli that are in some sense indigenous to their environments. Experiments of this sort have an ethological flavor. Natural stimuli are used instead of dots. The investigator plays with a cell, trying to discover clues that will indicate the optimal class of stimuli for that cell. Taking this approach, Lettvin and his colleagues argue that single cells are so complex in their function that the only way to describe them is in terms of animal behavior, not stimulus dimension-

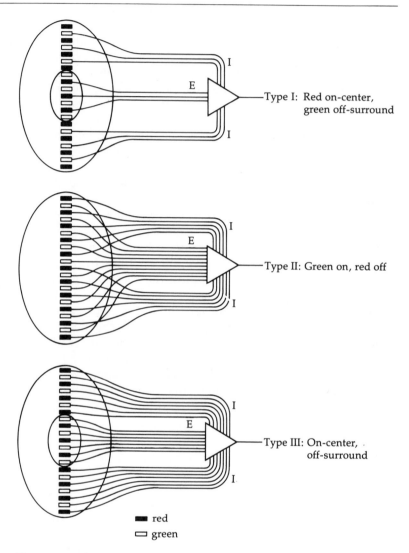

Type I: Red on-center,
green off-surround

Type II: Green on, red off

Type III: On-center,
off-surround

■ red
☐ green

Figure 5.12. *Types of lateral geniculate cells.* Lateral geniculate cells act to maintain both spatial contrast and color information. Type 1 maintains contact with one class of receptors in its center and with another class in its surround. Type 2 shows no spatial organization but, within its uniform receptive field, receives excitatory input from one class of cones and inhibitory input from others. Type 3, which functions to detect contrast without regard to color information, makes contact indiscriminately with the various classes of cones in both the center and the surround; one sector of the receptive field opposes the other. (From Wiesel, T. N., & Hubel, D. H. Spatial and chromatic interactions in the lateral geniculate body of the rhesus monkey. *Journal of Neurophysiology,* 1966, **29,** 1145. Used by permission.)

ality alone. The following is their account of the activity of a cell in the colliculus of the frog, which is not a part of the thalamocortical visual system.*

Let us begin with an empty gray hemisphere for the visual field. There is usually no response of the cell to turning on and off the illumination. It is silent. We bring in a small dark object, say 1 to 2 degrees in diameter, and at a certain point in its travel, almost anywhere in the field, the cell suddenly "notices" it. Thereafter, wherever that object is moved it is tracked by the cell. Every time it moves, with even the faintest jerk, there is a burst of impulses that dies down to a mutter that continues as long as the object is visible. If the object is kept moving, the bursts signal discontinuities in the movement, such as the turning of corners, reversals, and so forth, and these bursts occur against a continuous background mutter that tells us the object is visible to the cell.

When the target is removed, the discharge dies down. If the target is kept absolutely stationary for about two minutes, the mutter also disappears. Then one can sneak the target around a bit, slowly, and produce no response, until the cell "notices" it again and locks on. Thereafter, no small or slow movement remains unsignaled. There is also a place in the visual field, different for different cells, that is a sort of Coventry to which a target can retire and escape notice except for sharp movements. This Coventry, or null patch, is difficult to map. The memory that a cell has for a stationary target that has been brought to its attention by movement can be abolished by a transient darkness. These cells prefer small targets, that is, they respond best to targets of about 3 degrees.

There is also (we put this matter very hesitantly) an odd discrimination in these cells, which, though we would not be surprised to find it in the whole animal, is somewhat startling in single units so early behind the retina. Not all "sameness" cells have this property. Suppose we have two similar targets. We bring in target A and move it back and forth along a fixed path in a regular way. The cell sees it and responds, signaling the reversals of movement by bursts. Now we bring in target B and move it about erratically. After, a short while, we hear bursts from the cell signaling the corners, reversals, and other discontinuities in the travel of B. Now we stop B. The cell goes into its mutter, indicating that what it has been attending to has stopped. It does not signal the reversals of target A, which is moving back and forth very regularly all the time, until after a reasonable time, several seconds. It seems to attend one or the other, A or B; its output is not a simple combination of the responses to both.

These descriptions are provisional and may be too naturalistic in character. However, we have examined well over a hundred cells and suspect that what they do will not seem any simpler or less startling with further study. There are several types, of which the two mentioned are

*Reprinted from Lettvin, J. Y., Maturana, H. R., Pitts, W. H., & McCulloch, W. S., Two remarks on the visual system of the frog, *Sensory Communication*, W. A. Rosenblith (Ed.), by permission of The MIT Press, Cambridge, Massachusetts. © 1961 The MIT Press.

extremes. Of course if one were to perform the standard gestures, such as flashing a light at the eye, probably the cells could be classified and described more easily. However, it seems a shame for such sophisticated units to be handled that way—roughly the equivalent of classifying people's intelligence by the startle response [Lettvin et al., 1961, pp. 774–775].

The picture of this unit in the frog's visual system is very different from that obtained from a more conventional analysis of other animals such as the cat or the monkey. To reconcile the contradictory reports obtained from different studies, the argument is often made that the frog has a more sophisticated retina and brainstem than does the cat or monkey. Functions performed high in the more complex brain might, with less flexibility, be accomplished more peripherally in lower animals. Also, the answers one gets from nature may depend upon the questions that are asked. Lettvin and Hubel asked different questions. It is not clear which approach in the long run will yield the most satisfying answers.

Two Different Kinds of Seeing

In addition to the thalamocortical visual pathway of mammals, the visual areas of the brainstem play important roles in vision. Phylogenetically, the brainstem nuclei are older, more primitive structures. Some control the mechanics of the eye; for example, they regulate the pupillary reflexes, which adjust the size of the pupil to compensate somewhat for changes in lighting conditions. Other brainstem areas, one of which is the superior colliculus, are involved in more characteristically visual functions. The superior colliculus probably mediated much visually related behavior before the evolution of a substantial cortex, as in Lettvin's frog. But what functions does it perform in an animal with major cortical development?

Schneider made use of the fact that not all brain-damaged animals appear equally blind in all testing situations. Determining blindness often depends as much upon what an animal is required to do as upon what it is shown. Schneider chose the golden hamster, as Werblin and Dowling chose the mudpuppy, for reasons of scientific strategy. Unlike those of rats or cats, the superior colliculi of the hamster are not hidden beneath the cerebral cortex. Also, the constant activity of the hamster, who rarely stops looking for food, facilitates testing. Schneider found that hamsters that had their superior colliculi removed could search for food only by touch or smell and thus were, by this criterion, blind; they performed in the same manner as animals whose eyes had been removed. Surprisingly, animals that had had their visual cortices destroyed appeared normal; whereas they showed some difficulty in following moving seeds, they certainly did not seem blind. The superior colliculi allow the animal to orient itself to objects. But why don't animals with visual cortices removed also appear blind?

Visual cortex does not seem to be involved in localizing objects but rather in recognizing and identifying patterns. The determination of blindness, therefore, depends in part upon the animal's task. A thirsty animal can be tested in an apparatus with two doors, one striped and the other speckled. The animal is allowed to wander within the box but receives water only when he actually touches the proper door. Touching the other door is an error. This procedure allows equitable testing of the animal who has trouble orienting himself to objects but can still detect patterns. Hamsters without superior colliculi learn this discrimination task as quickly as do normals. Hamsters without a visual cortex, however, appear blind in this task. They cannot learn.

Without a superior colliculus, the hamster cannot orient itself effectively to a visual stimulus. Without a visual cortex, he cannot identify it. These two systems are not totally independent, of course; they are anatomically interconnected. One of the major pathways from visual cortex, for example, leads to the superior colliculus. Information from the superior colliculus is undoubtedly available to certain cortical areas such as the extrastriate cortex, which surrounds primary visual cortex.

The superior colliculus of the hamster may be exceptionally well developed, but a similar pattern has been reported in higher animals as well. For example, monkeys without visual cortex appear to be "pattern blind" but can locate objects moving in front of them. Localization and identification may be accomplished by these two visual systems in man as well.

Summary

The informational transformations that occur in the retina have been clarified by the study of the mudpuppy retina, in which single cells are of sufficient size to permit microelectrode recording. Receptors respond to stimulation by hyperpolarization. There is no evidence of any interaction among receptors; the receptive field of the receptor is the receptor itself. Receptors show a phasic response, a reduced tonic response, and a small off-response.

Horizontal cells, located near the receptor layer, branch laterally to make connections through their dendrites with many receptors. The receptive field of a horizontal cell is approximately the same size as its dendritic spread. Horizontals respond to stimulation by hyperpolarization and appear to sum the activity of the receptors that they innervate.

Bipolar cells, in the next layer of retinal tissue, begin the processes of visual feature extraction. The receptive field of the bipolar is differentiated into two regions: a central excitatory area and a surrounding antagonistic area. The response to excitation of the center may be either hyperpolarization or depolarization; stimulation of the surround acts to reduce either response. The strength of the bipolar response indicates the difference in the intensity of illumination between the center and the surround.

Amacrine cells show either the center-surround organization typical of bipolars or large, uniform receptive fields. Unlike the more peripheral neuronal elements, the amacrines respond to stimulation by depolarization and the generation of action potentials. Responding with one or two spikes to a change in illumination, amacrines perform a temporal transformation upon the stimulus. Large changes in stimulus intensity do not induce an increased number of spikes but rather reduce the latencies of these action potentials.

The ganglion cells, the axons of which form the optic nerve, also generate action potentials. These cells make connections with either bipolar or amacrine cells and show receptive field characteristics resembling either of these types. The ganglia generate frequency-coded spike trains, which relay information about amacrine or bipolar activity to the thalamus.

Most thalamic cells possess a circular center-surround organization. Little change in the structure of receptive fields is introduced in the thalamus. Some evidence suggests a heightening of center-surround antagonism at this stage.

Cortical cells continue the process of feature extraction begun in the retina. Simple cortical cells appear to combine the output of many thalamic cells to detect lines or edges. Such cells possess well-defined receptive fields with distinguishable excitatory and inhibitory regions.

Complex cortical cells, which seem to combine information from a number of simple cortical cells, respond to a line, in a specified orientation, anywhere within their receptive fields. Hypercomplex cortical cells are also sensitive to lines of a particular orientation but, in addition, require that the line be limited at one or both ends, giving rise to a functional corner detector.

Lateral geniculate cells that encode spatial contrast may also be color-sensitive. Two color systems are present in the lateral geniculate tissue. The red-green system responds to the difference in excitation between the red and the green cones in its receptive field. The blue-yellow system, which is far less prominent, opposes blue cones and the red and green cones, which together yield a spectral-sensitivity curve that peaks in the yellow region. Cells that perform both contrast and color detection make contact with one class of cones in their central region and with the other class (or classes) in the surrounding area of their receptive fields. Some thalamic cells are purely color-sensitive, whereas others serve only as contrast detectors. Still other cells, which appear sensitive only to the absolute intensity of stimulation, give neither color nor contrast information. By comparing the output of these various types of cells in a small area of the retina, the nervous system is provided with sufficient information to unambiguously decode color, contrast, and stimulus intensity.

Although the concepts discussed above are both powerful and logically elegant, some data suggest more complex interpretations of visual system function. For example, naturalistic investigations have indicated the presence of highly specific detection mechanisms that are uniquely adapted to the organism's probable environment.

Other visual systems within the brain contribute to the control of visual behavior in mammals. A brainstem system, which involves the superior colliculus and related nuclei, seems to control visually guided orienting behavior. Animals deprived of the superior colliculi cannot direct their behavior toward a visual stimulus, whereas animals in which the thalamocortical visual system has been lesioned cannot perform visual pattern recognition.

The visual systems of the mammalian brain function in concert with other brain systems to provide the organism with a detailed, flexible, and accurate map, or visual perception, of his environment. Visual perception must never be thought to result only from activity in the visual structures. It is a highly sophisticated process that demands the integration of activity in large amounts of brain tissue.

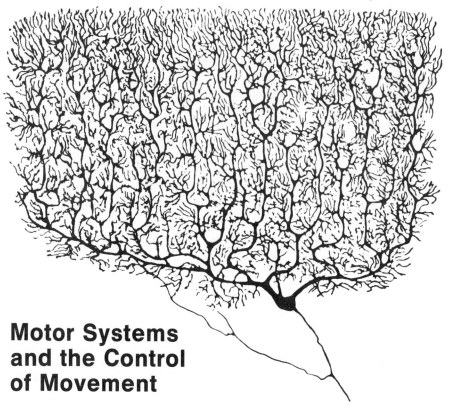

Chapter 6

Motor Systems and the Control of Movement

The study of behavior is the study of the activity of organisms, which ultimately depends upon the contraction of muscle tissue in complex patterns determined within the central nervous system. Muscle is the only bodily tissue that is capable of translating CNS information into behavior. Thus, it is reasonable to think of the bodily musculature as the sole output device of the information-processing system that is our brain and nervous system.

Muscle tissue can only contract. Behavior, therefore, must be built from patterns of contraction of the various muscles acting under CNS control on the noncontractile tissues of the body. These two factors, the structure of the CNS commands and the pattern of mechanical connection of the muscle tissue, determine the effect of a particular muscle on the environment. There is no essential difference among the muscle tissues used to speak, to walk, to shift the gaze, or to grasp a tool. For these reasons, an understanding of the function of muscle tissue and the nature of its control is essential for an understanding of the biological basis of behavior. Muscle and nervous tissue are similar in many ways and together form an integrated system that generates and controls the behavior of the organism.

Structure of Muscle Tissue

The discussion here focuses on the skeletal, or striated, muscles of the body. Other types of muscles, such as those found in the heart and in the viscera, are conceptually similar to skeletal muscle and, therefore, are not treated separately.

Each muscle is composed of long, thin fibers that lie lengthwise within the muscle. The fibers can be as long as 5 inches. In shorter muscle groups, all fibers extend the full length of the muscle and attach themselves to the connective tissue at each end. In longer muscles, individual fibers connect to other muscle fibers, and together they span the length of the muscle. Each muscle fiber is contained within its own cellular membrane.

Muscle fibers can be broken into still smaller units—fibrils and filaments. Figure 6.1 illustrates the arrangement of filaments within a fibril. There are two kinds of filaments, thick and thin, which are interlaced. The alternating bands of thick and thin filaments give skeletal muscle its banded, or striated, appearance. The light areas, which contain only thin filaments, and the Z lines, which provide a point of attachment, are the I bands. The sections that contain thick filaments and the ends of the thin filaments form the A band. The slightly lighter region in the center of the A band, which contains only thick filaments, is the H band.

When a muscle contracts, the length of the fibrils is shortened, but the lengths of the filaments remain the same. The thick and thin filaments move in relation to each other to produce contraction. The area in which thick and thin filaments overlap must increase if the fiber is to shorten. (See Figure 6.1.) Thus, during contraction, the thin filaments move into the H band and cause it to shrink. Or, if you prefer, the thick filaments move into the I band and make it shorter. The length of the A band, which is the length of the thick filaments alone, must stay the same. The interleaving of thick and thin filaments is repeated over and over again down the length of the fibril.

Most of the muscle fibers within any muscle are extrafusal fibers—the long, strong fibers that perform work in the muscle. They are innervated by alpha motor neurons—a class of large, fast nerve cells. The cell bodies of the alpha motor neurons are located in the

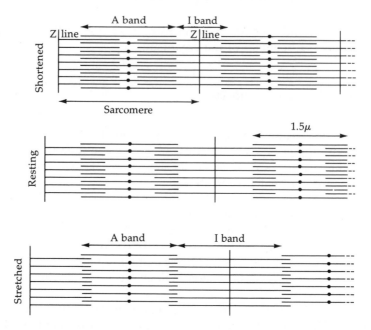

I band: Actin (thin) filaments (about 1μ long) on either side of Z line.

A band: Myosin (thick) filaments (about 1.5μ long) + partially overlapping actin filaments.

Figure 6.1. *The structure of muscle.* Muscles stretch and contract as the filaments within them move in relation to each other. The filaments themselves never change in length. The actin filaments enter the A band as the tissue contracts, increasing the amount of overlap between the thick and thin filaments. (From Katz, B. *Nerve, Muscle and Synapse.* New York: McGraw-Hill, 1966. Used by permission.)

spinal cord, and their endfeet rest on muscle tissues. The alpha motor neurons directly control muscle tension. The intrafusal fibers form a part of a specialized control device, the muscle spindle. Intrafusal fibers are innervated by gamma motor neurons, which are small in diameter and conduct nerve impulses relatively slowly.

The Neuromuscular Junction

In much the same way as neurons control other neurons, nerve controls muscle through a synapselike structure, the neuromuscular junction. Figure 6.2 illustrates the neuromuscular junction. Like the

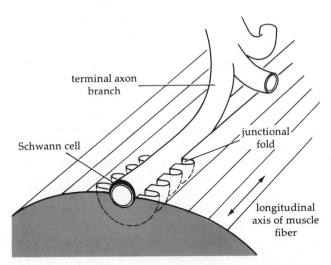

terminal axon
branch

Schwann cell

junctional
fold

longitudinal
axis of muscle
fiber

Figure 6.2. *The neuromuscular junction.* The neuromuscular junction is a folded
structure that allows maximal contact between the motor neuron and the muscle
fiber. (From Woodbury, J. W., Gordon, A. M., & Conrad, J. T. Muscle. In T.C.
Ruch, H. O. Patton, J. W. Woodbury, & A. L. Towe, *Neurophysiology, Second
Edition, 1965.* Used by permission of W. B. Saunders Company.)

neuronal synapse, a cleft separates the endfoot from the membrane of
the muscle fiber. Notice that the physical arrangement of the endfoot
and the muscle surface, the endplate membrane, permits extensive
contact. The efficiency of the neuromuscular junction as a transmission
device is due, in large measure, to this anatomical arrangement.

The neuromuscular junction functions like an excitatory synapse
in the CNS. A spike, generated in the motor neuron, travels down the
axon and, on reaching the endfoot, triggers the release of an excitatory
chemical transmitter, which, at the neuromuscular junction, is acetylcholine (ACh). As in synapses, the neurotransmitter is contained in
tiny spherical vesicles in the endfoot. The spike triggers the release of
the contents of some of the vesicles into the junction space. ACh crosses
the cleft and is taken up by the membrane or the endplate of the muscle
fiber. There it acts to open the endplate to permit the free passage of
small ions—most notably Na^+ and K^+—which in muscle, as in neuron,
depolarize the membrane, since the major ionic movement is Na^+ from
the outside to the inside. The resulting depolarization is the endplate
potential (EPP). The EPP, then, is a depolarizing response of muscle
tissue to the presence of ACh on the endplate itself. Depolarization
continues until the ACh is inactivated by the enzyme acetylcholine-
esterase (AChE) in the endplate region. Since AChE acts quickly, the
EPP is a brief response.

In addition to having synapselike structures, muscle fibers share another feature with neurons. The membrane of the muscle fiber is excitable, as is the membrane of the axon. Thus, the muscle fiber itself is capable of generating and propagating an action potential or spike. The mechanisms of membrane function are very similar in the two cases.

Since the neuromuscular junction is both large and efficient, the arrival of a spike in the motor neuron insures the generation of a spike in the muscle fiber. Thus, the neuromuscular junction, which has only one input, is a relaying device, the function of which is to reliably transmit to the muscle the pattern of excitation generated by the motor neuron that controls it. In contrast, central neurons can have many hundreds of synapses, which suggests an integration function.

The muscle action potential induces contraction in the muscle fiber. The nature of this coupling of electrical and mechanical events is not well understood; it is not known how the muscle spike triggers contraction. However, the relation between the two events is clear: the passage of the spike through a segment of muscle fiber is followed by a short contraction of the fiber. The mechanical response of the muscle to a single spike is a single contraction, or a twitch. All twitches are of the same amplitude and duration. Whole muscles produce graded, slow, sustained patterns of contracting by combining short twitches in many fibers. Thus, a slow movement is the result of the summation and integration of many twitches.

Motor Units

The basic functional unit of the motor system is not the muscle, which is innervated by many neurons and functions, therefore, in a complex manner. Nor is a muscle fiber, a single cell within a muscle, the basic unit; it is too small. The basic unit is a substructure of the muscle—the motor unit. The motor unit, composed of a single motor neuron and all the muscle fibers that it innervates, is the smallest functional element within the musculature. Since the neuromuscular junction is a very reliable transmission device, all muscle fibers of the motor unit are activated by each arriving spike in the motor neuron. Thus, the motor unit functions as an integrated system.

Motor units vary in size. In finely controlled muscles, a motor neuron will innervate only one or a few muscle fibers. The large and powerful muscles, which are less capable of precise control, are constructed from larger motor units comprised of many muscle fibers. When few motor neurons control many muscle fibers, the precision of movement is reduced. The contractile patterns of muscle fibers also differ in finely and coarsely controlled muscles.

Although nerve and muscle cells share two unique features—synapselike structures and excitable membranes—there are many differences between them. The principal difference is in output. Neurons can communicate with other neurons or with muscle fibers. Muscle fibers, however, translate their input into tension or movement and, in so doing, enable the nervous system to communicate with the environment.

Informational Control of Muscle

Sense Receptors in the Muscle

Muscular contraction is controlled by the level of activity in the alpha motor neurons. However, if a heavy object is held in the hand, an increase in alpha motor neuron firing, which would otherwise produce a large movement, might produce no movement at all. Discharge in the alpha motor neurons produces twitches in the muscle fibers and tension in the whole muscle, but movement depends upon both muscle tension and the load under which the muscle is placed. Alpha motor neuron activity determines only the amount of force a muscle can exert, not the length of the muscle once that force is applied. Length depends upon both force and load.

To move an arm to a particular position, the various muscles involved must reach specified lengths. Movement to a specified position requires accurate information about muscle length. This information is supplied by sensory receptors in the muscle group itself, which, together with a special type of muscle fiber, forms the muscle spindle.

Sense information must be used to ensure the execution of the command. As contraction takes place, sensory feedback is necessary to determine the amount of tension that is needed to bring the motion to a satisfactory conclusion. Similar problems exist in man-made systems. For example, to drive a car over flat country on open highway, the driver needs very little feedback to maintain a constant speed. One simply sets a foot on the accelerator and the engine puts forth a constant amount of energy. The car settles into an even cruising speed. In hilly areas, however, the load on the engine varies from mile to mile; more energy is needed to maintain speed against gravity when going uphill than when going down. The driver must vary the amount of gasoline that the engine receives if the car is to hold an even speed. If the effects of a command, in this case to the engine, are uncertain, then information about performance is needed to ensure that the command is properly executed.

Muscle Spindles

Muscle spindles both receive commands and relay information about their execution. The muscle spindle, a well-engineered device consisting of a receptor and an effector, provides the nervous system not only with information concerning the length of the muscle but also with corrective information that indicates the changes necessary to reach the desired length. The effectors in the spindle form a small collection of less than a dozen muscle fibers, the intrafusal fibers, which are very thin and weak compared with the strong extrafusal fibers that make up the rest of the muscle. No matter how firmly the intrafusal fibers contract, they cannot shorten the muscle by themselves. In the center of the intrafusal fibers, the muscle spindle is enlarged to form the nuclear bag (so named because it contains the nuclei of the intrafusal muscle cells). This area probably does not contract. The intrafusal fibers are controlled by a separate group of motor neurons, the gamma motor neurons.

Sensory fibers of the muscle spindle terminate on the nuclear bag. These fibers are of a size grouping designated 1-A, and the most important are those with annulospiral endings that wrap about the intrafusal fibers. The annulospiral endings are arranged so that they become mechanically deformed when the intrafusal fiber is stretched. Like many other somatosensory cells, these receptors depolarize and generate action potentials when they are distorted. Because of their unique physical arrangement, the annulospiral endings are activated when the intrafusal fibers are placed under tension. The 1-A fibers are the stretch receptors of the muscle spindle.

The axons of these stretch receptors enter the spinal cord through the dorsal root, where they synapse directly on the alpha motor neurons, which, in turn, innervate the extrafusal fibers of the same muscle. Figure 6.3 shows these connections in a simplified form. A word of caution here. The 1-A fibers have many endfeet and synapse upon cells other than the alpha motor neurons within the spinal cord. In a similar fashion, alpha motor neurons receive input from other cells besides the 1-A fibers. Nonetheless, the circuit shown in Figure 6.3 is one of the most important of the spinal reflex mechanisms. It can function to solve the tension, load, and movement problem. Perhaps as important for our purposes, it serves as an elegantly simple neuronal and mechanical device that controls a behavioral response in an intelligent way.

Suppose that a contraction movement is initiated with the gamma efferents instead of the alpha motor neurons. Discharge in the gamma system will cause the intrafusal fibers of the muscle spindle to

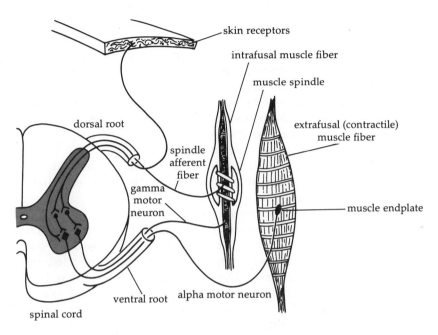

Figure 6.3. *The muscle-spindle system.* The relations among the muscle spindle, the whole muscle, and the afferent and efferent fibers that innervate them form the basis of the gamma motor neuron system. (From Thompson, R. F. *Foundations of Physiological Psychology.* © 1967 by Harper & Row, Publishers, Inc. Used by permission.)

try to contract, but, since these fibers are very weak, they cannot move the limb; only the extrafusal fibers produce overt movement. Instead, the muscle spindle will be put under tension. The degree of tension will depend upon the length of the whole muscle and the desired length of the intrafusal fiber. For any level of firing in the gamma-efferent system, an exact length of the muscle spindle is specified. The greater the activity in the gamma efferents, the more the muscle spindle will attempt to contract and the shorter the whole muscle will have to become for the spindle to be released from tension.

The rest of the argument is straightforward. As long as the muscle spindle is under tension the stretch receptors will be activated. The greater the amount of tension, the more the annulospiral endings will be deformed and the more these sensory cells will fire. The stretch receptors fire whenever there is a mismatch between muscle-spindle length and whole-muscle contraction that places the spindle under tension. Since the 1-A sensory fibers synapse directly upon the alpha motor neurons, the alpha motor neurons will be excited and will remain excited until the powerful extrafusal fibers shorten the muscle to the length prescribed by the level of gamma-efferent activity. At that length, the muscle spindle is no longer under tension and the input to the alpha motor neurons from 1-A fibers ends. If there is no load on the limb, the whole system comes to rest. But if there is a load, which acts to lengthen the muscle, the slight stretching of the whole muscle places tension again on the muscle spindles, which results in renewed 1-A firing to the alpha motor neurons. Therefore, the extrafusal fibers contract and maintain the desired position.

If the level of gamma-efferent activity drops and the limb is under load, the muscle will extend itself until the muscle spindle is again under tension. At this time, a new muscle length is established that is longer than before.

Load is often provided by weight, as shown in Figure 6.3. Under natural conditions, load may indeed be a weight, an object held in the hand, for example. However, a load may also be imposed by other muscles. In the limb the extensors and flexors are connected in a mechanically reciprocal manner across the joints so that contraction of one muscle group produces limb extension, whereas contraction of the other produces flexion. Background level of activity, or muscle tonus, produces a weak but continuous load on the opposing muscles.

Movement can be produced by activation of the gamma-efferent system, or the gamma and alpha motor neurons can work in concert, under central control. The fact that coordinated movement is still possible when all sensory feedback from the limbs is surgically eliminated demonstrates that purely central control exists.

The system composed of the gamma efferents, muscle spindles, 1-A fibers, alpha motor neurons, and extrafusal fibers is only one example of feedback control in the nervous system. There are many other feedback systems in the mammalian brain. The organization of the more complex systems, however, is not yet known in such detail. The muscle spindle uses feedback, or sensory information about muscle-spindle tension, to trigger action in the extrafusal muscle. The effect is to release the muscle spindle from tension. This feedback system acts in much the same way as does a household thermostat that controls a furnace and maintains room temperature at a predetermined level.

A movement that depends solely on this feedback mechanism is the knee jerk or stretch reflex. When the leg is hanging freely, a sharp tap on the tendon below the kneecap produces a kick, mediated by one of the fastest and simplest reflex movements known. When the tendon is tapped, the whole extensor muscle, including the muscle spindle, is quickly stretched. As a result, 1-A fibers discharge vigorously and synchronously, exciting the alpha motor neurons directly. Excitation is translated by the extrafusal fibers into a sharp, firm kick forward. The reflexive jerk of a muscle to stretch is rapid, since conduction in the 1-A fibers and the alpha motor neurons is relatively fast. Only these two classes of neurons are involved. As only a single set of synapses is employed, the reflex is monosynaptic. Most other reflexes involve additional neurons to relay signals between sensory and motor fibers. Multisynaptic reflexes are slower, however, since more neurons and synapses are involved.

Spinal Reflexes and Coordinated Behavior

In the complex neuronal connections of the spinal cord lie innate substrates of patterned behavior. An animal surgically deprived of all but the spinal control of his bodily musculature can be made to walk by stimulating the soles of its feet or by pulling on an extensor muscle. The naturalness of such reflex stepping is not impressive, but the movements are a testament to the sophistication of the spinal cord in organizing complex motor behaviors that involve the whole animal. This spinal organization must considerably ease the task of higher centers in directing motor activity in the normal animal. The cord functions as an intelligent, well-adapted machine that produces patterns of motor activity throughout the musculature that are normally supportive of centrally elicited movements. For example, in four-legged animals, reflexive withdrawal of a limb is automatically accompanied by extension of the opposite limb, which prevents the quadruped from falling. The same spinal mechanisms that are demonstrated in studies of reflexes are also operative if the command for movement is central rather than peripheral.

Viewed in a slightly different way, the system of spinal reflexes can be seen as an information coding device. For example, if the cord operated to translate a relatively simple command to tighten the flexors of a particular limb (a command that could take the form of central excitation of the alpha or gamma motor neurons directly involved) into more complex patterns of behavior, the total behavior would include relaxation of the extensors of the same limb and adjustments of all the other limbs in ways that would be normally adaptive. Such an arrangement is a coding system, since the original signal from the brain does not need to specify in detail—or at all, for that matter—the other adjustments that are to take place. The reflex machinery performs that function. As in pressing a button on an elevator, a simple command can cause the device to release a complex pattern of information. The signal gives permission to release a behavior, not instructions for its execution. The form of the behavior may be determined at least in part by the spinal machinery, whereas control may come from higher centers.

There is also a parallel with the sensory systems. There, input from many sense receptors converges on a single cell to define its receptive field. Patterns of organization in that receptive field cause the cell to respond in its characteristic manner, and we may speak of the cell as extracting some feature from the stimulus pattern. The edge detectors of the visual system are a fine example of extracting higher-order patterns from the complex retinal mosaic. As for the motor system, a higher-order central command for an action is elaborated through the spinal system, and finally translates into complex patterns of contractions, which vary in strength and in timing, in the enormous number of muscle fibers ultimately controlled by the cord.

Reciprocal Innervation.   One of the simplest and most basic spinal reflexes controls the activity of antagonist muscles. Paired antagonist muscles are mechanically connected to produce opposing movements. Reciprocal patterns of innervation coordinate the activity of such muscle pairs and ensure that, when one muscle contracts, its antagonist relaxes. The same input, peripheral or central, that excites one member inhibits the other. Flexor and extensor muscles, for example, are reciprocally innervated. (See Figure 6.4.) This spinal machinery ensures that muscles that are mechanically linked to each other are also neuronally connected in a manner that normally facilitates behavioral coordination. Reciprocal innervation is the nearly universal accompaniment of antagonistic structures. Similar arrangements are seen in the innervation of heart, smooth muscle, and glandular systems as well. The pairing of inhibition and excitation is important in the production of integrated behavior.

Larger Reflex Patterns.   The principle of selectively innervating opposing muscles in an excitatory and inhibitory manner may be extended across muscle groups to provide the basis for coordinated movements both within and across limbs.

When a spinal animal (one whose spinal cord has been cut to eliminate brain control of movement) withdraws its leg from a painful stimulus, the expected pattern of flexor excitation and extensor inhibition is apparent. This pattern is basic to the structure of the flexion reflex, mediated by reciprocal innervation. In addition to movement of the affected leg, however, the flexion reflex also induces movement of the contralateral leg, where the pattern is reversed. The extensors of the opposite leg are excited as the flexors are inhibited. Thus, the wounded animal is still able to stand. Such patterns of neuronal connection have been termed double reciprocal innervation.

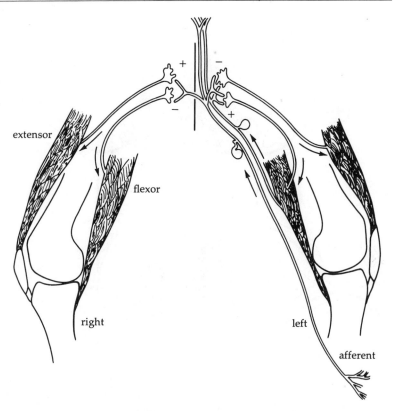

Figure 6.4. *Reciprocal innervation*. Reciprocal innervation across the spinal cord provides a basis for the coordinated control of pairs of limbs. The pattern of excitatory and inhibitory connections produces opposing patterns of extensor and flexor contraction in the two limbs. (From Sherrington, C. *The Integrative Action of the Nervous System, Second Edition*. New Haven: Yale University Press, 1947, p. 108. Used by permission.).

It should be noted that the form of the flexion, or withdrawal, reflex may vary with the location of the painful stimulus. The pattern of tensions in the muscles involved in withdrawal seems to change in a manner that would facilitate escape from the stimulus. For example, if the skin over an extensor is stimulated, the entire pattern of response is reversed. It is easy to imagine why that might be so. Figure 6.5 shows the pathways involved.

Reflex connections in quadrupeds transverse long distances in the spinal cord to coordinate the forepaws and hindpaws. These connections demonstrate the same set of principles as the connection between limb pairs do. Limbs on the same side of the body are reciprocal-

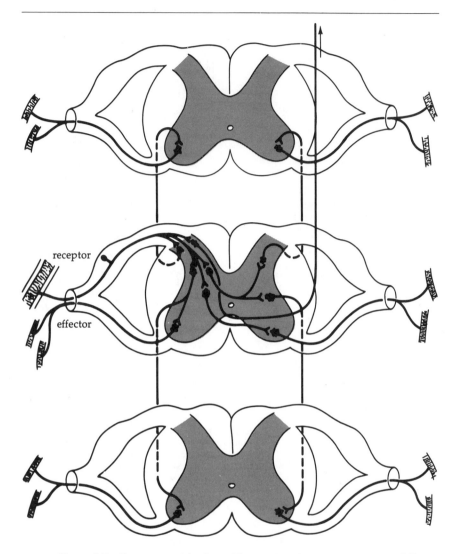

Figure 6.5. *Suprasegmental reflexes.* The pattern of connections among different segments of the spinal cord provides integrated input to muscles that are innervated at different levels. (From Gardner, E. *Fundamentals of Neurology, Fifth Edition,* 1968, p. 129. Used by permission of W. B. Saunders Company.)

ly innervated; the right hindlimb will extend if the right forelimb flexes, and vice versa. Or, extension of one forelimb leads to the extension of the opposite hindlimb. This arrangement is useful for both a moving and a standing animal.

Thus, the basic spinal arrangement of connections permits spinal animals to make walking movements without the intervention of any neurons above the neck. The degree of organization within this system is remarkable. Although such patterns of connection have a logical basis and can account for a great deal of the motor behavior of the spinal animal, the cord is more complex than the discussion has indicated. For example, local variations of these patterns often indicate finer modulation of behavioral control than would be possible if only the circuits outlined above were involved. Moreover, the variability of behaviors in the spinal animal is also inexplicable, given present knowledge. These complexities are superimposed on the basic spinal patterns of reflexive coordination.

Reflexes mediated by spinal connections employ the same neuronal elements that are available to brain mechanisms in carrying out centrally patterned behaviors. Similarly, the information that triggers reflexive responses in the spinal animal is also available to higher mechanisms in the normal animal.

Command Neurons and Centrally Patterned Behavior

Many actions can be viewed as whole, although complex, pieces of behavior. This is especially obvious in invertebrates, where the behavioral repertoire is highly stereotyped and quite limited. Each individual behavior is complex but, once begun, proceeds to completion in an exactly predictable fashion. Thus, the entire complex action pattern can be considered as a single behavioral unit. Such action patterns have been shown to be controlled by single command neurons in the invertebrate brain. Command neurons, when activated, trigger the release of the piece of behavior. For example, one command neuron in the crayfish releases a series of tail movements—a rhythmic waving back and forth. Dozens of motor neurons discharge repetitively in a precise, well-timed way to produce the rhythmic motion. The pattern of movement is unaltered if all sensory information from the tail is eliminated, indicating that sensory feedback is not used to regulate the movement. Moreover, all crayfish of a particular type show the same piece of behavior, which suggests that it is mediated by an innate, genetically determined brain mechanism.

The command neuron does not itself contain all the information necessary to perform the movement. It instead acts as a releaser, which activates complex neuronal networks of connection. These networks between the command neuron and the effectors must contain the information determining the spatial and temporal character of the movement. The output from the network plays upon the motor neurons to direct the motion of the tail. The command neuron, which gives permission, not instruction, is a trigger for the movement.

The behavior of man is not as stereotyped as the behavior of the crayfish. Man's behavior is characterized by flexibility. However, principles of neuronal organization that are obvious in lower forms are often present in higher animals as well. So it may be with command neurons. There are no known single cells that completely release complex behaviors in mammals, but populations of neurons in the brains of mammals must serve similar functions.

To produce complex, rhythmic patterned movements such as walking, there may be neuronal networks—probably at the brainstem and spinal levels—that generate the basic patterning of the movement. There a time dimension is added to spatial patterning. Certain spatial patterns of contractions must succeed and, in turn, be followed by other spatial patterns. Timing devices are vital to the production of coordinated sequences of behavior. Such neuronal networks may be triggered by populations of neurons located more centrally in the brain. The output of the network is undoubtedly modulated by sensory feedback from the musculature and is subject to spatial reflexive control. Figure 6.6 shows the arrangement of command, pattern-generator, and modulating, or adjustment, systems. The addition of afferent information, coupled with inclusion of the reflexive structure (which itself provides spatial coordination to movement), makes the behavior responsive to unexpected conditions. This responsiveness, in turn, somewhat alters the behavior pattern each time the pattern is played out. Complex temporal coordination, together with sensory feedback, renders mammalian movements more adaptive and less stereotyped than invertebrate behaviors. The command signals, however, are still releasers, not specifiers, of behavior.

Brain Mechanisms Controlling Movement

Structures above the spinal cord play more complex roles in the control of movement. Scientific investigation of these brain systems is more difficult, however. It is known, in general, what such mechanisms must do, but the difference between general and specific understanding is profound.

A few things are apparent. An animal deprived of the use of his higher structure loses the spontaneity, flexibility, and precision of his behavior. The spinal mammal shows no behavior that is not stimulus elicited and reflexive. But, because an animal whose entire nervous system is less complex than the dog's spinal cord is capable of

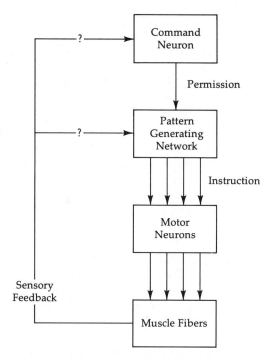

Figure 6.6. *Command neurons.* Command neurons permit the execution of a behavior but do not provide instructions for the resulting movements. Instructional information must be contained in neuronal pattern generating circuits between the command neurons and the muscle tissue. Sensory feedback may be employed in some instances to regulate the resulting behavior.

spontaneous behavior—that is, centrally directed, not stimulus-elicited, behavior—arguments about the loss of function in the spinal animal must be made very carefully. In no case should the spinal cord be considered the equivalent of the motor system in a simpler organism.

Central mechanisms modulate the performance of lower structures to achieve more organized and flexible behavior. Behavioral sophistication is not, however, a function only of motor systems. For example, the highly developed control of voice and hands in man may be largely a function of central development, but these motor skills should be placed in the larger context of man's expanded behavioral capacity. The distinction between sensory and motor structure in cortex is an intellectually dangerous and misleading practice. In an informal document, Towe has written that "one can hardly assign a primary role to the cerebral cortex, and particularly the pyramidal tract, in the initiation and control of movement. Nonetheless, the cerebral cortex clearly is involved in the regulation of behavior, and perhaps even of movement; the question is, How? It seems likely that the primary role of mammalian cerebral cortex is to continuously monitor the external environment and to forecast appropriate behaviors, immediate and more distant" (1971, p. 43). The idea of brain function as a process of generating models of the environment and predicting the consequences of behavior is of major importance. Notice that the appropriate unit of analysis changes as one progresses through the nervous system. At the spinal level, the events that occur are really movements. At cortex, the events are behaviors, perhaps expressible in any of a variety of movements. When an animal learns to find food in a maze, he learns not the movements but rather a behavioral sequence of locomotion. Flood the maze, and animals will swim to food. Bind them up, and—if they are hungry enough—they will roll their way to dinner, as Lashley has clearly shown.

Although such a characterization of higher function is accurate enough to be accepted, it is also frustratingly general. The question becomes one of how a particular piece of tissue contributes to behavioral, or even motor, control. If the brain makes models, predicts stimuli, readies output, triggers predefined behaviors, generates new behavioral sequences, monitors the output of the systems, and assesses the consequences, the valid questions of how and where and under what conditions quickly arise. Some answers concerning the more specifically motor systems of the brain follow.

The Pyramidal System

The pyramidal tract (so named because, as it passes through the brainstem, it forms a pyramid-shaped structure in the region of the medulla) is a large, complex fiber system that arises from cell bodies in the cortex and terminates in the motor areas of the spinal cord. Present only in mammals and exceptionally well developed in primates, the pyramidal tract is most prominent in man. Since it arises from cerebral tissue, its development across species more generally parallels the development of cortex.

Approximately one-third of the fibers in the pyramidal tract originate from cell bodies in the primary motor cortex. Others come from somatosensory areas, and a major portion of the remainder originate in other regions of the cortex. On anatomical grounds alone, one would not expect this fiber system to have a narrowly defined motor function. The fibers terminate on the interneurons of the spinal cord in most mammals, but in primates some of these fibers terminate directly—that is, monosynaptically—on the alpha motor neurons.

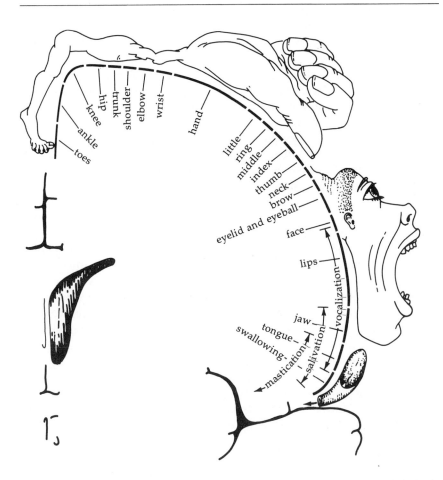

Figure 6.7. *The motor homunculus.* A precise topographic mapping of the body surface is maintained in motor cortex, but the proportion of cortex used to regulate a particular region of the body is determined not by the absolute size of that region but by the number of motor neurons that innervate it. The resulting distribution is shown in this motor homunculus, the size of which represents the amount of cortex involved in the control of its musculature. The face and hands are heavily innervated, as the illustration suggests. (From Penfield, W., & Rasmussen, T. *The Cerebral Cortex of Man.* © 1950 Macmillan Publishing Company, Inc. Used by permission.)

Although there is no behavioral effect when a single electrical shock is applied to the pyramidal tract, repeated stimulation will produce movement. The pyramidal tract fibers seem to produce their effects by selectively facilitating both excitatory and inhibitory reflexes of the spinal cord.

The pyramidal tract does not equally innervate all motor neurons in primates. Fibers controlling distal portions of the limbs tend to originate from small, well-defined regions of the cortex and, when stimulated, produce larger monosynaptic effects. This observation suggests an increased cortical role in controlling the precise movements of the fine musculature of the hand in primates—an interpretation congruent with the development of an opposing thumb and the appearance of tool-using behaviors.

The pyramidal system may serve a modulating, rather than a command, or releaser, function in the performance of skilled movement. Destruction of the pyramidal tract produces some loss in the precision of control of coordinated movement, but complex patterns of skilled behavior such as playing a musical instrument may still be retained. This conforms very closely to Towe's more general view of the cortex in the regulation of behavior.

That skilled behavior persists after pyramidal tract damage does not imply that the pyramidal tract neurons do not normally play an important role in the control of movement. Evarts has reported a series of experiments that investigate the role of pyramidal tract neurons in voluntary movement. The larger, rapidly conducting fibers in the pyramidal system appear to discharge only during movement, whereas the smaller, slower fibers show continuous activity. The rate of discharge varies either upward or downward during movement. Pyramidal tract neurons may also be involved in the initiation of learned movements. Following the onset of a conditioned stimulus that precedes the electromyographic activation of the muscles involved in the conditioned response, discharges in pyramidal fibers can be recorded. Thus, pyramidal tract activity is not solely a response to the activation of motor activity by other systems.

Evarts has argued that the primate motor cortex in primates functions as a servocontrol loop, with the pyramidal tract as the primary high-speed output system to the muscles. Such cortical connections may be involved in mediating learned responses to kinesthetic stimuli that occur with latencies as short as 30 to 40 msec.

The Extrapyramidal Motor Systems

All brain motor systems other than the cerebellar systems and the pyramidal system are termed extrapyramidal motor systems. However, many authorities doubt the usefulness of the grouping. It is very difficult to specify the features that unite these motor systems beyond the rather trivial distinction that they are neither cerebellar nor pyramidal. Further, pyramidal, cerebellar, and extrapyramidal circuits function together and complement each other in the control of motor activity. Thus, a functional distinction between these various systems is also of dubious value.

Perhaps it is best to consider the pyramidal system as a direct corticospinal pathway for motor control and the extrapyramidal systems as a set of parallel multisynaptic pathways. These multisynaptic pathways connect cortex, diencephalon, and lower brainstem with each other and with motor neurons in the spinal cord. Within the forebrain, the basal ganglia form a major part of the extrapyramidal motor pathways, as does the subthalamic nucleus. In the midbrain and hindbrain, various nuclei, including some in the reticular formation, serve extrapyramidal motor functions. The understanding of these multisynaptic influences on motor function is currently limited.

Cerebellum

The cerebellum is a convoluted structure behind the brainstem at the level of the metencephalon. The cerebellum has a primitive type of cortical organization. Its outer surface is gray matter—cell bodies and neuropile. Below the gray matter is white matter, the myelinated fiber tracts that bring information into and out of the cerebellum. An old brain structure, the cerebellum appears fully very early in evolution.

Because cerebellar circuits function to maintain posture and balance, to coordinate voluntary movements, and to regulate motor function at a high level, it must receive and transmit a large amount of information; the vast pattern of connections linking cerebellum with other brain and spinal structures suggests that it does.

Closely coupled with cerebral cortex, the cerebellum receives input from all sense systems. All cortical sensory and motor areas send fibers to and receive fibers from corresponding structures within the cerebellum. Cerebellum and cerebral cortex are reciprocally connected in a highly organized fashion. In addition to its outputs to the cerebral cortex, the cerebellum projects also to other motor systems of the brain.

Cerebellum is important to the coordinated control of muscular activity in both the absence and the presence of movement. The static functions include the maintenance and adjustment of muscle tone and posture. Electrical stimulation in different portions of the cerebellum can either increase or decrease muscle tone. Cerebellar adjustments of muscle tone are made through the gamma-efferent system. By determining the baseline tension in the muscle spindles, the tension of the whole muscle is controlled. Damage to the cerebellum can result in disorders of muscle tone, postural adjustment, gait, and balance.

One of the most interesting and revealing of all clinical syndromes is cerebellar damage that results in impairment of voluntary movement. The close connection of cerebellum and cerebral cortex suggests that the cerebellum is involved in high-order, or voluntary, behavior. Cerebellar damage may result in intentional tremors, irregular tremors that occur only during the execution of a voluntary movement. When a patient with cerebellar damage tries to move his hand to touch an object, for example, his hand may begin to shake. The intentional tremor, which is irregular and increases as the movement proceeds, is not simply a random disturbance but is the result of faulty attempts to correct movement as it progresses.

Complex movements are executed under guidance, and ongoing behavior monitored and compared with the planned movement. When deviations are detected, corrections are made. If sensory information is surgically eliminated, movement is less accurate, but there is no tremor. Tremor occurs when there is damage to the cerebellum, the device responsible for making the midmovement corrections. In intentional tremor, the cerebellum does not fail to correct; it corrects wrongly. Thus, movements become less accurate after the correction than they were before. This correction demands yet another correction, which of course is no more accurate than the first. The result is tremor, a pattern of correction and overcorrection which grows as the movement progresses. Each correction overshoots its mark. Weiner, the father of cybernetic theory, suggested that the cerebellum functions as a servomechanism—a self-adjusting controller—with negative feedback. In such a system, control is exerted not by simply instructing the muscle what to do but by providing information about how to change what it is doing into what it should be doing. The muscle-spindle system operates in a similar, but much more local, manner in adjusting for load. The cerebellum operates on a grander level and, in conjunction with cerebral cortex, assures that voluntary movements are properly executed and, perhaps, thus frees the cerebrum for other tasks.

Summary

Muscle tissue forms the effector systems of organisms and provides the only mechanisms by which CNS activity can be translated into behavior. Muscle and nervous tissues share many similar properties, including both excitable membranes and synapselike structures.

Muscle is composed of fibers that, in turn, are constructed of an orderly arrangement of fibrils and filaments. Single fibers contract as filaments move in relation to each other; filament length does not change. The activity of a single muscle fiber is controlled by the activity of the neuromuscular junction, which serves as a high-efficiency synapse between the endfoot of a motor neuron and the muscle fiber. Acetylcholine (ACh) is the transmitter at the neuromuscular junction in skeletal muscle and, as in a synapse, is inactivated in the postjunctional membrane. The effect of ACh is excitatory and ACh depolarizes the postjunctional membrane.

Depolarization of muscle tissue produces a propagated spike in the muscle fiber. By mechanisms currently unknown, a wave of mechanical contraction follows the electrochemical spike in the fiber. The arrival of a single spike at the neuromuscular junction induces a single spike and contraction in the muscle fiber. The contractions are short, uniform twitches. The smooth activity of the whole muscle is the result of spatial and temporal mechanical summation of the series of twitches.

Since the neuromuscular junction is highly efficient, the basic unit of motor function is comprised of a single motor neuron and the muscle fibers that it innervates. This motor unit always functions in a uniform manner with little variability. Large motor units compose coarsely controlled muscles, whereas a single motor neuron innervates many fewer muscle fibers in finely controlled musculature. Precision of movement is achieved in part by delicate control of the functional units within the muscle group.

In addition to the alpha motor neurons that innervate the extrafusal fibers of muscle, another motor system, the gamma-efferent system, is employed to control the intrafusal fibers of the muscle spindle. This latter system, together with the sensory neurons signaling tension in the intrafusal fibers, forms the basis for informational control of muscle. Gamma-efferent activity may specify a length at which the muscle spindle will no longer be under tension. Since the intrafusal fibers are incapable of directly moving the whole muscle, they may be removed from tension by sufficient contraction of the stronger extrafusal fibers. A spinal synaptic connection between the sensory fibers of the muscle spindle and the alpha motor neurons that innervate the same muscles forms a feedback loop that allows the gamma-efferent system to specify whole muscle length. As long as the muscle spindle is under tension, it activates the alpha motor neurons to cause contraction to the specified length. Thus, the muscle spindle functions as a feedback-control system, which partially solves the problem of maintaining control of muscle position under varying conditions of load.

Innate reflexive connections within the spinal cord, which facilitate the control of movement within the normal animal, serve as an information-storage device that encodes simpler central commands into a detailed temporal and spatial set of actions. Most of the prominent multisynaptic spinal reflexes operate by reciprocal innervation of antagonistically paired muscle groups. Under normal conditions, for example, flexor excitation is accompanied by extensor inhibition, which is mediated by reflexive spinal patterns of connections. These principles also appear in the suprasegmental reflexes, which coordinate the activity in the forelimbs and hindlimbs.

Central influences are of obvious importance in the control of behavior. Single cells that trigger complex series of movements have been identified in invertebrates. Single neurons or populations of neurons probably perform similar functions in man. Such units are permissive, not instructive, in their functions. The instructions must be buried in the neuronal networks that link command unit and muscle tissue.

In mammals, central processes provide the capacity for the flexibility, spontaneity, and precision in behavior that are unattainable by spinal mechanisms alone. However, the purely motor nature of such central control is debatable. Such capacities must be viewed in the larger context of behavior and its control.

Most notable in the primate and human brain among the various motor-related pathways is the pyramidal system, which originates in the cortex, not only in the motor areas but also in sensory and associational tissues. The pyramidal system seems to function by selectively modulating both excitatory and inhibitory processes within the spinal cord, although some fibers within the pyramidal system synapse directly upon alpha motor neurons. Destruction of the pyramidal tract results in a degradation of the precision of movement but not in an absolute loss in the capacity for skilled movement.

Central processes smooth, coordinate, and integrate behavior. Most notable in these respects is the cerebellum, damage to which may result in intentional tremor, which indicates that the normal function of the cerebellum is to correct movements while they are in progress.

The motor systems of the brain and the spinal cord constitute a sophisticated information-processing system that centrally merges with other information-processing functions of the organism. Using synaptic connections to form a hierarchy of control systems, the organism responds adaptively to environmental events. Specific functions are diffusely represented throughout the complex and integrated information-processing system.

Chapter 7

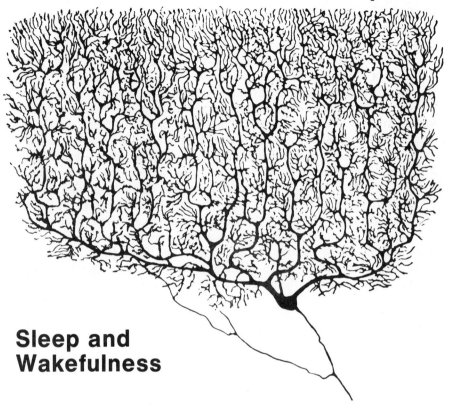

Sleep and
Wakefulness

Sleep and wakefulness represent different states of the nervous system, each characterized by a unique pattern of brain organization. The nature of these states and the brain mechanisms that organize them pose some of the most fascinating problems for neuropsychological research.

The early views of brain states were generally quite simple. Sleep and wakefulness were viewed as two levels on a continuum of arousal. The differences between them were thought to be more quantitative than qualitative. For example, it was held that the brain and the body exhaust themselves when awake; therefore, the organism becomes increasingly drowsy as fatigue increases until the organism can no longer maintain wakefulness and thus sleeps. Another view depicted wakefulness as the result of environmental stimulation. Stimuli keep the animal alert; in the absence of stimulation, the animal sleeps. Thus, according to this theory, the environment functions as the alarm clock for the organism. Both theories, of course, include some truth, but neither is adequate to account completely for changes in brain states that mediate sleep and wakefulness.

It is primarily brain physiology, rather than behavioral data, that demands a more complicated multiple-state theory of sleep and waking. It is now clear that there are at least three naturally occurring states of brain organization—two associated with sleep, the other related to wakefulness. Each depends upon different brain mechanisms for its occurrence, and each is an active state that is characterized by specific neurophysiological events; none occurs by default. For example, waking is not the absence of sleep but is rather one of the three unique brain states. Moreover, sleep and wakefulness do not together include all possible states of brain function. The coma, for example, which results from severe mechanical or pharmacological disruption of the brain, is not sleep. It is rather a condition of disorder, in which none of the brain mechanisms that normally organize the brain are capable of functioning adequately. Each of the natural states is characterized by a unique organization of brain activity.

Electroencephalographic Indications of Sleep and Waking

The physiological study of the states of the brain began in the late 1920s when Hans Berger applied the newly developed vacuum tube amplifiers to the human brain. Berger was able to accurately measure tiny waves of electrical activity at the human scalp, which are generated by the brain. At most, these changes are on the order of 1/10,000 volt (100 microvolts). The written record of these changes is the electroencephalogram (EEG), which shows striking differences in the various brain states. Primarily because it is one of the few measurements of brain activity that may be made on humans without surgery, the EEG is widely used in both clinical and research applications. Fortunately, the EEG is able to tell us something about brain function.

EEG recording usually involves the placement of rather large (¼ inch) metal-disc electrodes on the surface of the scalp. The voltage difference between these electrodes is first amplified and then displayed on a moving strip-chart recorder. The resulting graph (see Figure 7.1) plots instantaneous voltage on the y-axis as a function of time on the x-axis. The amplitude of the EEG refers to the amount of voltage change present, which appears as the peak-to-trough distance in the written record. Frequency of the EEG refers to the rapidity with which the EEG tracing reverses its direction of change. Low-frequency

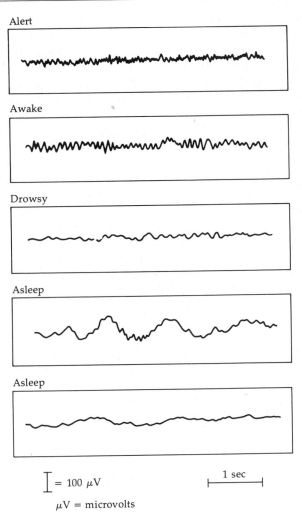

Alert

Awake

Drowsy

Asleep

Asleep

$\text{I} = 100 \ \mu V$ |— 1 sec —|

μV = microvolts

Figure 7.1. *Typical patterns of electroencephalographic (EEG) activity in man.* The rhythmic activity shown in the second trace (Awake) is the alpha rhythm. During REM sleep, the EEG resembles that of the awake, or alert, brain. (From Brazier, M. A. B. *The Electrical Activity of the Nervous System: A Textbook for Students.* © 1968 by Macmillan Publishing Company, Inc. Used by permission of Macmillan Publishing Company, Inc., and Sir Isaac Pitman & Sons Ltd.)

EEG activity changes its direction slowly; as a consequence, the period or length of each wave is long.

Since the EEG is recorded from relatively large electrodes on the scalp, it cannot reveal information concerning the function of a single cell in the manner of microelectrode recordings. Instead, the EEG reflects activity from masses of cells near the recording site and, therefore, gives information about the activity of populations of cells. For this reason, EEG may be appropriate for the analysis of brain states.

EEG activity is generated by the summation of cellular post-synaptic potentials, both excitatory and inhibitory. Large-amplitude waves in the EEG indicate synchronous activity in many cells. Conversely, very flat low-voltage EEG tracings suggest desynchronization and the relative functional independence of cortical cells.

Figure 7.1 shows typical EEG recordings obtained from a human subject. Although there are variations, both within and among people, the waking EEG is usually desynchronized, as in the top tracing, or shows an 8–12 Hz synchrony, as in the second tracing. The latter pattern, the alpha rhythm, has classically been described as an indication of relaxation. Current investigations indicate that this concept may be too simple. Other theories of the significance of the alpha rhythm have appeared recently. For example, it has been suggested that a great preponderance of alpha activity, especially in frontal areas of the brain, might signal a separate and special CNS state, since highly practiced Eastern meditators show exceptionally large amounts of alpha activity in frontal regions during contemplation. However, the conclusion that large amounts of frontal alpha constitute a special state seems premature at this point, especially when the enormous differences in the preponderance of the alpha rhythm among behaviorally normal people are considered.

Cortical desynchronization in the waking brain has traditionally been viewed as a function of arousal or heightened alertness. Orienting to a surprising stimulus, for example, typically blocks any ongoing alpha activity. Desynchronization, together with alpha-frequency activity, characterizes the waking EEG.

As one passes into sleep, the size of the EEG waves increases. The voltage, which reflects synchronization, grows, and the frequency of the waves decreases. Sleep spindles also appear in the EEG record. Sleep spindles are regular patterns of rhythmic activity that are initially very small but grow larger on each cycle until they dominate the record. Then the waves begin to diminish in size until they eventually disappear. The whole event, as it appears in the tracing, has the shape of a spindle (see Figure 7.2). These electroencephalographic events can be used to scale slow wave sleep into at least four stages (see Table 7.1).

As Figure 7.1 shows, the EEG is very slow in frequency and large in amplitude in slow wave sleep. The second sleep state is characterized by the presence of a desynchronized EEG. During these periods, a large number of sharp movements of the eyes are present, giving this state the name "rapid eye movement," or REM, sleep. The

Table 7.1.   *The four stages of nonREM sleep.*

Stage 1:   Record in which EEG alpha waves are slowed very slightly; seen in quiet relaxed wakefulness or as drowsiness supervenes.

Stage 2:   Record with spontaneous "sleep spindles"; runs of a few seconds' duration consisting of regular 14 to 15/sec. waves superimposed upon a low-voltage background with admixture of 3 to 6/sec. waves; a state from which the sleeper is readily aroused.

Stage 3:   Record with some sleep spindles but now on a background of slower 1 to 2/sec. delta waves; associated with sleep of intermediate depth.

Stage 4:   Record consisting entirely of high-voltage slow delta waves without spindling, associated with a phase of sleep in which the threshold for awakening is greatly elevated.

From Mountcastle, Vernon B.: Sleep, wakefulness, and the conscious state: Intrinsic regulatory mechanisms of the brain. In Mountcastle, Vernon B., editor: *Medical physiology*, ed. 13, St. Louis, 1974, The C. V. Mosby Co.; adapted from Dement, W., and Kleitman, N.: Cyclic variations of EEG during sleep and their relations to eye movements, body motility and dreaming, *Electroencephalogr. Clin. Neurophysiol.* 9:673, 1957. Used by permission.

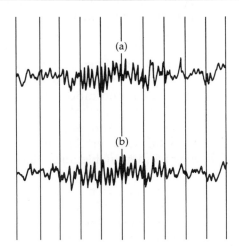

Figure 7.2.   *A pair of sleep spindles recorded simultaneously in the parietal (a) and the occipital (b) lobes of a human subject.*   (Adapted from Kleitman, N. Patterns of dreaming. In *Physiological Psychology: Readings from Scientific American,* W. H. Freeman and Company, 1971, p. 338. Used by permission.)

incidence of such movements is much reduced in slow-wave sleep. Notice the similarities between the EEG records when alerted and in REM sleep. The EEG indication of cortical arousal in the sleeping animal prompted Jouvet to call REM sleep "paradoxical sleep." REM sleep cannot be distinguished from wakefulness on the basis of surface EEG criteria alone. Other signs are needed to distinguish the two.

Thus, there appear to be at least three different normal states of brain organization: REM sleep, slow wave sleep, and wakefulness. Some have argued that slow wave sleep and wakefulness can each be further subdivided into separate, functionally distinguishable states, but such an analysis is beyond the scope of present evidence and of this text.

Wakefulness and the Reticular Activating System

The extensive study of the physiological mechanisms that determine central states of wakefulness began in 1949, when Moruzzi and Magoun reported that electrical stimulation of the brainstem reticular formation produces EEG arousal in the sleeping animal. Similarly, the early lesion studies of Lindsley reported that destruction of the reticular formation prevented an animal from ever awakening. Both lines of evidence suggest that the reticular information is instrumental for the initiation and maintenance of wakefulness and, therefore, consciousness.

The reticular formation is a complex core of neural tissue running from the spinal cord through the midbrain. Its relatively undifferentiated anatomy was initially interpreted as an indication of a functionally undifferentiated mass of tissue. It is now clear that this anatomical nonspecificity is more apparent than real. Although the reticular formation is not populated with many easily discernible landmarks, in the last two decades nearly 100 separate, identifiable nuclei have been described within it.

The reticular formation receives its name from its appearance as a densely interconnected network, or reticulum. The diversity of connections possible in this structure is obvious when the microanatomy of single cells is examined. Figure 7.3 shows the axons of a single cell in the reticular formation of a newborn rat. It is quite different from the simplified neurons illustrated in Figure 2.2. The widespread influence of this single reticular cell is quite impressive. As a whole, the reticular formation can influence activity in many areas of the brain. The exact nature of such influences is elusive, however.

The view of the reticular formation that emerged at the end of the 1950s was simple and exciting. The reticular formation was seen then as a nonspecific excitatory system that, when activated, arouses the cortex. Internally characterized by diffuse multisynaptic pathways, the reticular system receives its input from collaterals, or side branches, of the classical sensory-projection systems. Stimulation of any sense modality acts upon the same reticular core. The reticular system maintains

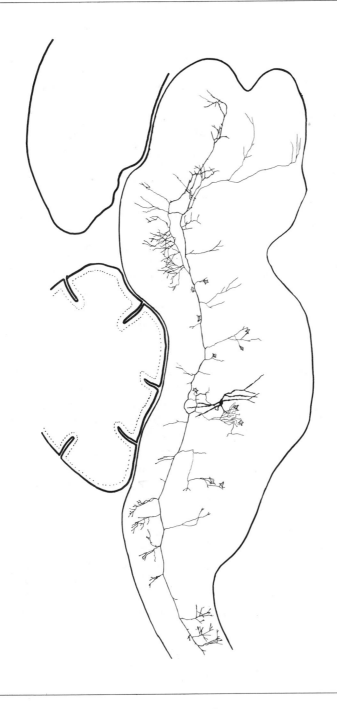

Figure 7.3. *A drawing of a single axon of a cell and its many branches in the reticular formation found in a 2-day-old rat.* (From Scheibel, M. E., & Scheibel, A. B. Structural substrates for integrative patterns in the brain stem reticular core. In H. H. Jasper, L. D. Proctor, R. S. Knighton, W. C. Noshay, & R. T. Costello (Eds.), *Henry Ford Hospital International Symposium: Reticular Formation of the Brain.* p. 46, © 1958 by Little, Brown and Company. Used by permission.)

wakefulness by maintaining an activating input to cortex. In the absence of input, according to the theory, wakefulness is not possible; sleep is produced by default, by a reduction in reticular formation activity. However, a more recent concept, of greater complexity and thus more fitting to the intricacy of the reticular system, has replaced the earlier, simple concept. The earlier view is not completely wrong, but a more detailed theory is needed to take into account the data that have more recently been acquired.

What are the difficulties with the simple reticular theory? First, not all sensory information is passed directly to the reticular formation. In the somatosensory system, for example, there is no collateral input from the medial lemniscus, which carries the bulk of detailed somatosensory information in the spinal cord. But the spinothalamic tract, which carries more general information—including signals indicating pain—does relay in the reticular formation. Input patterns to the reticular formation are thus more complex than was originally supposed.

Second, single units in the reticular formation may be limited in their response to sensory information. Single cells do not show the kind of homogeneous response to all input that was originally postulated. Further, Huttenlocher has shown that single cells do not respond uniformly to shifts from sleep into wakefulness, or vice versa. Contrary to expectation, most cells are more active in slow wave sleep than in quiet wakefulness, but some show exactly the opposite pattern. More interestingly, nearly all reticular formation cells studied doubled their rates of firing in REM sleep. The reticular formation cannot, therefore, be thought of as a simple system that increases its output with increasing arousal from sleep to wakefulness.

Another difficulty with the early work on the reticular system was in estimating the effect of lesions on postoperative behavior. In the early lesion studies, animals that received large, bilateral reticular formation lesions never regained wakefulness. Often death quickly followed the operation. More recently, it has been shown that, with proper nursing care, animals can be kept alive for much longer periods, and their recovery of function is substantial. There is a return to nearly normal behavior, including resumption of the sleep-wakefulness cycle with EEG arousal. If the lesion is made in two separate operations, instead of one, any disruption is markedly reduced. Although normally it may serve such a role, the reticular formation is not necessary for maintaining wakefulness in the animal.

The final blow to the simplified theory of reticular formation function was the discovery that the sleep states are the result of active processes and not simply the result of a decrease in wakefulness.

States of Sleep

Slow wave sleep is perhaps the least puzzling of the sleep states, although it is far from completely understood. Slow wave sleep is the first sleep of the night. As sleep begins, the cortex generates high-voltage slow waves that never occur in wakefulness. The muscles of the body are relaxed but not completely limp. The eyes do not move quickly. When awakened from slow wave sleep, the subject is groggy. Dreams are seldom reported, but, if they are, they are likely to be simple and primitive in structure; there is little if any cognitive elaboration.

REM sleep is quite different. Although it had been previously noted that the eyes may move in sleep, it was not until 1953 that the significance of these movements was realized. Aserinsky and Kleitman measured both the EEG and the eye movements of sleeping subjects. They found that periods of rapid eye movements (REM) occurred only during periods of cortical desynchronization. The REM period can be as short as a few minutes and as long as a half-hour. The eye movements of REM sleep are similar to the changes in fixation that occur in wakefulness, although they are not as rapid. Instead, they are very much like the movements of the eyes of a waking person imagining a visual scene with eyelids closed. This similarity suggested that REM periods might be associated with dreaming, and to test the hypothesis, Aserinsky and Kleitman awakened subjects from both REM and non-REM sleep. Most subjects reported elaborated dreams only when awakened during REM periods; more fully developed dreams were reported during the more intense REM periods.

REM sleep is accompanied by inhibition of the musculature of the body. In a cat, general muscular inhibition is especially striking. All tonic activation of the skeletal muscles is eliminated as the result of a brainstem inhibitory mechanism. The muscles are flaccid. The cat, unable to maintain its normal sphinx-like sleeping posture when the neck muscles are limp, lies on its side. Spinal reflexes are also blocked. Paradoxically, some phasic or transitory discharge, including the rapid eye movements themselves, occurs in motor fibers during REM. There may also be phasic movements of the muscles of the toes and lower legs; animals sometimes seem to be running in REM sleep. In cats, REM sleep is also characterized by an exceptionally large and stable discharge of cells in the hippocampus, which gives rise to the hippocampal theta rhythm, a regular waveform that repeats itself about five to seven times each second.

Another peculiar electrical pattern can be seen in recordings made during REM sleep. Sharp waves (PGO spikes, or ponto-geniculate-occipital sharp waves) originate in the pontine reticular formation (the portion of the reticular core near the pons) and proceed to occipital (visual) cortex through the lateral geniculate nucleus of the thalamus. In REM, PGO spikes occur at an average rate of 1 per sec. Similar waves appear frequently in wakefulness during visual attention.

During REM, there is a marked increase in the rate of firing of single cells in most brain structures, including cortex and reticular formation. These increases are rather nonspecific, as are increases in brain temperature and brain blood flow.

Is REM sleep a deeper sleep than slow-wave sleep? The question of depth of sleep is very difficult to answer. It assumes that the sleep states might be ordered on a simple scale; however, the two states are sufficiently different to require a more complex formulation. It may be argued that REM sleep is lighter because it resembles the waking, or stage-1, brain waves. Conversely, REM sleep may be deeper, since more reticular formation stimulation is needed to wake a cat from REM than from non-REM sleep. Furthermore, a small amount of reticular stimulation in REM will shift the EEG to slow wave sleep, but comparable stimulation in slow wave sleep wakes the animal. This finding seems to imply an ordering of states, with REM sleep being the deepest, but, when the complexity of these states is considered, other interpretations are possible.

Brain Mechanisms in Sleep

The conclusion that each of the sleep states depends upon a separate, active process within the brain rests not only on descriptive differences between the two states but also on experimental data. Slow wave sleep is absent in the newborn of some species and appears only as the nervous system matures. At birth, the baby shows only waking and REM patterns, which suggest that the slow wave sleep system is not yet operative. Furthermore, in the adult, drugs can selectively abolish one kind of sleep while the other sleep pattern remains quite normal. Although the effects of the sleep states are widely distributed within the brain, some restricted areas appear to be exceptionally important for the sleep states.

Much of the work of identifying the brain mechanisms that mediate the sleep states has been performed by Jouvet, who examined the roles played by the various neuronal transmitter substances in the brain. Although complicated, a coherent picture of brain function in sleep is developing. Major functional systems of the brain can be characterized by different neural transmitter substances. One system involves serotonin; others utilize the catecholamines dopamine and noradrenaline, both of which are formed from the same precursor dihydroxyphenylalanine, commonly called DOPA. Jouvet suggests that serotonin is involved in producing slow wave sleep and in triggering REM sleep, whereas the catecholamines are uniquely concerned with producing REM sleep. Of the wide variety of evidence in support of these ideas, the most convincing is the following.

Certain substances selectively modify the various central transmitters individually without affecting the others. P-chlorophenylalanine (PCPA) selectively inhibits the production of brain serotonin. For 24 hours after PCPA is injected, the organism shows completely normal behavior; the drug has no toxic effect of its own. During this time, the brain is using its pre-existing supplies of serotonin but is unable to manufacture more to replace them. After a day, the serotonin reserves are exhausted and the effects of diminished serotonin become apparent. There is a sudden reduction of sleep. A cat, which normally sleeps 70% of the time, becomes a total insomniac. The EEG is desynchronized, and the animal is quiet but wakeful. Neither slow wave nor REM sleep is present. The insomnia lasts until the 60th hour after injection, when the effects of the inhibitor begin to disappear.

Jouvet has demonstrated that serotonin depletion is responsible for the insomnia. PCPA blocks the production of serotonin by disrupting an event early in the long metabolic chain in which serotonin is produced. However, 5-hydroxytryptophan (5-HTP) is a product in the chain that is produced between the stage at which PCPA blocks and before the final production of serotonin. Therefore, 5-HTP can be converted into serotonin despite the presence of the inhibitor. Injected into the bloodstream, 5-HTP enters the serotoninergic systems of the brain. Very small injections of 5-HTP can restore available brain serotonin and thereby reinstate normal sleep patterns, even when the serotonin-deficient animal's insomnia is most pronounced. Recovery lasts a few hours until all available 5-HTP has been converted into serotonin. Then insomnia returns. This set of data suggests that serotonin must be available in serotoninergic neurons if normal slow wave sleep is to occur. Jouvet suggests that one of the products produced by the breakdown of serotonin after it has been used by the brain is responsible for triggering REM sleep.

The discovery that monoamines may be made to fluoresce when excited by ultraviolet light has provided a method by which these transmitters may be mapped in the brain. Through fluorescence microscopy, a large concentration of serotonin-rich neurons were discovered in the raphe nuclei of the midbrain tegmentum. Thus, the level of brain serotonin may be reduced surgically by removing the

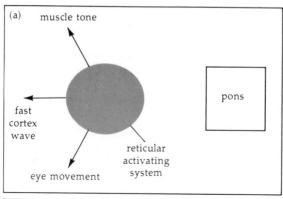

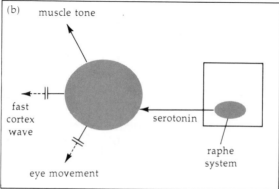

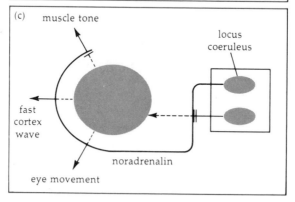

Figure 7.4. *Jouvet's theory of the biochemical basis of sleep.* The wakeful state is shown in (a). The release of serotonin by the raphe systems induces the shift to the slow-wave-sleep organization of the brain in (b). In (c), REM sleep results from the activation of the noradrenergic systems of the locus coeruleus. The REM state is similar to the wakeful organization in many respects. (Used by permission from Jouvet, M. The states of sleep. In *Physiological Psychology: Readings from Scientific American.* Copyright © 1967 by Scientific American, Inc. All rights reserved.)

raphe nuclei. If most (80%–90%) of these nuclei are destroyed, total insomnia results initially. After 4 days, some slow wave sleep appears, but never more than 10% of the time does the animal sleep. REM sleep does not occur. If the destruction is less complete, the animal shows more sleep, some of which is REM. Removing only the rostral raphe area produces wakefulness that alternates with REM sleep. Destruction of the more caudal raphe nuclei abolishes REM sleep altogether. The serotonin-rich raphe system may act as a trigger for REM sleep.

The serotoninergic-raphe system is not responsible for production of REM sleep. Control of REM sleep appears to involve the nucleus locus coeruleus, in the tegmentum near the pons. Cells there use noradrenaline at their synapses. When these noradrenergic nuclei are bilaterally removed, there is a total disappearance of REM sleep; the animal alternates naturally between slow wave sleep and wakefulness. The mechanisms underlying these latter two states appear to be undisturbed.

Removing the noradrenergic nuclei in the locus coeruleus results pharmacologically in a significant decrease in forebrain noradrenaline. Drugs that block noradrenaline synthesis also block REM sleep. Moreover, the rate of noradrenaline turnover in the brain increases in periods of intense REM sleep.

Noradrenergic systems, especially those in the locus coeruleus, are crucial to maintaining REM sleep. Jouvet has evidence that other transmitters in other systems also might be involved. The presence of other transmitters does not seem surprising in view of the radical change of brain function that characterizes the REM state.

Sleep Cycles

Slow wave sleep and REM sleep do not occur haphazardly throughout the night. Instead, beginning with slow wave sleep, the two kinds of sleep alternate. This pattern repeats itself at intervals of approximately 1.5 hours, as Figure 7.5 shows. Early in the night, the cycle is dominated by slow wave sleep, but, toward morning, the REM periods become increasingly long. The shift from slow wave to REM-dominated sleep is part of a daily cycle that continues through the waking hours. If one naps in the morning, much of the sleep is REM, whereas, later in the day, the time spent in REM decreases.

Sleep cycles are very regular. There are three major REM periods each night for 13 nights. Each REM period begins and ends at approximately the same time. There is some variation, which perhaps depends in part on the events of the day, but, despite these changes, the overall pattern of sleep remains substantially the same.

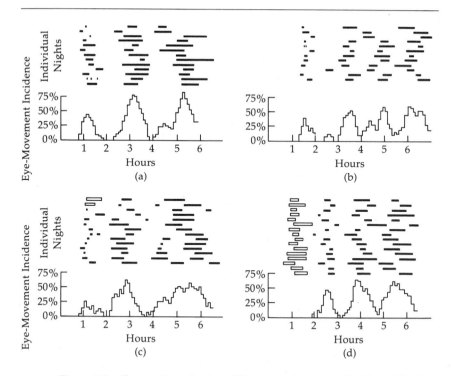

Figure 7.5. *Sleep patterns for four different people on several nights.* The bars indicate REM periods during a single night. The graphs beneath these bars show the incidence of REM averaged over the individual nights. Open bars indicate periods when REM was expected but did not occur. (From Dement, W., & Kleitman, N. Cyclic variations in EEG during sleep and their relation to eye movements, body motility and dreaming. *Electroencephalography and Clinical Neurophysiology,* 1957, **9,** 683. Used by permission.)

Consistency is found not only in the records of single individuals; the sleep records of different individuals also look very much alike. The sequence of three to four 90-minute cycles is nearly universal. The mechanisms that control sleep are largely internal and certainly very powerful, as similar patterns are seen in people sleeping under vastly different conditions.

Other cyclic changes throughout the night parallel the occurrence of eye movements and are undoubtedly linked to the REM sleep process. Penile erections in men, for example, occur regularly during REM sleep. Figure 7.6 shows the pattern of erection for one subject superimposed upon the REM record. The close correspondence between REM and erection may result from the general spinal inhibition accompanying REM, which produces a release from normal inhibitory

REM

Erection

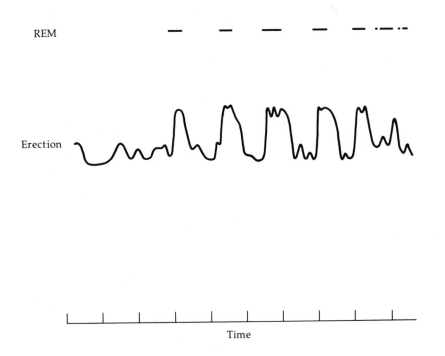

Time

Figure 7.6. *Penile erections appear to be related to the appearance of REM sleep in the night.* The dark bars indicate REM periods. The line tracing indicates the state of erection. (From Fisher, C., Gross, J., & Zuch, J. Cycle of penile erection synchronous with dreaming (REM) sleep. *Archives of General Psychiatry*, 1965, **12,** 36. Used by permission.)

control. It is tempting, however, to think that the erections are related to the psychoanalysts' argument that there is often a strong sexual component in dreams.

Sleep Deprivation

Since the sleep process is such an inescapable part of mammalian life, we naturally assume it must have great functional value. We seem to need to sleep, and we spend large parts of our life sleeping. What if we did not? That question suggests one of the few straightforward approaches to studying the function of sleep—the examination of the effects of sleep deprivation on both biology and behavior.

Since sleep occurs at the end of the day, many of the early theories suggest that sleep is a response to a gradually increasing level of some "fatigue substance." Similar mechanisms of chemical regulation are known in other biological systems. To test the fatigue-substance hypothesis, the biochemical changes that occur when an animal is deprived of sleep are analyzed. One simple and specific test is the attempt to identify a bodily substance that, when taken from a sleep-deprived donor, induces sleep if injected into a nondeprived recipient. No such substance has been found. Originally, it was thought that the substance might be found circulating in the blood. This is unlikely, however, since it is now known that Siamese twins who share the same cardiovascular system can show different sleep-waking cycle. If the fatigue substance exists, it is probably locally distributed within a specific brain structure.

There is, however, one positive set of findings from the biochemical sleep-deprivation studies that is of considerable interest. The body's use of energy undergoes radical changes when sleep is prevented. With increasing deprivation, more and more energy is required to do even the simplest of tasks. Coupled with this change in energy requirements is a drop in the production of adenosine triphosphate (ATP), a substance that provides cells with a source of energy. After four days without sleep, ATP synthesis virtually stops. Such disturbances in energy production and distribution might explain many of the psychological changes that accompany sleep loss.

Animals that have been deprived of sleep for several days show striking changes in their behavior. Caged animals may fight and kill each other. Humans often become depressed and listless, moody and irritable. Sleep loss appears to be highly stressful. Sleep-deprived humans are capable of optimal task performance only when they are interested; as the sleepless days pass, it becomes more difficult to maintain the motivation required for task performance. Subjects begin to hallucinate and show other signs of psychotic behavior. The cognitive and personality changes that occur in the prolonged absence of sleep are substantial.

Does the disruption of behavior following sleep loss arise from sleep deprivation in general or from the deprivation of only one of the two types of sleep? This question can be partially answered by observing the effects of selective sleep deprivation. To deprive the subject of REM sleep only, EEG and eye movements are monitored throughout the night. During slow wave activity, the subject is allowed to sleep, but, when signs of REM appear, he is awakened. Thus, he may have unlimited slow wave sleep but no REM sleep.

Both animals and humans deprived of REM sleep, which is normally the minor part of the sleep cycle, show increasing behavioral

disorganization with increasing REM sleep loss. Psychotic-like behaviors may also occur. Furthermore, it appears that the more the body
is deprived of REM, the stronger is the tendency to produce REM. The
number of awakenings required to prevent REM drastically increases
the longer selective REM deprivation is maintained. Figure 7.7 shows
that, by the 15th night, a subject had to be awakened nearly 20 times
each hour to prevent REM sleep.

When the subject is finally allowed to sleep naturally, after a
period of selective sleep deprivation, he shows extraordinary amounts
of REM. Sleep on these recovery nights often begins with a period of
REM (normal sleep virtually never begins with REM), and REM

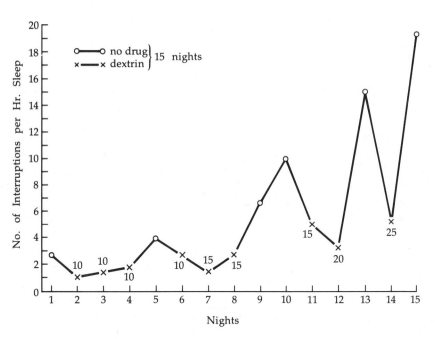

Figure 7.7.   *The effects of selective sleep deprivation on the pattern of sleep are quite
powerful.*   Subjects were awakened each time that they entered REM sleep. The
number of awakenings per hour are shown for 15 consecutive nights. In the last
night of REM deprivation, the subject was awakened, on the average, once every
3 minutes during the night. Dexedrine, a CNS stimulant, reduces the number of
necessary awakenings. (From Dement, W. C., Studies on the function of rapid
eye movement (paradoxical) sleep in human subjects. In *Aspects anatomo-
fonctionnels de la physiologie du sommeil*. Colloques internationaux du centre
national de la recherche scientifique #127. Paris: Centre National de la Recherche
Scientifique, 1965, p. 589. Used by permission.)

continues to dominate sleep throughout the night. The REM rebound suggests that REM sleep is governed by a mechanism, probably neurochemical, that builds up in the absence of REM and discharges during REM sleep.

Similar mechanisms seem to control slow wave sleep, which has been studied much less than REM. Volunteers are selectively deprived of stage-4 sleep by partially awakening them until another EEG pattern appears. These subjects, like REM-deprived subjects, need more stimulation more often each night to maintain partial deprivation. Furthermore, they show a rebound of stage-4 sleep on recovery nights.

It appears that sleep is necessary for maintaining normal patterns of behavior in mammals. Mechanisms that control the various sleep states are selective, and they are capable of controlling the sleep processes over long periods of time.

Summary

Wakefulness, slow wave sleep, and rapid-eye-movement (REM) sleep represent different states of CNS organization. Each state is the result of a distinct, active organizing process. Both REM sleep and wakefulness are characterized by cortical desynchronization in the electroencephalogram (EEG), whereas slow wave sleep is marked by slower high-voltage activity. Sleep spindles, a regular pattern of rhythmic activity, also appear in the EEG.

Wakefulness normally depends upon the activity of the reticular activating system, a densely and diffusely connected region within the brainstem that functions to arouse other brain systems from sleep and to activate the organism during wakefulness. Reticular formation receives input from most sensory systems and projects to widespread areas of the brain. Although recent studies indicate that recovery from reticular damage is possible, the reticular activating system normally is crucially important for the maintenance of electroencephalographic arousal.

Slow wave sleep is the first sleep of the night. In addition to the characteristic EEG signs, slow wave sleep is marked by muscular relaxation but not complete flaccidity, by a relative absence of rapid eye movements, and by little dream activity.

REM sleep is accompanied by a complete reduction of tonic muscle tone in the presence of some phasic muscle activity, including the rapid eye movements. The REMs resemble eye movements made during wakefulness. Centrally, the REM period is marked by an increase in the hippocampal theta rhythm and PGO spikes. Single cells in many brain areas display a high rate of firing during REM. One method of estimating the depth of sleep suggests that REM is the deeper of the two sleep states. Dreams commonly occur in REM sleep.

REM and slow wave sleep depend upon different brain systems for production. Slow wave sleep appears to be produced by a serotonin-dependent system in the raphe nuclei of the midbrain tegmentum. Substances that prevent the production of serotonin produce insomnia after normal brain reserves of serotonin are depleted. Pharmacological agents that restore brain serotonin induce sleep in the serotonin-deprived animal. Removal of the raphe nuclei results in near-complete insomnia; the absence also of REM sleep suggests that the slow wave system is responsible for triggering the onset of REM.

The REM organizing system appears to be located in the nucleus locus coeruleus and depends upon noradrenaline at its synapses. If this nucleus is removed, REM totally disappears, and the animal alternates between slow wave sleep and wakefulness. Also, there is a significant decrease in forebrain noradrenaline. Pharmacological inhibition of noradrenaline synthesis also prevents REM sleep.

Slow wave sleep and REM sleep alternate during the night in a well-controlled sleep cycle. Early in the night, slow wave sleep dominates, whereas later the duration of REM periods is increased. Such patterns are remarkably consistent, both within and among individuals.

Although searches for a "fatigue substance" that is accumulated during wakefulness and depleted during sleep have not been successful, it is known that some long-term mechanisms are involved in the control of the sleep states. Selective deprivation of REM sleep is debilitating and may lead to psychotic-like behavior. A compensatory increase in the amount of REM sleep follows the deprivation period. A similar rebound effect follows selective slow-wave sleep deprivation.

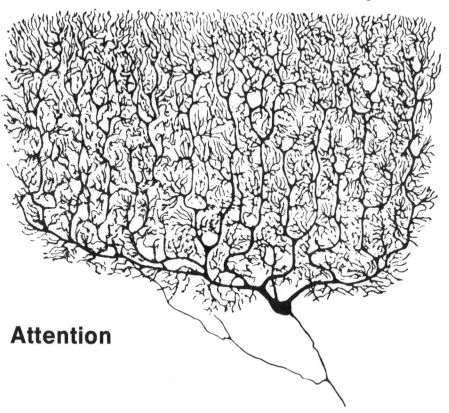

Chapter 8

Attention

"Everyone knows what attention is," wrote William James in 1890. "It is the taking possession by the mind, in clear and vivid form, of one out of what seems several simultaneously possible objects or trains of thought. Focalization, concentration of consciousness are of its essence. It implies withdrawal from some things in order to deal effectively with others, and is a condition which has a real opposite in the confused, dazed, scattered-brained state which in French is called distraction. . ." (James, 1890, pp. 403–404).

The terms have changed somewhat in 80 years. Discussions of "mind" have proved to be of little value in psychology. But the basic question of attention is still of primary importance for the understanding of behavior. Today, the term "selective attention" refers to those brain processes responsible for choosing from the great mass of sensory information presented to the receptors, which information will be fully processed and allowed to determine future behavior. For example, imagine that you are in a room filled with people. Everyone is talking while you eavesdrop, first on one conversation, then on another. Here you are using selective mechanisms of the brain to process speech sounds from one or two people and to discard a great many similar sounds.

Attention also has an intensive aspect. Everyone has had the experience of reading a novel that seems to go on and on and almost puts the reader to sleep. Then something interesting happens in the book that arouses the reader's attention. He awakens and is activated. He reads faster, intently absorbed in the book before him. All the while he has been paying attention to the novel; but when it became interesting, his brain was alerted. The increase in the processing capacity of the brain is the intensive property of attention. It may be a mistake to identify intensity with attention instead of with brain processing capacity more generally, but both selective and intensive properties are implicit in the normal usage of the word "attention." The fact that changes in selectivity and in processing capacity often occur together creates some of the many problems involved in the study of attention.

The Orienting Reflex

Among the earliest and most influential physiological studies of attentional mechanisms were those of the Nobel-Prize-winning physiologist I. P. Pavlov. In the course of his investigations of conditioned reflexes, Pavlov noticed that even the best-trained conditioned responses would fail to occur if something unusual distracted the animal. For example, one of Pavlov's assistants would laboriously teach a dog a new response. But when Pavlov entered the room to observe, the animal watched Pavlov and ignored the conditioned stimulus. This reaction Pavlov thought to be the response element of a reflex designed to orient the animal to novel, and perhaps biologically important, stimuli. He called it the orienting or "what-is-it" reflex.

The orienting reflex illustrates both the selective and the intensive dimensions of attention. Some selective changes are easily observed in animals. For example, dogs prick up their ears and point their heads toward the novel stimulus. Other changes are not so easily seen. For example, many selective processes do not involve changes in the musculature but occur entirely within the brain. Such selective processes are termed "central," since they take place in the more central portions of the nervous system, not in the periphery. While central processes may sometimes be demonstrated directly using electrical recording techniques, in most orienting-reflex experiments, central selective processes are not directly observed; instead they are inferred from changes in the animal's pattern of behavior.

Intensive changes are prominent in the orienting reflex. The animal shows many signs of increased arousal. The drowsy dog awakens; the waking dog becomes alerted. The pupils of the eyes enlarge as a sign of sympathetic activation. The blood vessels of the head dilate, while those in the rest of the body constrict. The electrical resistance of the skin (the galvanic skin response) decreases markedly, another sign of bodily arousal. The phsyiological mechanism giving rise to this resistance change is far from clear, but many investigators believe it to be related to the activation of sweat glands in the skin. The animal first holds his breath and then breathes more deeply and slowly. Tension of the skeletal muscles of the body increases. Heart-rate changes are variable, but usually the heart rate slows. The brain itself shows signs of activation. The slow, rhythmic electrical activity of the cortex is sharply attenuated, and the EEG pattern becomes one of desynchronized, low-amplitude activity.

The orienting reflex appears not only to direct the animal's attention toward the novel stimulus but also to prepare the animal through activation to deal more effectively with the novel event. The pattern of physiological changes described above, for example, charac-terizes a state of increased mental capacity. The activated desyn-chronized state of EEG activity is associated both with faster reaction times to sensory stimuli and with enhanced ability to make sensory

Table 8.1. *Bodily changes that characterize the orienting response.*

Local motor responses:	Orient animal toward stimulus. Ongoing activity inhibited.
General motor responses:	Increased electromyographic activity and muscle tone.
EEG:	Aroused pattern of cortical desynchrony.
Vascular changes:	Vasoconstriction in limbs. Vasodilation in head.
Heart rate:	Usually slows.
Electrodermal activity:	Galvanic skin response.
Respiration:	Breathing stops and then begins again with slow, deep breaths.
Pupil:	Pupillary dilation.

discriminations. Bodily changes also seem to be organized to prepare the animal for action.

Russian psychologists are careful to distinguish between the orienting reflexes described above and the defensive, or startle, reflexes. Physiologically, orienting and defensive reflexes differ only in the state of the blood vessels of the head. In the orienting reflex, the vessels dilate, whereas in the defensive reflex, they constrict. Overt bodily reactions in the two reflexes may also differ. The orienting animal always points toward the stimulus, but the defensive animal may prepare to attack or to retreat. The idea that the orienting reflex is a unique response to external stimuli that require the attention of the organism has been less well received outside the Soviet Union. Western psychologists typically do not make as firm a distinction between the physiological patterns of the orienting and defensive reflexes. The orienting reflex may represent a special case of a more general pattern of bodily response to information-processing demands on the brain and nervous system.

Since reflexes are generally thought to be stimulus dependent, considerable effort has been devoted to describing and categorizing the stimulus situations likely to give rise to the orienting reflex in man and animals. Attempts to define the eliciting conditions for the orienting reflex generally stress the following factors.

1. *Novelty*. The orienting reflex often occurs in response to stimuli that the animal has never seen before, but not all novel stimuli lead to orienting reflexes. Show a cat a Picasso sketch and it will not orient in the least, whereas some humans will orient to precisely the same stimulus if it is novel. Novelty is important, but novelty alone is not sufficient to specify which stimuli will lead to an orienting response.
2. *Intensity*. Loud sounds, bright lights, and other intense stimuli often produce an orienting response, although a defensive reaction may occur if the stimulus is too strong. However, in the context of other intense stimuli, the capacity of an intense stimulus to produce the response is reduced.
3. *Meaning*. Stimuli that are biologically important to an animal may continue to produce an orienting response long after the novelty of the stimulus disappears. For example, young foxes give an orienting response to the sound of mice squeaking at the foxes' first exposure to this stimulus. But with repeated presentations, the orienting response disappears or is habituated. If, however, the fox cub is given the opportunity to eat a mouse, the squeak takes on new importance. No longer will the orienting response to the sound habituate; instead, the stimulus will continue to produce a reliable orienting response every time it is presented.

Meaning is also an important determinant of the orienting response in man. The orienting response is reliably elicited in man by certain words or phrases; "watch out" or "fire" are verbal symbols capable of eliciting profound orienting responses under normal circumstances. In addition, one's own name serves as an adequate stimulus for an orienting reflex.

Organisms exhibit a certain amount of orienting behavior in learning situations. Whenever learning is possible, some aspect of the situation is likely to be novel, or unknown, to the animal. Therefore, it is reasonable that, when initially presented with the stimuli in a learned-discrimination task, for example, the subject shows strong orienting responses. As training proceeds, the orienting responses decrease. After the animal has mastered the task and his behavior appears automatic, the orienting responses to the discriminated stimuli are virtually absent. If the conditions of the experiment are changed, however, as when reinforcement contingencies are switched in reversal learning, the orienting responses reappear. The orienting response appears to follow task demands on the animal's capacity to process information.

Bodily Changes during Mental Activity

Even in situations where orienting to external stimuli is not of crucial importance, increasing the informational demands on the brain seems to arouse the activation systems within the brain. Arousal is reflected in alterations in skeletal and autonomic activity throughout the body. Some years ago, Daniel Kahneman and I performed a series of experiments to investigate pupillary change during mental activity, pursuing the discovery by Ekhard Hess that pupil diameter increases during mental multiplication. When a person is asked to remember for a short period of time a series of numbers that are slowly read to him, an increasing demand is placed on his short-term memory as each new digit is heard. Under these conditions, most people cannot remember more than seven or eight digits with accuracy; the demands on processing capacity, or attention, are too great for retention of longer series of numbers. If the subject slowly repeats the digits he has heard, the demands placed on the processing capacity are reduced as each digit is spoken. Only the remaining digits need to be held in the processing system. Therefore, as each digit is heard, load increases, and as each is spoken, load decreases.

If pupil size is measured during the performance of such a

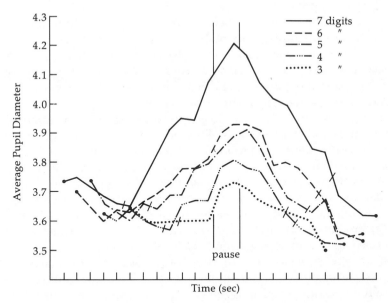

Figure 8.1. *Pupil diameter increases as load is placed on short-term memory (STM) and decreases as that load is removed.* Here, subjects are asked to repeat series of three to seven digits as pupil diameter is measured. Responses to series of different lengths are superimposed about the 2-second pause between listening and reporting. (From Kahneman, D., & Beatty, J. Pupil diameter and load on memory. *Science,* 1966, **154,** 1584. Copyright 1966 by the American Association for the Advancement of Science. Used by permission.)

memory task, pupil diameter quickly changes as the demands on the subject's attention vary. (See Figure 8.1.) Subjects were asked to remember series of three to seven digits read to them at the rate of one per second. Subjects were instructed to repeat the series at the same rate after a 2-second pause. Pupil diameter increased as each new digit was heard and decreased as each digit was spoken. Peak pupil diameter at the pause was greater as the number of digits to be remembered increased. Although pupil dilation is a component of the orienting response, it would be unreasonable to assume that the subject gives increasingly large orienting responses to each successive digit. Rather, moment-by-moment activation of the nervous system, as measured here by pupil diameter, seems to reflect demands on the subject's attention. Similar changes in other measures of sympathetic arousal, such as galvanic skin response and heart rate, have also been reported in this situation.

EEG Signs of Mental Activity

Physical signs of mental activity are seen not only in the peripheral structures of the body—the pupils, the skeletal muscles, the heart, and the blood vessels—but also in the brain itself. For example, desynchronization of the electroencephalogram (EEG) is a common sign of increased mental effort and has been classically considered a component of the orienting response. Other, more subtle changes that occur in brain activity in response to certain situations may be discovered by a more detailed analysis of EEG activity. One such pattern is the contingent negative variation (CNV). Walter, Cooper, Aldridge, McCallum, and Winter reported a very slow change in the electrical polarization of the cortex. The shift appears when an observer is signaled that an event is about to occur to which he must respond. Thus the experimental paradigm is essentially a reaction time problem with a warning stimulus. The signal to which the subject must respond is termed the "imperative stimulus" by Walter, since it is the event to which the subject must respond. The task is also analogous to a classical-conditioning paradigm, in which a neutral stimulus systematically precedes another stimulus that elicits a response from the organism. Following the warning signal by about a third of a second, the surface of the brain becomes increasingly negative until the stimulus to which the subject is to respond is presented. Shortly thereafter, the polarization of the surface of the brain returns to normal. The polarizing response does not appear when the second signal, the so-called imperative stimulus, or its functional equivalent, is not expected to occur. Thus, the name "contingent negative variation" was given to the response.

The CNV usually is largest at the vertex, or top, of the human brain, but it is recordable with diminished strength from many cortical areas. The CNV in a typical experiment is shown in Figure 8.2. A click serves as the warning stimulus and a flashing light as the imperative stimulus. The light is turned off when the subject presses his button.

Increasing cortical negativity has been thought to result from the buildup of electrical activity in the outermost dendrites of the cortical surface. Negative cortical shifts occur during stimulation of the reticular activating system. Similarly, cortical negativity increases when an organism is naturally awakened and increases still further with the organism's increasing alertness, as in orienting to a novel stimulus. Conversely, when an organism becomes sleepy, cortical negativity decreases, and the cortex becomes increasingly positive. For these reasons, the CNV can be thought to indicate a transitory state of increased arousal that is terminated after the response to the imperative stimulus. The CNV represents an intensive shift in attention.

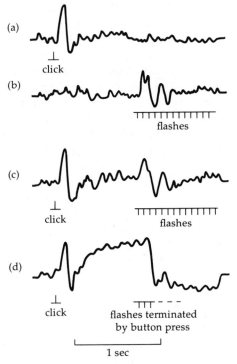

Figure 8.2. *Cortical responses to (a) a click, (b) flashes of light, and (c) both stimuli.* When the subject is instructed to terminate the flashes by pressing a button, the contingent negative variation appears (d). (From Walter, W., Cooper, R., Aldridge, V. J., McCallum, W. C., & Winter, A. L. Contingent negative variation: An electric sign of sensorimotor association and expectancy in the human brain. *Nature*, 1964, **203**, 381. Used by permission.)

The size of the CNV is related to factors that control the amount of attention that the subject must pay to the imperative stimulus. For example, the CNV is reduced when the very appearance of the imperative stimulus becomes highly uncertain. If the imperative stimulus is omitted in 50% of the trials, CNV amplitude drops. But if the imperative stimulus fails to appear only 20% of the time, the CNV remains. When the imperative stimulus is removed entirely, the subject soon learns not to expect to perform, and the CNV disappears. Also, if the subject is simply told that no imperative stimulus will occur, the CNV vanishes immediately. Whenever the subject determines that he does not need to prepare himself for the second stimulus, the CNV is diminished or disappears. Conversely, if the subject is instructed to pay careful attention to the imperative stimulus, the size of the CNV is increased. When subjects are rewarded for reacting quickly to the imperative stimulus, the CNV is enhanced. When reaction times are measured in a CNV task, faster reaction times are often associated with stronger CNVs, without special instructions to the subject. (See Figure 8.3.)

The contingent negative variation may also be measured in signal-detection tasks that employ a warning signal. For example, a CNV appears when subjects attempt to detect a faint tone that may follow a warning light flash. The CNV is larger when the subject successfully detects the tone than when he fails to detect a tone that was actually present. It is reasonable to infer that the subject paid more

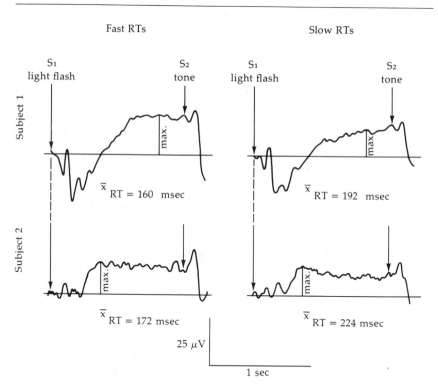

Figure 8.3. *CNV and reaction time.* The contingent negative variation (CNV) is usually greater when a subject responds quickly to the imperative stimulus than when he responds slowly. Here, data from two subjects who show this pattern are presented. Both reaction time and the CNV seem to change with shifts in the inferred level of attention. (From Tecce, J., & Scheff, N. Attention reduction and suppressed direct-current potentials in the human brain. *Science,* 1969, **164,** 332. Copyright 1969 by the American Association for the Advancement of Science. Used by permission.)

attention to the correctly detected signals than to the missed ones. Higher CNV responses are associated with more effective information processing.

Momentary changes take place in the brain in response to increased demands on its information-processing capacity. One such change, the CNV, appears to indicate increased cortical arousal. These shifts are transitory; they last only for the duration of the task, which ranges from a few to a dozen seconds. When the demand for increased attention is removed, these cortical processes return to more normal, chronic levels of activation. Such changes within the brain parallel changes in the autonomic nervous system.

In one of the few studies of single-cell activity and attention, Thompson and Bettinger report data similar to that seen in human EEG studies. They examined the response of small groups of neurons within the association areas of the cat's cortex, using a single electrode to record spikes from several nearby cells. When a novel stimulus is presented, cellular activity increases. Moreover, biologically important stimuli show the same effect on single-unit activity. Increases in the aggregated rate of firing appear when the cat is shown food. Firing returns to normal when the food dish is removed. Presentation of stimuli that are interesting to the animal increases activation of groups of cells in the association areas of the cat's brain and, almost certainly, elsewhere.

Selective Attention

The human brain must be viewed as an information-processing system with definite limits to its capacity. We cannot perceive at any moment all stimuli that present themselves to our sensory systems. For that reason, the selection of stimuli to be processed is an issue of crucial importance for understanding the behavior of organisms. Selective attention refers to those central processes that determine the selection of stimuli.

That there are limits to man's information-processing capacity should be obvious to anyone who has ever tried to read a book while listening to conversation. One task is accomplished at the expense of the other. Although one's eyes may continue to move across the page while listening, little of the written text will be comprehended. Certainly we can perform simple, well-learned functions while carrying out another task; with little difficulty, we can think or talk while walking. Sometimes, even a complex task with which we are very familiar can be performed at the same time we are doing something else, but little of the automatic task will be remembered. Many drivers have had the experience of becoming engrossed in conversation or in thought only to realize later that they have driven too far or have taken a familiar but currently inappropriate turn while their mind was otherwise engaged. However, when we try to carry out two different tasks, each of which places significant demands on the information-processing capacity of the brain, the limits of that capacity are all too readily apparent.

Capacity limits have often been demonstrated experimentally. For example, in the studies of digit-series memory and autonomic activity, a second task was introduced to verify that the demands placed on processing capacity increased with each digit heard and decreased with each digit reported. To increase the difficulty of the task, subjects were required to add 1 to each digit before repeating. In addition to the memory task, subjects were asked to watch a display that rapidly presented a series of single letters. After they had given the last digit of their response, they were asked if the letter K had been presented on the display. Sometimes it appeared; other times it was absent. If the K was presented, it occurred only once in one of five selected positions: (1) early in the presentation of the series, (2) near the end of the presentation, (3) in the pause in the middle, (4) early in the subject's response, or (5) as the subject was completing his report of all digits. Figure 8.4 shows both the structure of a single trial and some results from that experiment. Errors in the detection task varied directly with the load on short-term memory at the moment the target appeared. Since subjects were asked to perform the memory task correctly at all costs, the detection task suffered while memory performance was maintained. The brain's capacity to process simultaneously more than one stream of information is strictly limited.

The neural basis of selective attention can be examined by studying the response of the brain to the stimuli presented in two tasks. Investigations of these processes in recent years have examined either electroencephalographic or single-cell responses to single stimuli at various sites within the nervous system. Evidence of differential treatment of stimuli to the primary and secondary tasks is clear in at least certain structures of the nervous system.

Figure 8.4. *Information-processing load.* When subjects are required to listen to four digits, add one to each of the digits, and then report the transformed string, pupil diameter seems to reflect the level of mental activity necessary at each stage of the task. The limited capacity of the human brain as an information processor is shown by a parallel decrement in the ability of the subject to simultaneously perform a detection task. For details, refer to the text. (From Kahneman, D., Beatty, J., & Pollack, I. Perceptual deficit during a mental task. *Science,* 1967, **157,** 218–219. Copyright 1967 by the American Association for the Advancement of Science. Used by permission.)

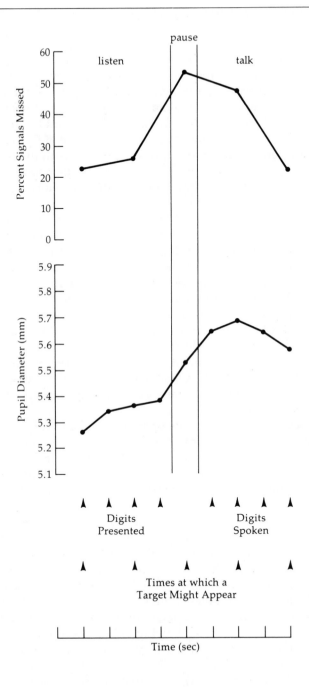

Peripheral Gating of Sensory Information

Selective-attentional mechanisms may function either by facilitating the selected sensory message or by simultaneously rejecting all other signals. Conceivably, the selective-attentional mechanisms might operate in both ways. The fundamental problems for the neuropsychological study of attention have been to identify and locate such attentional processes within the nervous system. Because of the relative simplicity of most peripheral nervous tissue compared with the central nervous system, many investigations have focused on the possibility of attentional control of sensory information at the receptor organ or within the first few relays of the sensory systems.

Certainly there is control of sensory information outside the central nervous system, if the mechanical structure of the sensory organs is to be considered. In vision, for example, the pattern of sensory information that falls on the retina is determined by the position of the eye. By controlling eye position, the brain selects from the possible visual stimuli present those stimuli that will receive visual processing. The eyes turn toward an unexpected stimulus as part of the orienting reflex. Further, in controlling accommodation and convergence, the distance from the eye at which objects will be in focus is determined. Mechanical adjustments in vision can serve selective-attentional functions. But such adjustments are gross and cannot account for the subtler phenomena that are critical to the understanding of selective attention in man.

Similar mechanical adjustments operate in the auditory system, but their connections with the processes of selective attention are less well established. Localization is less accurate in audition than in vision. Nonetheless, postural adjustments play a role in enhancing the reception of auditory signals, at least under extreme situations, as when one strains to attend to a speaker heard faintly in the distance.

More interesting in its possible connection with attention is the system of muscles in the middle ear that appear to function to protect the delicate inner ear from excessive stimulation. When activated, the middle-ear muscles impede the movement of the ossicles connecting outer and inner ear and reduce the amplitude of their vibrations by as much as 60 or 70 to 1. The middle-ear muscles are activated reflexively during chewing and swallowing, apparently to reduce the effects of these mechanical disturbances on hearing. Middle-ear muscles also contract immediately preceding each utterance of speech. But whether the middle-ear muscles are used for more than reflexive control of sound intensity is debatable indeed. They could be activated to suppress all incoming auditory information when attention is directed toward another of the sensory modalities such as vision or touch, but such a function has not been firmly established.

Whereas peripheral adjustments certainly can affect the selection and perhaps the intensity of incoming sensory signals, they cannot by themselves account for the complex selective processes that characterize human thought and behavior. Where within the nervous system do selective processes occur?

It is possible that complex decision processes in the thalamus or cortex could act to gate sensory information as it enters the sensory systems. Although the bulk of the nerve fibers connecting ear or eye to brain are afferent, or sensory, pathways, carrying information from the sense organs to more central structures, some efferent fibers carry information in the reverse direction, from the brain to the sense organs. The efferent fibers may serve to control the sensory information that the brain receives. Figure 8.5 shows the efferent and afferent connections for the auditory system. It has been postulated that efferent fibers are inhibitory and serve to gate sensory information that is not centrally attended to at that moment. But while the gating control function of the efferent fibers in attention is often mentioned, little direct evidence exists at present that supports this claim. There is, however, little question that these efferent fibers act to modulate sensory input. The question is whether this control is utilized in selective attention.

Hernandez-Peon and his coworkers in 1956 provided the first tentative, and now often-cited, evidence that attentional suppression of sensory information does take place peripherally. They recorded evoked responses to auditory clicks from the first sensory nucleus of the auditory system in the waking cat. The evoked potentials within the cochlear nucleus were significantly reduced in magnitude when the cat was shown a mouse behind a glass. Hernandez-Peon reasoned that the cat switched its attention away from auditory stimuli to the more interesting visual stimulus, but his conclusions appear to have been premature. The reduction in the response to clicks in the cochlear nucleus was later discovered by Worden and his colleagues not to be due to centrifugal efferent control at all. If the experiment is repeated using earphones instead of a speaker in the animal's cage, no reduction in the evoked response is seen. The changes originally reported are due entirely to the changes in the position of the cat's head and ears that occur when he orients to the mouse. Subsequent investigations have disclosed no change in the response of the lower sensory nuclei to sensory signals as shifts in attention occur.

This finding is consistent with recent behavioral findings concerning attentional processes in humans. Some years ago, Broadbent reported that, when subjects were instructed to attend to one of two simultaneously presented auditory messages and repeat the message

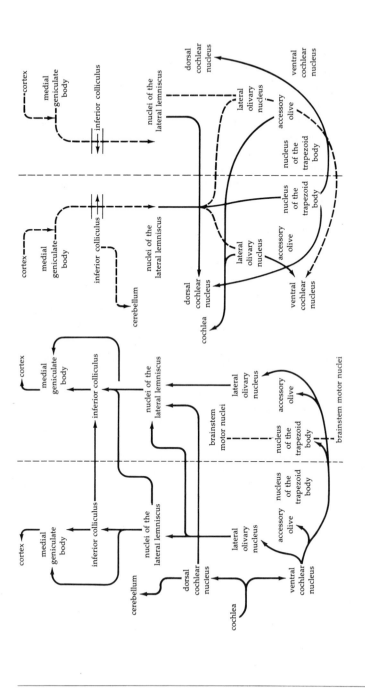

Figure 8.5. *Afferent and efferent connections in the auditory system.* Efferent pathways appear in all major mammalian sensory systems. Here, the afferent channels bringing auditory information to the cortex are shown on the left, and the corresponding efferent pathways are indicated on the right. No evidence yet exists to link these efferent pathways with the control of selective attention. (From Whitfield, I. C. *The Auditory Pathway*, Edward Arnold Publishers Ltd., London, 1967, p. 12. Used by permission.)

heard on the attended channel, most of the information in the ignored message was lost. A "channel" is the defining characteristic for one of the messages. People are able to track a channel by location of the sound source (right or left ear, for example), by voice quality (male or female), and by other similar characteristics. Subjects remember little or nothing of the rejected message. Switches from English to French and back again on the ignored channel are not noticed, nor is a change from normal to inverted speech recalled.

The evidence presented above would be compatible with the use of peripheral gating mechanisms for the unwanted channel. However, other data indicate that information in the rejected channel is fully processed and rejected centrally only after all analysis is completed. The semantic content of the ignored message is processed but, under most conditions, not allowed access to memory and response mechanisms. Although the rejected channel is normally ignored, the subject is likely to attend to it if his name is presented. Similarly, when subjects are instructed to attend to one ear but the content of the messages is occasionally switched between ears, listeners often follow the message to the other ear for a few words before returning to the proper channel. This suggests that sensory information is not peripherally gated but rather is fully processed before final rejection at high levels within the brain.

Other evidence from the study of lower species converges on this same conclusion. Wickelgren, for example, measured the evoked response to auditory stimuli throughout the brain over a large range of arousal conditions, from sleeping to fully alerted. The evoked responses recorded at the lower auditory stations—including the cochlear nucleus, the superior olivary nucleus, and the inferior colliculus—showed little alteration through the various conditions of arousal. However, auditory responses in the most central portions of the brain—the thalamus (medial geniculate nucleus) and cortex—changed dramatically with the animal's condition. The failure to find changes in the evoked responses low in the brain to large arousal shifts suggests that these centers would also show little differential response to ordinary changes in attention.

Cortical Evoked Responses and Attention in Man

A number of studies in the last decade have examined changes that take place, under a variety of conditions, in the cortical evoked response in man. These cortical responses to stimuli show extreme lability in their form, with considerable variation in both amplitude and latency. The largest waves occur between 75 and 500 msec following the presentation of the stimulus. These waves appear to be enhanced during conditions of heightened arousal and, perhaps, show differential shifts in selective attention.

Haider, Spong, and Lindsley provided solid evidence indicating that these cerebral events change, as does behavior, with shifts in arousal level. Subjects were placed in a vigilance situation, where they were required to watch for signals over a sustained period. Under these conditions, performance deteriorates as the subject becomes drowsy and inattentive, a common problem in watchkeeping tasks. For 80 to 100 minutes, subjects watched a light that flashed 110 times in each 5-minute period. Ten of those flashes were dimmer than the rest. The subject was to signal each time a dim flash appeared. EEG was recorded and the evoked response was computed separately for the bright flashes in each 5-minute period and for the dim flashes over the whole session. Cortical responses to the dim flashes were separated into detected and undetected stimuli. The evoked responses to the bright light were used to estimate arousal during each segment of the task. Figure 8.6 shows quite clearly a decrease in evoked-response amplitude as the task progressed. The detection performances of the subjects also deteriorated as time passed. Arousal and detection behavior appear to be correlated here.

When the evoked responses to the target stimuli are computed separately for hits and misses, a similar pattern develops (see Figure 8.7). The evoked response is larger to stimuli that are correctly identified as dim than to undetected signal stimuli. Detection performance may depend upon moment-by-moment variations in arousal and attention.

Cortical evoked potentials also are reduced for unattended stimuli in a selective-attention task, although the methodology and interpretation of the selective-attention experiments are still an issue of vigorous debate. One of the best experiments designed to test this hypothesis was reported by Donchin and Cohen, who measured the evoked responses to two kinds of visual stimuli when subjects were instructed to attend to one stimulus or the other. Subjects watched a screen on which appeared one of two forms, a disc or a star. The figures alternated randomly in time so that the exact moment of transition could not be anticipated. Concurrently, light flashes were randomly superimposed on the background. Subjects were asked to press a button either when the figures changed or when a flash occurred. The evoked response to the flashes was much larger when the subject attended to the flashes than when he attended to the figures. Since the time of presentation of the flashes and the figure changes was random, changes in general arousal are unlikely to mediate these effects. If the

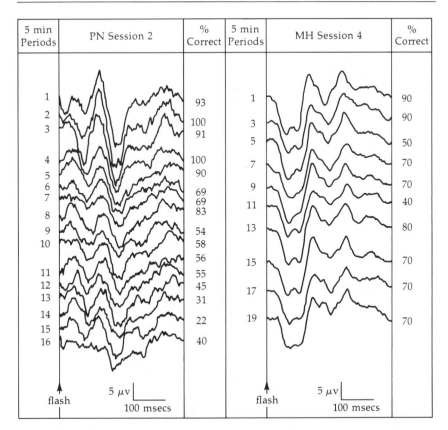

5 min Periods	PN Session 2	% Correct	5 min Periods	MH Session 4	% Correct
1		93	1		90
2		100	3		90
3		91	5		50
4		100	7		70
5		90			
6		69	9		70
7		69	11		40
8		83			
9		54	13		80
10		58			
		56	15		70
11		55			
12		45	17		70
13		31			
14		22	19		70
15					
16		40			

flash   5 μv   100 msecs   flash   5 μv   100 msecs

Figure 8.6. *Averaged evoked responses for 11 nonsignal stimuli presented in successive 5-minute segments of a vigilance task.* Decreases in evoked-response amplitude appear to be related to the efficiency of signal detection (indicated as percent correct) for two different subjects (PNO and MH). See text for further details. (From Haider, M., Spong, F., & Lindsley, D. Attention, vigilance, and cortical evoked-potentials in humans. *Science*, 1964, **145,** 180–182. Copyright 1964 by the American Association for the Advancement of Science. Used by permission.)

sequence were predictable, then the subject could ready himself for the delivery of the critical stimulus. These results suggest a central correlate of selective-attentional processes in man.

Momentary shifts in arousal occur in a task situation if the moment at which effort is required is known exactly. Davis, for example, measured the cortical evoked response to auditory stimuli in an auditory-discrimination task. Subjects listened to a sequence of four tones, each separated by 2.5 seconds. The first tone was a low-pitched warning signal. The second was a high-pitched tone that served as a

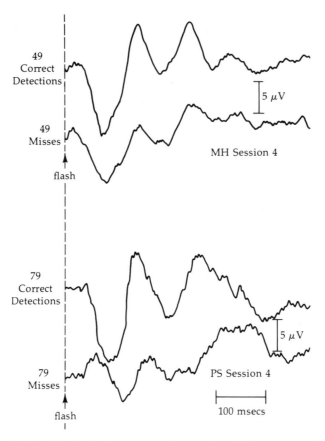

Figure 8.7. *Evoked responses.* Averaged evoked responses for successfully detected signals appear larger than the responses evoked by nondetected stimuli in a vigilance task for two subjects (MH and PS). Both the evoked response and detection performance may be related to the momentary level of activation or attention. (From Haider, M., et al. Attention, vigilance, and cortical evoked-potential in humans. *Science,* 1964, **145,** 182. Copyright 1964 by the American Association for the Advancement of Science. Used by permission.)

standard for judgment when a discrimination was required. The third, the test signal, was either slightly louder or softer than the standard. The fourth tone was like the second and served as a control for shifts of arousal throughout the trial. Figure 8.8 shows a typical pattern of evoked responses. When the subject was not attending to the series but instead was reading a magazine as the tones were presented, little difference in the evoked responses appeared. When he was asked to make a sensory discrimination, however, the evoked response to the critical stimulus increased in size. This augmentation of the cortical

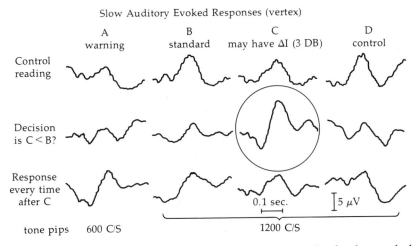

Figure 8.8. *Evoked responses and attention.* The amplitude of an evoked response appears to be augmented when a subject is required to process information contained in the signal. Here, the evoked response indicated by the circle shows this effect. See the text for further explanation. (From Davis, H. Enhancement of evoked cortical potentials in humans related to a task requiring a decision. *Science,* 1964, **145,** 183. Copyright 1964 by the American Association for the Advancement of Science. Used by permission.)

response to the stimulus depended upon making the judgment of louder or softer by pressing a button. No augmentation occurred when the subject was simply instructed to press the button every time the third tone sounded, indicating that the presence of a motor response was not in itself sufficient to increase evoked-response amplitude. Enhancement of the evoked response seems to reflect a momentary mobilization of attention to accomplish a difficult sensory task.

Summary

The term "attention" refers to two important processes that often occur simultaneously: (1) an intensive process, which is related to the information-processing capacity of the brain; and (2) a selective process, which determines which information from the vast amount present at the receptors will receive full processing.

Both processes are seen in the orienting reflex. Pavlov conceived of the orienting reflex, or "what-is-it" reflex, as a neuronal mechanism having as its adequate stimulus a novel event and as its response a constellation of arousal and information-gathering processes. The intensive dimension of the orienting reflex is shown by changes in central and autonomic processes reflecting arousal—that is, by pupillary dilation, vasodilation of the extracranial vasculature and vasoconstriction elsewhere in the body, activation of the galvanic skin response, increased muscle tension, EEG activation, and cardiac and respiratory changes. Selective aspects are seen in the orientation of the animal to the novel stimulus and the inhibition of ongoing behaviors. Stimuli capable of eliciting an orienting reflex are usually novel, intense, or meaningful. Under suitable conditions, verbal signals yield an orienting reflex in man.

Physiological changes occurring in the orienting reflex closely resemble the patterns of activation when informational demand is placed on the nervous system under nonorienting conditions. For example, pupillary dilation, cardiac change, and galvanic skin responses vary with demands placed on information-processing capacity in a short-term memory task. Both situations require the use of the brain's capacity to process information.

Central reflections of the intensification processes include cortical desynchronization and negative shifts in cortical polarization. The contingent negative variation (CNV) accompanies periods of readiness in a reaction-time task. The size of the CNV is related to the probability that the subject must perform and to the attentional demands the task places on the subject. Larger CNVs are associated with accurate sensory judgments. Investigations of attentional processes in animals have revealed alterations of aggregated cellular firing that occur in similar circumstances. Novel or meaningful stimuli trigger increased discharges in the association areas of the cat's cortex and, presumably, elsewhere. These changes together reflect momentary central and peripheral activation in response to increased demands for information processing and, possibly, for action.

Selective processes of attention appear to be mediated high within the nervous system, although mechanical components of the orienting response also serve to direct the animal toward relevant environmental stimuli. Early reports of gating information at the level of the receptors or at the lower sensory nuclei have been disconfirmed. Only the most central portions of the nervous system seem to alter their responses to stimuli on the basis of attentional factors.

The cortical evoked response in man reflects the simultaneous activation of a population of single cells within the vicinity of the recording electrode. The evoked response changes with attentional demands and appears in some instances to show selectivity.

Understanding the attentional processes, in both their intensive and selective aspects, is crucial to understanding the behavior of organisms. Current evidence suggests that attentional processes involve the highest structures within the nervous system and are fundamental to the processing of information by the brain.

Chapter 9

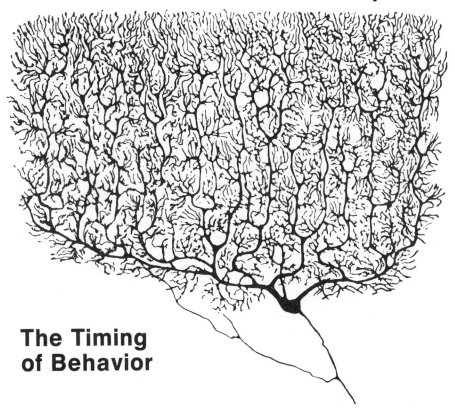

The Timing
of Behavior

Behavior always takes place in a specific context of other behaviors, each act both following and preceding other actions. This sequence is the temporal context of behavior, the study of which constitutes one of psychology's most important problems.

Psychologists have attempted to avoid the question of temporal order by concentrating on a very simple class of behaviors—unitary, stimulus-elicited responses. "Unitary" refers to a piece of behavior that can be construed to be a single event, or response, as defined in the experimental situation. "Stimulus-elicited" implies that the timing of the action relative to other behaviors of the organism is not important, since the behavior occurs in response to the stimulus. Eliciting stimuli can be simple. In classical conditioning, for example, the stimulus is often a signal such as a bell. But, for our analysis, other, more complicated events also constitute response-eliciting stimuli. Subjects may be asked to identify words as members of a word class, to predict the occurrence of an event in the future, or to answer a question with a "yes" or a "no." None of these situations demands temporally complex behavior from the subject. The problem of serial order and timing is avoided by examining "single" behaviors that subjects reliably produce in response to a manipulation by the experimenter.

Two questions are posed here. First, are any behaviors truly unitary? Even the simplest pieces of behavior, the most elemental of actions, involve a sequence of events. Just to say a word demands the movement of several muscle groups in a predefined order. The nervous system must initiate those movements in a precisely defined way to produce an intelligible bit of speech. So, at one level of analysis, even simple actions are sequential; but, at a higher level, it is sensible to think of a single word as a unitary response. In the context of a conversation, for example, single words seem to function as reasonably unitary events. The definition of "unitary" thus depends very much upon the level of analysis. In turn, the choice of the appropriate level of analysis depends upon the nature and the scope of the questions being asked. For example, to the mathematician programming a computer, the addition of two quantities is a unitary event. But, to the engineer building the computer, "addition" is the term for a complex series of precisely ordered electronic events. So it is with human behavior. Events that appear unitary at one level of analysis are sequential at a more molecular level. Although many of our most interesting activities can reasonably be described as single events, we must eventually come to grips with the temporal organization of our own behaviors.

The second question revolves around the words "stimulus-elicited." Are any of our interesting behaviors stimulus-elicited? Certainly some are. We leave an intersection when the traffic light turns green. We answer questions when asked. We turn our heads when our names are called. If it makes sense to call these environmental events stimuli, then we are certainly capable of responding to stimuli. The timing of such behaviors is relatively independent of factors within us and heavily dependent upon the timing of environmental events. In this sense, we function as asynchronous information processors, providing appropriate responses as they are called for by the environment. Asynchronous processors depend primarily upon external events to organize their behavior in time.

Behaviors do not have to be unitary to be stimulus-elicited. When you are asked about your activities of the previous evening, the initiation of your response is obviously stimulus-dependent. You find yourself saying things that you would never say unless someone had asked. But the response is not in any sense unitary; it is a complex series of words, properly chosen and produced to fit temporal orders prescribed by linguistic rules and arranged to convey the complex information that you wish to communicate. Clearly, nonunitary responses can be triggered by external stimuli (which, of course, may possess complex temporal order themselves).

Psychology has made relatively little progress in understanding complicated, internally sequenced behaviors, largely because the sheer complexity and variability of such behaviors are so great.

Temporally Ordered Behaviors

In contrast to the unitary behaviors discussed above, the units of a complicated, temporally ordered behavior such as language do not depend upon a series of external stimulus events to trigger their release. Most, if not all, of the temporal order is provided by the behaving organism itself. Since the behavior is much more complicated, it is also more difficult to understand.

The first theory proposed to explain temporally ordered behavior was a simple extension of the stimulus-dependent unitary-response theories. Serially organized behavior could be viewed as a series of unitary responses, with each unit being both a response to the previous unit and a stimulus for the subsequent unit. This is the response-chaining hypothesis. The rule for linking sequential units is learned association. A sentence, according to the response-chaining hypothesis, is nothing more than a series of words linked reflexively to each other. The theory has to its credit apparent conceptual simplicity; however, it is almost certainly wrong. Karl Lashley provided some of the most convincing criticisms of this simplistic view, and much of the following discussion is based on Lashley's analysis.

Lashley criticized the response-chaining theories on several grounds. First, there exists no unique ordering among words or even among parts of words. The series of muscular movements necessary to produce the word "right" are exactly the reverse of those needed to say the word "tire." Each motor act cannot lead exactly and reliably to another when each act occurs in virtually every order in ordinary speech. Proponents of the chaining theories initially phrased their arguments in terms of motor movements, and similar arguments have been made at higher levels of analysis. What word naturally and uniquely follows the word "right"? Such a question is clearly unanswerable, and yet must be answered if a chaining theory is to be plausible. Even a chaining theory that allows association between words more remote than immediate neighbors in the sentence cannot account for the production of speech. Lashley argued that the meaning of the sentence—the information that is to be transmitted—must exist in some other form in the brain. The interaction of the deeper representation, or meaning, with the rules of grammar and vocabulary produces intelligent, serially ordered speech. Lashley identifies a family of theories necessary for explaining ordered behavior. Such theories are very complex, since they simultaneously involve many levels of analysis, and finding the particular theory is therefore difficult.

Brain Mechanisms and the Serial Order of Behavior

Since timing is such an important part of the behavior of the animal, it is not surprising to find the temporal control of behavior widely distributed throughout the nervous system. Even the simple spinal cord has some temporal organization in its reflexive organization (see Chapter 6). Under the proper conditions, stimulation of the feet in a spinal animal can produce rhythmic movement, or reflex stepping, that is mediated entirely within the spinal cord. The spinal mechanisms are not the only neural circuits involved in producing serial movements such as normal walking, but they do make some contribution to the temporal ordering of these movements.

Temporal patterns are important in perception, although perhaps in a less obvious way than in behavior. Neurophysiologically, temporal transformations of sensory signals are apparent in several areas of the brain but most prominently in the thalamus. Recurrent inhibitory thalamic circuits relay a series of waves of activity to the cortex in response to a single brief sensory stimulus. Perceptually, the temporal nature of perception becomes apparent under special circumstances. For example, if a single square is briefly presented to an observer and followed some 100 msec later by two adjacent squares, only the latter stimuli will be consciously perceived, as if the perception of the first square was erased before it could be properly formed. This phenomenon is termed "backward visual masking," because the effect of the masking (second) stimulus seems to operate backward in time (which, of course, is not the case). Interestingly enough, the simple reaction time to the first stimulus remains unaltered by the presence of the mask; the observer responds to the first stimulus in the same amount of time whether or not the stimulus is consciously perceived. A somewhat similar phenomenon occurs when a single stimulus is briefly presented in a series of adjacent positions. If the presentation is timed properly, the series of discrete stimuli is transformed into the perception of a single stimulus that moves through space. This is the phenomenon of "apparent motion." In both these cases, the temporal patterns of stimulus presentation are crucially important in determining the resulting perception. Temporal factors are clearly of importance in perception.

Elsewhere in the brain, structures act to integrate or unify behavior in time. Temporal integration is most easily seen in motor structures, where the linkages between brain function and behavior are closest. For example, the cerebellum functions to guide, correct, and smooth the sequences of muscular contractions that together constitute bodily movements. It performs highly complex functions of temporal ordering. Temporal-sequencing mechanisms are also activated by central-motor-command units.

Karl Pribram and his associates have recently shown evidence for global temporal mechanisms in the frontal lobes of the primate brain. Pribram has for many years studied the behavior of monkeys with frontal-lobe lesions. These animals have been reported to show very poor short-term memory. The apparent failure to recall recent events comes not from an impaired memory mechanism but rather from a failure to properly attend to and encode the stimuli necessary to carry out the task. Pribram argues specifically that a function of the frontal cortex is to break the stream of sensation that constantly impinges on the animal into a series of discrete events. If Pribram is correct, the frontal cortex separates sensory input into a temporally ordered sequence of sensory events so that sensory information can take on meaning for the animal. The process of parsing sensory information aids information processing in much the same way as properly parsing a sentence aids in decoding its meaning. Parsing presumably operates through pathways linking the frontal cortex with the various sensory cortices. Electrical stimulation of the frontal cortex alters the electrically recorded responses of sensory cortex to sensory signals.

Normal animals can learn a delayed-alternation task, which can be thought of as a short-term memory problem requiring the animal to alternate in his choice of two responses, waiting a fixed amount of time between responses. Monkeys learn a right-left alternation task with a 5-second delay between responses in approximately 400 trials. But monkeys with frontal-lobe damage will not learn to perform correctly even if given 1000 trials of training. If frontally damaged animals cannot easily parse sensory input into reasonable chunks of experience, then they would be lost when trying to deal with a short-term memory problem. However, if the parsing of the experience is done for the animal by the experimenter, then frontally damaged animals learn as quickly as normal animals. For example, instead of presenting the animal with a series of choices every 5 seconds to which the animal is to respond R-L-R-L-R and so on, Pribram broke the sequence into a series of couplets, each separated by 15 seconds. Thus, the monkey would first respond R, and 5 seconds later the correct response would be L. Fifteen seconds would pass before the next two trials were presented. In this procedure, the stream of sensory input was broken into meaningful units by the task, not by the animal. Animals with frontal-lobe damage show the ability to remember discrete events but have a great deal of difficulty in imposing a proper serial order on a series of events occurring in the world about them. Such evidence suggests that the frontal cortex may be important in providing a serial order in perception.

Measuring Time

Often, more is required of an organism than simply to order events or behaviors in time. The absolute spacing of events in the flow of time can be very important. It means more to say "I'll meet you in 20 minutes" than to say "I'll see you later." The first statement measures the distance of events from each other in time; the second merely orders events.

Clocks are needed to measure time. Any physical event can be used as a clock, provided that it can be exactly repeated as many times as necessary. Thus, people can measure time approximately by counting slowly to themselves or employing similar strategies. Better clocks are more exactly repeatable. If any repeating physical process can be used as a clock, then the question is which of all the potential clocks are actually used. Are there rhythms in man that function as clocks to regulate behavior?

A biological clock should be relatively regular and independent of the events that it will be used to measure. Moreover, the period of the clock—the time necessary to execute completely one occurrence of the repeatable process—should be appropriate to the time scale of the behavior being regulated. The need for an appropriate time scale immediately suggests that there should be more than one biological clock. A clock that is appropriate for timing the daily cycle of sleep and waking would not be very useful for measuing the small intervals that are involved in the generation of speech. The first task requires a slowly changing clock (or a very large counting device); the second task requires a clock with a very short period.

Fast Clocks in Crabs and Lobsters

Since the vertebrate nervous system is extremely resistant to analysis at its higher, controlling levels, studying simpler nervous systems can help to provide answers to many important questions.

Often, such answers, first demonstrated in research on invertebrates, have later been found to hold true in higher forms. Thus, it is of more than passing interest to note that fast biological clocks, capable of controlling rhythmic behaviors, have been found in lobsters and hermit crabs.

Mendelson has reported the existence of single cells that act as clocks to control the rhythmic gill bailer movements in lobsters and hermit crabs. The gill bailer is directly controlled by 11 motor neurons, which are divided into two groups—one raising and the other lowering the paddle-like appendage. Normally, the two groups of neurons are alternately activated to produce an up-and-down movement of the bailer that forces water through the animal's gill chambers.

The motor neurons that directly control the two muscle groups of the bailer are themselves controlled by a very special cell, which Mendelson simply calls an oscillator. The oscillator is a small cell that shows no spike activity of its own. Apparently, the oscillator, like some other very small cells in the nervous system, is not large enough to need a spiking mechanism for internal communication. The electrical activity of the oscillator cell is shown in Figure 9.1. Notice that the cell regularly shifts between relative hyperpolarization and depolarization. The timing of the waves of polarization is exactly the same as that of the movements of the animal's bailer. These electrical events are not driven by rhythmic activity of neurons elsewhere in the nervous system. Instead, they directly govern the discharge of the 11 motor neurons. If the oscillator is artificially depolarized by a stimulating microelectrode, all activity in the levitator muscles stops while the motor neurons controlling the depressor muscles discharge. When the oscillator is hyperpolarized, exactly the opposite pattern appears. If the oscillator is allowed to run freely again, rhythmically changing its polarity, normal movements of the gill bailer occur.

Mendelson has isolated in this single neuron the clock responsible for timing a particular behavior. However, the behavior is not completely independent of activity elsewhere in the nervous system. The oscillator itself is regulated, but not paced, by the output of more central command interneurons. Excitatory command neurons synapse on the oscillator, effectively activating the neuron. Increasing excitatory input speeds the oscillator and renders the movements of the bailer more definite. Therefore, by controlling the discharge rate in the command fiber, the nervous system can activate and set the rate of the biological clock, which, in turn, directly controls the rhythmic, life-giving movement of the bailer.

The intracellular mechanism by which the clock generates the periodic oscillations is not known. It probably involves a metabolically driven pump that moves an ion such as sodium across the membrane to

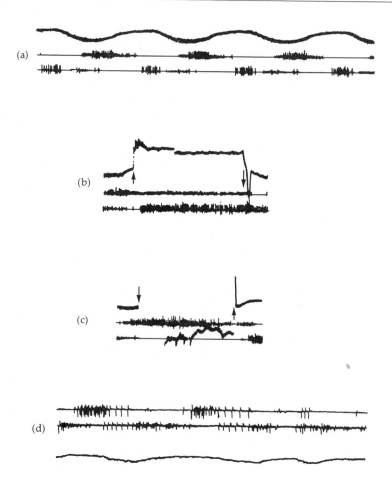

Figure 9.1.   *The activity of a fast clock in the nervous system of the lobster.*   (a) The upper trace shows the rhythmic intracellular potentials in the oscillator cell of the lobster. Beneath it are simultaneously obtained records from the two branches of motor neurons that the oscillator cell controls. Notice that the polarization of the oscillator cell determines which of the two muscle systems is activated. (b) When the oscillator cell is artificially depolarized, only one of the muscle groups is activated. (c) If the oscillator cell is hyperpolarized, the reverse pattern of motor activity is observed. The pattern of motor activity depends upon the polarization of the oscillator. (From Mendelson, M. Oscillator neurons in crustacean ganglia. *Science*, 1971, **171**, 1171. Copyright 1971 by the American Association for the Advancement of Science. Used by permission.)

produce periodic depolarization. That the rate of oscillation is very sensitive to the amount of available oxygen implies an active mechanism. A single cell can serve the function of a clock in the invertebrate's primitive nervous system.

Fast Clocks in Man

Biological clocks similar to those seen in lower animals probably exist in man. Certain kinds of internal fast clocks are well known and well studied. One example is the system controlling heartbeat in the cardiac muscle. Heartbeat is generated by cells within the heart itself. Its rate, however, may be modified by the activity of neurons within the central nervous system. Accurate clocks must also exist within the brain to control the timing of speech and other complex motor acts, but the nature of these neuronal mechanisms is not known.

Similarly, our sense of momentary time—that is, the duration of short events—probably depends upon biological clocks. These clocks appear to be sensitive to changes in metabolic rate. Because the rate of metabolism, in turn, depends partially upon temperature, patients with fevers consistently underestimate short time intervals. If asked to mark a 5-second interval, they will signal its passing in less than 5 seconds. The underestimation of time implies that the responsible biological clock is running faster than normal during fever. The same patients, by the way, can estimate 5 seconds more accurately when the fever passes.

The effect of body temperature on time estimation is not limited to the ill. Normal subjects also show similar effects when their body temperatures are artificially raised by a diathermy machine. Even normal daily fluctuations of body temperature affect time estimation. Subjects asked to indicate the end of a short interval will signal sooner when they are at their own daily peak temperature. Conversely, when the body temperature is naturally low, the estimate of a short interval is lengthened.

Timing in Perception

Timing is ordinarily discussed in terms of behavior marked by movement or action. In typing, for example, many groups of muscles must act in a precise order if the thoughts of the writer are to be understood. While behavior often seems discrete and ordered, perception seems to be either instantaneous or continuous. However, some recent evidence suggests that perception might not be continuous. Timing and sequencing of neural activity may be as important in perception as it is in action.

C. T. White and his colleagues performed an interesting series of experiments to study the ability of subjects to estimate the number of times a light flashed. The light flickered too fast for each flash to be counted. Thus, when the light was presented 14 times at 33-msec intervals, subjects reported seeing only four distinct flashes. What is important is not the number of flashes actually presented but the length of time the light was flashing. Subjects report seeing one flash for each 0.1 second (100 msec) during which the light flickered. If the same 14 flashes were presented more slowly so that the whole train of flashes took 0.6 second to present, subjects would say that they saw six flashes (one flash for each 0.1 second of flickering light). This finding suggests that perception is packaged into temporal units, each about 100 msec in duration. Extra flashes occurring within a 100-msec period are simply not perceived.

Harter and White have presented evidence suggesting that the parsing of a flash train into a sequence of observed flashes depends upon the cyclic changes in cortical excitability established by the first flash. (See Figure 9.2.) These changes and the excitability cycles to which they give rise may have as their basis a clocklike inhibitory-phasing mechanism in the thalamus. The thalamic inhibitory mechanism gives rise to a series of waves of electrical activity in the cortex (seen as late waves in the cortical evoked potential). The timing of these cortical waves is closely related to the periods in which additional percepts in the train of flashes are experienced. Flashes presented within an excitability cycle are grouped into a single perceptual unit in the brain and reported by the subjects as such. Thus, the thalamic mechanism responsible for the excitability cycles may function as a clock that controls the perception of sensory information.

Slow Clocks with Circadian Rhythms

It is not likely that the fast clocks used in timing perception or speech are also employed to control slower processes within the body. Slower events seem to be governed by their own clocks, which have periods more suitable to the time scale on which these events occur. Particularly important are the circadian rhythms, a term proposed by Halberg in 1959 to describe events having a time period of about one day (from the Latin *circa dies*). Circadian rhythms characterize many of the important biological functions of organisms.

Since many of the daily bodily rhythms are internally controlled by bodily clocks, moving between time zones can be upsetting, particularly when the transition is rapid and the necessary temporal adjustments are large. Wiley Post, the long-distance aviator, was the first to notice that a quick change between time zones is behaviorally disruptive. Particularly susceptible to time-shift disorganization are activity patterns such as the sleep-wakefulness cycle. The disruptive effects are accentuated in modern aircraft on intercontinental east-west flights. In relatively short periods of time, night changes into day, and vice versa. By studying the disruption of the normal temporal context,

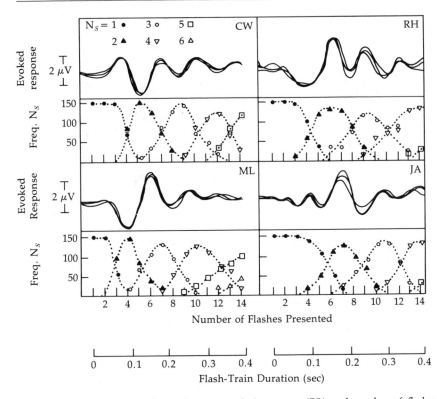

Figure 9.2. *The relation between evoked response (ER) and number of flashes perceived.* Beneath each ER, the number of times a flash train was perceived as a particular number of flashes (Ns) by the duration of the flash train for four different observers is shown. (From Harter, M. R., & White, C. Perceived number and evoked cortical potentials. *Science,* 1967, **156,** 407. Copyright 1967 by the American Association for the Advancement of Science. Used by permission.)

something may be learned of the circadian clocks and the processes they control.

Many interesting bodily events show a circadian periodicity. Of these, the sleep-wakefulness, or activity, cycle is the most obvious and the most often studied. Coupled with these changes in activity are alterations of other important bodily systems. Body temperature varies regularly throughout the day. Core temperature is highest during the waking hours and reaches a minimum during sleep at night. Peak temperature usually coincides with the daily period of maximal mental and physical efficiency. The timing of peak temperature differs among people, with early risers tending to show their thermal peak early in the day. The physiological basis underlying such individual differences is not known.

Biochemical systems also exhibit circadian rhythms. Regular oscillations appear in the excretion of such biologically important substances as catecholamines, the 17-ketogenic steroids, calcium, potassium, and sodium. Some of the biochemical changes are clearly related to behavior and to shifts of the activity cycle. Adrenalin secretion, for example, peaks during the day for normal non-nocturnal animals and reaches its lowest levels during sleep.

The susceptibility of the organism to toxic agents also shows a profound circadian rhythmicity. For example, a large dose of amphetamine is ten times more likely to be lethal when given at the peak of the activity cycle in the rat than when administered at the conclusion of the active phase. Similarly, a circadian variation is seen in mice genetically predisposed to epileptic seizure in the presence of loud noise. These mice are more likely to exhibit seizure leading to death when active than when sleeping. Similarly, many human epileptics display an increased probability of seizure during the waking hours. Reactions to other psychoactive agents show similar effects. A dose of alcohol sufficient to kill 60% of the mice that were injected when active produced only 12% morbidity when administered during sleep.

The circadian activity rhythms are exceptionally stable for organisms living in normal environments. Figure 9.3 shows 24-hour activity records for two rats housed in a laboratory that was illuminated from 6 A.M. until 6 P.M. During the night, the animals were in darkness.

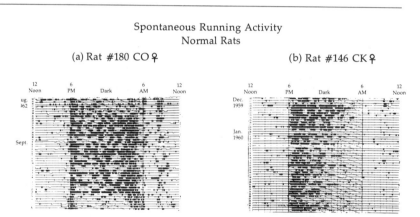

Spontaneous Running Activity
Normal Rats

(a) Rat #180 CO ♀   (b) Rat #146 CK ♀

Figure 9.3.   *Activity patterns for two normal rats in the laboratory environment.*   A thickening of the horizontal lines indicates an increase in activity. Notice both the characteristic differences in schedule between animals and the faithfulness with which each animal follows his own pattern. (From Richter, C. P. Sleep and activity: Their relation to the 24-hour clock. *Sleep and Altered States of Consciousness,* The Williams and Wilkins Company, 1967. Used by permission.)

The activity patterns of each animal were consistent from day to day. One rat began to move about immediately at the onset of darkness, whereas the activity cycle of the other began 2 hours later. During the night, these nocturnal animals were active. Housed in drum-like cages in which they could run, the rats would run as many as 4 miles each night. Toward morning, the period of inactivity began, and again each animal exhibited a characteristic time at which he terminated his activity phase.

Although activity cycles may be related to environmental stimuli, they are controlled by internal clocks. Periodic activity remains when animals are tested under conditions of constant illumination or are blind. Figure 9.4 shows the activity cycle of rats that had been surgically blinded. Notice that a periodicity still exists in the rats' behavior, but that the period is no longer exactly 24 hours, the length of a solar day. Nor is it exactly 24.8 hours, which would correspond to the period of the lunar day. Because the characteristic period varies among animals, they cannot be responding to the known geomagnetic forces. When freed of light and temperature fluctuations in the environment, the activity cycle reflects only the activity of internal circadian clocks.

The pattern of free-running motor activity devoid of environmental influence is extremely stable, as Figure 9.4 illustrates. Under laboratory conditions, the onset of circadian activation can be predicted within a few minutes of its actual occurrence. The range of characteristic periods among individual members of a species can be small indeed. For example, it deviates from 24 hours by not more than about 40 minutes for the flying squirrel. Why should activity be sequenced in exactly 24-hour intervals under more normal conditions? Environmental influences, particularly the daily changes in illumination and temperature, act to entrain the circadian rhythms of the biological clocks. Daybreak acts as a synchronizer to reset the clocks of organisms that sense its occurrence. Environmental stimuli do not impose a 24-hour rhythm upon the organism; instead, they trigger the onset of a rhythmic circadian process within the animal. Exogenous, or external, factors entrain an endogenous, or internal, rhythm. Because of the internal nature of the clocks, abrupt transitions between time zones become difficult.

Within the mammalian nervous system, there appear to be several circadian clocks, each controlling different bodily functions. The effect of environmental stimuli is to reset each of these clocks, separately correcting the small deviations from the 24-hour day inherent in such clocks. As a result, the several clocks produce an integrated and unified pattern of activity within the organism. However, when a significant alteration in the environmental entraining stimuli occurs, the multiplicity of clocks becomes evident. Various bodily processes

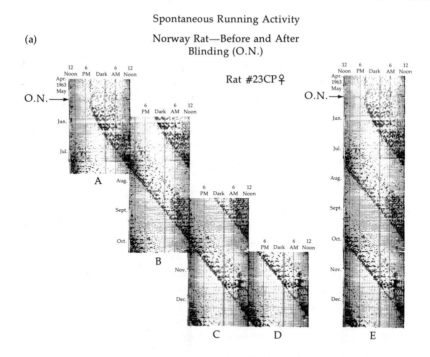

Figure 9.4. *Blinding eliminates the precise 24-hour rhythm of the rat's activity pattern.* (a) A blinded rat shows a characteristic free-running period of activity that is slightly greater than 24 hours. The graph on the left is staggered for continuity; on the right, successive days are aligned in a vertical column. (b) A rat that was blinded in January 1963. Notice the exact circadian entrainment before that date and the shift following surgery to a free-running period of less than 24 hours. (From Richter, C. P. Sleep and activity: Their relation to the 24-hour clock. *Sleep and Altered States of Consciousness*, The Williams and Wilkins Company, 1967. Used by permission.)

adjust to the new time at different rates. Not all systems are equally responsive to temporal change.

For example, in a Norwegian study, three groups of subjects attempted to live, respectively, 21-, 24-, and 27-hour days in an attempt to test the adaptability of the circadian systems. Some bodily functions adapted easily to the new schedule. Body temperature was quickly entrained. The rhythm of urinary secretion became established in less than 2 weeks. In 5 weeks, the excretion of 17-hydroxycorticosteroids had adapted to the longer or shorter days. Potassium excretion, however, remained fixed on a 24-hour rhythm. The concept of a single master circadian clock cannot account for such data. In the processes of adaptation, the organism simultaneously exhibits several different near-circadian periodicities.

Spontaneous Running Activity

(b)   Rat #224 CO ♂ WN

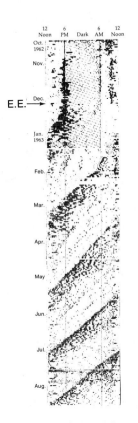
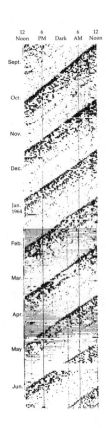

E.E.→

Similar findings are common when the period of the clock remains fixed at 24 hours but its phase or onset shifts. The time taken for different bodily systems to recover from time-zone change varies over a range of 1 to many days. For example, in a study of Air France pilots who fly from Paris to Anchorage, Alaska, it appeared that some hormonal systems remained phase-locked on Paris time, while others adapted to the local time in Alaska. In view of the temporal disintegration produced in east-west jet travel, it is not surprising to find behavioral disturbance as well. Subjective fatigue and slowed reaction time are common accompaniments to temporal stress.

A Circadian Clock in the Sea Hare

Because the mammalian brain is a complex structure composed of millions of individual neurons, researchers have attempted to find evidence of circadian rhythms in a simpler organism—one more tractable to neurophysiological study.

Felix Strumwasser has reported a series of experiments demonstrating a single neuron that acts as a circadian clock in the sea hare, a relatively primitive invertebrate about which much is known. The sea hare shows a circadian pattern in its behavior; it is active in the light portion of the day and quiescent in darkness. Activity begins near dawn and ends at dusk. The sea hare is a large invertebrate, but because its neurons are not myelinated, it is deprived of the primary mechanism utilized in vertebrates to achieve rapid communication over large distances. However, the sea hare possesses a few large fibers that transmit action potentials more quickly than do thinner, unmyelinated fibers. The large size of these key neurons results in a nervous system in which individual neurons may be visually identified and studied. Figure 9.5 shows the parietovisceral ganglion of the sea hare. Between 10 and 30 individual cells have been studied and numbered and can be readily identified in different specimens.

Using microelectrodes to record from single neurons, Strumwasser discovered a circadian rhythm in the firing of cell 3 (see Figure 9.5). Cell 3 characteristically emits bursts of spikes, which are separated by periods without action potentials. The rate of bursting increases dramatically at the expected dawn. (See Figure 9.6.) Clearly, the cell exhibits circadian behavior. Its behavior, as Figure 9.6 illustrates, represents the activity of a true cellular circadian clock. The response continues when the ganglia are removed from the animal and maintained in nutrient baths.

Cell 3 is not only able to generate circadian behavior but is also able to retain information about the temporal structure of the environment. Figures 9.7 and 9.8 show recordings made from two cells in isolation. The first recording (see Figure 9.7) was taken from an animal presented with only one light-dark cycle after a period of 1 week under constant illumination. Figure 9.8 shows the activity of another cell removed from an "experienced" animal, which had been exposed to 7 daily light-dark cycles. The cell taken from the animal with only 1 day's experience gave a high rate of bursting throughout the day, but its

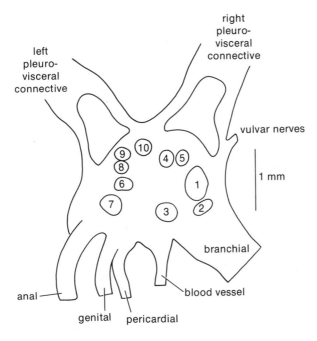

left
pleuro-
visceral
connective

right
pleuro-
visceral
connective

vulvar nerves

1 mm

branchial

anal

blood vessel

genital   pericardial

Figure 9.5. *The isolated parietovisceral ganglion of the sea hare.* Cell 3 and other clearly identifiable neurons are marked. (From Strumwasser, F. Types of information stored in single neurons. In C.A.G. Wiersma (Ed.), *Invertebrate nervous systems: Their significance for mammalian neurophysiology.* © 1967 by The University of Chicago Press. Used by permission.)

activity peaked 30 minutes after dawn. Although its behavior is poorly organized, as shown by the generally high response rate, the beginnings of a circadian pattern are present. The experienced cell demonstrated a well-developed circadian pattern of firing. Its general response rate was low, but at dawn it responded vigorously.

The oscillatory functions of these neurons must be intracellular, since the response persists in these cells in the absence of the remainder of the nervous system. The nature of the generating mechanism is not known, however. A micromolecular basis is suspected for the action of this cellular clock.

Summary

Behavior always takes place in a specific temporal context of other behaviors. The complexity of the stream of behavior is often avoided by studying stimulus-elicited, unitary responses. But re-

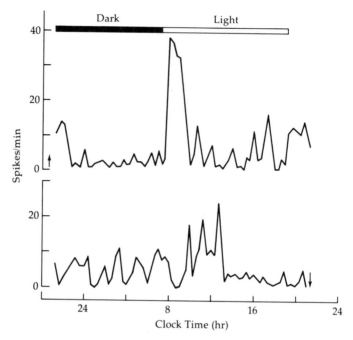

Figure 9.6. *Output of cell 3 as a function of time on two days following its removal from the animal.*   A peak of activity is seen quite clearly at dawn of the first day of recording. (From Strumwasser, F. The demonstration and manipulation of a circadian rhythm in a single neuron. In J. Aschoff (Ed.), *Circadian Clocks*, North-Holland Publishing Company, Amsterdam, 1965. Used by permission.)

sponses that are unitary at one level of analysis are temporally complex at other levels. The unity of the response is a useful hypothesis that facilitates analysis.

While many responses are stimulus-elicited, many complex behaviors are relatively independent of environmental factors and heavily dependent upon factors within the organism. Attempts to explain temporally complex behaviors as a series of chained, unitary events have been markedly unsuccessful. These difficulties are most apparent in language behavior, in which the role of internal temporal mechanisms is of obvious importance.

Problems of timing arise at every level of behavioral analysis, so it is not surprising to find that the mechanisms for the temporal control of behavior are widely distributed throughout the nervous system. Temporal organization is observed in the isolated spinal cord in the form of reflex stepping. Heart muscle contains its own timing devices to

Parabolic Burster, L/D:1, March 17

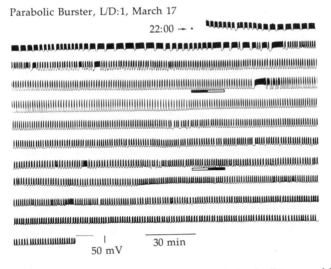

Figure 9.7. *Record of the spike activity of an isolated cell 3 removed from a sea hare exposed to 1 week of constant light, followed by one 24-hour light-dark cycle.* Circadian rhythmicity is present but very much attenuated in this temporally naive preparation. Bars indicate lights on and lights off. (From Strumwasser, F. Neurophysiological aspects of rhythms. In G. Quarton, J. Melnechuk, & F. O. Schmitt (Eds.), *The Neurosciences: A Study Program,* 1967, p. 527. Used by permission of the Rockefeller University Press.)

Parabolic Burster, L/D:7, May 4   22:00

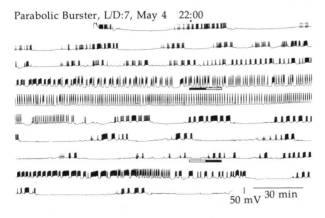

Figure 9.8. *Entrainment of circadian rhythm.* If the sea hare is exposed to seven light-dark cycles before removal of the circadian clock, more substantial entrainment of the circadian rhythm is seen in the isolated cell. (From Strumwasser, F. Neurophysiological aspects of rhythms. In G. Quarton, J. Melnechuk, & F. O. Schmitt (Eds.), *The Neurosciences: A Study Program,* 1967, p. 527. Used by permission of The Rockefeller University Press.)

regulate heartbeat. At higher levels, the cerebellum acts to guide, correct, and smooth the movements of the body in both time and space.

Mechanisms within the frontal cortex may function to parse the stream of sensory information into meaningful segments. A monkey with frontal lesions is incapable of learning a delayed-alternation task. However, a delayed-alternation task becomes possible for this monkey when the experimental situation is altered to provide the identifying temporal context that the monkey is no longer able to supply for himself. Temporal control is important in sensory as well as motor processes.

Organisms are not only able to order events in time but are also able to measure time through the use of biological clocks. Complex organisms have many such clocks, each well fitted to the function that it controls and to the periods that it must measure. A single cell, termed an oscillator, that functions as a clock has been isolated in the hermit crab and in the lobster. On command from more central structures, the cell controls the rhythmic movements of the animal's gill bailer. Although the periodicity of the movement is generated entirely by the oscillator cell, the rate of movement may be modulated by synaptic input. The oscillator cell not only orders the sequence of bailer movements; it also times the speed at which these ordered movements occur. Although the mechanism within the membrane that generates these timed potentials is not known, it appears to involve metabolic energy.

Similarly, man's sense of momentary time and the rhythmic movements of the human body may depend upon biological clocks. In man, the metabolic dependence of biological timing mechanisms is indicated by the characteristic shortening of estimated time intervals when body temperature is raised by either fever or environmental means. Evidence for fast clocks in the timing of perception indicates that perceptual events are grouped in 100-msec intervals. Perceptual grouping appears to be related to excitability cycles within the thalamocortical system.

Other bodily processes exhibit a much longer periodicity and are controlled by their own clocks, of which the circadian rhythms (of about 24 hours) are among the most common. Sleep-wakefulness, activity, body temperature, neuroendocrine activity, and even susceptibility to toxic agents show profound circadian periodicities. That separate clocks control such functions is evident from the differential time course of adaptation that the processes show following temporal disorientation.

Environmental stimuli do not impose a 24-hour rhythm on the organism. Instead, environmental stimuli, most notably light and temperature, act to synchronize, or reset, a rhythm that is intrinsic to the organism. When deprived of these environmental influences, the circadian clocks may run freely and exhibit a periodicity of about, but not exactly, 24 hours. Little is known about the biological features of the circadian clocks in man.

Whereas populations of cells may act to perform clock-like functions in their aggregated activity, in invertebrates, single cells have been isolated that possess a circadian rhythmicity. In the sea hare, a single identifiable cell controls the activity cycle and retains its clock-like features even after removal from the organism. Furthermore, this cell is capable of encoding and retaining temporal information about its environment.

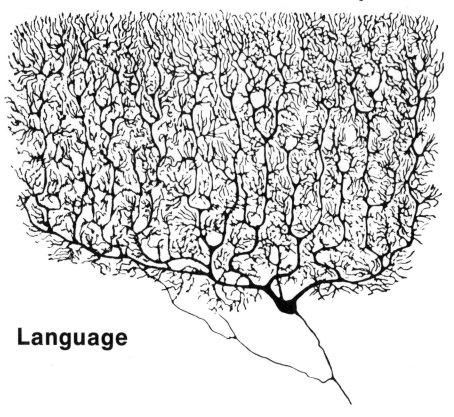

Language

The use of language is one of the most important aspects of human behavior. In all human societies, people use language to communicate in speech. Complex societies maintain a secondary coding system—written language—to further extend the possibilities of communication. Language permits the easy and flexible exchange of information, allows novel information to be expressed, permits reference to things and events that are far removed from the language users both in time and in space, and enables the efficient transfer of information across generations. Thus, human culture rests firmly on the human's use of language, and language, as we will see, depends upon specialized processes within the human brain. Language, its physiological foundations, and its evolutionary history are the subject of this chapter.

The Structure of Language

The brain processes that mediate language usage in man must be complex, since language itself is a complicated, hierarchically organized system for the representation and restructuring of information. It is useful therefore to first examine the structure of the language system without regard to brain mechanism before turning to the more difficult question of the relations between brain function and language.

The language system permits the communication of meaningful information in speech. Thus, at a minimum, language must be organized at two levels: (1) a semantic level, which is concerned with the organization of meaning, and (2) a phonological level, which involves the description of speech sounds. The set of rules necessary to translate between these two levels is the grammar of language. Notice that, in this usage, grammar is a much broader concept than the prescriptive grammar taught in elementary schools. Prescriptive grammar deals primarily with the training of particular language-usage patterns in children who already have competence in the use of the grammatical rules necessary for the production and reception of speech. In the broader conception of modern linguistics, the grammar, although currently unspecified, must be capable of accounting for all aspects of the language process. The grammar is nothing more nor less than the system of rules necessary for pairing sound with meaning.

Between the semantic and phonological level of organization is a syntactic organization that has become exceptionally important in current linguistic thought. Figure 10.1 illustrates these three levels of organization and the grammars that link them. The syntactic structure is differentiated into a surface and deep structure, following the tradition of the transformational grammarian Chomsky. The surface structure contains all information necessary for the phonological representation of information. The phonological grammar interprets the surface structure into a series of speech sounds. The deep structure contains all information necessary for semantic interpretation, which is performed by the interpretative, or semantic, component of grammar. The transformational rules relate surface to deep structure, using only the formal syntactic rules governing the structure of sentences. The transformational grammar, according to Chomsky, operates without reference to either meaning (which is provided by the semantic rules) or phonological considerations. Others question the separability of the syntactic and semantic systems, arguing that syntactic ambiguity often can be resolved through the use of semantic information. The degree of separation of syntactic and semantic components has little bearing on our primary concern, the physiological basis of language. However,

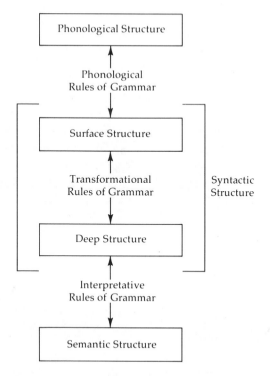

Figure 10.1. *The structure of language.*

the idea that the language system is hierarchically organized is essential to the understanding of these physiological mechanisms.

An example may help to clarify matters. Consider the spoken utterance "The ball was hit by the boy." On hearing such a sequence of speech sounds, we use the phonological component of the grammar to create a surface structure from these sounds. Absent from the surface structure is a great deal of acoustic information that is irrelevant for linguistic interpretation—for example, the pitch of the speaker's voice, a regional accent that may be evident in the spoken production, slight mispronunciations, and so on. The surface structure produced by the phonological component is a series of morphemes—linguistic units of meaningful speech such as root words, suffixes, and prefixes. In our example, each word is a single morpheme. The phonological grammar recodes information from the acoustic to the linguistic domain.

Within the syntactic structure, the transformational rules of the grammar map this surface structure onto an underlying deep structure. The nature of this deep structure is the subject of linguistic controversy and is only poorly understood. However, conceptually, it is the core linguistic representation of the sentence to which a variety of surface structures map and from which a variety of formally different surface structures may be generated. Perhaps in form the deep structure is more like the simple active kernel "The boy hit the ball," which is related by transformational or syntactic rules to a variety of related surface structures (for example, "The ball was being hit by the boy," "Did the boy hit the ball?" and so on). Thus, a single deep structure may map onto a variety of surface structures through the rules of the transformational grammar.

Conversely, a single surface structure may map onto two or more deep structures through the rules of the transformational grammar, in which case the sentence is ambiguous. For example, consider the sentence "Flying planes can be dangerous," for which ambiguity exists. One mapping leads to a deep structure that can generate the sentence "Flying planes *are* dangerous." It also may be transformed to another deep structure that can yield the sentence "Flying planes *is* dangerous." The meanings of the two deep structures are different; for that reason, the original sentence, "Flying planes can be dangerous," is ambiguous.

The question of meaning in ambiguous sentences relates to the poorly understood semantic system. The semantic component of grammar acts to interpret the information contained in the deep structure into the nonlinguistic form of the semantic, or meaning, system. The deep structure is thought to contain all linguistic information that is relevant to a semantic interpretation. The semantic system is the system of meaning, and the semantic rules attach meaning to deep structures.

The language system at its various levels performs radical restructuring of the form in which information is represented through the syntactic system to the semantic system. Similarly, in speech production, information is recoded in a series of forms from the semantic to the phonetic as acoustic patterns are generated in the vocal musculature. Liberman has suggested that the complexity of the language system is a necessary consequence of the fact that the various components of the system—the auditory system, the respiratory system, and the nonlinguistic cognitive systems—are poorly matched to each other, each evolving in response to different sets of evolutionary pressures. Long-term memory systems for information storage are certainly present and highly developed in species without language. Similarly, the auditory system, which in man is used to encode linguistic information, is a highly differentiated system that has developed in subhuman species in response to biological demands other than language use. And, although significant evolutionary changes characterize the vocal tract of man, these alterations are overlaid on the more basic properties of the respiratory system of which the vocal tract is a part. The complex hierarchical structure of the grammar may be necessary to coordinate these mismatched components into a single system. Grammar functions as a special interface to recode semantic representations of information into a form that is appropriate for acoustic transmission.

The result is that very different systems of rules or grammar operate at different levels in the general language system. In an analysis of the brain mechanisms mediating language, therefore, we would expect to find different mechanisms operating at different stages of language processing. And that, indeed, is the case.

The Vocal Apparatus

The vocal apparatus used by man in the production of speech is a special adaptation of the respiratory system. The larynx, for example, functions primarily as a valve that serves to prevent the entry of fluid or solid material into the lungs. In primates, the larynx is elaborated to form a double valve capable of locking air in the lungs and thereby providing a rigid support for the arms, which aids arboreal life. (We reflexively hold our breath while lifting with our arms by locking the larynx in its closed position.) In man, the lower portion of this valve, the vocal folds, or cords, is also used in the generation of speech sounds.

The larynx is located at the upper end of the trachea, or windpipe, which leads to the lungs. It is composed of cartilaginous material that projects forward, forming the Adam's apple of the neck. The soft, flap-like epiglottis is the upper valve of the larynx. The lower valve of the larynx is composed of the vocal cords, which are attached anteriorly to the Adam's apple and posteriorly to the arytenoids, which are also cartilaginous structures. This valve may be closed by muscular action, moving the arytenoids and vocal cords toward the midline and thereby closing the space between the vocal cords, which is the glottis. (See Figure 10.2.) In speech, the glottis is also closed, but pressure is simultaneously placed on the lungs to force air through the closed valve in 100 to 200 small puffs each second. The use of forced air to vibrate the vocal cords and produce sound is the process of phonation, which provides the acoustic basis for speech production. The resulting laryngeal tone in an adult male has a fundamental frequency of about 125 Hz and a complex harmonic structure of overtones at higher frequencies.

Vocal communication depends upon the modulation of the laryngeal tone. The pitch of speech may be varied by altering the

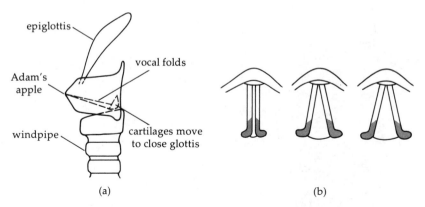

Figure 10.2. *The vocal apparatus.* (a) *A view of the larynx.* (From Miller, G. A., *Language and Communication.* Copyright © 1951 by McGraw-Hill, Inc. Used by permission of McGraw-Hill Book Company.) (b) *The opening of the glottis by movement of the arytenoids (the latter are shaded).* (From Denes, P. B., & Pinson, E. N., *The Speech Chain: The Physics and Biology of Spoken Language,* p. 58. Copyright 1963, Bell Telephone Laboratories, Inc. Used by permission of Bell Telephone Laboratories, Inc., and Anchor Books.)

tension of the vocal cords and the subglottal air pressure. Pitch carries phonemic information in some languages but not in English. The two other types of tonal modulation are linguistically important. Intensity changes do carry information and are produced by varying subglottal air pressure. Changes in the tonal or harmonic structure of sound also carry information; these changes are produced by varying the size and shape of the cavities of the throat and mouth, which change the resonance properties of these structures.

The cavities of the nose, throat, and mouth act as tuned resonators; that is, they act to amplify certain of the harmonics of the laryngeal tone and suppress other harmonics. Which harmonics are amplified is determined by the resonant frequency of these cavities, which in turn is determined by their size and shape. Since the size and shape of the nasal cavity is quite fixed, it is of little importance in the generation of speech. However, the resonances of the throat and mouth can be readily altered by muscular movements, and these movements provide the basis for the control of tonal quality in speech production.

Articulation is the process of adjusting the size and shape of the throat and mouth in the production of speech. For the vowels, the patterns of articulation are relatively simple. All vowels are voiced; that is, they are produced during the vibration of the vocal cords. (Unvoiced sounds do not employ the laryngeal tone.) The differences among

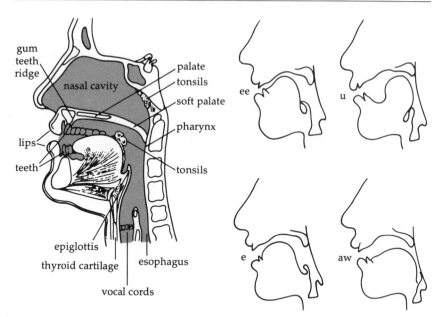

Figure 10.3. *A cutaway view of the vocal apparatus and positions of the tongue in the production of several vowels.* (From Denes, P. B., & Pinson, E. N. *The Speech Chain: The Physics and Biology of Spoken Language,* pp. 65 & 68. Copyright 1963, Bell Telephone Laboratories, Inc. Used by permission of Bell Telephone Laboratories, Inc., and Anchor Books.)

vowels are determined by the positions of the tongue and lips. Figure 10.3(b) shows the position of the tongue for several vowels. These positions may be classified by the part of the tongue that is maximally elevated (front, central, or back) and the relative height of the elevation (from high, or close, to low, or open). These coordinates may be mapped as the vowel quadrilateral shown in Figure 10.4, the edges of which describe the extreme positions of tongue movement. Vowels produced by intermediate positions within the vowel quadrilateral tend to be more neutral in character.

Vowels also may be defined in terms of lip position; in English, unlike some other European languages, lip and tongue position are closely related. Front vowels are made with the lips spread, whereas back vowels are produced with rounded lips. Lip and tongue position together completely determine the articulation of the English vowels.

The articulation of the set of English consonants is somewhat more complex, as both the place and the manner of articulation must be specified. Seven places of articulation are used in English (see Figure 10.5), in which a mobile articulator (the lower lip, the tip, front, and

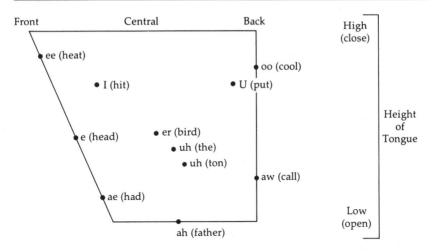

Figure 10.4. *The vowel quadrilateral, showing the tongue positions for the English vowels.* (From Denes, P. B., & Pinson, E. N., *The Speech Chain: The Physics and Biology of Spoken Language*, p. 72. Copyright 1963, Bell Telephone Laboratories, Inc. Used by permission of Bell Telephone Laboratories, Inc., and Anchor Books.)

back of the tongue, or the vocal cords) is brought into contact with a fixed articulator (the upper lip, the upper teeth, the gum ridge, the hard palate, the soft palate, or the glottis). These articulatory movements significantly alter the resonance properties of the vocal cavity and thereby change the quality of the emitted sounds.

Coupled with these places of articulation are five types of articulation. The plosive consonants, such as /p/ or /t/, are spoken by first stopping and then quickly releasing the flow of air at a point of articulation in the mouth. Fricative consonants, such as /f/ or /s/, are produced by constricting the flow of air, giving the resulting sound a hissing quality. Nasal consonants, such as /m/ or /n/, result from opening the passage between the mouth and nasal cavity. The semivowels /w/ and /y/ are produced by first forming an initial vowel position and then rapidly switching to the position for the vowel that follows the semivowel in the string of phonemes. The liquids /l/ and /r/ are articulated like vowels. The liquid lateral /l/ is produced by raising the tongue to permit the passage of air on either side, laterally. Figure 10.5 shows the combinations of place and manner of articulation that result in the English consonants.

The consonants and vowels of English are the phonemes of the language. Together, they compose a set of idealized speech sounds that may be combined in various orders to produce larger units of speech.

| | Manner of Articulation | | | | |
Place of Articulation	Plosive	Fricative	Semivowel	Liquids (including laterals)	Nasal
Labial (upper and lower lips)	p b		w		m
Labio-Dental (upper teeth and lower lip)		f v			
Dental (upper teeth and tip of tongue)		θ th			
Alveolar (gum ridge and tip of tongue)	t d	s z	y	l r	n
Palatal (hard palate and front of tongue)		sh zh			
Velar (soft palate and back of tongue)	k g				ng
Glottal (glottis and vocal cords)		h			

Figure 10.5. *Classification of the English consonants by place and manner of articulation.* (From Denes, P. B., & Pinson, E. N., *The Speech Chain: The Physics and Biology of Spoken Language,* p. 74. Copyright 1963, Bell Telephone Laboratories, Inc. Used by permission of Bell Telephone Laboratories, Inc., and Anchor Books.)

The individual speech sounds, as they are actually produced, not as they are ideally produced, are termed phones. Phones are the units with which speech-perception mechanisms must operate in phonological analysis.

The phonological grammar would be quite simple if each phoneme always resulted in the production of the same phone. However, phonemes in the speech string interact with each other so that the sound produced by a given articulatory act depends heavily upon the context in which it is placed. Therefore, the acoustic pattern generated by the production of a particular phoneme varies greatly as a function of preceding and subsequent phonemes. The sluggishness of the musculature itself apparently accounts for the overlap of successive phonemes in the actual speech signal. The acoustic patterns generated in articulating a series of phonemes overlap, and, therefore, a given phone may carry information about several adjacent phonemes. This is the principle of coarticulation. For this reason the phonological grammar must be more than a simple substitution code relating surface structure to sound pattern. The phonological constancy appears to exist not in the sound patterns produced in speech but in either the commands to the vocal musculature or, even more abstractly, the target positions toward which the various articulators move in the production of each particular phoneme. The phonological grammar must account for the interactions of adjacent phonemes in both the generation of speech sounds in speaking and in the interpretation of speech sounds in listening. Some investigators have suggested that the phonological problem in speech perception is to infer the set of articulatory commands that might have generated a speech string. Once a probable set of articulatory commands have been identified in the phonological grammar, the phonemic components of the speech string are also determined. Thus, the phonological grammar is complicated and serves to map a widely varied but lawful pattern of acoustic energy onto a set of phonemes, which may then be processed by the syntactic and semantic components of the grammar. In the theories of speech perception in which the listener covertly mimics the incoming speech and determines which of his own articulatory patterns match the perceived sound pattern, speech perception is said to proceed through analysis-by-synthesis. No adequate phonological theory of speech perception is currently available.

Brain Mechanisms Mediating Language

The most puzzling questions about the biology of language concern the brain mechanisms that have evolved for language processing. Where within the brain are these systems located? How are they organized? How do they perform their function of linking sound and meaning? How do they permit meaningful information to flow between auditory, articulatory, and cognitive systems of the brain? To answer such questions, it is necessary to study the human brain, since man is the only organism that unequivocally uses a true language. Thus, many of the techniques of physiological psychology that involve the use of subhuman species are not applicable to the study of language systems. Much of what is known about brain mechanisms mediating language was learned through the study of clinical patients, in whom, for example, patterns of brain damage may be correlated with functional disorders. Because of the limited number of patients available to the investigator at any particular time and the necessary requirement that clinical treatment be of primary importance, few well-controlled studies are possible. Nonetheless, even with these restrictions, much has been learned about the brain mechanisms that mediate language.

Evidence from the study of patients suffering unilateral brain lesions first suggested that language function is lateralized in the left cortex of the normal human brain. Since most brain functions are bilaterally represented in the mammalian brain, the lateralization of language function stands in marked contrast to the prevalent biological pattern. In right-handed patients with unilateral cortical injury, language function is usually severely impaired if the damage involves the left hemisphere; in cases of right-hemisphere damage, language competence is often preserved. This strongly suggests that it is the left hemisphere and not the right that normally mediates language in these patients, in which case the left hemisphere is said to be dominant with respect to language. In contrast, unilateral brain damage in left-handed persons is more likely to result in language dysfunction no matter which hemisphere is damaged, but the disorder is less likely to be as profound or as permanent as in right-handed patients with left-hemisphere damage. This pattern suggests that language function may be less completely lateralized in left-handed patients. More detailed analyses have confirmed these clinical observations.

Cerebral dominance for language may be determined in the clinic by temporarily disrupting the activity of one of the cerebral hemispheres and observing the effect on language. Using a technique originally developed by Wada, Brenda Milner and her colleagues have injected Sodium Amytal (amobarbital) on different days into the right and the left carotid arteries of several hundred patients. Each branch of the carotid supplies a single half of the brain with blood; therefore, it is possible to anesthetize one half of the brain while the other half remains functional. If the injected half is dominant for language, the patient becomes mute for several minutes, following which speech returns but with many errors of naming and ordering of language. Anesthesia of the nondominant hemisphere may result in a momentary loss of speech, but, after several seconds, language function returns, and the patient continues to speak without error.

In some patients, neither hemisphere appears dominant by the Wada test. In these patients, anesthesia of either hemisphere results in some impairment of language function but not in a complete disruption of language-processing capacity. In these patients, language function is said to be bilaterally represented.

Milner reports that 92 percent of right-handed patients clearly exhibit left-hemispheric dominance for language. Seven percent appear to be right dominant, and, in the remaining one percent, language function is bilaterally represented. This distribution is quite different from that observed in left-handed patients without childhood damage to the left hemisphere. Of these patients, 69 percent are left dominant, 18 percent are right dominant, and, in 13 percent, language is not lateralized. The normal pattern of left-hemispheric dominance for language is weak in left-handed patients, even among those without evidence of early left-hemisphere damage, which might force the acquisition of language function into the more normal right hemisphere. In left-handed adult patients with a medical history indicating early damage to the left hemisphere, recovery of language function after injury by the right hemisphere occurs frequently. Only 30 percent of these patients show the usual left dominance while a striking 54 percent appear right dominant; the remaining 16 percent demonstrate no clear lateralization. Language function appears to be lateralized in the left hemisphere in most people, a tendency that is somewhat weaker in left-handed persons. Early brain damage in the left hemisphere leads to a compensatory lateralization of language function in the right hemisphere. In some persons, neither hemisphere seems to be dominant for language.

Specific anatomical differences, which may be related to the functional lateralization of speech, also exist between the two cerebral hemispheres. For example, Geschwind has provided evidence that the area immediately behind the primary auditory cortex on the upper surface of the temporal lobe is typically larger by about 1 cm on the left than on the right cortex. A 1-cm difference represents an increase in the size of this small language-relevant area of about 33 percent in the left cortex as compared to the right. This tissue has been anatomically linked to the language-processing system of the brain, forming a part of Wernicke's area (see Figure 10.6). The size difference is not the result of learning, since it is also seen in the brains of newborn infants. Therefore, lateralization of language function may depend on genetic factors that induce differential anatomical development in the two cerebral hemispheres.

The phenomenon of lateralization is quite puzzling, since the rule of bilateral functional symmetry characterizes the evolution of the mammalian brain. Several suggestions have been made as to the reason that lateralization might have occurred, one of the most interesting of which has been proposed by Levy. The motor systems of each hemisphere control the musculature of the contralateral half of the body, but midline structures, such as the musculature of the vocal apparatus, may be controlled from either hemisphere. One possible consequence of lateralization therefore may be to eliminate conflicting commands upon the vocal musculature, in which the commands to the muscles of both sides are always symmetric. Through lateralization, bilateral influences

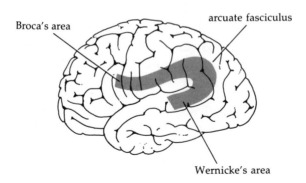

Figure 10.6. *The left hemisphere of the cerebral cortex.* Damage specific to Wernicke's area, Broca's area, or the arcuate fasciculus results in a characteristic and unique aphasia. (From Geschwind, N. The organization of language and the brain. *Science*, 1970, **170**, 941. Copyright 1970 by the American Association for the Advancement of Science. Used by permission.)

on the precision vocal apparatus are eliminated. Although Levy's hypothesis is plausible, like other answers to evolutionary questions, it is quite difficult to empirically substantiate.

The Study of Aphasia

More exact knowledge of the nature of the brain structures involved in language processing has come from the study of patients with language disorders resulting from brain damage, disorders which collectively are termed the aphasias. Various patients display different types of aphasias, but, in all cases, the disorder is linguistic in nature. By carefully determining the exact pattern of the aphasic deficit and comparing this information with neurological information on the localization of damage within the brain, the nature of the language systems of the cortex can be discerned.

Lenneberg (who, in an attempt to identify the various processes underlying language and thought, has analyzed in detail the clinical literature on language disorders resulting from brain damage) argues that two psychological processes depend upon different physiological mechanisms if each can occur without the other in different groups of patients. This criterion is termed double dissociation and is useful in providing a first approximation of the brain functions that underlie language. For example, verbal communication and nonverbal thinking may be physiologically separable, since, in senility, there is often a loss in nonverbal cognitive functioning while verbal communication remains intact. Conversely, in traumatic aphasia, speech can be lost without great impairment in nonverbal skills. Since the two kinds of disorders are doubly dissociated, the underlying processes may be relatively independent. However, these differences are relative. Although the loss is much greater for one skill than for the other, the surviving skill is not left absolutely intact.

Lenneberg has applied this analysis to clinical syndromes within the broad category of aphasia. Are there different, independent sets of language functions that depend on different physiological processes or even on different brain areas? The most common clinical classification of aphasias divides language skill into three parts: (1) *speech production aphasia,* in which, for example, the patient cannot speak but can listen and comprehend; (2) *cognitive aphasia,* in which the patient can say words but cannot speak intelligently or understand what is said to him; and (3) *word-presence aphasia,* in which the patient can understand and produce words but has difficulty locating the words needed for reasonable speech. Are these aphasias truly separable? Speech production and cognitive disorders are certainly independent; patients may show one syndrome but not the other. However, the independence of word presence and cognition is much more questionable since double dissociation has not been demonstrated for these classes of aphasia. Therefore, language rules and vocabulary do not appear to be physiologically separable. Grammar, in the broad sense of modern linguistic theory, and vocabulary depend upon the same brain system.

Clinically, no brain damage short of widespread destruction in the dominant hemisphere completely abolishes language competence. Because the language system must depend upon rather general and delicately integrated brain processes, it is not surprising that a wide variety of brain disorders can produce quite similar language deficits. A complex system can be disrupted by any of a variety of disturbances. Because of the nonspecificity of many aphasias, Lenneberg argues that most language disorders reflect a general loss of integration. The logical contexts of thought and speech are disrupted. At the same time, a disturbance of temporal integration may be observed. Thus, many aphasias reflect a loss of the brain's ability to maintain its own organization.

However, many neurologists believe that further localization of the language processes within the brain may be possible. As long ago as 1874, Carl Wernicke argued that two relatively small areas within the left hemisphere are crucial to linguistic information processing and that, along with their interconnecting fibers, they form a definable speech system (see Figure 10.6). Most frontal is a cortical area named for

Paul Broca, who, in the latter half of the nineteenth century, held that damage to this area of the cortex produces aphasia. Broca's area lies immediately adjacent to the primary motor areas that control the organs of speech. To this structure, Wernicke added a second area, located in the temporal lobe near the primary auditory cortex. Wernicke's and Broca's areas are connected to each other by the arcuate fasciculus and are linked to corresponding cortical tissues within the right hemisphere by the corpus callosum. From this anatomical arrangement, Wernicke postulated that Broca's area may contain the neuronal machinery necessary to produce speech and may also contain the rules for the generation of speech. This would be the logical function of a language-processing area making intimate connection with motor structures.

Wernicke's area is located in the immediate proximity of the auditory cortex. The logical function of Wernicke's area would be decoding linguistic messages after processing by the auditory system. Both Broca's and Wernicke's areas must be extremely complex in structure and function, since the use of linguistic symbols is a highly organized process. Simple rules do not govern the behavior of these areas.

That Wernicke's theory permits prediction of the nature of the aphasia resulting from specific lesions gives the theory considerable power. Geschwind has reviewed the literature describing aphasias resulting from stroke damage, in which detailed information is available concerning both the exact nature of the aphasia and the precise limits of cortical damage. The following discussion is based on Geschwind's analysis.

Damage to Broca's area produces a characteristic aphasia in which speech is hesitant and poorly articulated. This would be expected, since the hypothesized speech-generating mechanism has been disrupted in these cases. The deficit, however, is not merely motor. The ability to generate linguistically correct strings of words is also impaired. Patients with damage in Broca's area typically omit the small connecting words of speech—for example, the "ands," "ifs," and "buts" in English. Such patients produce sentences only with great difficulty. Similar disturbances are present in writing, which is a secondary adaptation of speaking. Aphasics with damage in Broca's area are able to write no more easily than they speak. The same neuronal machinery that mediates speech is also involved in the production of the written symbols of that speech.

Patients with cortical damage confined to Wernicke's area are also aphasic, but the deficit is of a different nature. These patients speak easily and without hesitation, but their words convey little meaning. Strings of words may be correctly formed, but usually they are devoid of meaningful content. Such aphasics are no more coherent when writing. Furthermore, they cannot comprehend the meaning of words, whether written or spoken. Neither blind nor deaf, Wernicke's-area aphasics are nonetheless unable to extract meaning from language.

Geschwind and others have proposed that other more specific types of aphasia result from unusual and highly specific lesions that destroy particular sets of connections between Broca's and Wernicke's areas and other structures within the brain. For example, Geschwind reports a rare case of word deafness without other linguistic deficits. The patient had normal hearing acuity when measured by the conventional means with pure tones. He could speak fluently and, with equal ease, both read and write. But he could not comprehend the spoken word. Autopsy revealed that most of the speech-related structures of the brain, including both Broca's and Wernicke's areas, were normal. The lesion had severed only the connections between Wernicke's area and the auditory cortex, both the direct connections with the left hemisphere and the callosal connections to the right temporal lobe. In this patient, the deprivation of auditory input in the speech areas gave rise to the limited impairment of the aphasia.

Other specific language disorders may result from equally well-defined lesions. For example, one stroke patient could not read (alexia), although he was fully capable of writing and verbally processing language. His stroke also produced total blindness in the right visual field. A postmortem examination revealed that, as expected, the left visual cortex was destroyed. Additionally, part of the posterior corpus callosum was damaged. Thus, no visual information could reach the speech areas of the left cortex. The patient displayed normal acuity in the left visual field (using the right visual cortex), but the visual features that were extracted there could not gain access to the language-processing system. All other pathways in the system were operative so that the speaking, hearing, and writing of linguistic symbols were not impaired.

Alternate Lateralization and the Recovery of Function

The detailed study of aphasia is most frequently accomplished in the victims of strokes, a disorder that most often occurs late in life. Severe disruption of speech often appears immediately after the stroke and during the initial period of adjustment and recouperation from injury. The aphasia that remains after 6 months is usually permanent. Recovery of the lost language functions seldom ensues.

A strikingly different pattern is seen in children with unilateral cortical injury. Damage to the left temporal lobe in prelanguage children is no more debilitating than comparable damage to the right temporal lobe. In the 2-year-old, functional lateralization is not yet established. Aphasias resulting from left-hemisphere damage in slightly older children indicate the emergence of functional lateralization, but such aphasias quickly pass as the right hemisphere recovers the lost language functions. The process of recovery is usually not immediate. The right hemisphere appears to pass through the normal developmental stages for speech acquisition, but at a faster rate than that which characterizes initial learning. At puberty, this plastic property of the brain is greatly reduced; no longer is recovery from a major aphasia likely. The early teens mark the end of the capacity of the right cortex to learn the rules of language, which coincides with some estimates of the attainment of full maturity in the development of brain structure.

Electrical Mapping of the Language System

Penfield and Roberts approached the study of brain mechanisms in language in a somewhat different manner, stemming from their major interest in the surgical treatment of epilepsy. Epilepsy results from damage or irritation of brain tissue. The damage may be produced by a tumor, by blood clots, or by other pathogenic processes. The affected cortex usually continues to function but will, on occasion, begin to discharge spontaneously in an uncontrolled manner. If the damage is confined to a small cortical area, it is said to form an epileptic focus. Epileptic discharges at the focus disrupt the normal patterns of activity in this tissue and so provide a clue as to the normal functioning of the affected area of the cortex. The exact nature of the behavioral disruption depends upon the size of the discharge and the location of the epileptic focus within the brain. If the focus is in a motor area, a train of rhythmic movements may be evoked. If it is in a sensory area, various primitive sensations (for example, buzzing noises or light flashes) may be experienced. Often, however, the pathological discharge is not confined to a small area of tissue, in which case little may be learned about the localization of cortical functions from examination of the seizure-produced disruptions.

Information about speech mechanisms can be gained from an examination of the speech disorders that sometimes occur during limited seizures. Speech is disrupted when the epileptic focus is located in a language-relevant area of the brain. If the epileptic focus is centered in the speech motor areas, as shown in Figure 10.7(a), the patient may emit a vowel cry as the seizure begins. The vocalization is not, however, complex, as in normal speech. Foci along the central sulcus or in the supplementary motor areas have this effect.

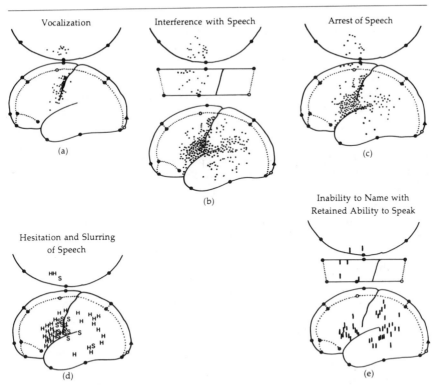

Figure 10.7. (a) *The areas within the left cortex where electrical stimulation of the epileptic brain produces vocalization.* The dots are concentrated in the speech motor area. A similar distribution of points may be seen on the right hemisphere. (b) *Areas within the left cortex at which electrical stimulation interferes with speech.* These points include large areas of the frontal, parietal, and temporal cortex, including Broca's and Wernicke's areas. Such points are seen only in the left hemisphere under the usual conditions of dominance. Stimulation in the right cortex does not interfere with either the production or comprehension of speech. (c) *Speech arrest.* Electrical stimulation of these points leads to a complete arrest of speech, probably by interfering with either speech organization or speech motor areas. (d) *Temporal disruptions.* Stimulation at these points produces either hesitation or slurring in speech, indicating a disruption of its temporal fabric. (e) *Areas in which stimulation can produce an inability to name a specific object.* Otherwise, speech is apparently normal. The distribution of points is similar to that seen in (b) through (d), with one exception: no points are included in the speech motor area. Stimulation along the motor strip induces a mechanical distortion of speech, preventing the observation of purely cognitive effects, if any should exist. (Redrawn from Penfield, W., & Roberts, L. *Speech and Brain Mechanisms*, pp. 121–124 & 127. © 1959 by Princeton University Press. Used by permission of Princeton University Press.)

All other effects of seizure on speech are negative. The production or comprehension of speech is disrupted. A patient may know that he is being addressed during an attack, but he is unable to understand the meaning of what is said. Similarly, a patient who is speaking may find himself mute, quite against his will. Disruptions of language may arise from foci in temporal, parietal, and frontal areas of the dominant cortex. Because the location of the disease process is often only vaguely known, it is difficult to map out speech areas by mapping epileptic foci.

Since removing a critical speech area in the adult brain results in an aphasia and not removing an epileptic focus means continued seizure, it is necessary to determine with some certainty whether the tissue to be removed is a part of the language system of the cortex. Initially, speech areas were avoided by excising only foci that lay far forward in the frontal lobe or far back in the occipital lobe of the dominant hemisphere. Penfield then discovered that direct electrical stimulation of the human brain could be used to identify speech-relevant areas, permitting the safe removal of at least some disordered tissue without affecting speech. This procedure, which permits a more detailed analysis of cortical function during speech, requires that the patient be awake during surgery and free to converse as electrical stimulation is applied.

Electrical stimulation prevents normal functioning of the cortical area beneath the electrode and, perhaps, elsewhere. Stimulation of a sensory area may produce elemental sensations such as colored patterns for visual cortex stimulation, but it also renders the area inoperative for processing normal stimuli. Similarly, in speech-involved areas, electrical stimulation prevents normal function.

As is the case with pathological irritation (epilepsy), electrical activation of the motor areas along the central sulcus in either hemisphere may produce vocalization. See Figure 10.7(a). The areas involved are always close to those that directly control the vocal apparatus. Words are never spoken during stimulation of the cortex; rather, the patient makes simple vowel cries that may or may not be sustained. Often, the vowel is coupled with a consonant. Normal speech of the patient is disrupted during stimulation of the speech motor area. Damage to or removal of this area is associated with speech-production aphasias.

Aphasias characterized by loss of syntactic or semantic function have been reported with tissue damage in many parts of the temporal, parietal, and frontal lobes of the dominant hemispheres. Similar results are seen when electrical currents are used to disrupt normal function in these areas. Figure 10.7(b) shows areas in which electrical stimulation of the brain produces interference with language function. A substantial area of the left cortex is involved.

Figure 10.7(c) shows points for which an absolute arrest of ongoing speech is seen. Notice the similarity to the distribution of points shown in Figure 10.7(b), which maps interference more generally.

The distribution of points at which electrical stimulation has produced disruptions of the temporal fabric of speech is shown in Figure 10.7(d). Again, note the similarity to the two previous maps. Here, ongoing speech continues throughout stimulation, but its fine timing is impaired. The patient either produces hesitation, by lingering too long on pauses, or slurs his speech, by elongating or shortening parts of the spoken word.

Word-presence aphasias are usually accompanied by more general linguistic difficulties. Figure 10.7(e) shows those areas in which stimulation produces an inability to name specific objects, while the more general capacity for speech is retained. Again, the distribution of sites is similar to that shown for interference more generally, with one exception: no points along the central sulcus are included, undoubtedly because stimulation in that area systematically interferes with the production of speech. Therefore, the ability to produce names cannot be evaluated in that tissue, since speech production is not possible.

The effects of stimulation are specific to the speech areas. Stimulation in other cortical areas produces no disordering of speech. However, at a point within a speech area that yields interference, the effects of stimulation are not consistent. Disruption usually occurs probabilistically, with stimulation sometimes interfering with speech and other times not. This suggests that a particular small part of the language system need not always be involved in mediating a language function; sometimes, but not always, it may be dispensable.

Penfield's data on electrical stimulation agree with the general clinical localization of speech function. Language competence in the adult depends upon the functional integrity of a large part of the dominant left cortex. When its integrity is compromised, by cortical destruction, by epileptic discharge, or by direct electrical stimulation, disruption of language function occurs.

Commissurotomy and Language Function

In certain epileptic patients, the epileptic seizure involves discharges across the corpus callosum. The corpus callosum is a bridge of fibers that links the two halves of the cortex (see Figure 10.8). Cell bodies in either half of the brain send their axons (which together form the corpus callosum) to the corresponding points in the contralateral hemisphere. To confine the epilepsy to one hemisphere, the corpus callosum and the anterior commissure (a similar but much smaller structure) were severed in 16 patients in an operation known as commissurotomy. The primary results of commissurotomy are simple

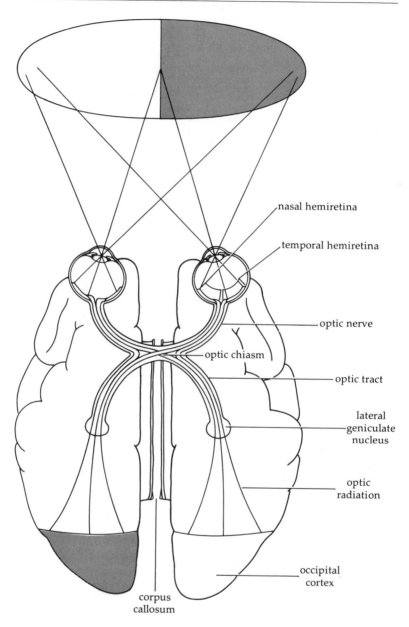

Figure 10.8. *A diagram showing the left and right cerebral cortices from above and the visual input to them.* In the split-brain operation, the corpus callosum is severed. All visual input in the left visual field is projected onto the right hemiretinas and relayed to the right cortex. Similarly, visual stimuli falling on the left hemiretina are transmitted only to the left cortex. No direct communication between the two cortices is possible.

and surprising. First, the epilepsy becomes relatively controlled. Second, there is relatively little impairment in the general behavior or mood of the patients. Third, the operation seems to result in the creation of two separate conscious mental spheres in the two cerebral hemispheres, each able to gain its own separate knowledge and to independently control the behavior in the portion of the body to which it is connected. The severing of the corpus callosum and the anterior commissure creates two cognitively functioning neocortices that share a common body and brainstem. The left cortex can speak fluently, but the right hemisphere may also possess some rudimentary language competence.

Commissurotomies on lower animals were done in the early 1950s by Myers and Sperry in the study of the behavioral functions of the neocortex. These investigators reported that, in cats, tasks learned by one hemisphere could not be performed by the other without separate training. Both half-brains, however, could be taught with equal ease. Outside these special testing situations, the cats appeared perfectly normal.

In man, as in lower vertebrates, the separated half-brains are fully capable of issuing contradictory orders to the musculature that they control, if they are operating on different sets of information. For example, when a human split-brain patient solves a manual puzzle for which one half-brain has been shown the correct answer, one hand works by trial and error while the other proceeds directly toward the solution. Either hand may grasp a block that the other has used or wants to place in position, and one hand may seize the other and force it away from the puzzle. Such behavior suggests true functional independence of the separated hemispheres.

In order to learn more about the capacity of each of the isolated hemispheres to process language, Sperry, Gazzaniga, and others have extensively studied patients in whom the corpus callosum had been severed. These investigations require that information be made available to each of the hemispheres separately. Therefore, auditory stimuli cannot be used to test the linguistic capacity, since auditory signals from the two ears are mixed in the brainstem auditory nuclei and are thereby available to both halves of the cerebral cortex. Visual stimuli, however, are more suited to the task. As Figure 10.8 illustrates, fibers of the optic nerve divide at the optic chiasma and become the optic tracts. Fibers originating in the nasal hemiretina (the half of the retina, divided vertically, that lies nearest the nose) cross at the chiasma and proceed to the contralateral geniculate nucleus and, through the optic radiations, to the occipital cortex. Fibers originating in the temporal hemiretina do not cross at the chiasma and make connections in the ipsilateral thalamus. Therefore, an object placed in the left visual field is imaged on the right hemiretina of each eye and information about the object is available at the lateral geniculate nucleus and the occipital cortex in the right side of the brain. If the corpus callosum has been severed, no information about the object is available in the left cortex. Similarly, stimuli in the right visual field are processed by the left hemisphere. Therefore, visual information can be selectively presented to only one cortex in the commissurotomized patient.

The sense of touch is also separated in the two brains. Most somatosensory pathways in man are crossed, so that the left brain receives information from the right side of the body and vice versa. Integration of somatosensory information across the midline of the body is apparently achieved by the corpus callosum. Similarly, in the control of movement, the right motor cortex directs the activity of the left half of the body. Thus, the right cortex controls the left hand but not the right. The bilateral separation of touch and movement is nearly complete. There is, however, some small ipsilateral influence, which, for most purposes, is negligible.

The separation of vision, touch, and movement permits independent evaluation of the language competence of each cerebral hemisphere. After brain bisection, the left hemisphere retains perfect language competence. Any information presented to that brain can be communicated since there is no measurable impairment of language or speech function in the left cortex.

In the right hemisphere, however, a very different pattern is seen after brain bisection. Not unexpectedly, the right hemisphere is mute. Under no conditions can information known only to the right hemisphere be spoken. Nor can the right hemisphere use the left hand to write, even though cortical control of the hand's musculature is unimpaired. The right cerebral cortex simply lacks the neuronal machinery necessary to generate language.

The ability of the right hemisphere to comprehend language can be tested by presenting verbal material visually, allowing only the right brain to see the message, and testing for comprehension with nonverbal motor responses. Using these procedures, in the cases reported by Gazzaniga, one patient failed to show any comprehension in the right hemisphere. But, in three other cases with minimal pathological brain damage, the right hemisphere did exhibit a limited capacity for linguistic comprehension.

Gazzaniga tested the right hemisphere by briefly flashing a word onto the subject's right hemiretina. The patient was then required to point to the correct item on the table. The right cortex has little trouble in processing a word like "knife" and pointing the left hand to a knife. But since the left hemisphere does not know the stimulus words, and the right hemisphere cannot produce speech, the patient cannot verbally report the stimulus. Similarly, when the right hemisphere is visually presented with a concrete noun, the left hand can point to the appropriate written word. Moreover, the patient may use his left hand under the direction of the right hemisphere to assemble simple concrete nouns like "dog" from single letters.

Strangely enough, the right cortex appears to be able to process only certain classes of words. Concrete nouns may be represented in the right cortex, but nouns derived from verbs apparently are not. Patients apparently cannot process nouns such as "locker" or "teller" in the right brain, whereas other "-er" nouns, such as "butter," "letter," or "water," are handled with ease. Simple adjectives also may be present in the vocabulary of the right hemisphere; shown a picture of a steaming cup of coffee, the patient can point out the word "hot" in a list of adjectives.

The right cortex seems unable to process verbs. When the right brain is visually presented with simple one-word commands such as "smile," "laugh," "frown," or "nod" (all movements that are bilaterally controlled), the patient cannot respond. This is not a motor deficit but truly a disorder of comprehension. If the right brain is shown a picture of the movement, there is no trouble in carrying out the command. The right cortex can process graphic, but not language-like, symbols of actions.

The nondominant right hemisphere of the commissurotomized patient may acquire language function if the bisection occurs early in life. One of the 16 commissurotomized patients was 13 years old at the time of the operation. Immediately following surgery, the patient gave no evidence of language processing in the right hemisphere. Seven years later, however, the patient's status was quite different; he could report verbally one to three digits or letters presented visually to the right hemisphere. Moreover, he was able to perform tasks that require the integration of information between the two hemispheres. Presumably, the brainstem mechanisms assumed some functions for hemispheric communication normally provided by the corpus callosum. Older patients do not show such recovery of function.

That each hemisphere may develop complete language competence if deprived of connections to the other hemisphere is shown in rare cases in which the corpus callosum is congenitally absent. Agenesis of the corpus callosum results from accidents in the fourth month of pregnancy. Such persons are typically asymptomatic, exhibiting no behavioral signs of the gross anatomical abnormality. One such patient, a 19-year-old college student who was admitted to the clinic for headaches, was able to completely integrate information from the two hemispheres, presumably through a somewhat enlarged anterior commissure and through brainstem pathways. Wada's test showed each hemisphere to be completely capable of mediating normal language. In the absence of the linking corpus callosum, two separate and equal language systems developed.

The study of split-brain man confirms the analysis of brain function in language in cases of aphasia. The ability to utilize language appears to depend upon a specifiable set of cortical structures, primarily in the left parietal, temporal, and frontal areas; corresponding tissues in the right hemisphere are unable to process most linguistic symbols.

The Evolutionary Basis of Language

Language represents an important development in the evolution of the human brain. It both provides internal flexibility in organizing thought and behavior and establishes an information-rich system of communication among members of the species. Language usage is undoubtedly most developed in man, but it would aid the understanding of human brain and behavior to search for precursors of this remarkable capacity in infrahuman species. Is man the only organism that is able to process linguistic information, or is there continuity of language-processing capacity in evolutionary development?

Certain cases of reputed language usage in lower species can be immediately discarded. Parrots, for example, can be trained to speak whole sentences, but clearly these birds are not language users. They are incapable of combining linguistic elements in a flexible manner to communicate information. Instead, they are mimics. They are as likely to imitate a frequently heard sequence of words as they are any other sound in their environment, including the squeaking of a cage door and similar noises. Perhaps more interesting is the case of the porpoise. Recently, a series of reports have claimed the production of English words by these remarkably intelligent animals. However, serious methodological flaws have plagued this research and such reports have only minimal acceptance to date.

The investigation of language capacity has often turned to subhuman primates, since brain structure in these species most closely resembles that of man. The similarities have fostered the hope that, if prelinguistic capacity is to be seen in any species other than man, it is most likely to be found in the primates, particularly in the chimpanzee. Not only is the chimpanzee perhaps the most intelligent of the infrahuman primates, it is also a uniquely social animal. The chimpanzee interacts easily in a learning situation and appears to form strong bonds with its human handlers.

Psychologists have made several attempts to teach chimpanzees to use the English language in speech. Similar projects have also been undertaken by others who maintain these animals as pets. All such endeavors have been strikingly unsuccessful. The seriousness of these attempts should not be doubted. Winthrop Kellogg and his wife, for example, raised a chimpanzee, Gua, with their own son. Gua gave evidence of understanding a sizable number of words, but she never spoke.

Recently, however, strong evidence has indicated that the chimpanzee may be language competent but possesses no physiological capability for speech. These animals may learn to process language-like symbols presented by nonvocal means. Premack has taught his chimp, Sarah, to use plastic symbols in a manner suggestive of a language-competent brain. Gardner and Gardner have trained their chimpanzee, Washoe, to use the American Sign Language, as employed by the deaf. Both series of experiments indicate that the chimpanzee may possess the necessary brain processes to use a language, at least in limited form. The ability to use symbolic units in a logical structure may not be limited to man. Although our speech sounds are unique to our species, the structural basis of language may be less unique. The problems of defining language competence in another species are incredibly difficult, but it is clear that a symbol-using ape who follows logical rules in symbolic communications is, at the least, an interesting middle case between parrot and man.

Premack and the Gardners have approached the problem of language training in somewhat different manners. Premack first established a set of behaviors that he believed the animal must exhibit to be said to use language. He then devised a set of training procedures that induced Sarah to produce these behaviors. Sarah was required to learn to manipulate the plastic words appropriately to obtain food. A social interaction was mapped onto the plastic language. Sarah learned (1) the use of words; (2) sentences, both simple and compound; (3) questions; (4) the use of language (rather than the objects to which the words refer) to teach language; (5) class concepts such as color, shape, and size; (6) "is" and "is not"; (7) the quantifiers "all," "none," "one," and "several"; and (8) the logical connective "if-then." Sarah performed beautifully in training and gave every evidence of mastering the exemplars listed. She can use the plastic words to generate sentences as well as to answer questions or to receive and issue commands. Nonhuman primates can be taught, or perhaps merely taught to express, a logical symbolic language that embodies some of the more important aspects of human language.

The Gardners trained Washoe in a less formal manner, which approximated more closely the way in which language is taught to the human child. Washoe was placed in a nonconfining environment with human companions who communicated among themselves only through the use of sign language. Washoe's imitation was encouraged. Playing, as well as the use of appropriate sign language communication within the context of the game, was emphasized. At the same time, observers carefully examined and coded Washoe's language-using behavior, extracting orderly data from the complex social interactions. Washoe, like Sarah, shows signs of language competence. Unlike chimpanzees in the natural environment, Washoe demonstrates the capacity to use names to refer to objects and to relations between objects. Without such training, chimpanzees appear to signal only motivational and emotional states in their communications. The development of naming behavior constitutes a use of language.

The chimpanzee, like the human child, generalizes a newly learned word to a variety of appropriate referents. These may include the naming of the object as it appears in pictures or other contexts. Also like the human child, the chimpanzee commits errors of overgeneralization and misapplication of the newly acquired name, which result from an inappropriate limiting of the concept. For example, as Washoe began to use the sign for "flower" with increasing frequency, misapplications began to appear. She employed the sign in the absence of flowers, when the word "smell" would have been more appropriate. For example, she made the "flower" sign when opening a pouch of tobacco and when looking into a kitchen as food was being prepared. After introduction of the sign for "smell," Washoe was able to differentiate correctly between the two concepts as new instances arose for their application. Occasionally, however, she errs and reverts to the inappropriate "flower" sign. Such errors resemble closely the mistakes of human children learning language.

In man, language performs the important internal function of facilitating thought. Washoe also shows some behavior that may indicate an internalized use of language. For example, she has been observed sitting by herself, leafing through a picture book, and naming, in sign language, each object that she sees. Occasionally, she corrects herself when she misnames a picture. She also has been observed on occasion making signs to herself in a mirror. Both these cases suggest that Washoe may be using the externally visible language function for some unknown internal purposes.

The behavior of both Sarah and Washoe suggests that the use of language may not be limited to man. The chimpanzee brain may be capable of learning and correctly using a language of symbols devised originally for use by humans. A careful and detailed examination of language use in these animals may reveal information about the structures and processes within the human brain that are important in the use of language.

Summary

Language is a hierarchically organized system that is capable of systematically relating sound and meaning. It is useful to think of three levels in the structure of language: (1) a phonological level of sound patterns, (2) a syntactic level that comprises the surface and deep structural systems, and (3) a semantic level at which meaning is organized. Grammar is the set of rules linking semantic meaning and sound, with different subsets of the grammar operating at different levels of the hierarchy. The phonological grammar maps the surface structure into sound pattern and vice versa. The transformational syntactic grammar relates surface and deep structure. The semantic component of grammar maps deep structure into the nonlinguistic system of meaning.

Speech sounds are generated in man by the coordinated activity of the vocal apparatus. Voiced sounds are produced by modulation of the laryngeal tone, changing the resonance properties of the throat, mouth, and nose by articulatory movements. The effects of individual articulatory commands interact in normal speech so that speech sounds produced by a given articulatory act depend heavily upon the speech context in which they occur. This complicates the processes of speech production and perception.

The importance of particular brain structures to these processes is apparent in patients in whom relatively localized damage has produced a specific language deficit, or aphasia. In most people, aphasia results only from damage to the left cortex, indicating that the left cortex is normally dominant for language. Dominance does not appear to be irreversibly established until puberty. In younger children, damage to the left cortex may produce aphasia, but recovery of the lost language processes, which normally ensues, indicates a recovery of function, probably by the right hemisphere.

The aphasias are often divided into three broad classes: speech-production aphasia, cognitive aphasia, and word-presence aphasia. The first of these appears to depend upon brain processes that are different from those of the other two, as indicated through the use of double dissociation of clinical syndromes to determine independence of process. Sometimes, more specific localization of function and identification of process are possible. Patients with lesions in Broca's area appear to have lost the neuronal structure necessary for the production of intelligent speech, suggesting that Broca's area contains the rules for the generation of phonologically correct speech. Patients with cortical damage exclusively in Wernicke's area produce phonologically competent speech, but their speech is incoherent and carries no meaning. Wernicke's area may, in part, be responsible for the extraction of meaning from the spoken word, a function suggested by its proximity to the auditory areas of the cortex. Disruption of the connections between these areas produces the expected forms of aphasia.

The mapping of speech areas of the brain produced from the study of aphasic patients is confirmed in its broad outlines by the use of stimulation techniques. Because electrical stimulation of the brain prevents normal functioning of the affected areas, electrode placements may be mapped for the production of vocalization, the general interference of speech, the arrest of speech, disruption of timing, and interference with cognitive language functions. Stimulation is not as specific as are lesions, since, in the epileptic brain, electrical events are likely to be conducted from the point of stimulation to other, unspecifiable areas within the brain.

If the corpus callosum and the anterior commissure are severed, the cerebral hemispheres are isolated from each other. The left hemisphere retains perfect language competence. The right hemisphere does not permit either speech or writing, but it appears to retain certain rudimentary forms of linguistic information. It may recognize some simple concrete nouns but not verbs. It is, however, able to process pictorial information.

Since language appears to be deeply linked to cortical structures within the highly developed human brain, it is not surprising that language behavior is not observed in other species in their natural environments. High primates, such as the chimpanzee, possess a cortex that resembles man's in many important ways. The chimpanzee can be trained to use an artificial language if the language does not require the use of vocal mechanisms. One chimpanzee has been trained to produce language-like behavior by manipulating plastic symbols. Another has learned at least limited use of the American Sign Language, as employed by the deaf. These experiments indicate that the infrahuman primate brain may be capable of language and suggest that internal, language-like mechanisms of information processing might be used in these species in the absence of specific training. The experiments also suggest a continuity of language-like behavior among the primates.

Chapter 11

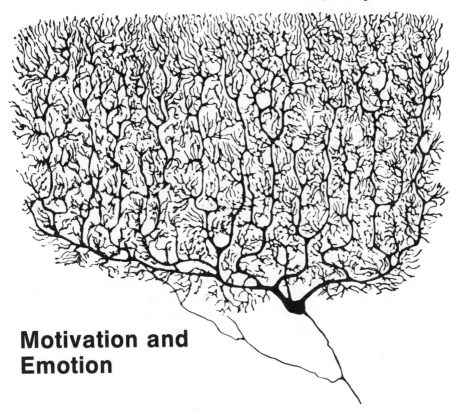

Motivation and Emotion

Some objects in the environment are biologically important to living organisms. Food, water, and other living creatures are necessary for survival. The way in which an animal will behave toward any of these objects depends not only on the object but also upon factors within the animal. For example, normally a person will not eat if he has just eaten. If asked, one would reply that he was hungry before but felt full after eating. Motivation is a term used by psychologists to denote internal processes such as hunger that serve to direct the behavior of the organism.

Motivational processes are inferred from changes in the direction, intensity, or persistence of behavior. Hunger, thirst, sexual attraction, and similar internal variables can never be directly observed. Instead, motivational states are inferred. Motivational constructs are abstractions within psychological theory that are useful for the analysis and prediction of behavior and conventionally have been employed to account for three facts about behavior:

1. The same stimulus object elicits very different responses from the same animal at different times. Psychologists usually think of a stimulus object as the controller of behavior, but the response of an organism to even the most important of stimuli is variable. Food will be eagerly sought out and consumed on some occasions, whereas at other times, it will be ignored. In the case of food and water, changes in motivation are cyclic.

2. At certain times, some objects are more attractive than are others. To a food-deprived animal, a tasty morsel has great incentive value, but after eating, the same bit of food seems far less attractive.

3. Objects also can serve as reinforcers, or rewards. To a hungry pigeon, grain is a highly attractive goal object. If the animal is to be trained to perform some task, therefore, grain can be used as a reinforcer.

The concept of motivation is employed to explain very subtle behaviors. It is no surprise, therefore, that the neural processes underlying motivation are incompletely understood. Some firm information, however, concerning the control of basic bodily needs such as food and water intake, the brain mechanisms involved in reward and punishment, and the physical changes that accompany emotion, is available.

Motivation and the Concept of Homeostasis

Certain of the common motivational states such as hunger and thirst are closely linked to the acquisition of substances necessary for the maintenance of life. The processes controlling feeding, water intake, and body temperature are regulated in a particular way, which Cannon termed homeostatic.

The blood and the lymph of the body are fluids that bathe the cells of living animals. The composition of both fluids is closely regulated to provide a stable internal environment in which individual cells may prosper. For the organism living in a changing and sometimes hostile outer environment, many complex adjustments are required to maintain internal consistency. Changes that act to preserve a constant internal environment are homeostatic. Animals with extensive homeostatic mechanisms are able to exist in a greater range of environments than are animals with more limited capacities to adjust. For example, because cold-blooded animals lack important mechanisms for maintaining the constant internal temperature at which cellular life can exist, they are behaviorally limited to environments that are continually moderate. Thus, in northern climates, frogs can gather food and live on the land in the summer but, in winter, must live deep in a pond if they are to survive. They lack the homeostatic temperature-regulating mechanisms necessary to function in an environment that differs markedly from the necessary internal temperature.

Homeostatic mechanisms are, by necessity, feedback-controlled devices. Like a modern heating and air-conditioning system, bodily thermal-regulation systems must have sensors that provide information about the temperature to be regulated. In addition, there must be criteria information, which specifies the range of temperatures acceptable to the system. In architectural heating systems, the criterion temperature is provided by setting a dial on the thermostatic control. The thermostat also contains a sensor that signals room temperature. If room temperature is too low, the furnace is activated until room temperature reaches an acceptable level. If it is too hot in the room, another effector mechanism, the cooling system, is employed. Crucial to the operation of homeostatic-regulation systems in both man and machine is the use of feedback information. Feedback information can also be thought of as the measurement of the effects of the heating and cooling mechanisms on the regulated environment. By comparing this information with the criteria defining desired temperatures, heating and cooling mechanisms can be brought into play as they are needed and terminated when they have achieved their desired effect. Homeostasis is an important concept for understanding many of the motivational regulatory systems of the body.

Hunger and the Control of Feeding

A proper balance of nutrients and other substances required for cellular metabolism must be maintained in the internal environment to preserve the integrity of the organism. Nutrients can be obtained only by feeding, at least in the long run, and, therefore, it is not unreasonable to expect that feeding behavior is related to homeostatically controlled processes within the organism.

Any homeostatic system must possess information about the current state of the variable to be controlled. We know that animals eat when they are food deprived, but which of the many changes occurring in the ingestion and subsequent utilization of food are monitored to control feeding behavior? No one variable studied to date appears to be completely satisfactory in accounting for the homeostatic regulation of feeding. Indeed, several variables may be involved in this complex system. Most evidence, however, points to a constituent of the blood as the regulated quantity. When the blood from a well-fed rat is injected into a hungry animal, the hungry rat stops eating and appears sated. However, if the animal receives a transfusion from another hungry rat, he continues to eat. Something in the blood appears crucial to the control of feeding. A chemical component of the internal environment appears to be measured and regulated by the homeostatic system.

What is that component? A likely candidate is blood glucose. Blood glucose is used in cellular metabolism as an energy source that supports cellular activity. The blood-glucose level is usually low in a food-deprived animal but rises quickly after feeding. Since glucose is so nutriently important for the organism, it would not be surprising to find that the blood-glucose level controls feeding in some direct way. However, a simple glucostatic theory appears to be inadequate. In certain diseases, such as diabetes mellitus, blood-glucose levels are chronically high, yet the patient eats. However, the utilization of blood glucose is quite low in these patients, leading Mayer to argue that the regulated variable in the control of feeding is an index of glucose utilization, which appears as the difference between the amount of circulating glucose in the arteries and the veins. The difference between these two values is utilized.

Neural mechanisms controlling food intake not only must instigate feeding when the animal needs nutrients but must also terminate feeding. Although the brain mechanisms controlling hunger satiety are not well understood, they appear to depend on the hypothalamic nuclei. Nuclei in the lateral hypothalamus seem to be involved in hunger and the initiation of feeding. Stimulation of the lateral hypothalamus, for example, leads to eating even in an animal that is satiated. Destruction of the lateral portion of the hypothalamus results in hypophagia, a lack of eating, which leads to starvation. Also involved in the control of food intake is the ventromedial nucleus (VMH) of the hypothalamus, which has been implicated in the control of satiety and the termination of feeding. VMH and lateral hypothalamus appear to be reciprocally related. Stimulation of VMH prevents eating even in a food-deprived animal. If VMH is destroyed, the organism seems unable to terminate feeding. Humans with brain tumors in the VMH cannot curb their food intake.

Similarly, animals with VMH damage eat excessively and produce large increases in body weight. The inactivation of VMH need not be permanent to affect feeding; injection of an anesthetic into the VMH seems to disinhibit feeding mechanisms in the lateral hypothalamus and induce eating in a previously sated animal.

Many areas of the brain in addition to the VMH and lateral hypothalamus are involved in the regulation of hunger and eating behavior. Although important, these nuclei must be thought of as working in conjunction with other areas in both the brainstem and the cortex to adequately account for the subleties of food-orienting behavior.

Thirst and the Regulation of Water Intake

Drinking is also a homeostatically controlled process but in some respects a separate process from feeding. There are important relations between the two mechanisms, since both interact to affect the internal environment. But the mechanisms controlling hunger respond to different sets of control variables.

What are the internal events that trigger thirst? Clearly, they are not peripheral. Cannon originally proposed that the drying of salivation in dehydration produced thirst and drinking, but more must be involved than simply the drying of salivation. Both men and dogs deprived of their salivary glands show normal control of water intake, although some differences in the timing of drinking occur. Water intake is too important a function to be entrusted to an organ system such as the salivary glands, which is subject to frequent disruption during the ingestion of food and other substances.

If peripheral factors in the mouth and throat are not crucial to the regulation of thirst, then where do the signals triggering thirst originate? Current research suggests that there may be at least two relatively independent bodily control systems that regulate water intake. Drinking may result when an organism becomes dehydrated. In simple dehydration, the fluid volume of both the intracellular and extracellular spaces is reduced and the concentration of solutes in both solutions increases. Thirst increases under such conditions.

Thirst also increases when only intracellular, and not extracellular, dehydration takes place. The increase in thirst may result from the ingestion of sodium salts, which increase the amount of sodium in the extracellular fluid. Since sodium does not cross the neuronal membrane with ease, the concentration of intracellular sodium does not increase. Under these conditions, the movement of water from the intracellular to the extracellular compartments of the brain produces a relative dehydration of only the intracellular spaces.

To account for the relation between intracellular dehydration and thirst, special sensory cells, or osmoreceptors, have been postulated to exist in the anterior hypothalamus of the brain. Osmoreceptors are thought to be large cells that change their rates of firing (or the rates of firing of some nearby cells) as they change in size. When their interior volumes shrink as a result of general dehydration, they send signals that trigger thirst. But such cells should also respond when sodium salts are used to induce thirst. Ingestion of sodium salts increases the amount of sodium in the extracellular fluid. The neuron's membrane is semipermeable, and, under most conditions, sodium is one of the ions that can cross the membrane only with great difficulty. Therefore, the intracellular concentration of sodium does not increase.

It is useful to think of the membrane as a structure with tiny pores. Water can cross the membrane freely if it gains access to the pores, but a solute like sodium cannot pass through it. In a state of continuing random motion, molecules of all sorts continuously contact the membrane. When sodium contacts a pore, it temporarily prevents other ions from using the pore. Therefore, an extracellular molecule of water is less likely to cross the membrane, since the chances are greater that a sodium ion will block its inward passage. But, on the inside, there is relatively little sodium, and water can pass freely into the extracellular space. Therefore, water will tend to move out of an area of dilute solute into an area of concentrated solute, if the solute cannot cross the membrane itself. This process will continue until the concentration of the solute is the same on the inside and the outside. Osmolarity is the ratio of solute to solvent particles in a solution. Thus, a cell that changes its size as a function of the concentration of sodium in the extracellular fluid could function as an osmoreceptor. When extracellular sodium is increased, such a cell shrinks. When extracellular sodium concentration is decreased, as happens following drinking, the cell expands. If such a cell is placed in pure water, it will expand until it bursts.

An osmoreceptor could sense the state of absolute cellular hydration and relay that information to other neuronal systems to permit corrective measures to be taken. One such corrective measure is to increase the water content of the body by the production of thirst-induced drinking. Another measure is to conserve the water immediately available within the body. Thus, at the same time as thirst is generated, there is also a release of antidiuretic hormone (ADH) from the pituitary gland. ADH is manufactured in the hypothalamus and transported to the pituitary, where it is released into the blood on neuronal command from the hypothalamus. ADH acts upon the kidney to increase the reabsorption of water from the kidney, which results in a low volume of highly concentrated urine, minimizing the loss of water by the body. In addition, in relative dehydration, the excretion of sodium in the kidney is also increased, and thus the source of the disparity between intracellular and extracellular fluid volumes is reduced.

The osmometric control of thirst and ADH output appears to

perform a balancing function for the organism. ADH is normally released by the pituitary at a relatively low rate. Only during states of hydration, in which both the intracellular and extracellular fluid volumes are increased by excessive water intake, does the release of ADH stop completely. In the absence of ADH, large volumes of urine are rapidly formed in the kidney, permitting the discharge of extra liquid by the organism. Osmometric control of water balance through the regulation of water intake and water output, therefore, may extend through a wide range of organismic conditions, from hydration through normal water balance to dehydration.

Hypothalamic osmoreceptors cannot, however, be the only mechanism operative in the control of thirst. Drinking and thirst result from a sudden loss of extracellular fluid, even though no alteration in the composition of the fluid occurs. For example, in the thirst arising after blood loss, osmolarity remains unaffected as the extracellular-fluid volume decreases dangerously. Some sort of volumetric control of fluid intake must also exist.

A situation similar to that arising from blood loss occurs in cases of extracellular sodium depletion, which results in a movement of water from the extracellular to the intracellular compartment and, therefore, in a sharp reduction of blood volume, which, in turn, reduces the blood supply to the bodily organs. Under such conditions, organisms drink, as they must, to restore the lost extracellular fluid. But, in this case, drinking cannot be under the control of osmoreceptors, since these cells are maximally hydrated and enlarged. Again, a volumetric mechanism is needed, which, in addition to producing thirst, also triggers the release of a vasoconstrictor, which limits the size of the vascular bed that the blood must fill and thereby partially restores blood pressure. In addition, the reabsorption of sodium by the kidney, which reduces further sodium depletion, is also increased.

Little is known about the postulated volume receptors. Even their location within the body is in doubt. It is likely, however, that special tissues in the kidney function as volume receptors. When blood flow through the kidney is reduced, thirst develops, without any alteration of the osmolarity of the fluids involved. The kidneys may release a substance that triggers the production of angiotensin, which could trigger receptors located somewhere within the brain to produce both thirst and a release of ADH. The relations between the kidney and the brain in sensing reductions of extracellular fluid remain to be clarified. It has even been suggested that the volume receptors are not in the kidney but are instead located within the heart and major blood vessels. But, whatever the case, it seems that a system of volumetric control must parallel the osmometric control system to account for important facts in the regulation of thirst and drinking.

Reward and Punishment Areas of the Brain

The control of bodily temperature, food intake, and water balance constitutes a relatively well-defined problem in the study of motivational systems of the brain. Some understanding has been gained of the internal stimuli used to regulate these vital processes and of the brain structures responsible for maintaining them within proper limits. However, motivational concepts are also necessary to explain behaviors far more subtle and variable than those concerned with the regulation of body temperature, food intake, and water balance. Is it possible to locate structures within the brain that mediate reward and punishment? That is, can animals who are neither hungry nor thirsty be motivated to perform arbitrarily defined tasks to receive or escape electrical stimulation of such structures? In 1954, Olds and Delgado discovered independently that the answer to these questions was yes.

Olds and Milner were interested in the motivational effects of electrical stimulation of the reticular arousal systems of the brainstem. Fine electrodes were permanently implanted within the rat's brain so that they could be used to deliver electrical stimulation after the animal had recovered from surgery. Long, flexible wires, suspended from above the animal's cage, permitted the animal's free movement during electrical stimulation. Since Miller had suggested earlier that electrical stimulation of the brain might be aversive (see below), Olds tested for possible aversive effects of stimulation by applying current to the animal's brain when the animal entered a particular quadrant of his cage. One rat did not avoid the portion of the cage in which he received shock; instead, he appeared to be coming back for more. That electrical stimulation increased the probability of the response made by the animal immediately prior to stimulation fits the classical definition of positive reinforcement.

Experimental error contributed a great deal to Olds' discovery. The electrode that he had hoped to place in the reticular formation had strayed far from its mark; it was lodged in the septal area of the forebrain instead. Although the positive-reinforcement systems of the brain are quite extensive, the placement of the electrode in the septal area was particularly fortunate, since the septum is one of the most potent of the reward sites. The relation between stimulation and reward was therefore quite apparent in the animal in which it was observed.

Olds and Milner confirmed this observation by making electrical stimulation of the brain (ESB) contingent on the animal's pressing a lever in his cage. If the electrodes were properly positioned, the animal would respond vigorously to receive ESB. Response rates of 2,000 presses per hour for a 24-hour period were not uncommon.

The possibility always exists, however, that ESB does not really reinforce but simply mimics certain aspects of naturally occurring reinforcers. Therefore, it was important to validate the correspondence between ESB and other rewards across a wider variety of situations and measures. The results of such investigations have been encouraging. Animals bar press for ESB in a Skinner box. ESB systematically increases the speed with which an animal moves down a runway if he receives ESB at the end. Animals will cross painful shock grids to obtain ESB and will choose ESB over other rewards under appropriate conditions. ESB can be used to generate secondary reinforcers (stimuli that become rewarding only after having been paired with a potent reinforcer). Although some controversy remains concerning the nature of ESB reward, the relationship of ESB to natural rewards, and other matters, there is little doubt that ESB at appropriate sites within the brain can serve as a potent reinforcer of behavior.

Olds endeavored, in a massive set of experiments, to map the reinforcement systems of the brain by measuring the effectiveness of ESB in reinforcing lever pressing at various loci throughout the brain. The results of these studies pointed to the limbic structures, especially to the hypothalamus.

The limbic system is an area of the brain long associated with emotions and emotional behavior. MacLean chose the term limbic or "border" system to describe a series of structures that surround the brainstem just below the cerebral cortex. The two great rings of tissue forming the limbic system are the hippocampus and the cingulate gyrus (see Figure 11.1). Two subcortical nuclei, the amygdala and the septum, are important parts of this system. Thalamic and hypothalamic nuclei also form part of the limbic brain, as do certain major connective pathways, including the fornix and the medial forebrain bundle. Disorders in the limbic system have long been associated behaviorally with emotional disturbance.

Limbic system areas are among the most potent of the positive reinforcement sites, although the relative efficacy of individual placements varies quite widely. The septum, amygdala, cingulate gyrus, and hippocampus have all been implicated in the reward system. The lateral portions of the hypothalamus also show positive effects. In fact, the single most potent tissue for rewarding ESB is the medial forebrain bundle, which is located in the lateral hypothalamus. Some placements within the reticular formation, as well, exhibit reward properties. From such anatomical evidence, it appears that the reward system of the mammal involves a considerable amount of forebrain tissue. Its interconnections allow communication with the cortex, with the extensive limbic and hypothalamic structures long associated with both vegetative function and emotion, and with the arousal systems of the

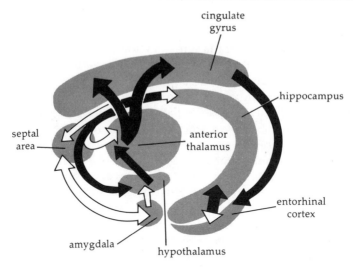

cingulate
gyrus

hippocampus

septal
area

anterior
thalamus

entorhinal
cortex

amygdala

hypothalamus

Figure 11.1. *The major structures of the limbic system and their interconnections.*
(From McCleary, R. A., & Moore, R. Y. *Subcortical Mechanisms of Behavior: The
Psychological Functions of Primitive Parts of the Brain.* New York: Basic Books,
1965, p. 32. Redrawn by permission.)

brainstem. But, despite its widespread ramifications, the reward system is discretely organized and has a complex structure and definitive
limits.

The reward system appears to depend heavily on a single
neurotransmitter, norepinephrine, in its synaptic connections. Ad-
renergic-blocking agents, which interfere with the release, or utilization, of norepinephrine, interfere with the operation of the reward
system and either decrease the rate at which an animal will bar press to
receive positively reinforcing ESB or raise the effective threshold of the
electrical stimuli needed to observe ESB-motivated behavior. Conversely, drugs that facilitate adrenergic activity seem to increase the
motivational efficacy of positive ESB, either increasing the rate of
operant responding or lowering the ESB threshold. Moreover, microanatomical evidence also supports the adrenergic hypothesis of
reward system action. The most potent structure for positive reinforcement, the medial forebrain bundle, contains norepinephrine in particularly large quantities, suggesting a pharmacological as well as neuroanatomical specificity in the positive reinforcing systems of the brain.

In the same year in which Olds first published his remarkable
observations on ESB, Delgado, Roberts, and Miller reported that ESB
delivered to some areas within the hypothalamus appeared punishing

to the cat. Animals would learn to perform a task to escape ESB at these sites. When stimulated, the cats displayed bodily signs of fear. Delgado, Roberts, and Miller had discovered the complement to Olds' pleasure areas, the hypothalamic aversive areas of the brain. Subsequent work with mapping firmly established both sets of findings. Most limbic areas show positive reinforcement effects to ESB, although in many places these effects are quite mild. Other sites show aversion, but, in rats, the aversive system is far less extensive than is the system of positive reinforcement. Although some areas appear clearly negative in their reinforcing effects, usually the aversive systems are closely intermixed with positively reinforcing structures. Thus many electrode placements give ambivalent effects, which produce both positive and negative reinforcement, the balance of which sometimes depends on the strength of electrical stimulation employed.

How is electrically produced reinforcement related to naturally occurring reinforcements? Does electrical stimulation act upon those brain structures that normally mediate reinforcement from environmental stimuli? Olds provided data that indicate that indeed ESB and natural reinforcers operate through the same channels within the limbic system. Olds implanted electrodes in castrated male rats and determined that those placements were, in fact, reinforcing. He then examined the effects of increased natural drive on lever pressing by depriving the animals of food on one occasion and by injecting them with androgen, a sexual stimulant, at another time. Rats with laterally placed electrodes tended to increase their response rates when injected with androgen and decrease it when deprived of food. Rats with more medial stimulation sites showed just the opposite pattern. Hunger tended to facilitate lever pressing, whereas sexual activation inhibited it. Rats with electrodes between these two extremes showed enhanced responding when either drive state, hunger or sex, was activated. Rewards appear to be controlled by two anatomically distinct reward systems within the brain. Because ESB may operate as a reinforcer through the same neuronal channels that mediate natural reinforcement, it is to be expected that a hungry animal will respond more to food-related reinforcement and less for sex-related ESB. Artificially produced drives appear to interact in much the same manner as do naturally occurring drive states. Drive state determines the attractiveness of the reinforcer or goal object.

Electrical stimulation of the brain can, under the best of circumstances, be a very powerful reinforcer. Routtenberg and Lindy demonstrated the power of ESB as a reinforcer by allowing rats access to both food and ESB for a 1-hour period each day. Rats with hypothalamic placements chose ESB and, by ignoring the food, produced dramatic losses in weight. Similarly, Olds presented data from a single animal allowed to press a lever for ESB at will for a 2-day period. The animal had pressed continuously for 26 hours when he fell asleep. As soon as he awoke, he again began pressing until he was finally removed from the box. In these cases, ESB appears to completely dominate the selection of responses by the organism.

Specific Motivational Effects of ESB

Since ESB in positive reinforcing areas interacts selectively with natural reinforcers, it is not surprising to find that stimulation of certain portions of the limbic and related systems results in motivational changes that are quite specific. In such sites, ESB has limited and predictable effects on behavior and on the expression of emotion. For example, electrical stimulation of specific points within the hypothalamic complex elicits apparently genuine aggressive behavior. Highly aggressive predatory attack can be obtained by stimulation of the perifornical area of the lateral hypothalamus. During such stimulation, the animal behaves as a hunter, quietly stalking its prey until the proper moment for attack, at which time he kills the stalked animal. Several factors suggest that the electrically induced hunting behavior is like natural hunting. First, the behavior depends on environmental factors. Aggression is much more likely to appear in the presence of an appropriate target organism than in its absence, but the presence of an apparently more powerful adversary can inhibit attack altogether. Moreover, during ESB of these sites, animals will perform a task for which the sole reward is access to an appropriate target organism. Electrically induced aggression appears to function as a drive state.

Stimulation in more medial regions of the hypothalamus appears to elicit a very different, defensive attack, in which the animal seems more intent on frightening away another animal than on hunting it. Such an attack is usually accompanied by noise and species-specific posturing. Similar effects can be obtained by electrical stimulation of the amygdala.

Sexual behavior can also be triggered by stimulation of hypothalamic areas. For example, stimulation of the lateral anterior hypothalamus greatly increases the level of sexual activity in the male rat. A continuous erection develops and, if a female is also present, near continuous copulation and ejaculation may be observed. All such behavior immediately ceases if ESB is discontinued. Stimulation of other hypothalamic areas may result in sexual responses of other forms, such as ejaculation without erection in the male rat. It should be remembered that the control of visceral and autonomic functions is a role that has been traditionally assigned to the hypothalamus. Such functions are not incompatible with the control of the expression of emotion, aggression, and sexuality.

The effects of ESB on behavior are not always positive. Sometimes the response of the organism is to terminate a particular type of ongoing behavior. Delgado, for example, has reported the results of a series of experiments with monkeys in which portions of the caudate nucleus, one of the limbic structures, were stimulated. The inhibition of motivated behavior was often the result. For example, stimulation of a particular caudate site appears to inhibit feeding. The monkey only casually examines a banana during caudate ESB; without the electrical stimulus, he grasps and consumes a banana without delay. Stimulation of another caudate area seems to have an inhibitory effect on aggression. The rhesus is normally a ferocious monkey, but during ESB it becomes tranquil.

Caudate ESB can inhibit aggressive behavior in monkeys in complex social conditions. A monkey colony is dominated by an aggressive male, who maintains his position by subtle gestures and postures that threaten his subordinates. He enjoys a variety of privileges, including the first choice of mates and food. During caudate stimulation, however, the dominant male is no longer able to maintain his position by the communication of aggression. He sits quietly and peacefully in his cage as a new social order develops. At the termination of stimulation, however, he again takes charge of the community.

Electrical Stimulation of the Human Brain

Research using electrical stimulation in the human brain has been quite limited, as one might expect. Investigators in clinical settings have reported the effects of ESB in man in cases where ESB was employed for primarily therapeutic reasons, but, because of the small number of such cases and the lack of appropriate control, the interpretation of these reports is difficult. Nonetheless, the results of the studies tend to confirm and extend the concept of limbic-system control of reinforcement and affect developed in the study of lower mammals. The effects of ESB and the anatomical distribution of ESB reinforcement appear to be substantially the same for man as for other species.

For a number of years, Heath has examined the effects of ESB in man. Human patients, unlike lower animals, can verbally express the subjective effects of ESB. In a recent summary of this work, Heath describes the effects of positively reinforcing ESB as follows:

> With septal stimulation the patients brightened, looked more alert, and seemed to be more attentive to their environment during, and for at

least a few minutes after, the period of stimulation. With this basic affective change, most subjects spoke more rapidly, and content was more productive; changes in content of thought were often striking, the most dramatic shifts occurring when prestimulation associations were pervaded with depressive affect. Expressions of anguish, self-condemnation, and despair changed precipitously to expressions of optimism and elaborations of pleasant experiences, past and antici-pated. Patients sometimes appeared better oriented; they could calculate more rapidly and, generally, more accurately than before stimulation. Memory and recall were enhanced or unchanged. Psychomotor activity accelerated during stimulation. Subjects were not informed when stimuli were applied. When questioned concerning changes in mental content, they were generally at a loss to explain them. For example, one patient on the verge of tears described his father's near-fatal illness and condemned himself as somehow responsible, but when the septal region was stimulated, he immediately terminated this conversation and within 15 seconds exhibited a broad grin as he discussed plans to date and seduce a girl friend. When asked why he had changed the conversation so abruptly, he replied that the plans concerning the girl suddenly came to him. This phenomenon was repeated several times in the patient: Stimulation was administered to the septal region when he was describing a depressive state, and almost instantly he became gay. Another severely agitated and depressed subject whose verbalizations expressed self-condemnation and hopelessness (a condition that had prevailed for over 2 years) smiled broadly and related a sexual experi-ence of his youth within one minute after onset of septal stimulation.

Striking and immediate relief from intractable physical pain was consistently obtained with stimulation to the septal region of three patients with advanced carcinoma, two with metastases from primary breast carcinoma to bone and one with carcinoma of the cervix and extensive local proliferation. The patients were stimulated at intervals ranging from twice a day to once every 3 days over periods of 3 weeks to 8 months. Stimulation to the septal region immediately relieved the intense physical pain and anguish, and the patients relaxed in comfort and pleasure [Heath, 1964, pp. 224–225].*

Conversely, electrical stimulation of the brain in areas known to be aversive often is reported to elicit a mental state of fear. Erwin has described cases in which ESB of medial thalamic regions produces acute anxiety in human subjects. The feeling is apparently quite real, like being missed by a speeding automobile, one patient reported. Fear, like other intense emotions, produces changes in the activity of the autonomic systems of the body. That the patient also reported feeling a chill pass down his back suggests that such changes are directly related to electrical stimulation of limbic nuclei. Since the ESB was applied only

*From Heath, R. G. Pleasure response in human subjects to direct stimulation of the brain: Physiological and psychodynamic considerations. In R. G. Heath (Ed.), *The Role of Pleasure in Behavior*, Hoeber, 1964. Used by permission.

to one side of the brain, the chill was also experienced as unilateral, as it occurred in the contralateral half of the body.

The experience of pleasure or anxiety may be directly proportional to the strength of the stimulating current. Erwin describes the case of a female patient who was hospitalized for acute anxiety attacks leading to suicidal attempts and continuing agitated depression. Electrical stimulation of the dorsolateral nucleus of the thalamus produced typical anxiety attacks in this patient. The intensity of the attack could be controlled by simply adjusting the level of ESB. Threshold levels of stimulation produced only mild anxiety, but the terror of the attack could be increased by increasing stimulating current. Erwin remarked that "one could sit with one's hand on the knob and control the level of her anxiety" (Delgado, 1969, p. 135).

Similar relationships exist between the intensity of ESB and the strength of its rewarding effects in animals. If the electrode is situated in a purely reward area, increasing current density increases the rate at which the animal will bar press to obtain it. If, however, the electrode is placed in a mixed area or near a mixed area, the relation between strength of ESB and its behavioral effects is less predictable. Because increasing current density also increases the area within the brain affected by ESB, adjacent limbic areas become involved at higher current levels. If those areas are functionally antagonistic, mixed effects will begin to appear.

As do the animal experiments, studies of humans suggest that ESB and environmental reinforcers may utilize the same brain structures in achieving their effects. Stimulation of the septal area of the limbic system in man tends to induce sexually oriented behavior. The septal area is also critically involved in sexual activity in the absence of electrical stimulation of the brain. Figure 11.2 shows EEG activity recorded from many brain sites while the patient was alert and relaxed. Compare Figure 11.2 with Figure 11.3, which shows EEG recorded from the same sites during orgasm. Activity in the septal areas shows a sudden shift to epileptiform patterns of spikes and slow waves at about 1 to 2 per second. This shift is taken to represent intense septal activation with ramifications elsewhere in the limbic system, including the amygdala. Notice little change elsewhere in the brain, except for artifacts produced by intense muscular activity and bodily movement.

Peripheral Factors in Emotion

Central mechanisms, located primarily within the limbic system of the brain, are necessary in the normal activation of the emotions. But are they sufficient? Strong emotions have long been known to produce

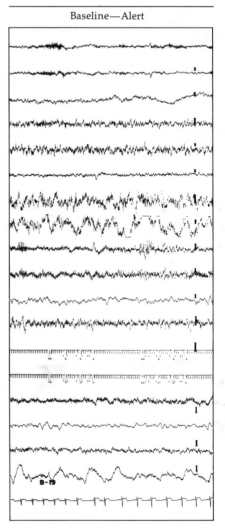

Baseline—Alert

left frontal to left temporal scalp

right frontal to right temporal scalp

left frontal cortex

central midline to right frontal cortex

right frontal to right temporal cortex

left occipital cortex

left amygdala

right amygdala

left cerebellar dentate

left cerebellar fastigius

left anterior septal region

right midseptal region

time code, generator machine 1

time code, generator machine 2

left caudate nucleus

left posterior septal region

right posterior ventral lateral thalamus

right central nucleus

electrocardiogram

Figure 11.2. *EEG recorded from both the surface of the brain and deeper structures during a period of alert relaxation.* (From Heath, R. G. Pleasure and brain activity in man: Deep and surface electroencephalograms during orgasm. *Journal of Nervous and Mental Disease*, 1972, **154**, 10. © 1972 The Williams & Wilkins Co., Baltimore. Used by permission.)

dramatic changes in the pattern of bodily functioning. Would fear be different without its chills and shudders? Visceral changes that usually accompany emotion seem to be necessary for normal emotional expression.

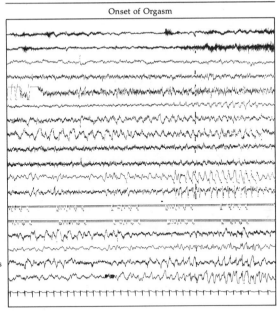

	Onset of Orgasm
left frontal to left temporal scalp	
right frontal to right temporal scalp	
left frontal cortex	
central midline to right frontal cortex	
right frontal to right temporal cortex	
left occipital cortex	
left amygdala	
right amygdala	
left cerebellar dentate	
left cerebellar fastigius	
left anterior septal region	
right midseptal region	
time code, generator machine 1	
time code, generator machine 2	
left caudate nucleus	
left posterior septal region	
right posterior ventral lateral thalamus	
right central nucleus	
electrocardiogram	

Figure 11.3. *EEG recorded during the onset of orgasm.* For explanation, see text. (From Heath, R. G. Pleasure and brain activity in man: Deep and surface electroencephalograms during orgasm. *Journal of Nervous and Mental Disease,* 1972, **154,** 11. © 1972 The Williams & Wilkins Co., Baltimore. Used by permission.)

William James, the first great American psychologist, argued strongly for the importance of visceral sensation in emotion. He proposed that the feelings associated with emotional behavior arise from the perception of the autonomic responses that are produced reflexively by the occurrence of the exciting event. Others have challenged James' view on a number of critical issues, three of which will concern us here. First, if James were correct, then the artificial induction of visceral activity should produce emotion of some sort. Second, different visceral patterns should accompany perceptibly different emotional states. Finally, the interruption of sensory pathways from the visceral organs to the brain should result in substantial changes in the quality of emotional experience. Each of these predictions has been, in part, borne out. Schachter has recently examined closely the status of James' peripheralist theory, which is now 80 years old. Much of the following is drawn from Schachter's analysis.

Maranon was one of the first to test the hypothesis that artificially induced changes in autonomic activity might lead to the experience of emotion. Maranon injected 210 volunteers with adrenalin, an agent that produces a sympathetic pattern of visceral arousal similar to that seen during intense emotion. All subjects reported significant physical changes, such as sweating, increased heart rate, and flushing. But most (71 percent) subjects reported no emotional experience. Of the remaining subjects, the great majority reported "cold" emotion or "as if" emotion. "I feel as if I were afraid, but I am not" would be a typical subject's report. A few subjects did experience true emotion, but those volunteers were people for whom a strong emotional memory had been suggested. For example, if prior discussions revealed concern about a sick child, the same subject broached after the adrenalin injection would produce a full reaction of grief or fear. Autonomic activation by an injection of adrenalin is not by itself sufficient to elicit emotional response.

Schachter and Singer pursued the interaction of sympathetic activation and cognitive factors in an ingenious experiment involving the secret administration of adrenalin. They reasoned that most of the subjects in Maranon's study attributed the physical changes that they experienced to the drug that they were given. The signs of autonomic arousal in Maranon's study would not be attributed to emotion, since a display of emotion would not be plausible under those circumstances; only subjects to whom emotionally powerful memories were available had the cognitive set that would permit the experience of bodily changes as emotional changes.

By administering adrenalin disguised as a vitamin, Schachter and Singer deprived their subjects of a simple cognitive explanation for the changes that would occur. Some subjects were then told that the vitamin produced side effects similar to those that they would actually experience. Other subjects were told nothing. All subjects were then placed in a social situation designed to produce either anger or euphoria. In the anger condition, subjects were treated brusquely and required to fill out a questionnaire composed of increasingly personal and insulting items (for example, "With how many men [other than your father] has your mother had extramarital relationships? Four or under, 5–9, 10 and over.") In the euphoria condition subjects were treated kindly and each put in the company of a playful accomplice of the experimenter. The results indicate that subjects who were informed of the drug effects were far less likely to show emotion than were those who were ignorant. But, in those uninformed subjects, visceral arousal could give rise to either euphoria or anger, depending on the cognitive set induced by environmental cues.

The extent of emotionality elicited by an emotionally laden stimulus grows with increasing autonomic arousal. Singer examined fear responses in rats given either adrenalin, a placebo (an inert substance), or chlorpromazine, which blocks the action of adrenalin and other adrenergic compounds. The three groups of animals then could be characterized as having heightened, normal, or suppressed visceral responsiveness. Fear was measured by observing the rat's behavior for species-specific signs of fearfulness: urination, defecation, freezing, trembling, and face washing. Injection of the drugs by themselves produces no noticeable changes in emotionality. But, if the pretreated animals are placed in a fear-producing situation—a box with loud buzzers, ringing doorbells, and bright flashing lights—the expected differences appear. Rats given adrenalin were most fearful, whereas those receiving pretreatment with chlorpromazine showed the least emotionality. Autonomic activation makes important contributions to emotion, but, by itself, it is insufficient to elicit emotion.

The second prediction of James' theory of emotion is that discriminably different visceral responses should occur in discriminably different emotions. There is now some evidence for characteristically different responses in the viscera for different emotional states. Wolf and Wolff, for example, have shown that different patterns of response occur in the stomach wall of a human subject under conditions of fear and hostility. Specific changes in other autonomic response systems during the experience of emotion have also been reported. For example, Funkenstein found differential changes in diastolic and systolic blood pressure, heart rate, and peripheral skin resistance, which distinguish the autonomic response in fear and anger. But the action of the internal organs is notoriously labile. It would be a mistake to think that each emotion reliably leads to one, and only one, pattern of autonomic response.

A third prediction of a peripheralist theory such as James' is that the interruption of sensory pathways linking the viscera and brain should produce substantial changes in the quality of emotional experience. Avoidance tasks are often used to test fear-based behavior. Animals trained to respond to avoid a painful stimulus continue to respond even after sympathectomy, which severs most connections between viscera and brain. Learned emotional behavior does not seem to depend on the maintenance of visceral input.

If, however, sympathectomy is performed before training, a very different pattern develops. Sympathectomized dogs learn an avoidance task very slowly, and, unlike normals, they extinguish the learned behavior very quickly. Normal dogs extinguish avoidance behaviors only with great difficulty, if they extinguish at all.

A distinction must be made, therefore, between emotional behavior and emotional experience, or feeling. Schachter finds support of the view that disruption of visceral input may significantly affect experience while leaving old, well-learned emotional behaviors unchanged in an experiment of Hohmann. Hohmann studied 25 patients in the Spinal Cord Injury Service at the Veterans Administration

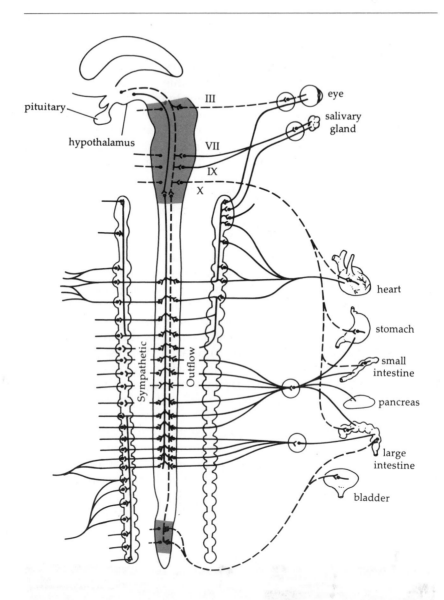

Figure 11.4.   *The autonomic nervous system and the organs that it innervates.* (From Gardner, E. *Fundamentals of Neurology, Fifth Edition,* 1968, p. 232. Used by permission of W. B. Saunders Company.)

Hospital in Long Beach, California. He asked the patients to recall emotion-arousing experiences subsequent to their injury and then to recall a comparable incident before the injury took place. The patients were instructed to compare the intensity of the emotional feelings that they experienced in each of the situations. Their responses were coded to constitute the basic data of the investigation.

These patients all had completely severed spinal cords. Above the level of the cut, the brain could maintain normal communication with the viscera, but, below the injury, none of the normal pathways remained. Thus, patients with high breaks received very little visceral input, whereas patients with low breaks had nearly normal sensory input from the autonomic nervous system. When patients are separated into groups by spinal level of injury, the results of Hohmann's study are clear. The higher the break, the less feeling remained in the experience

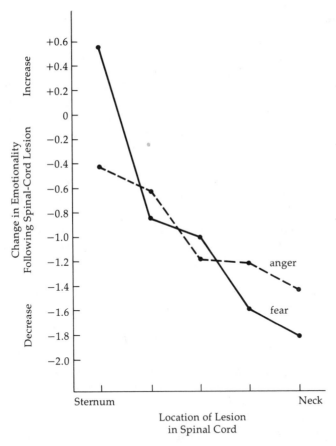

Figure 11.5. *Changes in rated emotional feeling before and after lesion of the spinal cord for patients with lesions at different levels.* Higher lesions deprive the patient of more autonomic input and result in larger reported changes. (From Schachter, S. *Emotion, Obesity, and Crime*, p. 51. Copyright 1971 by Academic Press, Inc. Used by permission.)

of emotion (see Figure 11.5). Emotions do not seem as intense with part of the communication from the viscera removed.

Emotional behavior does not disappear in these patients. They say that they still act emotionally when the situation warrants but that the feeling is gone. Unlike Maranon's subjects, who felt "as if" they were aroused, the spinal patients say that they are aroused but do not feel it. As one remarked, "It's a mental sort of anger," and that is very different from bodily anger.

Peripheral factors, along with more central activation, are necessary for the normal expression of emotion. Motivation often reflects integrated processes throughout the entire nervous system.

Summary

Motivational processes are always inferred from changes in the direction, intensity, and persistence of behavior. Motivational processes cannot be directly observed. Motivational concepts are useful for explaining and predicting the behavioral variability of an organism's response to a stimulus object over time, the variation in the incentive value of stimuli, and the reward properties of high-incentive stimuli. The brain processes that mediate these subtle phenomena are incompletely understood.

Some motivational processes such as the control of hunger and thirst can be considered homeostatic. They act to maintain certain important variables within desired limits. Homeostatic mechanisms must have sensors to provide information concerning the variable under control, predefined goal states to specify the desired region, and connection with effectors to permit adaptive responding when the desired limits are exceeded.

The controlled quantity in the feeding-regulation system has not yet been positively identified; it is probably, however, a constituent of the blood. Blood glucose has often been suggested as the crucial variable. More than one variable may be involved in the complex feeding-regulation system.

Hypothalamic areas are implicated in the control of feeding. The initiation of feeding depends upon activation of the lateral hypothalamus, whereas the termination of hunger depends in part upon the action of the ventromedial nucleus of the hypothalamus (VHM). Lesions in the VMH lead to obesity, as the animal cannot curb his food intake at normal levels. Satiety can be artificially induced in a food-deprived animal by electrical stimulation of the VMH.

Like eating, drinking is also homeostatically regulated. Peripheral variables such as mouth dryness have been postulated to instigate thirst, but they appear to be of little actual importance.

Instead, cellular osmolarity seems a more likely candidate for the controlled process. Osmoreceptors have been postulated to exist in the anterior hypothalamus. However, that drinking behavior can be modified by changing the volume of the extracellular compartment without affecting osmolarity indicates the existence of other controlled variables in the regulation of water intake.

Other brain structures, primarily within the limbic system, seem to perform more general motivational functions to mediate the control of reward and punishment. Stimulation of reward areas increases the probability of actions that immediately precede the onset of stimulation, while stimulation of punishment areas produces the opposite effect. That electrically elicited drive states seem to interact with naturally occurring drives suggests that both utilize the same brain structures.

Electrical stimulation of the brain (ESB) can act as a very powerful reinforcer. Animals will choose ESB in preference to food or, if allowed uninterrupted bar pressing, will continue to work for ESB as long as wakefulness can be maintained.

The reinforcement systems of the human brain seem to follow the same mapping established for lower mammals. ESB in man produces marked alterations of mood, affect, and behavior. ESB in rewarding areas has been employed to ameliorate the effects of intractable pain in certain patients. The effective changes induced by ESB are fully elaborated within the autonomic nervous system. The bodily signs of emotion accompany ESB within the limbic system.

Peripheral factors contribute to the normal experience of emotion. For example, the administration of adrenalin, a sympathetic activating agent, will not normally induce emotion, although the bodily signs of intense emotion will be present. When given secretly, however, and when an appropriate cognitive state is provided, adrenalin facilitates the expression of emotion. Sympathetic activation can be interpreted as either joy or anger, depending upon situational determinants. If, however, the autonomic arousal can be ascribed to the drug, the experience of emotion is considerably less likely.

The pattern of visceral response is not the same for all emotional states. Fear and anger, for example, produce reliably different responses in both the cardiovascular and the gastrointestinal systems. The extent of autonomic specificity is not great, however. Fine distinctions of emotion are not likely to depend upon fine differences in the pattern of autonomic response.

Depriving the organism of visceral input seems to reduce the intensity of emotional feeling, but, under many circumstances, emotional behavior remains unchanged. Motivation and emotion depend upon integrated processes in both the central and the peripheral nervous systems.

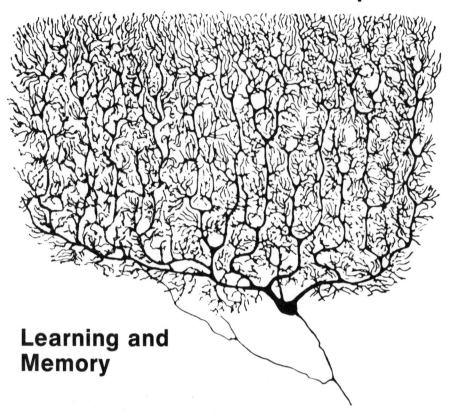

Chapter 12

Learning and Memory

The higher animals have survived and prospered largely because they are adaptable, changing their behavior on the basis of previous experience. Of course, learning is not all that distinguishes the quick from the dead in the animal kingdom. Higher animals also process information in more sophisticated ways than lower animals do and are more flexible in the manner in which they can organize responses. But learning is crucial. Higher organisms can better use past experience to modify future behavior.

What is learning? The answer to such a question seems very easy. However, a formal definition of learning has been notoriously difficult to provide, since learning is a process that cannot be directly observed. Instead, it must be inferred from the behavior of organisms. Only behavior can be measured to discern probable internal processes. Learning has been defined as the process that produces a relatively permanent change in behavior resulting from practice. However, not all behavioral change is attributable to learning. For instance, behavior changes when an animal becomes fatigued, but fatigue is not learning. The speed and accuracy of performance of even a highly skilled typist deteriorate after many consecutive hours of work. Changes due to fatigue are not attributed to learning since they are not relatively permanent. The definition of learning also excludes behavioral changes produced by drugs, motivational changes, and maturation, since none of these changes depend upon practice as conventionally understood. Learning is the process of storing information in memory.

How Many Memories Are There?

There may be, for example, special memory systems for motor tasks, other memory systems for verbal tasks, and still other memory systems for perceptual information. However, evidence for this kind of proliferation of memory systems is very scant. Strong evidence exists for at least three different memory systems that are based not on the quality of information to be stored but on the newness of information within the system. (See Figure 12.1.) One memory system, sensory memory, holds incoming information for a fraction of a second until other systems can process it. Another memory system, short-term memory (STM), stores information for short periods of time, minutes or hours; it appears to function as scratch-pad memory, controlling ongoing behavior. Long-term memory (LTM), a third information-storage system, permanently retains information. Consolidation is the hypothesized process of building long-term memory, probably from information stored in short-term memory.

Sensory Memory

Although the physical basis of sensory memory is unknown, there are several plausible mechanisms. The time scale of sensory memory is similar to that of neuronal after-events in many sensory

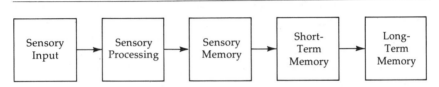

Figure 12.1. *One of the possible sets of relations linking sensory memory, short-term memory, and long-term memory.*

systems; therefore sensory memory could depend upon the lingering activity in sensory cells of the thalamus and cortex. Prolonged discharges would preserve sensory information for short periods of time.

Sensory memory probably occurs in all sensory systems. Although normally we are not aware of its existence, under special circumstances its action can be directly observed. A tachistoscope, for example, is used to present a visual stimulus of a few milliseconds' duration. The image appears to linger after the presentation is over. You can experience this phenomenon for yourself by first shutting your eyes for a few seconds, then rapidly opening and closing them. The image does not disappear abruptly but instead fades. The lingering image is sensory memory in vision.

Some devices exploit sensory memory to achieve their desired effect. For example, both motion pictures and television employ a series of images, which are joined together in sensory memory to form one continuously moving picture. Without sensory memory, a succession of still pictures would be experienced, as when the speed of a home movie projector is reduced or when a televised image is rebroadcast slowly. The limits of sensory memory are passed and the illusion of movement disappears.

Sensory memory is nonselective. In vision, the whole memory of a briefly presented scene fades together. The capacity of sensory memory to store information, therefore, is large, but sensory memory is impermanent. There is much more information in sensory memory than can ever be passed to other systems in the brain.

George Sperling provided an elegant demonstration of the large information capacity of visual sensory memory. Sperling used a tachistoscope to display both an array of nine letters, arranged three by three, and a marker pointing to one of the letters. The marker appeared after the array had vanished. The subject was asked to report the letter that was in the position indicated by the marker. Since the letters were no longer physically present when the marker appeared, the subject had to use sensory memory to produce the correct answer. Figure 12.2 shows this experiment graphically. By varying the amount of time between presenting the array and the marker, the decay of information in the sensory memory can be charted, as shown in Figure 12.3. The subject's performance deteriorates as the interval is lengthened. At about 0.5 second, the curve stabilizes. If no marker is presented, the subject can recall four or five letters when asked several seconds later. Presumably, he has had time to transfer this information to another form of memory in the 500-msec period before the image faded. Sperling's experiment tells us two things: the duration of sensory memory and the rate at which information can be read from it. If the subject is shown the marker while the sensory image still remains, he can use the image to

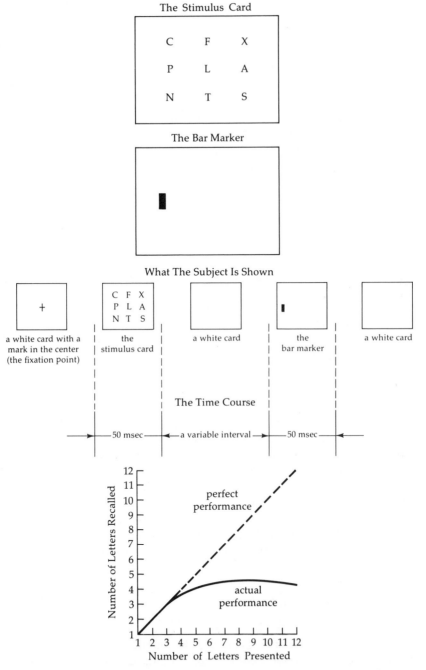

Figure 12.2. *The Sperling experiment.* (From Lindsay, P., & Norman, D. *Human Information Processing: An Introduction to Psychology.* © 1972 by Academic Press, Inc. Data taken from Sperling, G. Information in a brief visual presentation, unpublished doctoral dissertation, Harvard University, 1959. Used by permission.)

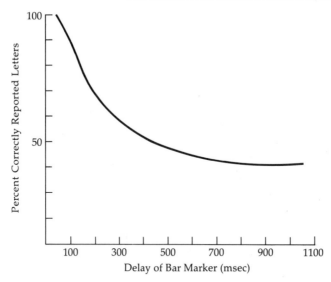

Figure 12.3. *Decay of sensory memory.* Sperling's results suggest that sensory memory decays in a few hundred milliseconds. Beyond that time, the subject appears unable to report from sensory memory the item indicated by a marker. (From Lindsay, P., & Norman, D. *Human Information Processing: An Introduction to Psychology.* © 1972 by Academic Press, Inc. Data taken from Sperling, G. Information in a brief visual presentation, unpublished doctoral dissertation, Harvard University, 1959. Used by permission.)

produce the correct answer. But, after the image has faded, he must rely on other, more stable memories.

Thus, for extremely short periods of time, we remember a great deal of information. However, most of that information is quickly lost. What happens to the information that is later remembered? Those few items must be transferred from sensory memory to another brain system (probably short-term memory) which functions to hold information.

Short-Term Memory

Short-term memory functions to retain information for immediate use. The span of STM, measured in minutes or hours, depends upon factors such as the species of the animal and the complexity of the information being processed. Short-term memory appears to serve at least two purposes. One is to guide behavior—that is, to allow the organism to utilize recently acquired information to modify his actions.

Animals can learn to perform a task by using only STM without the benefit of more permanent information storage. The other probable function of STM is to hold information while a more permanent memory is being formed.

Why postulate a short-term memory at all? In some experiments, there appears to be a period following the acquisition of new information by the organism in which long-term memory is not yet established. Consolidation, or the process of building long-term memory, presumably takes some time. During this period, and for some time thereafter, some other memory mechanism must be operative.

One line of evidence for a separate STM is based on cases of traumatic amnesia, or the loss of memory as a result of a sudden and significant disruption of brain activity, such as a blow to the head that renders the organism unconscious. Amnesia may also result from a major epileptic seizure, during which the activity in many areas of the brain is disrupted. Any of a number of other events might produce traumatic amnesia, but all have in common the thorough disruption of normal patterns of activity.

Surprisingly, not all memories disappear. Indeed, if there is not permanent brain damage, most memory is retained. Only the memories for very recent events, events that occurred immediately preceding the disruption, are lost. It has therefore been postulated that for these events no permanent memory had yet been established. Traumatic amnesia appears to interfere only with short-term memory, not with permanent memory.

The disappearance of short-term memory tells us something about its nature. Because it seems to be fragile and is lost when the pattern of activity in the brain is radically altered, STM is often considered to be an activity trace in which information is encoded as a particular pattern of neuronal firing. If a pattern is disrupted, the information it represents will be irretrievably lost.

Various neuronal mechanisms could serve the function of an activity trace for short-term memory. Donald Hebb, among others, has suggested that information may be temporarily stored in the firing of a closed chain of neurons. In such an arrangement, one cell excites a second, which excites a third, and so on. A closed chain is formed when one of the neurons synapses on the original unit. A closed chain can be self-sustaining; once activated, it remains active until disrupted, either by additional input or by degenerative influences such as the instability of single cells within the chain.

There is no reason to believe that such a chain would be a simple circle of neurons. Indeed, if that were the case, information would be lost completely if any one of the neurons failed to properly relay its message. However, the same principle could operate in an infinitely more complicated system. Many closed circuits of neurons could be arranged to form a closed, highly interconnected system, in which the activity of any one cell would be relatively unimportant, but in which the whole circuit could achieve some stability over time. This circuit would allow information to be retained by the nervous system while a more permanent trace is being formed. Of course, the circuit could not withstand a severe blow, such as epileptic seizure, that would simultaneously alter the firing of all cells within the circuit. Although difficult to test directly, closed-circuit concepts are consistent with what is known about the nature of the short-term memory trace.

Short-term memory and its disruption can be studied in the laboratory by electrically inducing epileptic-like seizures in animals (and sometimes in man). The application of a large, pulsating current across the brain to upset its delicate balance of activity results in seizure and convulsion. Electroconvulsive shock (ECS) both mimics epileptic attack and produces traumatic amnesia.

Beginning with the experiments of Duncan in 1949, ECS has been used to study short-term memory and the time course of consolidation. In these experiments and in many of the others that followed, the organism was quickly trained to perform a task. At some later time, ECS was administered. After a suitable period for recovery (often a day or a week), the organism was again tested on the original task. In most experiments, subsequent performance was better in animals for which the ECS and the training were separated by a relatively long period. From such data, estimates were made of the probable time course of consolidation for that combination of species and task. The greatest interval separating training and ECS for which an impairment could be measured was usually taken as the time necessary for relatively complete consolidation.

Various methodological difficulties arose in this research. For example, ECS seems to produce amnesia, but it also is very unpleasant. In some animals, aversive effects accumulate over time and interfere with the straightforward interpretation of the experiment. An animal may not perform a previously learned task for which he earns a pleasurable reward, not because ECS blocks memory but because the ECS is punishing. One way to avoid this methodological difficulty is to use a passive-avoidance task. A rat is placed on a small platform above a wire-mesh floor, which can be electrified to give painful foot shock when the animal steps down. Normal rats quickly leave the pedestal to explore the cage. The average time taken to step off the platform is short. If the floor is electrified, the animal quickly learns to remain on the platform; one trial is enough for a normal animal. When placed on the platform again, he does not leave and thereby passively avoids the unpleasant foot shock. If, however, the animal is given ECS immediately after foot shock, an interesting situation develops. If ECS is merely painful but does not actually produce amnesia, then the ECS should join with the foot shock in punishing the animal for leaving the platform. But, if ECS is an amnesic agent, then, when tested later, the animal should remember neither the ECS nor the foot shock and should naively step off the platform. In fact, if ECS immediately follows foot shock, the animal fails to passively avoid the wire-mesh floor that had been the source of pain. Thus, ECS appears to produce genuine traumatic amnesia.

ECS can be used to measure the amount of time necessary for the animal to consolidate information into permanent memory. If ECS given 45 seconds after a trial produces amnesia, whereas ECS given 60 seconds after a trial does not, then it can be argued that a long-term memory is sufficiently established between 45 and 60 seconds to permit use of the learning at a later time. Such time values are common for rats in a passive-avoidance task, but much longer estimates have been reported for the time course of consolidation in other experiments. Both species and task may be important in determining the speed with which permanent memory is established. Genetic factors may also play a role. Rats bred for their ability to learn seem to consolidate information more quickly than rats bred for stupidity.

The speed of consolidation of long-term memory can also be manipulated experimentally. For example, in some species, the brain can be artificially cooled without doing damage to tissue. Cooling the brain appears to slow the rate of activity of the consolidation mechanism as well as slowing brain processes more generally. Also, pharmacological agents can be employed to alter the rate of consolidation, as estimated by the ECS method. For example, strychnine apparently blocks transmission in certain inhibitory neurons within the brain. Given in large doses, strychnine is lethal; but, in small doses, strychnine appears to speed the consolidation of information in animals. Strychnine apparently removes some unknown inhibitory influences that act on the hypothesized consolidating processes of the brain.

Finally, it should be pointed out that consolidation is not presumed to be an all-or-nothing affair. The representation of information appears to become more complete, or robust, as the fixation of memory proceeds. When consolidation is prematurely interrupted, the strength of the resulting memory is more or less proportional to the time elapsing before disruption. As incomplete representations of information seem to be possible, data from such experiments must be interpreted probabilistically.

Long-Term Memory: Consolidation

Permanent memory is not likely to be based on activity traces but, instead, probably depends upon physical changes in the structure of the nervous system. The notion of structural traces as the basis of long-term memory has much to recommend it. First, LTM can survive many assaults on the activity of the brain. That LTM is not destroyed by electroconvulsive shock, epileptic seizures, or long periods of coma seems to rule out activity traces, as commonly understood, as the substrate on which permanent memory is based. The fact that memory can remain intact in man for many years without apparent rehearsal of information suggests instead a structural change of some permanence. The idea of a permanent structural change corresponds well with data showing that certain chemicals that interfere with the capacity of the brain to make structural changes prevent the consolidation of permanent memory.

Neurons, like other living cells, accomplish many of their life functions, including self-modification, through the construction of complex proteins. Plans for these proteins are contained in the genetic code of the deoxyribonucleic acid (DNA) molecules. Specific information is extracted from the immensely long DNA chain by a ribonucleic-acid (RNA) molecule in the process of transcription. Information is transcribed onto the RNA molecule, which becomes in some sense the mirror image of the DNA master plan. But RNA, no matter what its configuration, is of little direct use to the cell in carrying out its functions. Crucial proteins must be formed by using information contained in the RNA. Protein synthesis, or translation, is carried out in the ribosomes of neurons. Messenger RNA specifies the complex sequence of amino acids that are to be used in the construction of the particular protein. Antibiotics injected directly into the brain interfere with the process of translation. Puromycin, an antibiotic, disrupts protein synthesis by attaching itself to the growing amino acid chain, thereby breaking it off prematurely. Cycloheximide, another antibiotic that disrupts protein synthesis, acts in a different manner; it severely slows the rate of translation. Both drugs, when injected over brain tissue, prevent the construction of new proteins in neurons.

If consolidation of memory depends upon the construction of proteins, then blocking the process of consolidation with antibiotics is a very likely possibility. It is difficult to conceive of a cellular basis for permanent memory that does not involve proteins. For example, the physical basis of memory may be a newly grown endfoot that makes a connection where none existed before. It may be the production of an enzyme that increases the efficiency of an already existing synapse. It may involve the alteration of a cellular membrane to modify the efficiency of current flow within a cell. It may depend upon the production of a specific protein that can be recognized by another protein, in much the same way that cells remember an irritant in allergic reactions. The point is that there are many possible cellular events that could, separately or in combination, serve to store information permanently. Although we do not know what mechanism is actually used, it is a good bet that the mechanism, whatever it may be, involves the construction of proteins to record what has been learned. Other possibilities exist, but evidence from experiments using antibiotics suggests that proteins play a crucial role in the establishment of permanent memory.

Bernard Agranoff developed a very successful method for studying the consolidation process using goldfish. (The goldfish distinguishes itself in the laboratory by being small, inexpensive, trainable, and easy to inject cerebrally.) The task is a simple one: the fish learns to escape, and then to avoid, electric shock. Figure 12.4 shows a fish in a two-compartment training tank, or shuttle tank. The barrier separating the tank into compartments lies within an inch of the surface. The fish is first placed in the darkened tank for 5 minutes. Then a light is turned on in the fish's compartment. A pulsing electric shock is applied 20 seconds later. If the fish has crossed to the other side, he does not feel the shock. Thus, the fish can escape the shock by crossing the barrier. If he swims over before the shock is applied, but after the light is turned on, he avoids the shock completely. Both the shock and the light are terminated 20 seconds after the shock was introduced. The procedure begins again 20 seconds later, but this time the fish must cross the barrier in the opposite direction (hence the term "shuttle tank").

Most goldfish escape shock without training, but very few avoid shock without practice in the task. In the first ten trials, a goldfish will

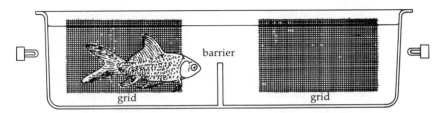

Figure 12.4. *The shuttle-box training situation for goldfish.* (Used by permission from Agranoff, B. W. Memory and protein synthesis. *Scientific American,* 1967, **216**(6), 115. Copyright © 1967 by Scientific American, Inc. All rights reserved.)

avoid shock about 20% of the time. If given unlimited training, a goldfish can reach about 80% avoidance. In the remaining trials, the goldfish escapes shock.

Not only can normal goldfish learn to avoid electric shock, but they can also remember what they have learned. As shown in Figure 12.5a, the goldfish is given 30 training trials, 20 on one day and 10 later. The fish resumes the learning task as he left it. Whether 3 or 30 days intervene, the fish shows perfect memory for what he has learned. The information about the task is consolidated.

Can an antibiotic, puromycin, be used to block the consolidation process? It can, if injected before the hypothesized protein-dependent consolidation process is completed, as shown in Figures 12.5b–12.5d. The needle indicates the time at which a small quantity of puromycin was injected over the fish's brain. By 1 hour after removal from the task situation, the protein-dependent phase of the consolidation process appears to have been completed. The animals remember as much as untreated animals do when tested several days later. But, if the drug is injected immediately following training (Figure 12.5d), no memory is formed. When tested later, the fish appears to be learning the task anew. He behaves as though he retained nothing from his previous training. Figure 12.5c indicates that the consolidation process is not an all-or-nothing phenomenon; when puromycin is injected ½ hour after leaving the shuttle tank, the animal retains an incomplete representation of his former learning. He performs during retest at a level somewhere between that of an untreated animal and a naive, or immediately injected, animal. Some information seems to be present, but not as much as if the consolidation process had been allowed to progress to completion.

Goldfish can learn a task normally, even when a protein-dependent consolidation process is completely blocked, as shown in Figure 12.5e. Puromycin is given before the first learning trial. The fish learn perfectly but remember nothing when tested some days later. These data suggest that, in the goldfish, task learning involves only short-term memory. An active, protein-independent representation of the task information is used to learn the avoidance response. Therefore, blocking protein synthesis has no effect on the ability of the fish to learn.

Another interesting, and somewhat puzzling, finding is shown in Figure 12.5f. The consolidation process apparently does not begin during learning, nor does it necessarily begin immediately afterwards. In these experiments, consolidation seems to be triggered by removing the animal from the testing tank and returning it to its home. Agranoff and his colleague, Davis, suggest that consolidation is blocked when the animal is in an environment, such as the training tank, that is

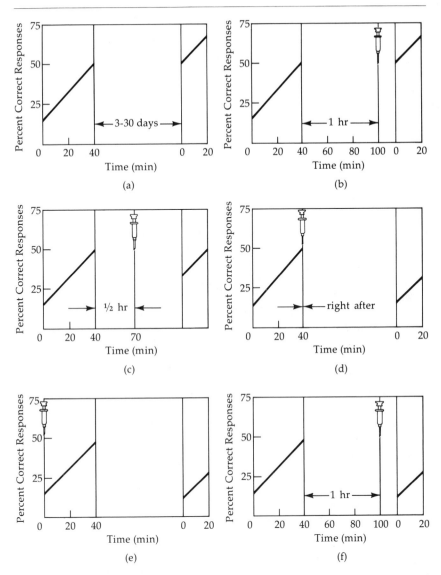

Figure 12.5. *Effects of protein-synthesis inhibition on performance.* (a) Normal goldfish show retention for avoidance learning over a period of 3 to 30 days. (b) Injection of puromycin 1 hour following training and return to the home tank does not disrupt this learning. (c) A similar injection at ½ hour reduces the information retained by about ½. (d) Injection immediately following training prevents consolidation and retention. (e) Injection prior to training does not prevent learning but does prevent retention. (f) If the fish is allowed to remain in the testing situation for 1 hour after training and is then injected with puromycin, no retention is seen. The consolidation process apparently depends upon environmental factors that trigger or inhibit its initiation. (Used by permission from Agranoff, B. W. Memory and protein synthesis. *Scientific American*, 1967, **216**(6), 121. Copyright © 1967 by Scientific American, Inc. All rights reserved.)

associated with a large amount of stimulation. They believe that the consolidation process takes place during relatively quiet periods. The fixation of permanent memory, therefore, appears to depend upon both temporal and environmental factors. But, whenever it occurs, fixation of permanent memory depends physiologically upon the brain's ability to synthesize new proteins.

Effects of Arousal on the Consolidation of Memory.   The capacity of the brain to form permanent memory may also depend upon the occurrence of exciting, arousing, and perhaps, sometimes, rewarding events in the environment. Consider the following experiments.

Barondes and Cohen employed a very short-acting antibiotic, cycloheximide, during training. The drug lost effect before short-term memory had disappeared. Could the learned information be consolidated in that period after training when both STM is present and the protein-synthesis capacity of the brain has returned? Under normal conditions, it apparently cannot.

Barondes and Cohen trained rats to choose the lighted arm of a simple T-maze to escape shock for five out of six consecutive trials. Untreated rats showed excellent retention when tested 3 hours, 6 hours, or 7 days later. Rats given cycloheximide 30 minutes before training could remember equally well at 3 hours, but, if tested at 6 hours or 7 days, they recalled little. Usually, massive interference with brain protein synthesis is necessary to prevent consolidation. At 3 hours, the blocking effects of the drug had nearly dissipated. Only 19% of the inhibition of protein synthesis remained, and yet information available within the brain at 3 hours was not consolidated.

However, the consolidation process can be triggered once the effects of the drug have disappeared. Barondes and Cohen found that, if they administered a single foot shock 3 hours after training, the rats showed perfect retention when tested 7 days later. But, when foot shock was given at 6 hours, the rats remembered virtually nothing when tested later. Foot shock triggered the consolidation of memory only when the information to be consolidated was available in short-term memory and the brain had recovered its capacity to synthesize proteins.

Possibly the arousing effects of foot shock are not crucial. Instead, shock may serve to remind the rat of the shock he previously received in training, and thereby induce rehearsal. This hypothesis, however, seems to be ruled out by other experiments; similar results can be obtained for tasks that are entirely positively rewarding and that involve no foot shock at all during training.

Foot shock apparently acts to arouse the animal. Similarly, natural reinforcements might trigger the consolidation of memory by their arousal functions. Barondes views consolidation as a concomitant of some portions of the arousal process. To test the idea that it is the arousing aspect of the foot shock that is important, critical changes were made in the experimental procedure. Instead of using foot shock to trigger consolidation, injections of amphetamine were employed, since amphetamine produces arousal. Corticosteroids, chemicals released within the organism during periods of stress and arousal, were also used. As before, injections of either substance produced no effect if given 6 hours after training, when the short-term memory of the task was no longer present. But, if injected at 3 hours, rats showed memory when tested the following week. Increasing arousal by any of these means appears to induce consolidation of material present in short-term memory only if the brain has recovered its capacity to produce proteins.

Such results are exciting because they seem to suggest a link between the action of environmental rewards and the consolidation of information by the brain. But other explanations, perhaps more prosaic, are possible and must be considered. Certainly, matters must be more complex than these data suggest. For example, both rewarding and aversive reinforcement have markedly different effects on learning in many situations, and their effects can be distinguished from the effects of arousal per se. It seems unlikely that the formation of memory is related to arousing stimuli in a simple manner.

Robert Livingston has put forth the theory that momentary arousal may function to inform the memory system that an important event has occurred. The arousal is not selective; everything present in short-term memory is printed in long-term memory. Information need not be causally related to the stimulus triggering arousal; temporal contiguity is sufficient. Since arousal appears to trigger the transfer of all information from short-term to long-term memory, an organism would be more likely to recall events of biological consequence. The cost of such a system would be the simultaneous inclusion of irrelevant information in long-term memory.

Alternatives to the Consolidation Hypothesis. The STM-consolidation-LTM model has been widely supported by researchers investigating the biological substrates of memory. The model contains a set of concepts that are useful in gaining insight into the ways in which the brain might store information. But the consolidation hypothesis is not the only hypothesis capable of explaining the observable phenomena of experimentally induced amnesia.

Donald Lewis has pointed out several alternatives to the consolidation hypothesis, all originating in Tolman's classic distinction between learning and performance: organisms may learn and remember information even though they may not show it in their current behavior. The failure of performance is not necessarily a failure of learning; it may be an effect of motivational or other factors. Specifically, ECS and other amnesic agents may not disrupt the consolidation of memory per se. They may, for example, simply introduce confusion into the filing or coding processes of memory so that the information will be more difficult to find at a later time. ECS could also interfere with retrieval processes to split the memory from its original context. Or the ECS could act to remove the motivation for the animal to recall information acquired immediately before ECS administration. These hypotheses represent viable, but relatively unstudied, alternatives to the consolidation hypothesis. Consolidation is merely a first step in processing information through a long-term memory system. There is little reason to be sure that it is not other steps that are, in fact, disrupted.

Consolidation theory, although still certainly the dominant concept of experimental amnesic phenomena, does not explain easily certain peculiarities in the data of some experiments. For example, in some situations, the measured time for consolidation is only a few seconds. If consolidation indeed takes place within only a few seconds, then perhaps the disruptive effects of ECS reported in other situations that extend into tens of minutes or into hours are attributable to other interactions between ECS and performance. The wide variety of consolidation times reported in the literature suggests that ECS may operate in more than one disruptive manner, each with its own reasonable time course. Further, experimental amnesia can be eliminated in the passive-avoidance task if the animal is completely familiarized with the environment before the training trial. Even in situations in which effective amnesia has been apparently produced, the use of a reminder cue will often reinstitute the learned performance, which indicates that the disruption may not occur in the fixation of memory but, rather, in its addressing and retrieval. The possibility always exists that ECS and other amnesic agents have more than one effect. The disruption of consolidation may well occur, but not all disruptions of performance necessarily indicate that a memory has not been formed.

Amnesias and the Structure of Human Memory

The concept of separable short- and long-term memory systems within the brain, perhaps linked by a consolidation process, was originally developed from the examination of amnesic patients. Although the study of clinical cases—the so-called "experiments of nature"—is difficult, it can also be rewarding, since only with clinical cases can the processes of the human brain be examined.

One of the most interesting analyses of the structures of clinical amnesias has been provided by Warrington and her colleagues, Weiskrantz and Shallice. These investigators have employed sophisticated measurement techniques borrowed from experimental psychology to assess more exactly the nature of the deficit in various cases.

Warrington argues that the structure of memory may be revealed in the search for its components, which may be differentially affected by disease processes. If two patients can be found, one with a functioning STM but without LTM and the other with the reverse pattern of pathology, then strong evidence exists for the structural separation of these processes within the brain. Such evidence would meet the criterion of double dissociation, which is often used in the analysis of clinical pathology (see, for example, the discussion of aphasias in Chapter 10).

The typical amnesic patient exhibits marked defects in what might be called long-term memory, but the characteristics of short-term memory are often quite normal. For example, the memory span of amnesic patients (the number of items that they can hold temporarily in memory) does not differ significantly from normal. Short-term memory, as measured by the length of time a single item can be retained when active rehearsal is prevented, is also much the same in amnesic patients as in matched nonamnesic control subjects. Disease processes therefore may interfere with long-term information processing but leave the capacity to recall information over short periods intact.

Some evidence indicates that the opposite pattern of disorder also occurs, fulfilling the criterion of double dissociation. Warrington and Shallice have described a series of tests made on one patient with a disturbed auditory STM system. The patient appeared to have retained an essentially normal LTM for auditory information in the presence of a severely impaired STM system. Such data suggest that the simple hypothesis depicted in Figure 12.1 must be modified to provide alternate pathways by which information can enter the LTM system. Evidently information must not necessarily pass through STM to be encoded in LTM.

Another interesting feature of the clinical literature is the apparent importance of the hippocampus in the formation of permanent memory. Early clinical evidence and interpretation suggested that patients with bilateral hippocampal damage suffered a defect of consolidation; while still able to recall events preceding brain injury, they were apparently unable to fix information concerning more recent events. An initial difficulty of the concept appeared when numerous attempts to test the effects of hippocampal damage on LTM in animals failed to replicate the clinically observed pattern. Under proper conditions, animals could retain information learned after bilateral removal of the hippocampi.

However, hippocampally damaged animals show gross behavioral deficits. They appear to have great difficulty in inhibiting ongoing behavior. They can, for example, learn to choose the right arm of a T-maze to receive a food reward in the same number of trials as the normal animal, but they can learn to reverse the discrimination only with great difficulty. If the reward is moved to the left arm of the maze, the hippocampal animal appears unable to adapt to the changed conditions and inhibit the previously learned response. Therefore, it is not surprising that hippocampally damaged animals, when compared with normal animals, show very little extinction of habits. Here, the hippocampus appears to be involved in the inhibitory control of behavior, not the consolidation of memory.

This interpretation is further supported by a detailed examination of performance in a learning task in hippocampally damaged humans. Such patients exhibit an astonishingly high rate of "intrusions" in a list-learning task. Intrusions are wrong answers that were correct answers on a previously learned list. Such responses were quite evidently learned but could not be suppressed when no longer relevant. Warrington and Weiskrantz provided evidence that the performance of these amnesic subjects improves when they are given partial information about the correct response at the time recall is tested. Such information evidently aids in inhibiting the troublesome false positive responses. Some of the apparent amnesic effects of hippocampal damage may therefore be attributable to a generalized deficit of behavioral inhibition. Considering the phylogenetic importance of the hippocampus and its proximity to the language-relevant areas of temporal and parietal cortex, however, it is by no means clear that other behavioral effects of the massive damage to the forebrain are not also present.

Searching for Memory within the Brain: Lesion Experiments

Since permanent memory presumably involves structural changes within the nervous system, it should be possible to locate those changes. Can any part of the brain be removed to selectively deprive the organism of the memory of an event? There are many difficulties with lesion methods, but they represent a straightforward attack on the problem of the localization of memory. Other techniques have also been employed. Tissue can be examined for subtle changes after massive learning experiences, or the electrical activity of the brain can be measured to find physiological signs of altered brain functioning. Both these approaches will be considered later. First we shall concern ourselves with the question of brain lesions and memory.

The lesion and ablation approach to the localization of memory was pioneered, although certainly not originated, by Karl Lashley, an American psychologist who spent over 30 years in what he called the search for the "engram," another term for the permanent memory trace. His work is instructive, since it points the way to a very general concept of the higher brain processes.

When Lashley began his work, the dominant psychological and physiological theories of learning were based on the concept of the reflex arc. In the spinal cord, simple behaviors could be explained by tracing a burst of excitation from sensory receptors into the spinal cord, sometimes through interneurons within the cord, and out again through the motor neurons to the muscle. To study complex behaviors, this linear concept was extended, with little real evidence, into the brain. The conditioned reflexes of Pavlov's animals were thought to be produced by a long reflex arc that began at the sense receptor, proceeded to the corresponding sensory cortex, through the association areas of the cerebral mass, to the motor cortex, and back down the spinal cord into the motor neurons. Lashley began his work by trying to interrupt this chain.

Animals were trained to perform one of many tasks, either simple or complicated, that involved directly one or several of the sensory and motor systems. To interrupt the reflex arc, a portion of the brain was either cut or removed, before or after training. Animals were tested to discover either how much they could remember or how easily they could learn a new task. By these methods, Lashley hoped to discover the importance of particular areas of the brain in either constructing or retaining the memory of a task. The results of these experiments are interesting.

The simple reflex arc as originally conceived appears not to exist. Lashley first began to doubt the linear reflex model when he discovered that rats trained to produce a discriminative response to a visual stimulus showed no loss in accuracy when the entire motor cortex was removed. Therefore, the motor cortex could not be a single necessary bridge linking stimulus to response. Even in the most complicated visual discriminations for which a rat can be trained, lesions that separated the visual and motor cortices produced no impairment of performance. The same holds true with more complicated tasks in more complicated animals. Monkeys were trained to open latch-boxes—a kind of mechnical puzzle. Then the motor areas of their cortices were removed. Immediately thereafter, they became paralyzed, but after some weeks the paralysis disappeared. When tested again, they opened the boxes perfectly without any exploration. Clearly, the memory for motor acts is not kept exclusively in the motor cortex. Nor is the motor cortex a necessary pathway in the execution of a motor habit.

Similar experiments were performed to interrupt other supposed cortical pathways of the reflex arc. Drastic incisions were made to cut the cortical tissue in many directions over its length and breadth. Even for the most complicated habits, transcortical conduction does not seem to be an essential part of the reflex arc; only lesions in the pathways bringing sensory information to the brain made any difference. It appears that the hypothesized reflex pathways, if they exist at all as the neuronal basis of memory, are not specific and localized but must be multiple and diffuse.

If we examine the so-called association areas of the cortex, a similar pattern emerges. The association areas received their name from the belief that, simply because they lie between sensory and motor cortex, they must contain the associations linking perception and action. Lashley's ablation experiments clearly demonstrate that, for simple sensorimotor habits, the memory trace is not laid down in any specific portion of the association areas. Removal of this tissue does not disrupt simple sensorimotor habits. The association areas do not constitute a necessary, vulnerable link in the hypothesized chain of the reflex arc.

Sensory areas of the cortex present a somewhat different picture when simple discrimination tasks are used. Lashley's data indicate that, if an animal learns a visual-discrimination task and the visual cortex is then removed, the animal seems to retain nothing. He can relearn the task at exactly the same rate with which he first learned it. Neither savings nor impairment is evident. Instead of the visual cortex, an older visual area in the brainstem, the optic tectum, is apparently employed to process the sensory signals. If the optic tectum is also removed, the animal cannot learn a simple visual discrimination. Therefore, one might conclude either that the original engram is located in the visual cortex or that the visual cortex normally processes the sensory signals, which become diffusely encoded in memory through- out wide regions of the brain. In the absence of the visual cortex, the optic tectum can perform that function.

Within the visual cortex, and within the other sensory cortices as well, a special relation between cortical area and habit retention is found. Lashley used the term "equipotentiality" to describe the fact that, within a sensory area, any small patch of tissue is capable of mediating the entire simple sensory habit. An animal trained to discriminate various visual figures, for example, can continue to discriminate with only 1/16 of his visual cortex remaining. The phenomenon of equipotentiality of sensory areas makes sense when one thinks of two facts. First, to make a visual pattern discrimination, the animal must have output from a form-recognizing analyzer. Second, the whole of the visual cortex is similarly constructed; different areas within it correspond to different areas of the visual field, and such areas are functionally equivalent. It makes little difference whether a driver sees a red traffic light in the upper right or in the upper left of the visual field; he stops to avoid a potential accident or arrest. And so with the rat. He may be blind in all but a small area of his visual field, but in that area he knows the difference between a square and a circle.

A very different situation occurs when complex behaviors or habits are analyzed. For a complicated maze task, the removal of even small amounts of tissue seems to affect performance. A 5% loss may be barely noticeable, but, if half the cortex is removed bilaterally, the animal will be unable to run a maze correctly. Equivalent losses of habit are seen when a fixed amount of cortex is bilaterally removed, no matter which cortical areas are excised. Lashley termed this phenomenon "mass action." The data seem to show that the mere presence of cortical tissue contributes to the efficiency of recalling old memories. That larger lesions are more likely to disrupt crucial sensory pathways offers some explanation for mass action, but it is by no means the only factor. The destruction of sensory areas produces a far greater disruption of a complex habit than does the removal of the corresponding sensory organs. A rat blinded by the removal of his eyes can learn a complicated maze; a rat without visual cortex learns only with great difficulty.

Similarly, in the association areas, destruction seems to produce not a lack of information necessary to perform a difficult task but a disruption of some higher schemata or conceptual systems that control behavior. For example, monkeys were trained to perform a series of discriminations in all sense modalities in which they were required to pull strings attached to stimuli. After massive removal of cortical tissue, they could not perform correctly. Had they forgotten all they knew? Perhaps, but, when laboriously retrained to perform just one of the discriminations, they could again perform all the rest without additional training. What appears to have been lost was not specific information but the rules and relational concepts, or organizational strategies, necessary for successful task performance.

Lashley's work typically involved bilateral destruction of homologous cortical areas, with all tissue being removed in a single operation. When such extensive surgery is performed in two successive operations, with adequate time for recovery between them, the disruptive effects of brain damage can be markedly attenuated. For example, when animals are tested for acquisition of a light-dark discrimination that involves a reversal component (the animal must learn to inhibit a previously effective behavior), animals with both hippocampi removed in a single operation show profound performance decrement. If the hippocampi are removed in two separate, unilateral operations, however, animals learn the discrimination in much the same manner as do animals who underwent comparable operative procedures but without the actual removal of brain tissue. Neither group of hippocampally damaged animals had use of these structures, but their ability to perform a new task differed greatly as a function of the manner in which the forebrain damage was inflicted.

Little is known about the brain mechanisms involved in the recovery of function obtained with the two-stage operations. Apparently, other brain tissues assume functions once performed by the hippocampus. The process seems to be facilitated by a period in which one hippocampus is present and the other is absent from the forebrain. This points to one of the serious problems of the ablation method. If something is removed and the behavior being studied is intact, one can legitimately conclude that the excised tissue was not necessary for the behavior in question. One cannot conclude, however, that the excised tissue was not normally involved. The problem becomes more difficult when ablation leads to deterioration of performance. Does the inability to carry out a previously learned task mean that the information is gone? Not necessarily. The experiment above would point to another, more general deficit. An analogy is often drawn between investigating the function of the brain by removing tissue and studying the function of a radio by removing a tube or transistor. Pull out one component of the radio, and the music stops playing. Do you know what the function of the removed component was? If a truly reasonable view of the function of the brain is to be developed, lesion and ablation studies should be combined with other investigative tools that have different sets of limits and weaknesses.

The Anatomical Localization of Memory

The problem of localization of memory has been approached in a different manner by Kretch and Rosenzweig. Instead of removing brain tissue, they have employed anatomical and biochemical techniques to search for differences between the brains of animals given enriched environments and those of animals given impoverished environments. These investigators reasoned that animals raised in an impoverished environment have less opportunity to learn, since the availability of novel information is reduced. The impoverished animals are housed alone in small cages; they neither see nor touch other animals. The lighting is dim, and the cage room is quiet. Unlike their impoverished littermates, rats reared under enriched conditions have an enhanced opportunity to explore and learn about their world. They are raised with a dozen other rats in a large, well-lighted cage. Each day new toys are introduced for their use. Often they are removed from the cage and placed in a novel, interesting environment, which they investigate. After a month of exposure to their environments, they are given formal training in maze learning and other tasks. At the end of these experiences, the brains of these rats are removed and compared with the brains of the impoverished rats. Any systematic differences between the brains of the enriched rats and the impoverished rats might be due to the opportunity for learning, although many other differences obviously exist between these two extreme environments.

The environmental differences do produce measurable, stable changes in the brain of the rat. As with the lesion experiments, wide areas of the cortex seem to be involved. Cortical weight is greater by 4% in the rats raised in the enriched environment, but there is no difference in the weight of subcortical structures. In the standard enriched environment, the occipital, or visual, cortex shows the largest change, 6%, whereas the somatosensory areas show the smallest changes, averaging about 2%. As Lashley noted, the visual cortex seems to be especially important in normal learning. If, however, animals are raised in total darkness, the occipital cortex withers. But animals raised in a darkened, enriched tactile environment develop heavier somatosensory areas. Cortical brain weight seems to increase with use of the cortical area.

There are no differences in the number of neurons in the cortices of animals raised in different environments. Instead, in enriched rats, the gray matter, the cortical areas composed of cell bodies and dendrites, becomes thicker. The extra weight appears to be related to a proliferation of glial cells. Whereas glia may have information-processing functions of their own that are at present unknown, they also are known to perform nutritive functions for neurons. Thus, an increasing number of glial cells in an area may reflect increases in the metabolic demands of the neurons that they service.

Changes in brain weight and glial-cell proliferation are limited to the cortex in the rat. Within the cortex, changes in brain weight appear to be somewhat responsive to the sensory modality within which the opportunities to learn are presented. Biochemical differences that parallel changes in brain anatomy also occur. Rats raised in enriched environments show more acetylcholinesterase (AChE) and cholinesterase (ChE) activity than do their littermates raised in isolation. AChE and ChE are enzymes that inactivate a probable brain neurotransmitter, acetylcholine (ACh). The measurement of the destructive enzymes is used as an indirect measure of the abundance of the neurotransmitter in the brain.

The anatomical and biochemical analysis of the enriched-environment experiments seems to suggest that the engram may be cortically located, but, within the cortex, the permanent representation of information is probably quite diffuse.

The Electrophysiological Localization of Memory

The engram may also be sought by examining the responses of single cells of the brain during learning. O'Brien and Fox measured electrophysiological activity in cats being trained to produce leg flexion to a flash of light. Their investigations provided some very interesting data on the cellular changes that may be involved in learning.

To record from single neurons requires very delicate techniques and electrodes almost microscopically fine. Thus, it is difficult to work with a freely moving animal. O'Brien and Fox used curare to paralyze the animal during the experiment so that, while no leg movement could actually occur, the neuronal changes taking place might be observed. Microelectrodes were placed in the somatosensory area at a point that received input from the rear contralateral paw, to which shocking electrodes were applied to deliver the unconditioned stimulus (UCS). The conditioned stimulus (CS) was a flash of light.

Some individual cells in the somatosensory cortex responded naturally not only to foot shock but also to light flashes. Of those cells, some responded to light by increasing their rate of firing; other cells responded with decreases. Similarly, some cells showed inhibitory, whereas others showed excitatory, responses to foot shock. The sign (increasing or decreasing) of the cell's response to one stimulus gave no information about the response of the cell to the other stimulus. The responses to the two stimuli seemed unrelated.

During classical conditioning, the CS and UCS were systematically paired. Not all cells showed conditioning. Many neurons in the somatosensory cortex were unaffected in the learning process. However, some cells did change their characteristic responses to the CS. These were cells that were initially responsive to the light before training began. Cells that originally responded by increasing their firing rate when the light appeared responded after conditioning in an inhibitory manner. Conversely, cells that initially were inhibitory became excitatory in the presence of the light. It appears, then, at least for the cat in this task, that learning at the cellular level might involve dramatic changes in the response of a cell to a stimulus.

Cells that responded most vigorously, either by increasing or by decreasing their firing rates before conditioning, were the cells that showed the largest changes in training. Cells that were only weakly linked to the stimulus showed little conditioning. Moreover, when the whole conditioning procedure was repeated several times, cells that were initially conditionable remained conditionable, whereas cells that did not train remained refractory.

The timing of the conditioned cellular response was also different in conditioned excitatory and conditioned inhibitory cells. Cells that became excitatory displayed their peak response about 0.3 second following the CS, whereas conditioned inhibitory cells responded maximally 0.3 second before the UCS. Conditioned excitation appears to be linked in time to the presentation of the CS. Conditioned inhibitory cells are temporally tied to the UCS.

The peculiar pattern of timing may be related to another difference between the two types of conditionable cells, a difference of responding in extinction. A conditioned response is extinguished by the continuous presentation of the CS without the UCS. Thus, the animal received light flashes but not shocks. During extinction, the learned response disappeared, and the conditioned cellular responses also extinguished. Conditioned excitatory cells responded to at least 15 presentations of the CS alone before they reverted to their former inhibitory pattern. They extinguished in approximately the same number of trials as was needed for the behavior to disappear. Conditioned inhibitory cells, which were linked in time to the UCS, extinguished in one or two trials. Thus these responses disappeared when the UCS was removed.

Conditioning may be localized not in the gross anatomy of the brain but in its microanatomy. Conditionable cells may be located in many areas of the brain. That hypothesis was not tested by O'Brien and Fox. But whether a cell conditions or not appears to depend upon its receiving input from the proper sources. In O'Brien and Fox's study the finding that only cells that initially responded to the CS showed changes during learning suggests a switching among pre-existing pathways.

Olds has recently begun a more extensive analysis of single-unit activity during learning. He and his colleagues have postulated that learning involves the rerouting of signals along various microanatomical pathways within the brain. Excitation arising from a sensory signal would be expected to follow a pre-existing pathway into the brain until the synapses encoding the learned change are encountered. At the point of encounter, excitation would be diverted onto a new or alternate pathway that itself may be complex and many-staged. The alternate pathway may or may not be preformed. No alterations in synaptic conductivity need necessarily occur along it. But, according to Olds' theory, synaptic change is necessary at least at the rerouting point. Since an entire new pathway is opened by the conditioned change, changes in activity following learning would be observable in any of the cells comprising the alternate pathway. Olds reasons that the original point in the new path may be discriminated from all others on the basis of its latency. The cell that responds most rapidly to the CS would be the cell at the switching point, the site of the neuronal engram. Responses in cells further along the new path must of necessity appear after excitation has passed the switch point and, therefore, show a longer latency.

To search for the engram in this manner necessitates observation of a large number of cells, the formation of a stable picture of their responses before conditioning, and the formation of an equally stable representation of responses after conditioning. Olds first measured the responses of cells from various portions of the brain to a high-pitched tone, a low-pitched tone, and the delivery of a food pellet by a noisy dispenser. After a stable pattern of response had developed to these stimuli when presented separately, one of the tones was paired with the delivery of food (positive conditioned stimulus, or CS+). The other tone was never accompanied by food (negative conditioned stimulus, or CS−). Most rats quickly learned to move to the dispenser following the presentation of the CS+.

Some of the cells studied showed statistically reliable changes in response to the conditioned stimuli after pairing with food delivery (31 of 443 cells measured, or about 7%) that occurred at extremely short latency (20 msec or less). These short-latency conditioned cells were present at all levels of the brain, but they were not evenly distributed in all structures. For example, the responsive units of the thalamus were confined to the posterior nucleus and were absent elsewhere. The short-latency conditioned thalamic units were relatively nonspecific and showed a conditioned change to both the positive and the negative conditioned stimuli.

In contrast, specific responses were seen in frontal and parietal cortex and in portions of the hippocampus. Although the size of the learned response was small, it was specific. It occurred only following the CS+. No generalization to the CS− was seen. As O'Brien and Fox had previously reported in their analysis of units in the area of the cortex, the sign of the prelearning response to CS+ changed with conditioning. The latency of these changes was an astonishingly short period, 6 msec, following the arrival of the tone at the rat's ear. If the logic of these experiments is accepted, these data strongly implicate cortical neurons as the units in the brain that may alter their conductivity to channel excitation onto an alternate pathway in learning. Further data are clearly necessary to determine the utility of the latency-mapping approach to the search for the engram, but the possibility of mapping the learning systems of the brain by electrical recording is indeed exciting.

Summary

Learning is a process that cannot be directly observed. Instead, it must be inferred from the behavior of organisms. Learning is often defined as a process that results in a relatively permanent change in behavior as a function of practice. This definition of learning excludes behavioral changes attributable to fatigue, pharmacological agents, motivational changes, and maturation.

Several mechanisms for the retention of information, which differ from each other in the age of the information they store, are present in the mammalian brain. Sensory memory stores incoming sensory information for a fraction of a second until other memory mechanisms can process it. Short-term memory (STM) holds information for minutes or hours and serves to control ongoing behavior. Long-term memory (LTM) contains relatively permanent representations of information, which can exist throughout the life of the organism. The process of forming LTM is consolidation.

Sensory memory is closely linked with perceptual processes. Indeed, the lingering activity of sensory neurons within the thalamus and cortex may provide the neuronal substrate for its action. Sensory memory is not selective but momentarily retains all information available to it.

Selective processes are introduced by the STM system, in which the information-processing capacity is strictly limited. In addition to its behavioral control functions, STM probably stores information during the process of consolidation. STM may depend upon specified patterns of maintained activity such as complex closed loops of neurons, since disruption of cortical activity erases STM. Electroconvulsive shock is often used to terminate STM in studies of the consolidation process.

The rate at which LTM is formed depends in part upon the species of the organism and the nature of the information being consolidated. Within a species, genetic factors are also involved, since rats that are bred for learning ability show more rapid consolidation than rats that are not. The rate of consolidation can be speeded by reducing the inhibitory control of cortical processes and slowed by reducing the metabolic rate.

The process of consolidation results in the formation of LTM through the construction of brain proteins. Antibiotics that impair cerebral protein synthesis prevent consolidation. In the goldfish memory, the escape-avoidance task consolidates over the period of an hour after the fish's removal from the testing tank. If the antibiotic is injected before training, the fish learns normally by using only STM, but no LTM record for the event is established. The onset of the consolidation process appears to be controlled in part by the environment and is not initiated as long as the fish remains in the testing situation.

Physiological arousal, whether induced by foot shock, amphetamine, or corticosteroids, may act to trigger the transfer of information from STM to LTM. Such transfer is nonspecific; all information in STM is permanently encoded, regardless of its relationship to the arousing stimulus. This mechanism would increase the likelihood of retaining information concerning biologically important events.

The best current evidence suggests that the LTM system is not localized in any limited region of the brain. Rather, plasticity may occur in the multiple and diffuse pathways that mediate behavior throughout the forebrain. This view has received at least partial support from lesion, neuroanatomical, and electrophysiological investigations, although the issue is by no means closed. Lashley conducted a long series of experiments that seemed to indicate the diffuse nature of the memory systems. For many tasks, cortical sensory areas hold particular importance; but, within these areas, no particular sector is crucial. That each small area is capable of mediating the entire simple behavior indicated to Lashley the equipotentiality of sensory tissue. For more complex tasks, cortical destruction is more disruptive; but, again, within large limits, the locus of the bilateral destruction seems unimportant. Mass action refers to integrated functioning of the cortex in mediating complex behaviors; behavioral deficit increases with increasing tissue damage, regardless of the cortical locus of that damage.

If animals of common genetic characteristics are raised in environments that differ greatly in the amount of learning permitted, widespread differences in cortical development appear. Animals reared in enriched environments show increased proliferation of cortical glial tissue, which results in a slightly greater cortical weight than that of their littermates raised in an impoverished environment. The increase of glial tissue might reflect increased metabolic demands that cortical neurons place on that tissue during learning. The amount of growth within the cortex depends upon the dominant sensory modality within the environment. An enriched tactile environment encourages selective growth of the glia in the somatosensory cortex. Other evidence suggests an increase in the use of neurotransmitters throughout the cortex. No change in either brain weight or neurotransmitter activity is seen in subcortical tissues, which suggests a diffuse cortical representation of memory.

Electrophysiological evidence suggests that the cellular change involved in learning may be discretely localized in the microanatomy but not confined to any particular region of gross anatomy. In one conditioning experiment, only cells that initially responded to the conditioned stimulus showed modification when the CS was paired with the unconditioned stimulus. The conditioned change appeared as a shift in the nature of the response from excitation to inhibition, and the reverse. Conditioned excitatory changes were linked to the arrival of the CS and extinguished at the rate that characterizes behavioral extinction. Conditioned inhibitory units are linked in time to the arrival of the UCS and extinguish in one trial. Such large and dramatic changes in cellular function during the acquisition of a conditioned response are limited to those neurons that were initially capable of responding to both stimuli. However, this evidence does not imply the absence of other, perhaps even more primary, conditioned changes elsewhere in the brain.

Glossary

A bands. The dark bands in striated muscle in which thick (myosin) and thin (actin) filaments overlap.

Ablation. See Lesion.

Absolute refractory period. The period of time (about 1 msec) after an action potential is initiated during which another action potential cannot be triggered.

Accessory structure. A specialized mechanical structure in which a receptor or system of receptors is embedded. May function to filter or select information.

Accommodation. In vision, the focusing of the lens of the eye. (See also Convergence.)

Acetylcholine. A neurotransmitter substance that serves to excite and contract muscle when released at the neuromuscular junction and is also a transmitter substance at some central synapses. Abbreviation: ACh.

Acetylcholinesterase. The enzyme that rapidly inactivates acetylcholine. Abbreviation: AChE.

Actin. The protein of thin muscle filaments that acts with myosin to contract the muscle.

Action potential. A stereotyped propagated sequence of cell membrane potential changes that occurs in the excitable membrane of neurons. Also referred to as a neuronal spike.

Activity trace. A hypothetical representation of short-term memory in which information is stored as a pattern of activity in a closed neural circuit.

Adaptation. In sensory systems, the decrease in response that occurs in some receptors when a stimulus is repeatedly presented.

Adenosine triphosphate. A substance that is a source of energy for cells. Abbreviation: ATP.

Adequate stimulus. The quality of stimulus to which a receptor is most sensitive.

Adrenalin. A chemical substance, produced by the adrenal gland, that acts to stimulate the heart and that has other autonomic effects of a sympathetic nature. Also known as epinephrine.

Afferent. Refers to nerve pathways that conduct impulses toward more central structures of the nervous system, as in sensory nerves.

Alexia. The loss of the ability to read.

Alpha motor neurons. A class of large, rapidly conducting neurons whose cell bodies are in the spinal cord and whose axons terminate on extrafusal muscle fibers. Activity in alpha motor neurons directly controls muscle contraction.

Alpha rhythms. An EEG pattern of 8–12 Hz and usually relatively high amplitude.

Amacrine cell. A type of neuron in the retina, the processes of which extend laterally. Amacrine cells receive input from bipolar cells and provide output to ganglion cells.

Amino acids. Organic compounds that join together to form proteins.

Amphetamine. A drug that acts as a CNS stimulant.

Amygdala. An almond-shaped collection of nuclei deep in the temporal lobe that forms part of the limbic system.

Analyzer. A neuronal system that extracts particular kinds of information from its input.

Androgen. A male sex hormone.

Angstrom. One hundred-millionth of a centimeter (10^{-8} cm).

Annulo-spinal endings. The endings of muscle spindle sensory neurons that wrap about intrafusal fibers. When the intrafusal fiber is stretched, the annulo-spinal endings are mechanically deformed, and spikes are generated.

Antagonistic surround. In differentiated receptive fields, an outer border that, when activated, counteracts the effects of stimulation in the central region.

Antagonist muscles. Muscle pairs that produce opposite movements—for example, an extensor and flexor of a joint.

Anterior. Toward the nose of a four-legged animal along the nose-to-tail axis.

Anterior commissure. A bundle of fibers connecting phylogenetically older portions of the right and left cerebral hemispheres.

Antibiotics. Drugs that destroy bacteria or inhibit their growth.

Antidiuretic hormone. A substance produced in the hypothalamus and transported to the pituitary gland where it may be released into the bloodstream, causing the kidney to reabsorb water. Abbreviation: ADH.

Aphasia. In general, the loss of the use of language.

Aqueous humor. The fluid in the eye between the cornea and the lens.

Arcuate fasciculus. A bundle of nerve fibers connecting Wernicke's area and Broca's area, as well as other cortical areas.

Arousal. A behavioral state characterized by a high degree of activation or alertness. Also refers to the EEG pattern accompanying this behavioral state, characterized by low-voltage, fast-desynchronized activity (beta rhythms).

Articulation. The act of joining. In speech, the placement of a movable articulator (for example, the tip of the tongue) on a fixed articulator (for example, the upper teeth) resulting in a particular speech sound.

Artifact. Something that is artificial, or not normally present. With reference to the EEG an artifact is an electrical potential that is not produced by the brain—for example, muscle artifact produced by electrical activity in muscles.

Arytenoids. Cartilaginous structures of the posterior larynx to which the vocal cords are attached.

Association areas. Cortical areas that are neither clearly sensory nor clearly motor in nature.

Attenuate. To make weaker.

Auditory nerve. The cranial nerve leading from the cochlea to the cochlear nucleus of the medulla that transmits auditory information from the ear to the brain.

Autonomic nervous system. In vertebrates, the portion of the peripheral nervous system controlling internal organs and glands. It is composed of the sympathetic and parasympathetic divisions.

Axon. The extension from the nerve cell body, composed of excitable membrane, which normally transmits nerve impulses away from the cell body.

Backward visual masking. The masking of a visual stimulus by another stimulus that is presented later in time. (See also Masking.)

Bailer. See Gill bailer.

Ballistic. A movement or behavior that is totally determined before its execution; that is, it does not depend on feedback.

Barbiturates. A class of drugs used as sedatives.

Basal ganglia. A collection of gray-matter nuclei at the base of the cerebral hemispheres that includes caudate nucleus, putamen, and globus pallidus.

Basilar membrane. A membrane running the length of the cochlea that is important in frequency analysis.

Beta rhythm. An EEG pattern consisting of low-voltage, desynchronized waves from 13 to approximately 30 Hz.

Binocular. Refers to the viewing of objects with both eyes simultaneously.

Bipolar cell. A type of neuron in the retina, the processes of which connect receptors and horizontal cells with retinal ganglion and amacrine cells.

Brain. In vertebrates, the portion of the central nervous system within the skull. In invertebrates, a specialized anterior portion of the nervous system.

Brainstem. The part of the vertebrate brain consisting of the medulla, the pons, and the mesencephalon.

Broadly tuned receptors. Receptors that respond to several qualities of stimuli.

Broca's area. An area of cortex important in the production of spoken and written language, found in frontal lobe of the left hemisphere near the primary motor areas, which control the organs of speech.

Capacitive charge. An electrical charge (voltage) on a membrane, produced when particles of opposite charge are separated by a membrane and congregate along it.

Cardiovascular. Refers to the heart and blood vessels.

Carotid artery. A major artery supplying the head and brain.

Cartilaginous. Made of cartilage.

Catecholamines. A class of chemicals including the neurotransmitters noradrenaline (norepinephrine) and dopamine.

Caudal. Toward the tail of a four-legged animal along the nose-to-tail axis.

Caudate nucleus. A telencephalic structure that forms a neostriatal portion of the basal ganglia.

Cell. The smallest structural unit of an organism considered to have life. Consists of cytoplasm and specialized structures, all surrounded by a membrane.

Central nervous system. In vertebrates, the brain and spinal cord. Abbreviation: CNS.

Central sulcus. The sulcus separating the frontal and parietal lobes.

Centrifugal. Pathways conducting impulses away from the cerebral cortex. Efferent.

Cephalic. Refers to the head, or head end of the body or nervous system.

Cerebellum. The large, bilaterally symmetric, cortical structure of the metencephalon important in coordination of motor behavior.

Cerebral aqueduct. The narrow canal found in the mesencephalon connecting the fourth ventricle of the metencephalon with the third ventricle of the diencephalon.

Cerebrum. The part of the brain occupying the most anterior part of the CNS, consisting of cortex and underlying white matter. In man, it is the largest structure in the nervous system.

Channel. A pathway for information, defined by any of many possible signal parameters.

Chloride. The ionized form of chlorine. In the nervous system, it is found in highest concentrations in the extracellular fluid. Symbol: Cl⁻.

Chlorpromazine. A tranquilizing compound that acts in part to block the action of adrenalin and other adrenergic compounds.

Chromophore. A chemical that shows a pattern of selective light absorption.

Cilia. In organ of Corti, tiny projections from the hair cells to the tectoral membrane that are displaced by vibrational movements of the basilar membrane.

Ciliary muscle. The muscle of the eye that controls the shape of the lens for visual accommodation.

Cingulate gyrus. A gyrus of neocortex that runs parallel to the corpus callosum and is a part of the limbic system.

Circadian rhythm. A recurring pattern of events, the period of which is about 24 hours.

Classical conditioning. A type of training that pairs the presentation of a neutral stimulus (conditioned stimulus, or CS) with another stimulus (unconditioned stimulus, or UCS), which elicits a natural response (unconditioned response, or UCR) in an animal. After training, the formerly neutral stimulus, when presented alone, now elicits a response also (the conditioned response, or CR). The UCR and CR are similar though not always identical.

Coarticulation. The representation within a single phone of information from two or more adjacent phonemes.

Cochlea. The spiral-shaped organ of the inner ear where frequency analysis and transduction of vibrational energy into patterns of neuronal activity take place.

Cochlear duct. The portion of the cochlea between the basilar and Reissner's membranes that contains the hair cells, also known as scala media.

Cochlear microphonic. A potential recorded in the cochlea that is an electrical replica of the vibrations of the basilar membrane.

Cochlear nucleus. The first relay nucleus in the auditory pathway, found in the medulla.

Coding. The representation of information in a systematic, consistent form, usually for the purpose of transmitting the information.

Cognitive aphasia. A type of loss of language competence in which the patient can produce words but cannot use them intelligently, either in speech production or perception.

Collaterals. Secondary branches of an axon.

Command neuron. A neuron that, when activated, triggers the release of a specific behavior.

Commissure. Any bundle of fibers connecting corresponding parts of the right and left sides of the brain or spinal cord.

Commissurotomy. The lesioning of a commissure.

Complex cortical cell. A class of cells in visual cortex that respond most strongly to stimuli such as lines of light of specific orientation anywhere in the receptive field of the cell.

Compression function. A receptor stimulus-response relationship that compresses a large range of stimulus intensity onto the limited range of neuronal response, with decreasing sensitivity at increasing levels of stimulation.

Concentration. In reference to ions, the number of ions in a specific volume of fluid.

Concentration gradient. The rate of change of concentration in a region of a solution in which differing concentrations of a substance exist. A substance diffusing down its concentration gradient would be moving from an area of higher concentration to one of lower concentration.

Conditioned response. A response elicited by a stimulus as a result of conditioning. Abbreviation: CR.

Conditioned stimulus. A stimulus that was neutral before conditioning but that elicits a specific conditioned response after training. Abbreviation: CS.

Conditioning. The training of a new response in an animal.

Conductance. A measure of the ease with which electrical charges move through a medium.

Cones. Visual receptors of the fovea that are responsible for high-acuity color vision.

Consolidation. A hypothetical process that converts information in short-term memory into a more permanent form in long-term memory.

Constrict. To contract or make smaller.

Contingent negative variation. A slow negative potential that occurs at the surface of the brain when an observer is signaled that an event to which he must respond is about to occur. Abbreviation: CNV.

Contralateral. Refers to a point on the opposite side of the body.

Contrast detection. The detection of the difference between levels of stimulation in different parts of a receptive field; not the detection of absolute levels of stimulation.

Convergence. In a neuronal system, the channeling of information from several sources or neurons to one location or neuron. (See Divergence.) In vision, the directing of the two eyes inward so that they point directly at a nearby object.

Convulsion. Very strong, involuntary contraction of skeletal muscles.

Cornea. The transparent structure of the anterior of the lens of the eye.

Coronal plane. A flat section perpendicular to the horizontal, dividing the body into front and back portions.

Corpus callosum. The massive bundle of nerve fibers connecting the right and left cerebral hemispheres of the mammalian brain.

Corticosteroids. A class of chemical released by an organism during stress or arousal.

Cranial nerves. Nerves of the peripheral nervous system that enter the brain directly, as opposed to spinal nerves that enter the CNS at the spinal cord.

Critical band. A range of sound frequencies that interferes with the detection of a pure tone.

CS−. Negative conditioned stimulus—a stimulus that is never followed by reinforcement.

CS+. Positive conditioned stimulus—a stimulus that is always followed by reinforcement.

Cuneate nucleus. The medullary nucleus of the lemniscal system where dorsal column fibers originating in the arms and upper body terminate. (See Gracilis nucleus.)

Curare. A drug that paralyzes skeletal muscles.

Cycloheximide. An antibiotic that interferes with protein synthesis.

Cytoplasm. The complex fluid substance consisting of proteins, other organic materials, and ions, all contained in water, that is separated from the extracellular fluid by the cellular membrane.

Decibel. A unit of measurement of the ratio between two quantities, as the logarithm of the ratio times 10 if the quantities are power, or times 20 if they are voltages. In acoustics, a decibel scale of sound-pressure ratios is used to measure sound intensity.

Deep structure. A structural level in the syntactic system that may be directly interpreted by the semantic grammar into the nonlinguistic semantic system of meaning. (See also Surface structure.)

Defensive reflex. A reflex similar to the orienting reflex in which attention is directed to a potentially threatening stimulus. In the defensive reflex, the blood vessels of the head constrict, whereas, in the orienting reflex, they dilate.

Delta rhythm. An EEG pattern consisting of high-voltage 0.25–4 Hz waves.

Dendrite. The branched extension of the nerve cell that receives input from other neurons and that transmits information (electrotonic and sometimes spike potentials) toward the cell body.

Depolarization. A change in the membrane potential of a cell such that its interior becomes less negative.

Depressor muscles. A group of muscles that, with the levitator muscles, control the movement of the gill bailer of some invertebrates.

Desynchrony. In EEG, low-voltage, fast activity—thought to result from neuronal activity that is not closely coordinated among large groups of neurons. (See Synchrony.)

Diabetes mellitus. A disease in which carbohydrates cannot be metabolized and utilized as food. It is characterized by high levels of blood glucose.

Diastolic blood pressure. The arterial pressure of the blood, measured between contractions of the left ventricle.

Diathermy machine. A device that artificially raises the temperature of the body by passing electrical current through it.

Diencephalon. The part of the brain consisting of the thalamus, subthalamus, and hypothalamus. Literally, the "interbrain."

Diffusion. The spreading of ions or particles throughout a solution.

Dihydroxyphenylalanine. The chemical precursor of noradrenalin and dopamine. Abbreviation: DOPA.

Dilate. To expand or make larger.

Discs. In reference to photoreceptors, the specialized structures of the outer segment of the photoreceptor that contain photochemicals and where the initial electrical response to light occurs.

Disinhibition. The removal of inhibition.

Distal. Toward the periphery of the nervous system, or farther from a point of reference. (See Proximal.)

Divergence. In a neuronal system, the channeling of information from one source or neuron to multiple locations or neurons. (See Convergence.)

DNA. The molecule responsible for transmitting genetic information from generation to generation and which contains information necessary for the synthesis of proteins in the body. Deoxyribonucleic acid.

Dopamine. A possible CNS neural transmitter.

Dorsal. Toward the back or top side of a four-legged animal, with reference to the horizontal plane.

Dorsal column. A lemniscal system fiber tract in the dorsal portion of the spinal cord that carries somatosensory information.

Dorsal root. A sensory spinal root. The portion of a dorsal spinal nerve between the spinal cord and the dorsal root ganglion.

Double dissociation. A technique of analysis to determine that two brain functions are physiologically different and separable, by demonstrating in one group of patients the retention of one function and the loss of the other and, in another group, the reverse pattern of impairment.

Double reciprocal innervation. A pattern of innervation of muscle groups such that contraction of a flexor and relaxation of the extensor in one limb (as in reciprocal innervation) are accompanied by the opposite pattern in the contralateral limb (that is, contraction of the extensor and relaxation of the flexor).

Drift. Slow movement of the eyes away from a point of fixation.

Early receptor potential. A nonionic electrical photochemical receptor response recorded in rods in response to flashes of light. Abbreviation: ERP.

Effective range of stimulus intensity. The range of stimulus intensity between threshold and an upper boundary, beyond which the response to increasing stimulus intensity is not reliable.

Effector. Cells in muscles or externally secreting glands.

Efferent. Refers to nerve pathways that conduct impulses away from a central structure of the nervous system, as in motor neurons.

Electroconvulsive shock. An electrical current applied across the skull that may result in convulsions and memory loss. Abbreviation: ECS.

Electrode. An electrical conductor used in recording electrical activity of the brain.

Electroencephalogram. A graph or other record of the summated, relatively low-frequency (less than 100 Hz), electrical activity of the brain. In humans, it is typically recorded from disc-shaped electrodes placed on the scalp. Abbreviation: EEG.

Electromyographic. Refers to the measurement of electrical potentials produced by the muscles.

Electrotonic conduction. Passive propagation of potential changes along a membrane.

Embryological. Pertaining to the early patterns of growth and development of an animal following conception.

Encephalization. The progressive increase in relative size and importance of the cerebral hemispheres found in phylogenetically higher species.

Endfoot. The terminal enlargement of the axon, containing neurotransmitter and forming the axonal portion of the synapse.

Endolymph. The fluid in the cochlear duct of the inner ear.

Endplate potential. The depolarizing potential seen in muscle fibers at the neuromuscular junction, in response to the release of acetylcholine. Abbreviation: EPP.

Engram. The hypothetical permanent-memory trace in the brain.

Entorhinal cortex. An area of neocortex adjacent to the hippocampus through which hippocampal afferents pass.

Entrain. A process in which one rhythmic function is brought into synchrony with another such function.

Enzyme. Any of the many types of proteins that control chemical reactions of living tissues.

Epicritic sensation. High-acuity sensation, as in touch and temperature. (See Protopathic sensation.)

Epiglottis. A soft flap-like structure that acts as a valve to close the upper entrance to the larynx.

Epilepsy. A category of disease characterized by abnormal brain-wave patterns, loss of consciousness, sensory disturbances, involuntary movements, and/or convulsions.

Epileptic focus. A small, restricted area of brain tissue that shows the large electrical discharges characteristic of epilepsy.

Epileptiform. An EEG pattern that is epileptic in nature—synchronous, high-amplitude activity.

EPSP. Excitatory postsynaptic potential. A temporary and partial depolarization in a postsynaptic neuron, resulting from synaptic activity.

Equilibrium. The state in which electrical and chemical (that is, concentration) forces are in balance and there is no net force on a species of ion tending to move it either into or out of the cell.

Equilibrium potential. The potential that a species of ions contributes to the membrane potential when the species is in equilibrium.

ESB. Electrical stimulation of the brain.

Ethological. Refers to the study of the behavior of animals, usually in their natural environment.

Evoked potential. A change in brain electrical activity (potential) evoked or elicited by a stimulus.

Evoked response. See Evoked potential.

Excitable membrane. Any cell membrane that demonstrates the Hodgkin cycle.

Excitatory. Refers to a depolarizing, neuronal membrane-potential change that tends to produce an action potential. In systems of neurons, refers to the increase of activity in a neuronal system by the activation of another neuronal system.

Excitatory angle. The range of angles of the position of a limb that produce a response in an individual cell in the joint receptor system.

Excitatory postsynaptic potential. See EPSP.

Extensor. A muscle that acts to extend a joint.

External ear. See Outer ear.

Extinction. A process in which a learned response fails to occur after the removal of reinforcement.

Extracellular fluid. In the nervous system, the liquid found outside of nerve cells and glia.

Extrafusal fibers. The long, strong fibers of striated muscle that predominate and that are responsible for contracting the muscle. (See Intrafusal fibers.)

Extralemniscal pathways. Somatosensory pathways that do not form part of the lemniscal system.

Extraocular muscles. The muscles attached to the outside of the eyeball that control its position.

Extrapyramidal motor systems. Motor pathways that are not part of the pyramidal tract.

Extrinsic muscles. The extraocular muscles.

Fasciculus. A bundle of nerve fibers.

Feedback. A concept in which the outcome of a particular process or event is used to control future outcomes. The flow of information from the output to the input of a controlled process.

5-hydroxytryptophan. A chemical precursor of serotonin. Abbreviation: 5-HTP.

Flaccid. Limp, relaxed, soft.

Flexor. A muscle that acts to flex a joint.

Fluoresce. To emit light when stimulated with light energy of higher frequency.

Forebrain. The telencephalon and the diencephalon of the brain.

Fornix. A fiber bundle that connects hippocampus with the septal area.

Fovea. The small central part of the retina that is specialized for high-acuity vision.

Frequency following. In audition, the firing of an auditory neuron in phase with acoustic stimulus.

Fricative consonant. A speech sound produced by the forced passage of air through a constricted portion of the vocal tract.

Frontal lobe. The most anterior lobe of the cerebral cortex.

Gamma motor neurons. The class of motor neurons that terminate on intrafusal fibers.

Ganglion. A definable concentration of nerve cells.

Ganglion cell. A retinal neuron that receives input from bipolar and amacrine cells, the axons of which leave the eye, forming the optic tract.

Gastrointestinal. Refers to the stomach and intestines.

Gate. To control the passage of.

Generalization. In discrimination learning, a measure of the extent to which stimuli different from the original CS elicit the learned response.

Generator potential. The graded dendritic potential produced in a sensory neuron by receptor activation.

Geomagnetic. Refers to the magnetic field of the earth.

Gill bailer. A structure in the gills of hermit crabs and some other invertebrates that moves water through the gills with fast rhythmic oscillatory movements.

Glia. A class of cells found in the nervous system serving a supportive and nutritive role for neurons. They are possibly important in regulating ionic concentrations in the nervous system as well.

Glottis. The opening between the vocal cords of the larynx.

Glucoreceptors. Cells that can signal the level of glucose in the body.

Glucose. A liquid mixture of the sugar dextrose.

Glucostatic theory. The theory that hunger is regulated by the level of glucose in the blood.

Gracilis nucleus. The medullary nucleus of the lemniscal system where dorsal-column fibers originating in the legs and lower body terminate. (See Cuneate nucleus.)

Graded potential. A potential change that varies continuously as stimulus strength or synaptic activation is varied.

Grammar. The total set of rules relating speech sounds and meaning.

Grand mal seizure. A seizure characterized by loss of consciousness and violent jerking movements.

Gray matter. Areas of the CNS composed mainly of cell bodies. (See White matter.)

Gyrus. Any of the raised portions of the folded surface of the cerebral hemispheres.

Hair cells. In reference to audition, the auditory receptor cells of the organ of Corti.

H bands. The lighter areas in the center of the A bands of striated muscle which contain only thick (myosin) filaments.

Hemiretina. Half of the retina divided vertically. The nasal hemiretina is the medial half of the retina, toward the nose. The temporal hemiretina is the lateral half of the retina, toward the temple.

Hemispheres. The two lateral halves of the cerebrum or cerebellum.

Hertz. Cycles per second. Abbreviation: Hz.

Hierarchical. A multilevel organization of control.

Hindbrain. The part of the brain consisting of the metencephalon and the myelencephalon.

Hippocampus. A three-layered cortical structure at the base of the cerebral hemispheres that is part of the limbic system.

Histology. See Microanatomy.

Hodgkin cycle. The positive feedback cycle responsible for producing an action potential. Depolarization of the neuronal membrane beyond the threshold increases membrane permeability to sodium, which allows more sodium to enter the cell, which further depolarizes the cell; this sequence continues to repeat.

Homeostasis. A condition of stability in the bodily systems that is maintained by feedback control.

Homologous. In anatomy, tissues having the same structure, position, and embryological origin. For example, the two cerebral hemispheres are completely homologous structures.

Horizontal cell. A type of neuron in the retina that receives input from many different visual receptors through processes that extend laterally; it sends output to bipolar cells.

Horizontal plane. A flat section, parallel with the ground, dividing the body into an upper and lower portion.

Hormone. A chemical secreted by glands that regulates the activity of other organs.

Hydrated ions. The form ions take in water—water molecules bond weakly with the ions, increasing their effective radius.

Hypercomplex cell. A class of cells in visual cortex that respond most strongly to lines of light of specific orientation anywhere in the receptive field that terminate at or before an adjacent inhibitor area. Sometimes termed "corner detectors."

Hyperpolarization. An increase in the voltage gradient across the membrane such that the interior of the cell becomes more negative.

Hypothalamus. A relatively small but important structure in the caudal portion of the diencephalon that consists of a number of nuclei and is involved in the regulation of bodily processes such as feeding, drinking, and temperature maintenance.

I bands. The light areas of striated muscle in which thin (actin) filaments are found.

Iconic. Refers to a symbolic pictorial representation of information.

Imperative stimulus. A signal to which a subject must respond.

Inactivation. In reference to membrane permeability, the process in which the temporary change in permeability of the neuronal membrane to an ion (for example, Na^+) is reversed.

Incus. One of three small bones in the middle ear that serve to transmit air-driven vibrations from the outer to the inner ear.

Inferior colliculi. Nuclei protruding from the dorsal surface of the mesencephalon that are involved in auditory perception.

Information transduction. The transfer of information from one form to another (for example, from light energy to neuronal spike trains).

Infrahuman. An animal below man on phylogenetic scales—hence, any nonhuman animal.

Inhibitory. In single neurons, refers to a neuronal membrane change in the hyperpolarizing direction tending to prevent the initiation of an action potential. In systems of neurons, refers to the reduction of activity in a neuronal system by the activation of another neuronal system, as in the cortical inhibition of a subcortical area.

Inhibitory postsynaptic potential. See IPSP.

Inner ear. The part of the ear including the cochlea and semicircular canals.

Inner segment. The anterior portion of the photoreceptor.

Intensity (of a stimulus). The energy of a stimulus.

Intentional tremor. Muscular tremor that is only seen during the performance of voluntary (intended) movements. (See Tremor "at rest.")

Interneuron. Short-axoned neurons that serve neither an afferent nor efferent function but connect neurons within the CNS.

Intracellular fluid. The liquid substance found inside cells.

Intrafusal fibers. The thin muscle fibers that do not themselves directly produce muscular contraction but form the motor component of the muscle spindle and therefore are involved in monitoring and regulating whole muscle length.

Intrusions. In a verbal learning task, intrusions are wrong answers that were correct answers on previous tests.

Invertebrate. An animal without a backbone.

Ion. An atom that has either lost or gained one or more electrons and hence has a net electrical charge.

Ipsilateral. Refers to a point on the same side of the body.

IPSP. Inhibitory postsynaptic potential. A temporary hyperpolarization in a postsynaptic neuron as a result of synaptic activity.

Iris. The pigmented membrane of the eye, located posterior to the cornea.

Kinesthesia. The sense of the position and movement of the joints and muscles.

Krause endbulbs. Sensory receptors in the skin that were thought to be exclusively receptors of cold temperatures.

Labile. Unstable.

Larynx. The structure comprising muscle and cartilage at the top of the trachea that is important in the production of speech sounds.

Latency. The time from a stimulus to the response to that stimulus at either the behavioral or neuronal level.

Lateral. Away from the center, or midline, of an organism.

Lateral cervical nucleus. The nucleus of the cervical section of the spinal cord in which fibers of the spinocervical pathway synapse.

Lateral differentiation. The concept that more lateral structures of the nervous system are increasingly specialized in function.

Lateral geniculate nucleus. The thalamic relay nucleus of the visual system that receives impulses from the retina via the optic tract and sends impulses to visual cortex via the optic radiations.

Lateral inhibition. A mechanism of sharpening in which a neuron in a sensory system will, when excited, act to inhibit surrounding neurons.

Lateralization. The specialization of the left or right side of the brain to mediate specific functions, such as language.

Lateral lemniscus. An auditory pathway that conveys information about acoustic stimuli from the superior olive of the medulla to the inferior colliculus of the mesencephalon.

Lemniscal system. A somatosensory pathway including the dorsal-column fibers of the spinal cord, medial lemniscus of the brainstem, and ventrobasilar nuclear complex of thalamus. Also included are the spinocervical pathway and fibers of the ventrolateral tracts.

Lesion. The destruction or removal of brain tissue, or the result of that destruction or removal.

Levitator muscles. A group of muscles that, with the depressor muscles, control the movement of the gill bailer of some invertebrates.

Limbic system. A set of interconnected brain structures, including the hippocampus, cingulate gyrus, amygdaloid complex, septum, and hypothalamus, that is implicated in the control of emotion.

Liquid consonant. A sound that is produced without a narrowing of the vocal tract and that may be prolonged, like a vowel.

Local potential. A potential change across a neuronal membrane that is produced in a restricted region and is not actively propagated but spreads electrotonically.

Long-term memory. Memory that is relatively long lasting; permanent memory. Abbreviation: LTM.

Malleus. One of three small bones in the middle ear that serve to transmit air-driven vibrations from the outer to the inner ear.

Masking. The interference with the detection of one stimulus by the presentation of another stimulus.

Mechanoreceptors. Sensory receptors that respond to physical displacement.

Medial. Toward the center, or midline, of an organism.

Medial forebrain bundle. A fiber bundle that passes from olfactory areas, through the lateral hypothalamic area, and to caudal brainstem regions. Electrical stimulation of the medial forebrain bundle is positively reinforcing.

Medial geniuclate nucleus. The thalamic relay nucleus of the auditory system that receives information from the inferior colliculus and sends information to auditory cortex.

Medial lemniscus. A fiber tract, conveying somatosensory information, that arises in the cuneate and gracilis nuclei and passes through the brainstem to the ventrobasilar nuclear complex of the thalamus.

Medulla. The most caudal part of the brain, important in control of such vital bodily processes as respiration and blood circulation.

Meissner's corpuscles. Sensory receptors of the skin that were thought to respond to touch or pressure.

Membrane. The thin structure surrounding each cell and some cell parts such as the nucleus. More generally, a layer of tissue that covers or divides a bodily organ.

Membrane potential. The electrical potential (voltage) difference between the inside and outside of a cell membrane, stated in reference to the inside of the cell. For example, if the interior of a neuron were 70 mV more negative than the extracellular fluid, the membrane potential would be −70 mV.

Memory trace. A hypothetical representation of stored information in the brain. (See Activity trace and Structural trace.)

Mesencephalon. The relatively undifferentiated part of the brain that is between the diencephalon and the metencephalon. Literally, the "midbrain".

Metabolism. The set of all chemical processes by which life is maintained, including the production of chemical substances necessary for the organism and chemical reactions that produce energy needed by the organism.

Metencephalon. The part of the brain consisting of the cerebellum and the pons.

Microanatomy. The anatomy of small structures in tissue, visible only microscopically.

Microelectrode. An electrode usually used for recording electrical activity from single neurons. The diameter of its tip is about 1 micron.

Micromolecular. Refers to molecules that are relatively small (would not include large molecules such as proteins).

Micron. One millionth of a meter. Symbol: μ.

Midbrain. The mesencephalon.

Middle ear. The part of the ear between the tympanic membrane and the oval window including the malleus, incus, and stapes.

Middle-ear muscles. Tiny muscles of the middle ear that, when contracted, render the malleus, incus, and stapes less efficient in transmitting air-driven vibrations to the inner ear.

Millisecond. One thousandth of a second. Abbreviation: msec.

Millivolt. One thousandth of a volt. Abbreviation: mV.

Miniature endplate potentials. Small uniform depolarizations of the postsynaptic element of the neuromuscular junction membrane that probably result from the release of the transmitter contents of a single synaptic vesicle.

Mitochondria. Small structures found in the cytoplasm of the cell that are important in metabolism.

Modality. Any one of the senses (for example, taste or touch).

Modulate. To regulate.

Monoamines. A class of chemicals including the neural transmitters noradrenalin and dopamine, which are catecholamines, and serotonin, which is an indolamine.

Monosynaptic. Refers to a neural circuit involving only two neurons and one synapse.

Monotonic. Steadily increasing or decreasing.

Morphemes. The smallest meaningful units of speech—that is, root words, suffixes, and prefixes.

Motor neuron. A neuron that terminates on muscle tissue and acts to control the contraction of that muscle.

Motor unit. The functional unit of the musculature, composed of a single motor neuron and all of the muscle fibers that it innervates.

Multisynaptic. Refers to a neural circuit involving two or more synapses.

Muscle fibers. The elongated cells of muscle tissue that contract.

Muscle fibrils. The bundles of muscle filaments within a muscle fiber.

Muscle filaments. Strand-like structures in muscle cells that are made of actin or myosin. The displacement of the two types of filaments in relation to one another is responsible for the contraction of muscle.

Muscle spindle. A structure found in muscle tissue important in the control of muscle contraction, consisting of intrafusal fibers, sensory receptors, and afferent and efferent neurons.

Myelencephalon. The most caudal part of the brain consisting primarily of the medulla, which connects the spinal cord with higher portions of the brain. Literally the "spinal-cord brain."

Myelin. The white, fatty substance surrounding portions of nerve axons that acts to increase the speed and efficiency of spike production.

Myosin. The protein of which thick muscle filaments are constructed and that, together with actin, produces contraction of muscle.

Nasal consonant. A consonant that involves resonance of the nasal cavity in its production.

Neospinothalamic system. A collection of ascending somatosensory fiber tracts in the ventrolateral portion of the spinal cord that have been found with certainty only in the higher primates and man.

Neural transmitters. Chemical substances, released into the synaptic cleft by a presynaptic neuron, that diffuse across the synaptic cleft and excite or inhibit the postsynaptic cell.

Neuro-. Pertaining to nerves or the nervous system.

Neuroanatomy. The science of the structure of the nervous system.

Neurochemical. Chemical events in nerve cells.

Neuromuscular junction. The synaptic-like structure in which a motor neuron makes contact with muscle tissue.

Neuron. A nerve cell, including all of its processes.

Neurophysiology. The science of the function of the nervous system.

Neurosciences. The sciences of the nervous system, including its structure, function, biochemistry, and pharmacology.

Nodes of Ranvier. Gaps in the myelin sheath of an axon that allow for saltatory conduction of action potentials.

Noradrenalin. A neural transmitter. Also referred to as norepinephrine.

Norepinephrine. A neural transmitter. Also referred to as noradrenalin.

Nuclear bag. The enlarged central portion of an intrafusal fiber.

Nucleus. A group of nerve cell bodies in the central nervous system. In reference to cells, the spherical subcellular structure found in cells that contains chromosomes.

Occipital lobe. The most posterior section of the cerebral cortex, which serves primarily a visual function.

Off response. A response of a receptor or neuron to the termination of a stimulus.

1-A fibers. A class of rapidly conducting afferent nerve fibers.

On–off cells. Receptors or neurons that respond both to the onset and termination of a stimulus.

On response. A response of a receptor or neuron that occurs when a stimulus is applied to a sensory system.

Operant conditioning. A type of training in which a reinforcement is presented immediately after a desired behavior is emitted, thereby altering the subsequent probability of the behavior.

Opsin. A class of molecule that combines with retinene (11-*cis* form) to form the photochemicals of visual receptors.

Optic chiasma. The point of crossing of the optic nerves.

Optic nerve. The nerve that transmits visual information from the retina toward the lateral geniculate body, forming the optic tract as it passes through the optic chiasma.

Optic radiation. The fiber pathways leading from the lateral geniculate body to the visual cortex.

Optic tectum. An area of the visual system near the superior colliculus in the mesencephalon.

Optic tract. The collection of nerve fibers between the optic chiasma and the lateral geniculate nucleus, formed as the optic nerve enters the optic chiasma. (See Optic nerve.)

Organ of Corti. The receptor organ of the inner ear that transduces sound-driven movements of the basilar membrane into patterns of neuronal activity.

Orienting reflex. A reflex in which attention is directed to a new stimulus.

Oscillator. A type of neuron found in invertebrates that shows no spiking but shows a very regular spontaneous pattern of depolarizations and hyperpolarizations. More generally, a system that generates regular cyclic changes.

Osmolarity. The concentration of all particles in a solution.

Osmometric. Refers to the measurement of osmolarity.

Osmoreceptors. Neurons that change their firing rate as their volume is altered in response to changes in concentrations of salts, ions, and other chemicals in the extracellular fluid.

Ossicles. The bones of the middle ear—malleus, incus, and stapes—that transmit air-driven vibrations from the outer to the inner ear.

Outer ear. The part of the ear including the pinna (the fleshy structure of the ear that lies outside the skull) and the external auditory meatus (canal-like opening leading from the pinna to the tympanic membrane).

Outer segment. The posterior portion of the photoreceptor that is layered in its structure.

Oval window. The membrane-covered, oval-shaped opening separating the middle and inner ear, through which the vibrational energy of the stapes is transmitted to the cochlea.

Pacinian corpuscle. A pressure-sensitive receptor with a complex laminated structure.

Paradigm. A model or example of a concept. For instance, a Pavlovian training situation is referred to as the classical-conditioning paradigm.

Paradoxical sleep. REM sleep.

Parasympathetic nervous system. The division of the autonomic nervous system arising from the cranial nerves and the spinal nerves in the neck and lower back region, which serves vegetative functions such as digestion and sleep.

Parietal lobe. The section of the cerebral cortex posterior to the frontal lobe, anterior to the occipital lobe, and superior to the temporal lobe.

Parse. To break into a series of meaningful units.

Passive avoidance. An experimental situation in which an animal can avoid punishment by not responding, hence remaining passive. An example is a situation in which an animal avoids electrical shock by not stepping down from a platform onto a grid floor.

P-chlorophenylalanine. A chemical that inhibits the production of serotonin. Abbreviation: PCPA.

Percept. A term for the product of a perceptual process.

Peri-. Around.

Perilymph. The fluid of the inner ear, not including the endolymph of the cochlear duct.

Peripheralist theory. A theory that emphasizes events in the body or the periphery of the nervous system as opposed to the brain. For example, the peripheralist theory of emotion proposes that sensation in visceral organs produced reflexively by events is responsible for emotional feelings.

Peripheral nervous system. In vertebrates, the portion of the nervous system outside the brain and spinal cord, including the autonomic nervous system.

Permeability. The property of a membrane that allows substances to pass through it.

Phase. A particular point in a cyclical event. Two cyclical events that show the same phase at the same time are said to be in phase.

Phasic. In reference to receptors, a response that occurs only to changes in the stimulus. More generally, a response that is short lasting in the presence of continuing stimulation.

Phone. A speech sound as produced.

Phoneme. The smallest unit of speech that is used to distinguish different spoken utterances in a particular language.

Phonetic. Related to speech sounds.

Phonologic. Refers to speech sounds.

Phonology. The study of speech sounds, both phones and phonemes.

Phylogenetic. Pertaining to the evolutionary relationships of organisms.

Pineal gland. A small gland-like body of uncertain function that is attached to the roof of the third ventricle of the diencephalon.

Pituitary gland. A neuroregulatory gland attached to the hypothalamus by a stalk-like appendage.

Placebo. A substance or treatment that has no specific effect of its own, used in experiments as a control procedure.

Place theories of quality. Theories that propose that different qualities of the stimulus are mediated by separate neuronal systems—for example, in audition, the theory that sound frequency is coded by the place on the organ of Corti where auditory nerve fibers originate.

Plasticity. The ability of specific parts of the nervous system to change their function—for example, in learning.

Plosive consonant. A speech sound produced by the sudden release of air previously occluded at some point in the vocal tract.

Polarization. The production of an electrical potential (voltage) difference in different parts of a structure—for example, across the membrane of a neuron.

Pons. The brainstem portion of the metencephalon.

Ponto-geniculate-occipital spikes. EEG spikes or sharp waves appearing in REM sleep that originate in the pontine reticular formation and proceed to the lateral geniculate nucleus and occipital (visual) cortex. Abbreviation: PGO spikes.

Posterior. Toward the tail of a four-legged animal on the nose-to-tail axis.

Postsynaptic. In a synapse, the neuron or neuronal membrane contacted by the endfoot.

Potassium. A metallic element found in the nervous system in the ionized form with highest concentrations in the intracellular fluid. Symbol for the ionized form: K^+.

Precursor. A chemical from which another chemical is produced. More generally, something that precedes another thing.

Presynaptic. In a synapse, the neuron or neuronal membrane that releases neurotransmitter into the synaptic cleft.

Primates. The order of higher mammals consisting of prosimians, monkeys, apes, and man.

Processes. The axonal and dendritic projections from the cell body of a neuron.

Productive aphasia. See Speech-production aphasia.

Propagation. The active process by which an action potential is passed along the length of an axon.

Protein. Large molecules that are essential building blocks of living things, composed of chains of amino acids.

Protopathic sensation. In the body, senses of pain and temperature that are poorly localized. (See Epicritic sensation.)

Proximal. Toward the center of the CNS, or closer to a point of reference. (See Distal.)

PSP. Postsynaptic potential—either an EPSP or IPSP.

Psychoactive drugs. Drugs that affect states of consciousness and the functioning of the brain, affecting behavior.

Pupil. The opening of the iris of the eye through which light passes to reach the retina.

Pure tone. The sound that is produced by a perfect sinusoidal vibration.

Puromycin. An antibiotic that interferes with protein synthesis.

Pyramidal tract. The large descending pathway, consisting of axons of neurons in motor, somatosensory, and other cortical regions, that passes through the medullary pyramids. Present only in mammals, it is especially well developed in higher primates.

Quality (sensory). The type of energy of a stimulus.

Quantity (sensory). The intensity of a stimulus.

Raphe nuclei. A group of nuclei in the midbrain tegmentum.

Rapid-eye-movement sleep. A stage of sleep characterized by a low-voltage, desynchronized EEG and rapid movements of the eyes. Abbreviation: REM sleep.

Receptive field. The area in the periphery in which stimulation alters the response of a sensory neuron.

Receptor. A type of cell at the periphery of the nervous system that recodes the energy of a physical stimulus into a neuronal representation.

Receptor potential. A graded electrical potential in a sensory receptor that varies as a function of stimulus input.

Reciprocal innervation. A pattern of innervation of antagonist muscles such that contraction of one of the muscle pairs is accompanied by relaxation of the other.

Recoding. Changing the representation of information from one form to another.

Recurrent. Returning toward the source. A recurrent neuronal pathway is one through which neuronal output returns as input, either excitatory or inhibitory, via one or more intervening neurons.

Reflex. An automatic, involuntary response to a stimulus.

Reflex arc. The neural circuit of a reflex, from the sensory organ through the CNS to the muscle or effector organ.

Reflex stepping. The reflexive movements of the legs resembling walking, in animals having only spinal control of movement, in response to touching the bottom of the feet or to stretching leg extensor muscles.

Reinforcement. In operant conditioning, an event following a response that alters the subsequent probability of the response. In classical conditioning, the unconditioned stimulus with which a conditioned stimulus is paired. Loosely, positive reinforcement is reward and negative reinforcement is punishment.

Reissner's membrane. A membrane in the cochlea.

Relative refractory period. The period after the absolute refractory period of an action potential in which a second action potential may be triggered only by a larger than normal stimulus.

Resonance. The intensification of particular frequencies of vibration. In vocalization, the alteration of the quality of speech sounds by the cavities of the mouth, nose, and throat.

Response-chaining. An explanation for complex behavior in which a response serves as a stimulus for the next response in the chain.

Reticular activating system. A collection of pathways in the reticular formation thought to act to produce behavioral and electroencephalographic arousal.

Reticular formation. A central core of relatively undifferentiated tissue running the length of the brainstem.

Retina. The structure in the posterior of the eye containing the photoreceptors and a network of neurons.

Retinene. A molecule that, in the 11-*cis* form, is bound with a large opsin molecule to form a photochemical. When a photon of light is absorbed by a photochemical, retinene is likely to change to the all-*trans* form, and rhodopsin will then split into retinene and opsin.

Retinotopic. The orderly representation of visual information in visual-system structures by the location of the stimulus on the retina.

Reversal. In learning, a situation in which a response opposite to one previously learned must be acquired.

Reward system. A collection of brain structures in which electrical stimulation has rewarding properties. Includes the septum, amygdala, hippocampus, and lateral hypothalamus.

Rhodopsin. The photochemical of the rods.

Ribosomes. Small cytoplasmic structures that contain RNA and are active in protein synthesis.

RNA. Nucleic acid molecules that, with DNA, control the protein synthesis in the cell. Ribonucleic acid.

Rods. Visual receptors of the periphery of the retina.

Rostral. Toward the nose of a four-legged animal along the nose-to-tail axis.

Round window. A round membrane-covered opening in the cochlea.

Ruffini corpuscles. Sensory receptors in the skin that were thought to exclusively signal warmth.

Saccade. A rapid movement of the eyes from one point of fixation to another.

Sagittal plane. A flat section perpendicular to the horizontal and parallel to the midline, dividing the body into left and right portions.

Saltatory conduction. The skipping of a propagated action potential from one node of Ranvier to another, along the length of an axon.

Sarcomere. One segment of a muscle fibril, bounded by Z lines.

Saturation. The failure of a receptor to reliably signal stimulus intensity at high levels of stimulation.

Sclera. The tough white outer covering of the eyeball.

Sea hare. A type of molluscan marine invertebrate. Also called *Aplysia*.

Secondary reinforcer. A stimulus that becomes reinforcing only after being paired with an already reinforcing stimulus.

Seizure. An epileptic convulsion.

Selective attention. The process of determining which stimuli receive further processing.

Semantic. Related to meaning.

Sensor. A device that provides information about a physical quantity. For example, a thermometer is a sensor of temperature.

Sensory image. The detailed representation of perceived objects in sensory memory.

Sensory memory. A memory system that stores a great deal of sensory information for very short periods of time until portions are processed by other memory systems.

Septum. A midline structure of the limbic system, situated caudal to the corpus callosum, in which ESB is positively reinforcing.

Serotonin. A proposed neural transmitter implicated in the control of sleep. Also called 5-HT (5-hydroxytryptamine).

17-hydroxycorticosteroids. A class of hormones that are released into the blood by the outer layer (cortex) of the adrenal glands and that can be measured in the blood or urine.

17-ketogenic steroids. A class of hormones that includes male sex hormones.

Sharpening. A process in which a broadly tuned response in a sensory system is rendered more selective.

Sharp wave. An EEG wave that is larger in amplitude than background activity and that has a duration of more than 1/12 sec and less than 1/5 sec.

Short-term memory. A memory system of relatively short duration—that is, a few seconds, minutes, or hours. Abbreviation: STM.

Simple cortical cell. A class of cells in visual cortex that responds most strongly to stimuli such as lines of light of specific orientation and location in the visual field.

Skinner box. A box containing a bar or panel that an experimental animal must learn to press in order to receive a reward.

Slow waves. EEG waves of 1/8 sec or greater duration.

Slow-wave sleep. The stage of sleep characterized by slow EEG waves.

Sodium. A metallic element that is present in the nervous system in ionized form, with highest concentrations in the extracellular fluid. Symbol for the ionized form: Na$^+$.

Sodium Amytal. A sedative barbiturate compound.

Solute. A chemical that is dissolved in another substance.

Soma. The neuron cell body.

Somatosensory. Refers to bodily senses including touch, pressure, temperature, and pain.

Somatosensory cortex. The primary somatosensory receiving area in the parietal lobe of the cortex.

Spatial summation. The summing of PSPs produced at two or more synapses in one postsynaptic cell.

Species. In reference to ions, an ion of a particular type—for example, K$^+$.

Spectral absorption characteristics. The particular pattern of light wavelengths that are absorbed by a substance.

Speech-production aphasia. The loss of speech production without impairment of speech perception.

Spike. With reference to the EEG, a sudden large potential of less than 1/12 sec duration, which is often epileptiform in nature. With reference to single cells, see Action potential.

Spinal cord. The portion of the central nervous system contained in the spinal column.

Spinal nerves. The nerves of the peripheral nervous system that enter the CNS at the spinal cord. (See Cranial nerves.)

Spindles. Short series of EEG waves of a particular frequency, initially low in amplitude, that increase and then decrease, forming a spindle-like pattern.

Spinocervical pathway. A lemniscal-system pathway in which fibers enter the spinal column through dorsal roots and proceed upward to the lateral cervical nuclei of the spinal cord where they synapse.

Spontaneous activity. In neurons, activity in the absence of specific sensory stimulation.

Stage-1 sleep. A state of drowsiness or relaxed wakefulness defined by an EEG record with slightly slowed alpha (8–12 Hz) waves.

Stage-2 sleep. A state of light sleep defined by an EEG with sleep spindles. Several second periods of 14 to 15 Hz waves superimposed on a low-voltage background activity with 3 to 6 Hz waves are also present.

Stage-3 sleep. A state of sleep of intermediate depth defined by an EEG record with some sleep spindles superimposed on a background of slow 1 to 2 Hz waves.

Stage-4 sleep. A state of sleep defined by an EEG record of high-voltage delta (4 Hz or slower) waves without spindling.

Stapes. One of three small bones in the middle ear that transmit air-driven vibrations from the outer to the inner ear.

Startle reflex. See Defensive reflex.

Stretch reflex. The monosynaptic spinal reflex that results in contraction of a muscle when that muscle is stretched.

Structural trace. A hypothetical representation of information in long-term memory by an unknown physical change in neuronal structure.

Strychnine. A CNS stimulant.

Substantia gelatinosa. A region of the gray matter of the spinal cord where some dorsal-root fibers terminate, in which control of information about painful stimulation is thought to occur.

Substrate. Underlying mechanism or basis.

Sulcus. Indentations of the folded cortical surface of the cerebral hemispheres that separate the gyri.

Superior colliculi. Bilateral nuclei protruding from the dorsal surface of the mesencephalon that are involved in visual perception.

Superior olive nucleus. A nucleus of the auditory pathway, found in the metencephalic brainstem.

Surface structure. A structural level in the syntactic system that may be directly interpreted by the phonological grammar into a series of speech sounds. (See also Deep structure.)

Sympathectomy. An operation that removes some of the sympathetic connections between visceral organs and the CNS.

Sympathetic nervous system. The division of the autonomic nervous system arising from the length of the spinal cord that serves primarily to activate internal organs for action. (See also Parasympathetic nervous system.)

Synapse. The place at which two neurons make a functional connection. Usually found at the point where the axon of one neuron transmits nerve impulses to the dendrite, cell body, or endfoot of a second neuron.

Synaptic cleft. The physical gap (200 angstroms) at the synapse between the presynaptic and the postsynaptic neuron that is filled with extracellular fluid.

Synaptic conductivity. The relative ease and efficiency with which presynaptic events influence postsynaptic events.

Synaptic vesicles. Small spherical structures found in the synaptic endfoot that contain neural transmitter.

Synchrony. Refers to events happening at the same time. In EEG, high-voltage patterns of brain-wave activity, such as the alpha rhythm, which are thought to be produced by nearly simultaneous cyclical activity in a large number of neurons. (See Desynchrony.)

Syndrome. A set of symptoms that characteristically occur together.

Syntax. The rules of organization of words into larger units, such as phrases or sentences.

Systolic blood pressure. The arterial pressure of the blood measured during ventricular contraction.

Tachistoscope. A device used to present visual stimuli of short duration.

Tectorial membrane. The membrane of the organ of Corti against which cilia of the hair cells are displaced by vibrations of the basilar membrane.

Tegmentum. A region of the mesencephalon immediately ventral to the cerebral aqueduct.

Telencephalon. The most rostral part of the brain, consisting of the cerebral hemispheres and some underlying structures, including portions of the limbic system. Literally, "end brain" or "far brain," reflecting its rostral location.

Temporal lobe. The portion of the cerebral hemispheres beneath the temple of the skull that is inferior to the frontal and parietal lobes and anterior to the occipital lobe.

Temporal summation. The summing of PSPs produced at a single synapse when action potentials arrive in quick succession.

Thalamus. The rostral portion of the diencephalon, consisting of a number of nuclei serving sensory relay and other less clearly defined functions.

Theta rhythm. An EEG pattern of cyclical 4 to 7 Hz waves.

Threshold (of a neuron). The level of membrane depolarization in the axon hillock or axon at which an action potential is initiated.

Threshold (of a sensory stimulus). The point at which a sensory stimulus may be first detected reliably as its intensity is increased.

Tonic. In reference to receptors, a response that is sustained for the duration of the stimulus. More generally, a response that is maintained for a relatively long time.

Tonotopic. The orderly representation of frequency in the auditory system, in which single neurons with similar frequency response characteristics are adjacent to each other.

Tonus. The weak, continuous level of contraction of a muscle.

Topographic. An orderly representation of sensory information in the CNS in which a stimulus applied to a particular point on the body is represented in a specific location in a somatosensory projection area, such that the spatial relations among bodily points are preserved.

Trachea. The cartilaginous tube-like structure leading from the bronchial tubes of the lungs to the larynx. Also called the windpipe.

Tract. A bundle of nerve fibers in the CNS having the same origin and destination.

Transcription. The process of the transfer of information from a DNA molecule to a messenger RNA molecule.

Transformational grammar. The set of rules relating deep and surface structures.

Translation. The process of transfer of information from a messenger RNA molecule to a protein, as an ordering of amino acids in protein synthesis.

Trapezoid body. A nucleus in the auditory pathway in the medulla.

Traumatic amnesia. Amnesia produced by injury.

Tremor. A trembling or vibratory motion, usually involuntary.

Tremor "at rest." Muscular tremor in the absence of voluntary movements (that is, at rest). (See Intentional tremor.)

Trichromaticity theory. A theory of color vision that states that there are three types of visual color receptors, each responding to light of a different wavelength (that is, to a different color).

Tuning curve. A plot of the stimulus energy needed at various frequencies to produce a specified change in the rate of firing of a cell in the auditory system.

Tympanic membrane. The thin membrane separating the outer and inner ear, commonly referred to as the eardrum.

Unconditioned response. An unlearned response to a stimulus. For example, a salivation response to meat powder placed in a dog's mouth would be an unconditioned response. Abbreviation: UCR.

Unconditioned stimulus. A stimulus that elicits an unlearned response. An example of an unconditioned stimulus would be meat powder that would elicit salivation when placed in a dog's mouth. Abbreviation: UCS.

Unit. In reference to neurophysiology, a single neuron.

Vascular bed. Refers to a set of blood vessels.

Vasculature. The system of blood vessels of the body, or any portion thereof.

Vasoconstriction. A decrease in the diameter of blood vessels.

Vasodilation. An increase in the diameter of blood vessels.

Vegetative function. Activity of the internal organs involved in nutrition and growth of the organism.

Ventral. Toward the front or belly side of a four-legged animal with reference to the horizontal plane.

Ventral root. A motor spinal root. The portion of a ventral spinal nerve between the spinal cord and its junction with the sensory component of the nerve.

Ventricles. Any of the four cavities in the brain filled with cerebrospinal fluid—the two lateral ventricles of the cerebrum and the third and fourth ventricles of the brainstem.

Ventrobasal nucleus. The nucleus located in the ventral portion of thalamus that receives somatosensory information from the medial lemniscus and projects to somatosensory cortex.

Ventrolateral tracts. Fiber tracts of the spinal cord that are found in the ventral lateral portion of the white matter and that carry somatosensory information toward the brain.

Ventromedial hypothalamic nucleus. A nucleus in the medial portion of ventral hypothalamus implicated in the control of satiety. Abbreviation: VMH.

Vertebrate. An animal with a backbone—that is, a mammal, bird, fish, reptile, or amphibian.

Vertex. The most rostral portion of the cerebral cortex.

Vestibular system. The collection of structures important in balance, including the semicircular canals of the middle ear, vestibular nerve and nuclei, and associated CNS pathways.

Visceral. Refers to the internal organs of the body, especially those of the abdomen.

Visual field. The portion of the environment that can be seen at a particular fixation.

Vitreous humor. The thick fluid posterior to the lens of the eyeball.

Volumetric. Refers to the measurement of volume.

Wernicke's area. A small area of the superior temporal cortex of the left hemisphere near primary auditory cortex that is involved in language function.

White matter. Areas of the CNS composed almost entirely of axons, the myelin sheaths of which give these areas a white appearance. (See Gray matter.)

White noise. An auditory stimulus with equal energy at all audible frequencies.

Word-presence aphasia. A descriptive term for a loss of language competence in which the patient has difficulty locating the words needed for reasonable speech.

Z lines. The areas on striated muscle where the thin actin filaments attach to one another, found in the I band.

References

Agranoff, B. W. Agents that block memory. In G. C. Quarton, T. Melnechuk, & F. O. Schmitt (Eds.), *The neurosciences: A study program.* New York: Rockefeller, 1967.

Agranoff, B. W., Davis, R. E., & Brink, J. J. Chemical studies on memory fixation in goldfish. *Brain Research,* 1966, **1,** 303–309.

Alpern, M., Lawrence, M., & Wolsk, D. *Sensory processes.* Monterey, Calif.: Brooks/Cole, 1967.

Andersson, Bengt. Thirst—and brain control of water balance. *American Scientist,* 1971, **50,** 408–415.

Arbib, M. A. *The metaphorical brain.* New York: Wiley-Interscience, 1972.

Aserinksy, E., & Kleitman, N. A motility cycle in sleeping infants as manifested by ocular and gross bodily activity. *Journal of Applied Physiology,* 1955, **8,** 11–18.

Barondes, S. H. Multiple steps in the biology of memory. In F. O. Schmitt (Ed.), *The neurosciences: Second study program.* New York: Rockefeller, 1970.

Barondes, S. H., & Cohen, H. D. Arousal and the conversion of short-term to long-term memory. *Proceedings of the National Academy of Science,* 1968, **61,** 923–929.

Basmajian, J. V. Electromyography comes of age. *Science,* 1972, **176,** 603–609.

Beidler, L. M., & Reichardt, W. E. Sensory transduction. *Neurosciences Research Program Bulletin,* 1970, **8**(5).

Bennett, E. L., Diamond, M. C., Krech, D., & Rosenzweig, M. R. Chemical and anatomical plasticity of the brain. *Science,* 1964, **146,** 610–619.

Berger, H. Hans Berger on the electroencephalogram of man. *Electroencephalography and Clinical Neurophysiology,* 1969, Suppl. 28.

Berlucchi, G. Cerebral dominance and interhemispheric communication in normal man. In F. O. Schmitt & F. G. Worden (Eds.), *The neurosciences: Third study program.* Cambridge, Mass.: M.I.T. Press, 1974.

Bernard, C. *An introduction to the study of experimental medicine.* New York: Dover, 1957.

Bishop, M. P., Elder, S. T., & Heath, R. G. Intracranial self-stimulation in man. *Science*, 1963, **140**, 394–396.

Bodian, D. The generalized vertebrate neuron. *Science*, 1962, **137**, 323–326.

Bodian, D. Neurons, circuits, and neuroglia. In G. C. Quarton, T. Melnechuk, & F. O. Schmitt (Eds.), *The neurosciences: A study program*. New York: Rockefeller, 1967.

Brazier, M. A. B. *The electrical activity of the nervous system*. New York: Macmillan, 1960.

Bredberg, G., Lindeman, H. H., Ades, H. W., West, R., & Engstrom, H. Scanning electron microscopy of the organ of Corti. *Science*, 1970, **170**, 861–866.

Broadbent, D. E. Division of function and integration of behavior. In F. O. Schmitt & F. G. Worden (Eds.), *The neurosciences: Third study program*. Cambridge, Mass.: M.I.T. Press, 1974.

Broadbent, D. E. *Perception and communication*. Oxford: Pergamon, 1958.

Bronowski, J., & Bellugi, U. Language, name and concepts. *Science*, 1970, **168**, 669–673.

Broughton, R. J. Sleep disorders: Disorders of arousal? *Science*, 1968, **159**, 1070–1078.

Brown, P. K., & Wald, G. Visual pigments in single rods and cones of the human retina. *Science*, 1964, **144**, 45–52.

Bullock, T. H., & Horridge, G. A. *Structure and function in the nervous systems of invertebrates*. Vols. I & II. San Francisco: Freeman, 1965.

Bullock, T. H. Operations analysis of nervous functions. In F. O. Schmitt (Ed.), *The neurosciences: Second study program*. New York: Rockefeller, 1970.

Bullock, T. H. Neuron doctrine and electrophysiology. *Science*, 1959, **129**(3355), 997–1002.

Butter, C. M. *Neuropsychology: The study of brain and behavior*. Monterey, Calif.: Brooks/Cole, 1968.

Cannon, W. B. The James-Lange theory of emotions: A critical examination and an alternative theory. *The American Journal of Psychology*, 1927, **39**, 106–124.

Chomsky, N. The formal nature of language. In E. H. Lenneberg, *Biological foundations of language*. New York: Wiley, 1967.

Chorover, S. L., & Schiller, P. H. Short-term retrograde amnesia in rats. *Journal of Comparative & Physiological Psychology*, 1965, **59**(1), 73–78.

Chow, K. L. Effects of ablation. In G. C. Quarton, T. Melnechuk, & F. O. Schmitt (Eds.), *The neurosciences: A study program*. New York: Rockefeller, 1967.

Cuénod, M. Commissural pathways in interhemispheric transfer of visual information in the pigeon. In F. O. Schmitt & F. G. Worden (Eds.), *The neurosciences: Third study program*. Cambridge, Mass.: M.I.T. Press, 1974.

Darwin, C. J. Ear differences and hemispheric specialization. In F. O. Schmitt & F. G. Worden (Eds.), *The neurosciences: Third study program*. Cambridge, Mass.: M.I.T. Press, 1974.

Davis, H. Enhancement of evoked cortical potentials in humans related to a task requiring a decision. *Science*, 1964, **145**, 182–183.

Davis, H. Psychophysiology of hearing and deafness. In S. S. Stevens (Ed.), *Handbook of experimental psychology*. New York: Wiley, 1951.

Davis, H. A model for transducer action in the cochlea. *Cold Spring Harbor Symposia of Quantitative Biology*, 1966, **30**, 181–189.

Delgado, J. M. R. *Physical control of the mind*. New York: Harper & Row, 1969.

Delgado, J. M. R., Roberts, W. W., & Miller, N. E. Learning motivated by electrical stimulation of the brain. *American Journal of Physiology*, 1954, **179**, 587–593.

Dement, W., The effect of dream deprivation. *Science*, 1960, **131**(3415), 1705–1707.

Dement, W., & Kleitman, N. Cyclic variations in EEG during sleep and their relation to eye movements, body motility, and dreaming. *Electroencephalography and Clinical Neurophysiology*, 1957, **9**, 673–690.

Denes, P. B., & Pinson, E. N. *The speech chain: The physics and biology of spoken language.* Garden City, N.Y.: Anchor Books, 1973.

Descartes, R. *Passions of the soul.* (Trans. A. P. Torrey.) New York: Henry Holt, 1892.

De Valois, R. L. Analysis and coding of color vision in the primate visual system. In *Sensory receptors.* Cold Spring Harbor, N.Y.: Cold Spring Harbor Lab. of Quant. Biology, 1965.

De Valois, R. L., & Jacobs, G. H. Primate color vision. *Science*, 1968, **162**, 533–540.

De Valois, R. L., Jacobs, G. H., & Abramov, I. Responses of single cells in visual system to shifts in the wavelength of light. *Science*, 1964, **146**, 1184–1186.

Dingman, W., & Sporn, M. B. Molecular theories of memory. *Science*, 1964, **144**, 26–29.

Donchin, E., & Cohen, L. Average evoked potentials and intra-modality selective attention. *Electroencephalography and Clinical Neurophysiology*, 1967, **22**, 537–546.

Dowling, J. E. Foveal receptors of the monkey retina: Fine structure. *Science*, 1965, **147**, 57–59.

Dowling, J. E. The sight of visual adaptation. *Science*, 1967, **155**, 273–279.

Duncan, C. P. The retroactive effect of electroshock on learning. *Journal of Comparative and Physiological Psychology*, 1949, **42**, 32–44.

Easton, T. A. On the normal use of reflexes. *American Scientist*, 1972, **60**, 591–599.

Eccles, J. C. *The neurophysiological basis of mind.* Oxford: Clarendon, 1953.

Eccles, J. C. *The physiology of nerve cells,* Baltimore: Johns Hopkins Press, 1957.

Eccles, J. C. *The physiology of synapses.* New York: Academic Press, 1964.

Egeth, H. Selective attention. *Psychological Bulletin*, 1967, **67**, 41–57.

Eldredge, D. H., & Miller, J. D. Physiology of hearing. *Annual Review of Physiology*, 1971, **33**, 281–309.

Engstrom, B., & Engstrom, H. Structural and physiological features of the organ of the Corti. *Audiology*, 1972, **11**, 6–28.

Evans, C. R., & Mulholland, T. B. (Eds.) *Attention in neurophysiology.* New York: Appleton-Century-Crofts, 1969.

Evarts, E. V. Unit activity in sleep and wakefulness. In G. C. Quarton, T. Melnechuk, & F. O. Schmitt (Eds.), *The neurosciences: A study program.* New York: Rockefeller, 1967.

Evarts, E. V. Relation of pyramidal tract activity to force exerted during voluntary movement. *Journal of Neurophysiology*, 1968, **31**, 1–13.

Evarts, E. V. Motor cortex reflexes associated with the learned movement. *Science*, 1973, **179**, 501–503.

Evarts, E. V., Bizzi, E., Burke, R. E., Delong, M., & Thach, W. T., Jr. Central control of movement. *Neurosciences Research Program Bulletin*, 1971, **9**(1).

Fehr, F. S., & Stern, J. A. Peripheral physiological variables and emotion: The James-Lange theory revisited. *Psychological Bulletin*, 1970, **74**, 411–424.

Feldman, S. M., & Waller, H. J. Dissociation of electrocortical activation and behavioural arousal. *Nature*, 1962, **196**, 1320–1322.

Field, J., Magoun, H. W., & Hall, V. E. (Eds.) *Handbook of physiology: Neurophysiology, I.* Washington, D.C.: American Physiological Society, 1959.

Field, J., Magoun, H. W., & Hall, V. E. (Eds.) *Handbook of physiology: Neurophysiology, II.* Washington, D.C.: American Physiological Society, 1960a.

Field, J., Magoun, H. W., & Hall, V. E. (Eds.) *Handbook of physiology: Neurophysiology, III.* Washington, D.C.: American Physiological Society, 1960b.

Fuster, J. M. Effects of stimulation of brainstem on tachistoscopic perception. *Science,* 1958, **127,** 150.

Fuster, J. M. Excitation and inhibition of neuronal firing in visual cortex by reticular stimulation. *Science,* 1961, **133,** 2011–2012.

Gardner, E. *Fundamentals of neurology.* Philadelphia: W. B. Saunders, 1968.

Gardner, R. A., & Gardner, B. T. Teaching sign language to a chimpanzee. *Science,* 1969, **165,** 664–672.

Gazzaniga, M. S. *The bisected brain.* New York: Appleton-Century-Crofts, 1970.

Gazzaniga, M. S. One brain—Two minds? *American Scientist,* 1972, **60,** 311–317.

Geschwind, N. The organization of language and the brain. *Science,* 1970, **170,** 940–944.

Glassman, E. The biochemistry of learning: An evaluation of the role of RNA in protein. *Annual Review of Physiology,* 1969.

Glickman, S. E. Perseverative neural process and consolidation of the memory trace. *Psychological Bulletin,* 1961, **58,** 218–233.

Goldstein, M. L. Physiological theories of emotion: A critical, historical review from the standpoint of behavior theory. *Psychological Bulletin,* 1968, **69,** 23–40.

Graham, C. H. (Ed.) *Vision and visual perception.* New York: Wiley, 1965.

Granit, R. *Receptors and sensory perception.* New Haven: Yale University Press, 1955.

Granit, R. *The basis of motor control.* New York: Academic Press, 1970.

Green, D. M., & Swets, J. A. *Signal detection theory and psychophysics.* New York: Wiley, 1966.

Gregory, R. L. *Eye and brain.* New York: McGraw-Hill, 1966.

Gulick, W. L. *Hearing: Physiology & psychophysics.* New York: Oxford, 1971.

Gurowitz, E. M. *The molecular basis of memory.* Englewood Cliffs, N.J.: Prentice-Hall, 1969.

Haider, M., Spong, R., & Lindsley, D. B. Attention, vigilance, and cortical evoked potentials in humans. *Science,* 1964, **145,** 180–182.

Hammes, G. G., Molinoff, P. B., and Bloom, F. E. Receptor biophysics and biochemistry. *Neurosciences Research Program Bulletin,* 1973, **11**(3).

Harmon, L. D. , & Knowlton, K. C. Picture processing by computer. *Science,* 1969, **164,** 19–28.

Hartline, H. K. Visual receptors and retinal interaction. *Science,* 1969, **164,** 270–277.

Heath, R. G. Pleasure response in human subjects to direct stimulation of the brain: Physiologic and psychodynamic considerations. In R. G. Heath (Ed.) *The role of pleasure in behavior.* New York: Hoeber, 1964.

Heath, R. G. Pleasure and brain activity in man. *The Journal of Nervous and Mental Disease,* 1972, **154,** 3–18.

Hebb, D. O. *The organization of behavior.* New York: Wiley, 1949.

Hebb, D. O. The role of neurological ideas in psychology. *Journal of Personality,* 1951, **20,** 39–55.

Hebb, D. O. *Textbook of psychology.* (3rd ed.) Philadelphia: W. B. Saunders, 1972.

Hernandez-Peon, R. Reticular mechanisms of sensory control. In W. A. Rosenblith (Ed.), *Sensory communication*. New York: Wiley, 1961.

Hernandez-Peon, R., Scherrer, H., & Jouvet, M. Modification of electric activity in the cochlear nucleus during "attention" in unanesthetized cats. *Science,* 1956, **123,** 331–332.

Hess, E. H. Altitude and pupil size. *Scientific American,* 1965, **212**(4), 46–54.

Hillyard, S. A., Squires, K. C., Bauer, J. W., & Lindsay, P. H. Evoked potential correlates of auditory signal detection. *Science,* 1971, **172,** 1357–1360.

Hodgkin, A. L. The ionic basis of nervous conduction. *Science,* 1964, **145,** 1148–1154.

Hoebel, V. G. Feeding: Neural control of intake. *Annual Review of Physiology,* 1971, **33**.

Holubar, J. *The sense of time: An electrophysiological study of its mechanisms in man.* Cambridge, Mass.: M.I.T. Press, 1969.

Horridge, G. A. *Interneurons.* San Francisco: W. H. Freeman, 1968.

Hubel, D. H., & Wiesel, T. N. Receptive fields of single neurons in the cat's striate cortex. *Journal of Physiology,* 1959, **148,** 574–591.

Hubel, D. H., & Wiesel, T. N. Receptive fields of optic nerve fibers in the spider monkey. *Journal of Physiology,* 1960, **154,** 572–580.

Hubel, D. H., & Wiesel, T. N. Integrative action of the cat's lateral geniculate body. *Journal of Physiology,* 1961, **155,** 385–398.

Hubel, D. H., & Wiesel, T. N. Receptive fields, binocular interaction and functional architecture of the cat's visual cortex. *Journal of Physiology,* 1962, **160,** 106–154.

Hubel, D. H., & Wiesel, T. N. Shape and arrangement of columns in the cat's striate cortex. *Journal of Physiology,* 1963, **165,** 559–568.

Huxley, A. F. Excitation and conduction in nerves: Quantitative analysis. *Science,* 1964, **145,** 1154–1159.

Jacobson, M. Development of specific neuronal connections. *Science,* 1969, **163,** 543–547.

Jacobson, M. Development, specification, and diversification of neuronal connections. In F. O. Schmitt (Ed.), *The neurosciences: Second study program.* New York: Rockefeller, 1970.

James, W. *The principles of psychology.* Vols. I & II. New York: Dover Press, 1890.

James, W. The physical basis of emotion. *Psychological Review,* 1894, **1,** 516–529.

Jasper, H. H. (Ed.) *Reticular formation of the brain.* Boston: Little, Brown, 1958.

John, E. R. Electrophysiological studies of conditioning. In G. C. Quarton, T. Melnechuk, & F. O. Schmitt (Eds.), *The neurosciences: A study program.* New York: Rockefeller, 1967.

Jouvet, M. Neurophysiology of the states of sleep. In G. C. Quarton, T. Melnechuk, & F. O. Schmitt (Eds.), *The neurosciences: A study program.* New York: Rockefeller, 1967.

Jouvet, M. Biogenic amines and the states of sleep. *Science,* 1969, **163,** 32–40.

Kahneman, D., & Beatty, J. Pupil diameter and load on memory. *Science,* 1966, **157**(3756), 1584.

Kahneman, D., Beatty, J., & Pollack, I. Perceptual deficit during a mental task. *Science,* 1967, **157**(3785), 218–219.

Karlin, L. Cognition, preparation and sensory evoked potentials. *Psychological Bulletin,* 1970, **73,** 122–136.

Katsuki, Y. Neural mechanisms of auditory sensation in cats. In W. A.

Rosenblith, (Ed.), *Sensory communication*. New York: Wiley, 1961.

Kellogg, W. N. Communication and language in the home-raised chimpanzee. *Science*, 1968, **162**, 423–426.

Kimble, D. P. *The anatomy of memory*. Palo Alto: Science and Behavior Books, 1965.

Kimble, D. P. *The organization of recall*. New York: The New York Academy of Sciences, 1967.

Kleitman, N. Patterns of dreaming. *Scientific American*, 1960, **203**(5), 82–88.

Lansing, R. W., Schwartz, E., & Lindsley, D. B. Reaction time and EEG activation under alerted and non-alerted conditions. *Journal of Experimental Psychology*, 1959, **58**, 1–7.

Lashley, K. S. The problem of serial order in behavior. In L. A. Jeffress (Ed.), *Cerebral mechanisms in behavior*. New York: Wiley, 1951.

Lashley, K. S. In search of the engram. *Physiological Mechanisms in Animal Behavior, Society of Experimental Biology Symposium No. 4*, 1950, 454–483.

Leibovic, K. M. (Ed.) *Information processing in the nervous system*. New York: Springer-Verlag, 1969.

Lenneberg, E. H. Brain correlates of language. In F. O. Schmitt (Ed.), *The neurosciences: Second study program*. New York: Rockefeller, 1970.

Lenneberg, E. H. *Biological foundations of langauge*. New York: Wiley, 1967.

Lenneberg, E. H. On explaining language. *Science*, 1969, **164**, 635–643.

Lettvin, J. Y., Maturana, H. R., McCulloch, W. S., & Pitts, W. H. What the frog's eye tells the frog's brain. *Proceedings of the IRE*, 1959, **47**, 1940–1951.

Lettvin, J. Y., Maturana, H. R., Pitts, W. H., & McCulloch, W. S. Two remarks on the visual system of the frog. In W. A. Rosenblith (Ed.), *Sensory communication*. Cambridge, Mass.: M.I.T. Press, 1961.

Levy, J. Possible basis for the evolution of lateral specialization of the human brain. *Nature*, 1969, **224**, 614–615.

Lewis, D. J. Sources of experimental amnesia. *Psychological Review*, 1969, **76**, 461–472.

Liberman, A. M. The specialization of the language hemisphere. In F. O. Schmitt & F. G. Worden (Eds.), *The neurosciences: Third study program*. Cambridge, Mass.: M.I.T. Press, 1974.

Liberman, A. M., Cooper, F. S., Shankweiler, D. P., & Studdert-Kennedy, M. Perception of the speech code. *Psychological Review*, 1967, **74**, 431–461.

Lindsay, P. H., & Norman, D. A. *Human information processing*. New York: Academic Press, 1972.

Lindsley, D. B. Attention, consciousness, sleep and wakefulness. In J. Field, H. W. Magoun, & V. E. Hall (Eds.), *Handbook of physiology: Neurophysiology, III*. Washington, D.C.: American Physiological Society, 1960.

Lindsley, D. B., Schreiner, L. H., Knowles, W. B., & Magoun, H. W. Behavioral and EEG changes following chronic brainstem lesions in the cat. *Electroencephalography and Clinical Neurophysiology*, 1950, **2**, 483–498.

Livingston, R. B. Reinforcement. In G. C. Quarton, T. Melnechuk, & F. O. Schmitt (Eds.), *The neurosciences: A study program*. New York: Rockefeller, 1967.

Loewenstein, W. R. The generation of electric activity in a nerve ending. *Annals of the New York Academy of Science*, 1959, **81**, 367–387.

Lowenstein, O. *The senses*. Baltimore: Penguin Books, 1966.

Luce, G. G. *Biological rhythms in psychiatry and medicine*. (USPHS Publication No. 2088) Washington, D.C.: United States Government Printing Office, 1970.

Lynn, R. *Attention, arousal and the orientation reaction*. Oxford: Pergamon Press, 1966.

Mackay, D. N. Evoked brain potentials as indicators of sensory information processing. *Neurosciences Research Program Bulletin,* 1969, **7**(3).

MacKenzie, N. *Dreams and dreaming.* New York: Vanguard, 1965.

Mackworth, J. F. Vigilance, arousal and habituation. *Psychological Review,* 1968, **75**, 308–322.

MacLean, P. D. Psychosomatic disease and the "visceral brain": Recent developments bearing on the Papez theory of emotion. *Psychosomatic Medicine,* 1949, **11**, 338–353.

MacNeilage, P. F. Motor control of serial ordering of speech. *Psychological Review,* 1970, **77**, 182–196.

Magoun, H. W. *The waking brain.* (2nd ed.) Springfield, Ill.: Charles C Thomas, 1963.

Marks, W. B., Dubelle, W. H., & MacNichol, E. F., Jr. Visual pigments of single primate cones. *Science,* 1964, **143**, 1181–1183.

Margules, D. L., & Olds, J. Identical "feeding" and "rewarding" systems in the lateral hypothalamus of rats. *Science,* 1962, **135**, 374–375.

Mark, V. H., & Ervin, F. R. *Violence and the brain.* New York: Harper & Row, 1970.

Marsh, J. T., Worden, F. G., & Hicks, L. Some effects of room acoustics on evoked auditory potentials. *Science,* 1962, **137**, 281–282.

Mayer, J. Glucostatic mechanisms of regulation of food intake. *New England Journal of Medicine,* 1953, **249**, 13–16.

Mayer, J., & Sudsaneh, S. Mechanism of hypothalamic control of gastric contractions in the rat. *American Journal of Physiology,* 1959, **197**, 274–280.

McGaugh, J. L. Time dependent processes in memory storage. *Science,* 1966, **153**, 1351–1358.

McGaugh, J. L., & Dawson, R. G. Modification of memory storage processes. In W. K. Honig & P. H. R. James (Eds.), *Animal memory.* New York: Academic Press, 1971.

McLennan, H. *Synaptic transmission.* Philadelphia: W. B. Saunders, 1970.

Melton, A. W. Implications of short-term memory for a general theory of memory. *Journal of Verbal Learning and Verbal Behavior,* 1963, **2**, 1–21.

Melzack, R., & Wall, P. D. Pain mechanisms: A new theory. *Science,* 1965, **150**(3699), 971–979.

Mendelson, M. Oscillator neurons in crustacean ganglia. *Science,* 1971, **171**, 1170–1173.

Miller, G. A. *Language and communication.* New York: McGraw-Hill, 1951.

Miller, G. A. The magical number seven, plus or minus two: Some limits on our capacity for processing information. *Psychological Review,* 1956, **63**, 81–97.

Miller, J. F., Moody, D. B., & Stebbins, W. C. Evoked potentials and auditory reaction time in monkeys. *Science,* 1969, **163**, 592–594.

Millikan, C. H., and Darley, F. L. *Brain mechanisms underlying speech and language.* New York: Grune and Stratton, 1967.

Milner, B. Brain mechanisms suggested by studies of temporal lobes. In F. L. Darley (Ed.), *Brain mechanisms underlying speech and language.* New York: Grune & Stratton, 1967.

Milner, B. Hemispheric specialization: Scope and limits. In F. O. Schmitt & F. G. Worden (Eds.), *The neurosciences: Third study program.* Cambridge, Mass.: M.I.T. Press, 1974.

Milner, B., Branch, C. & Rasmussen, T. Observations on cerebral dominance. In A. V. S. de Reuck & M. O'Connor (Eds.), *Ciba foundation symposium on disorders of language.* London: Churchill, 1964.

Milner, B., & Penfield, W. The effect of hippocampal lesions on recent memory. *Trans. American Neurological Association,* 1955, **80**, 42–48.

Milner, P. M. *Physiological psychology.* New York: Holt, Rinehart and Winston, 1970.

Mokrasch, L. C., Bear, R. S., & Schmidt, F. O. Myelin. *Neurosciences Research Program Bulletin,* 1971, **9.**

Moruzzi, G., & Magoun, H. W. Brainstem reticular formation and activation of the EEG. *Electroencephalography and Clinical Neurophysiology,* 1949, **1,** 455–473.

Mountcastle, V. B. *Interhemispheric relations and cerebral dominance.* Baltimore: Johns Hopkins Press, 1962.

Mountcastle, V. B. The problem of sensing and the neural coding of sensory events. In G. C. Quarton, T. Melnechuk, & F. O. Schmitt (Eds.), *The neurosciences: A study program.* New York: Rockefeller, 1967.

Mountcastle, V. B. *Medical phsyiology.* Vol. 2. St. Louis: Mosby, 1968.

Mountcastle, V. B., Poggio, G. F., & Werner, G. The relation of thalamic cell response to peripheral stimulus varied over an intensive continuum. *Journal of Neurophysiology,* 1963, **26,** 807–834.

Mountcastle, V. B., & Powell, P. S. Neural mechanisms subserving cutaneous sensibility, with special reference to the role of afferent inhibition in sensory perception and discrimination. *Bulletin of the Johns Hopkins Hospital,* 1959, **105,** 201–232.

Neff, W. D. (Ed.) *Contributions to sensory physiology.* Vol. I. New York: Academic Press, 1965.

Neff, W. D. (Ed.) *Contributions to sensory physiology.* Vol. II. New York: Academic Press, 1967.

Neff, W. D. (Ed.) *Contributions to sensory physiology.* Vol. III. New York: Academic Press, 1968.

Neisser, U. *Cognitive psychology.* New York: Appleton-Century-Crofts, 1967.

O'Brien, J. H., & Fox, S. S. Single cell activity in cat motor cortex, I: Modifications during classical conditioning procedures. *Journal of Neurophysiology,* 1969a, **32,** 267–284.

O'Brien, J. H., & Fox, S. S. Single cell activity in cat motor cortex, II: Functional characteristics of the cell related to conditioning changes. *Journal of Neurophysiology,* 1969, **32,** 285–296.

Olds, J. Physiological mechanisms of reward. In M. R. Jones (Ed.), *Nebraska symposium on motivation.* Lincoln, Nebr.: University of Nebraska Press, 1955.

Olds, J. Self-stimulation of the brain. *Science,* 1958, **127**(3294), 315–324.

Olds, J. Hypothalamic substrates of reward. *Physiological Review,* 1962, **42,** 554–604.

Olds, J., & Milner, P. Positive reinforcement produced by electrical stimulation of septal area and other regions of rat brain. *Journal of Comparative Physiological Psychology,* 1954, **47,** 419–427.

Olds, J., & Olds, M. E. Drives, rewards, and the brain. In *New Directions in Psychology.* Vol. 2. New York: Holt, Rinehart and Winston, 1965.

Olds, J., Segal, M., Hirsh, R., Disterhoft, J. F., & Kornblith, C. L. Learning centers of rat brain mapped by measuring latencies of conditioned unit responses. *Journal of Neurophysiology,* 1972, **35,** 202–219.

Palay, S. L. The morphology of synapses in the central nervous system. *Experimental Cell Research,* 1958, **5,** 275–293.

Palay, S. L. Principles of cellular organization in the nervous system. In G. C. Quarton, T. Melnechuk, & F. O. Schmitt (Eds.), *The neurosciences: A study program.* New York: Rockefeller, 1967.

Papez, J. W. A proposed mechanism of emotion. *Archives of Neurological Psychiatry*, 1937, **38**, 725–743.

Pavlov, I. P. *Conditioned reflexes*. Oxford: Oxford University Press, 1927.

Pearlman, A. L., & Daw, N. W. Opponent color cells in the cat lateral geniculate nucleus. *Science*, 1970, **167**, 84–86.

Penfield, W., & Perot, P. The brain's record of auditory and visual experience. *Brain*, 1963, **86**, 595–696.

Penfield, W., & Roberts, L. *Speech and brain mechanisms*. New York: Atheneum, 1966.

Pfeiffer, R. R., & Molnar, C. E. Cochlear nerve fiber discharge patterns: Relationship to the cochlear microphonic. *Science*, 1970, **167**, 1614–1616.

Ploog, D. Social communication among animals. In F. O. Schmitt (Ed.), *The neurosciences: Second study program*. New York: Rockefeller, 1970.

Ploog, D., & Melnechuk, T. Primate communication. *Neurosciences Research Program Bulletin*, 1969, **7**(5).

Ploog, D., & Melnechuk, T. Are apes capable of language? *Neurosciences Research Program Bulletin*, 1971, **9**(5).

Poggio, G. F., & Mountcastle, V. B. A study of the functional contributions of the lemniscal and spinothalamic systems to somatic sensibility. *Bulletin of the Johns Hopkins Hospital*, 1960, **106**, 283–316.

Polyak, S. L. *The retina*. Chicago: University of Chicago Press, 1941.

Premack, D. A functional analysis of language. *Journal of the Experimental Analysis of Behavior*, 1970, **14**, 107–185.

Premack, D. Language in chimpanzee? *Science*, 1971, **172**, 808–822.

Pritchard, R. M., Heron, W., & Hebb, D. O. Visual perception approached by the method of stabilized images. *Canadian Journal of Psychology*, 1960, **14**, 67–77.

Quarton, G. C., Melnechuk, T., & Schmitt, F. O. (Eds.) *The neurosciences: A study program*. New York: Rockefeller, 1967.

Ratliff, F. *Mach bands: Quantitative studies on neuronal networks in the retina*. San Francisco: Holden-Day, 1965.

Richter, C. P. Sleep and activity: Their relation to the 24-hour clock. In *Association for Research in Nervous and Mental Disease*. Vol. 45. *Sleep and altered states of consciousness*. Baltimore: Williams & Wilkins, 1967.

Richter, C. P. Inborn nature of the rat's 24-hour clock. *Journal of Physiological Psychology*, 1971, **75**, 1–4.

Rosenblith, W. A. *Sensory communication*. Cambridge, Mass.: M.I.T. Press, 1961.

Rosenzweig, M. R. Environmental complexity, cerebral change, and behavior. *American Psychologist*, 1965, **20**, 321–322.

Ruch, T. C., & Patton, H. D. (Eds.) *Physiology & biophysics*. Philadelphia: W. B. Saunders, 1965.

Schachter, S. *Emotion, obesity and crime*. New York: Academic Press, 1971.

Schachter, S., & Singer, J. E. Cognitive, social, and physiological determinants of emotional state. *Psychological Review*, 1962, **69**(5), 379–399.

Scharf, B. Fundamentals of auditory masking. *Audiology*, 1971, **10**, 30–40.

Schmitt, F. O. (Ed.) *The neurosciences: Second study program*. New York: Rockefeller, 1970.

Schneider, G. E. Two visual systems. *Science*, 1969, **163**, 895–902.

Scoville, W. B., & Milner, B. Loss of recent memory after bilateral hippocampal lesions. *Journal of Neurology, Neurosurgery and Psychiatry*, 1957, **20**(11), 11–19.

Shallice, T., & Warrington, E. K. Independent functioning of verbal memory stores: A neuropsychological study. *Quarterly Journal of Experimental Psychology*, 1970, **22**, 261–273.

Sheer, D. E. (Ed.) *Electrical stimulation of the brain.* Austin, Texas: Univ. of Texas Press, 1961.

Sherrington, C. S. *The integrative action of the nervous system.* (2nd ed.) New Haven, Conn.: Yale Univ. Press, 1947.

Siegel, P. V., Gerathewohl, S. J., & Mohler, S. R. Time-zone effects. *Science,* 1969, **164**, 1249–1255.

Simon, H. A. *The sciences of the artificial.* Cambridge, Mass.: M.I.T. Press, 1969.

Sokolov, E. N. Neuronal models and the orienting reflex. In M. A. B. Brazier (Ed.), *The central nervous system and behavior.* New York: Josiah Macy Jr. Foundation, 1960.

Sokolov, E. N. Higher nervous functions: The orienting reflex. *Annual Review of Physiology*, 1963, **25**, 545–580.

Sokolov, E. N. *Perception and the conditioned reflex.* New York: Pergamon Press, 1963.

Somjen, G. *Sensory coding in the mammalian nervous system.* New York: Appleton-Century-Crofts, 1972.

Sperry, R. W. Cerebral organization and behavior *Science,* 1961, **133**, 1749–1757.

Sperry, R. W. Lateral specialization in the surgically separated hemispheres. In F. O. Schmitt & F. G. Worden (Eds.), *The neurosciences: Third study program.* Cambridge, Mass.: M.I.T. Press, 1974.

Spong, P., Haider, M., & Lindsley, D. B. Selective attentiveness and cortical evoked responses to visual and auditory stimuli. *Science,* 1965, **148**, 395–397.

Stein, D. G., Rosen, J. J., Graziadei, J., Mishkin, D., & Brink, J. J. Central nervous system: Recovery of functions. *Science,* 1969, **166**, 528–530.

Stellar, E., & Sprague, J. M. *Progress in physiological psychology.* Vol. 1. New York: Academic Press, 1966.

Stellar, E., & Sprague, J. M. *Progress in physiological psychology.* Vol. 2. New York: Academic Press, 1968.

Strumwasser, F. Neurophysiological aspects of rhythms. In G. C. Quarton, T. Melnechuk, & F. O. Schmitt (Eds.), *The neurosciences: A study program.* New York: Rockefeller, 1967.

Studdert-Kennedy, M., Lieberman, A. M., Harris, K. S., & Cooper, F. S. Motor theory of speech production: A reply to Lane's critical review. *Psychological Review*, 1970, **77**, 234–249.

Tecce, J. J. Attention and evoked potentials in man. In D. I. Mostofsky (Ed.), *Attention: Contemporary theory and analysis.* New York: Appleton-Century-Crofts, 1970.

Tecce, J. J., & Scheff, N. M. Attention reduction and suppressed direct current potential in the human brain. *Science,* 1969, **164**, 331–333.

Teuber, H. Why two brains? In F. O. Schmitt & F. G. Worden (Eds.), *The neurosciences: Third study program.* Cambridge, Mass.: M.I.T. Press, 1974.

Thompson, R. F. *Foundations of physiological psychology.* New York: Harper & Row, 1967.

Thompson, R. F., & Bettinger, L. A. Neural substrates of attention. In D. I. Mostofsky (Ed.), *Attention: Contemporary theory and analysis.* New York: Appleton-Century-Crofts, 1970.

Tobias, J. V. *Foundations of modern auditory theory*. New York: Academic Press, 1970.

Tomita, T., Kaneko, A., Murakami, M., & Pautler, E. L. Spectral response curves of single cones in the carp. *Vision Research*, 1967, **7**, 519–531.

Towe, A. L. In Evarts, E. V., Bizzi, E., Burke, R. E., DeLong, M., & Thach, W. T., Jr. (Eds.), *Central control of movement. Neurosciences Research Program Bulletin*, 1971, **9**(1), 43.

Treisman, A. M. Selective attention in man. *British Medical Bulletin*, 1964, **20**, 12–16.

Tunturi, A. R. Anatomy and physiology of the auditory cortex. In G. L. Rasmussen and W. F. Windle (Eds.), *Neural mechanisms of auditory and vestibular systems*. Springfield, Ill.: Charles C Thomas, 1960.

Uttal, W. R. Emerging principles of sensory coding. *Perspectives in Biology and Medicine*, 1969, **12**, 344–368.

Valenstein, E. S. *Brain stimulation and motivation: Research and Commentary*. Glenview, Ill.: Scott Foresman, 1973.

Valenstein, E. S., Cox, V. C., & Kakolewski, J. W. Reexamination of the role of the hypothalamus in motivation. *Psychological Review*, 1970, **77**, 16–31.

Vanderwolf, C. H. Limbic-diencephalic mechanisms of voluntary movement. *Psychological Review*, 1971, **78**(2), 83–113.

von Békésy, G. Current status of theories of hearing. *Science*, 1956, **123**(3201), 779–783.

von Békésy, G. *Experiments in hearing*. New York: McGraw-Hill, 1960.

von Békésy, G. *Sensory inhibition*. Princeton, N. J.: Princeton University Press, 1967.

von Békésy, G. Problems relating psychological and electrophysiological observations in sensory perception. *Perspectives in Biology and Medicine*, 1968, **11**, 179–194.

von Békésy, G., & Rosenblith, W. A. The mechanical properties of the ear. In S. S. Stevens (Ed.), *Handbook of experimental psychology*. New York: Wiley, 1951.

Wald, G. The receptors of human color vision. *Science*, 1964, **145**(3636), 1007–1016.

Wald, G. Molecular basis of visual excitation. *Science*, 1968, **162**, 230–239.

Walter, W. G., Cooper, R., Aldridge, V. J., McCallum, W. C., & Winter, A. L. Contingent negative variation: An electrical sign of sensorimotor association and expectancy in the human brain. *Nature*, 1964, **203**(4943), 380–384.

Warren, R. M. Perceptual restoration of missing speech sounds. *Science*, 1970, **167**, 392–393.

Warrington, E. K., & Weiskrantz, L. An analysis of short term and long term memory defects in man. In J. A. Deutsch (Ed.), *The physiological basis of memory*. New York: Academic Press, 1973.

Webb, W. B. *Sleep: An experimental approach*. New York: Macmillan, 1968.

Weddell, G. Receptors for somatic sensation. In M. A. B. Brazier (Ed.), *Brain and behavior*. Vol. 1. Washington, D.C.: American Institute of Biological Sciences, 1961.

Weinberger, N. M. Attentive processes. In J. L. McGaugh (Ed.), *Psychobiology: Behavior from a biological perspective*. New York: Academic Press, 1971.

Werblin, F. S., & Dowling, J. E. Organization of the retina of the mudpuppy *Necturus maculosus*. II. Intracellular recording. *Journal of Neurophysiology*, 1969, **32**, 339–355.

Werner, G. The topology of the body representation in the somatic afferent pathway. In F. O. Schmitt (Ed.), *The neurosciences: Second study program.* New York: Rockefeller, 1970.

Werner, G., & Mountcastle, V. B. The variability of central neural activity in the sensory system, and its implications for the central reflection of sensory events. *Journal of Neurophysiology,* 1963, **26,** 958–977.

Wiesel, T. N., & Hubel, D. H. Spatial and chromatic interactions in the lateral geniculate body of the rhesus monkey. *Journal of Neurophysiology,* 1966, **29,** 1115–1156.

Willows, A. O. D., & Hoyle, G. Neuronal network triggering a fixed action pattern. *Science,* 1969, **166,** 1549–1551.

Wilson, D. M. Neural operations in arthropod ganglia. In F. O. Schmitt (Ed.), *The neurosciences: Second study program.* New York: Rockefeller, 1970.

Woolsey, C. N. Organization of somatic sensory and motor areas of the cerebral cortex. In H. F. Harlow & C. N. Woolsey (Eds.), *Biological and biochemical bases of behavior.* Madison, Wisc.: University of Wisconsin Press, 1958.

Young, J. Z. *A model of the brain.* London: Oxford University Press, 1964.

Index